KU-265-262

An Outline History of Poland

An Outline History of Poland

by Jerzy Topolski

translated by Olgierd Wojtasiewicz

Interpress Publishers
Warsaw 1986

On the cover: Details of Łukasz Evert's frieze *Casimir the Jagiellon Entering Malbork*, 1585

Graphic design by
Stanisław Kazimierczyk

Production editor:
Wiesław Pyszka

Genealogical tables compiled by
Antoni Gąsiorowski

Maps designed by
Ludwik Fijał
Maps based on *Historyczny atlas Polski*, PPWK, Warsaw

Graphic design of maps by
Jolanta Bylicka, Krzysztof Dulkowski and Mariusz Motyliński

Photographs by
S. Arczyński, B. J. Dorys, O. Gałdyński, Z. Gamski, S. Gawliński, J. Grelowski, J. Hattowski, T. Hermańczyk, W. P. Jabłoński, A. Kaczkowski, K. Kamiński, S. Kolowca, E. Kozłowska-Tomczyk, E. Kupiecki, J. Langda, E. Lewandowska, Z. Małek, W. Mądraszkiewicz, S. Michta, J. Morek, K. Niedenthal, P. Pierściński, Piotrowski, W. Prażuch, T. Przypkowski, H. Rosiak, Z. Siemaszko, J. Siudecki, W. Stasiak, J. Styczyński, J. Szandomirski, S. Turski, J. Tymiński, J. Uklejewski, W. Wolny, T. Zagoździński, and T. Żółtowska

Photographs by courtesy of
National Library, Central Archives of the Polish United Workers' Party Central Committee, Central Photographic Agency (CAF), Army Photographic Agency, Institute of Art of the Polish Academy of Sciences, Photo-Service of the Polish Interpress Agency

This is the two thousand one hundred and fifty-seventh publication of Interpress
This book appears also in German and Polish

Printed in Poland

ISBN 83-223-2118-x

Contents

Chapter VI. Poland under the Renaissance and the 'Democracy of the Gentry' (1501—1618)

Chapter VII. The Baroque and the Dominance of the Magnates (1618—1733)

Chapter VIII. The Age of Reason and the Age of Reforms. The Partitions (1733—95)

Chapter IX. The Beginning of Foreign Rule. Napoleon I and Poland The Duchy of Warsaw (1795—1815)

Chapter X. National Liberation Struggles of the Polish Nation. Collapse of Feudal Structures (1815—64)

Chapter XI. Advances of Capitalism in Poland. Struggle for National Identity. Regaining of Independence (1864—1918)

Chapter XII. Between the World Wars: Successes and Failures (1918—39)

Chapter XIII. Poland and the Poles During World War II. The Origins of People's Poland (1939—45)

Chapter XIV. Development of People's Poland. Formation of Modern Society and a Socialist Nation. Democratization of Cultural Life (1945—80)

Chapter I

Polish Territory in Antiquity (until the 6th century A.D.)

1. When does the history of Poland begin?

The history of Poland is usually described as having begun under the rule of Mieszko I, in other words at the time when Poland had already been formed as a state and information about it had been recorded by its contemporaries. But the state ruled by Mieszko I did not emerge suddenly in the form as suggested by these sources. Its emergence had been preceded by processes of long duration, among which of prior importance were the coming of the Slavs and their settling of the Polish lands, and the social, economic and cultural developments necessary for the evolution of a political organization at state level.

The origins of the Polish state, society, culture and nation are therefore connected with the settling of the Slavs, for from that time (c. 1500—500 B.C.) Polish territory was inhabited by the same people speaking the same language (Proto-Slavonic, Slavonic, and towards the end of the first millennium, Proto-Polish). During that millennium and during the next, a process took place of the history of Polish territory changing into the history of the Polish state, society and nation.

The Polish political organization, society and culture needed some two thousand years to take full shape. On the other hand, the history of the Polish lands at the time when they were inhabited by the various groups who had nothing to do with the later Polish population covers some 250,000 years if we count it from the appearance of man on those territories. Thus the history of Poland, including that of Polish territory, could be split into three periods:

(i) the history of Polish territory before the advent of the Slavs, from ca. 250,000 B.C. to ca. 1500—1300 B.C.;

(ii) the history of the formation of the foundation of the Polish society, culture, state and nation, from ca. 1500—1300 B.C. to ca. 500 A.D.;

(iii) the history of the Polish society, state, nation and culture, from ca. 500 A.D. until the present day.

This shows a constant acceleration of development and such density of changes that the periods of time are increasingly packed.

2. The earliest times

Before the advent of the Slavs, the Polish lands had been the scene of a long process of development and the coming and going of the various peoples who were then moving about in search of good living conditions. The stages of the historical development through which the Polish lands went in these times resembled those known from other parts of the world. It is worth while noting that Europe was then not a centre of civilization, and the differences in development among the various areas were small. Civilizational influence came mainly from the more advanced areas in the Near East and moved northwards. But these advances took place on a larger scale only in the Neolithic period, which in the case of the Polish lands lasted from ca. 4400 B.C. to ca. 1700 B.C., nearly three thousand years.

But the Palaeolithic period, marked by more primitive stone implements, witnessed many changes, too, although transition occurred at a very slow pace (the period lasted from ca. 230,000 B.C. to ca. 8000 B.C., i.e., for some 220,000 years), and also pertained to man himself as he was still in the process of evolution. The oldest traces of man, discovered by archaeologists in the Polish lands, date back to some 40,000 years. His predecessors were hordes of primitive hunters who knew how to make use of fire and simple stone implements. Their mode of existence did not differ from the standard ways of human life in the territory of present-day France (the Acheulian culture, so named after Saint-Acheul near Amiens) or Britain (the Clactonian culture, after Clacton-on-Sea in Essex). Probably toward the end of the Riss glacial stage that covered a large part of the Palaeolithic (from ca. 240,000 to ca. 120,000 B.C.) the Polish lands saw the appearance of the Neanderthal man (*Homo sapiens Neanderthalensis*), who was a product of the adjustment of primitive peoples to the persevering hard climate. At that time human beings could exist only on a narrow belt, some 200 kilometres wide, to the north of the Carpathians, not covered by glaciers. The climatic conditions resembled those of present-day Greenland. Neanderthal man used more differentiated flint implements. He lived gregariously and used caves as his permanent shelters and primitive huts made of branches as temporary shelters (for instance, when hunting, because hunting and food gathering were still the foundation of his existence). His mode of life was similar to that typical of other parts of Europe, and came to be called the Mousterian culture (after Le Moustier in France).

The next 50,000 years of the so-called Riss-Würm interglacial stage were marked by a warmer climate, which brought some progress in the life of man of that time. The next glaciation (Würm), which lasted for some 70,000 years, blocked the further development of Neanderthal man who had to succumb, some 40,000 years ago, to the more advanced Cro-Magnon man, who already resembled man as we know him today (*Homo sapiens*).

For some 30,000 years, until the Mesolithic period (the Middle Stone Age) Polish territory was inhabited by various human groups whose mode of existence is called by archaeologists the Aurignacian culture (from Aurignac in France), the Altmühl culture (named so after a locality near Hamburg), and the Magdalenian culture. The flint tools were being improved. This was particularly necessary because, in the form of sows, burins and drills, they had to be used for the production of objects made of horn and bone, frequently used raw materials. Hunting and food gathering still prevailed, but the importance of fishing increased. Trade in flint, mined in the Świętokrzyskie (Holy Cross) Mountains, occurred on a large scale.

The Mesolithic period (8000 to 4400 B.C.) saw a certain mixing of the populations of the Polish lands. The population characterized by the so-called Swiderian culture (named so from the locality Świdry Wielkie near Warsaw), which lived in the northern part of the Polish lands, migrated to Lithuania, Latvia, Estonia and Byelorussia (following the reindeer which were moving toward the Subarctic regions), and its place was taken by groups of people who came from the North-West and West. This was due to a considerable warming up of the climate in the Polish lands, which resulted in changes in the flora (including the appearance of mixed forests) and in the fauna (the appearance of aurochs, deer and wild boar). Certain technical progress was observable, too. The bow was used in hunting, fishing techniques were improved, the flint axe and the dug-out canoe bacame common. Next to the primitive huts built of tree branches, pit dwellings became the standard abode.

3. The agricultural revolution. The Neolithic period

The essential changes, however, were brought only by the next period, which began some six thousand years ago and lasted for about three thousand years until the Bronze Age. What were the changes? First, the advent in Polish territory of the so-called Neolithic (agricultural) revolution, which consisted of a gradual popularization of plant cultivation and animal breeding. It spread from the south — Mesopotamia, Palestine, Syria, Anatolia, across the Balkans — and within a few thousand years completely modified the living conditions. Hunting, food gathering and fishing, though still important, became secondary occupations. Polish territory saw the arrival, together with the new modes of life, of various groups from the Danubian basin. They were no longer the old hordes, but tribes of clans, interconnected by bonds of blood. The new settlers looked for fertile lands, black soil (*chernozem*) and loess. They exploited them for a number of years and then moved on. Later they would return to their previous tillage ground, which in the meantime had become covered with trees and shrubs. After slashing and burning these, they sowed wheat, barley, millet, some leguminous, fibrous and oleaginous plants and bred cattle, sheep, goats and pigs. The soil was broken up and softened with hoes and this is why that type of agriculture is now termed slash-and-burn hoe cultivation. Pottery, also unknown before, appeared in the Polish lands. Weaving developed, too. The agricultural population lived on the whole a settled life and cultivated the land jointly; there was no individual property. The division of labour among men and women was already noticeable. Beliefs consisted in the worship of Nature, combined with the agricultural cycle. The dead were buried or burned. There were still groups of the population occupied mainly with hunting and food gathering; they lived in the forests and often, when defending their areas, engaged in conflicts with the 'agriculturalists'.

In the Middle Neolithic period (ca. 3500 to 2500 B.C.) there was certain progress in agriculture, which consisted of plowing the soil with an ox-drawn furrowing plough, even though the hoe cultivation still prevailed. The Funnel Beaker culture, brought by a people of unknown origin, was superimposed, over vast regions of Europe, upon the old culture of Danubian origin, especially the Stroke-Ornamented Pottery culture and the Lengyel culture (the latter named so after the town of Lengyel in Hungary). The Funnel-Beaker culture covered most Polish lands. Animal breeding was intensified and economic life became brisker. In the Świętokrzyskie Mountains in Central Poland there was a flint mine, at that time the largest in Europe, with some 1,000 shafts. Barter included flint, and also cattle and amber. Imported bronze also appeared.

The Late Neolithic period (ca. 2500 to 1700 B.C.) saw the arrival in the Polish lands of groups bearing different cultures based more on hunting than on agriculture, because the advances of the agricultural revolution were very uneven. The most important event was the coming of a population whose culture was marked by pottery ornamented with cords impressed on soft clay (hence the name the Corded Ware culture). These people based their economic life on agriculture and pasturing, with a greatly increased use of horses. The Corded Ware culture covered the regions from the Rhine to the Volga and beyond and from the Danube to southern Scandinavia. It is believed, although the opinions on that point are not unanimous, that the carriers of the Corded Ware culture were the first wave of the Indo-European population that came to the forest-covered European territories from — as it is usually supposed — the Asian steppes. Later waves of the Indo-Europeans, more differentiated linguistically, came to Europe in the Bronze Age and were superimposed first upon the palaeo-European population and later one upon the other. Many of those new waves consisted of the now North European peoples, the Germans, the Balts and the Slavs. The latter two groups at first formed an ethnic and linguistic community, to be split only later into the Balts and the Slavs.

The identification where the Balto-Slavonic and later the Slavonic language group became isolated from the other Indo-European peoples is still controversial. It is assumed here that the process took place in the area between the middle course of the Dneper and the Odra, parallel to the arrival of new groups of the Indo-European population.

4. The Slavs in the Polish lands. The Bronze and the Iron Age

It took the Proto-Slavonic and the Slavonic population nearly one thousand years, from ca. 1500—1300 B.C. to ca. 500 B.C. (almost the whole Bronze Age and the early Iron Age), to settle in the Polish lands. These times saw the transition from the cultivation of the soil with hoes to the use of ox-drawn furrowing ploughs. The so-called Trzciniec culture (from the name of a locality in the Lublin region in Central Poland) was, as is often assumed, a product of those Proto-Slavs, who gradually superimposed themselves upon the local population, absorbed existing culture and imparted new features to it in the process. Next to the Trzciniec culture there was also the Pre-Lusatian culture, associated with the palaeo-European people called Veneti, who occupied the areas between the lower Vistula and the upper Warta. That culture, characterized by mound graves, was common to the mid-Danubian basin and later also spread to Moravia and Germany.

During some four or five hundred years in the early Bronze Age the Polish lands saw the emergence of the material (and probably also spiritual) culture called Lusatian, which supposedly evolved from the Proto-Lusatian and the Trzciniec culture. It is known to have had two varieties, the western (more advanced) and the eastern, the latter with cattle breeding prevailing over agriculture and with a stronger influence of the Trzciniec culture. The Neuri, whom Herodotus mentions to have lived in the 5th century B.C. to the east of the Bug, were, as is usually assumed, already Slavs.

The range of cultivated plants increased under the Lusatian culture to include several strains of wheat and barley, millet, peas, poppy, beans, lentils, garlic, flax, hemp and turnip. Animals bred included cattle, pigs, sheep and goats. There were some endeavours to keep bees. Pottery flourished as did such crafts as the processing of wood, bone, horn, and amber, and also plaiting and tanning. Canoes were dug out of tree trunks and, towards the end of the period, two-wheeled and four-wheeled carts were known. Trade was gaining in importance, bronze being largely used as money. The technique of soil cultivation and the search for new pastures made people change their living places frequently. A settlement might last for a number of years. Some settlements, however, were permanent in character, as evidenced by Biskupin, a fortified settlement from the period of the Lusatian culture.

In the later periods of the Bronze Age and the Lusatian culture, groups of clans began to combine into tribes of varying size. The wealth and the power of the chiefs of tribes and senior tribesmen increased. The search for new lands led to conflicts among tribes and also (as a reflection of the struggle for power) among senior tribesmen. This in turn resulted in the consolidation of the tribes and the emergence of new ones. The fortified settlements mentioned above were often the centres of the defence systems of the tribes. There were also conflicts between the settled population and the newly arriving tribes.

The Iron Age on Polish territory brought the development of a fairly homogeneous proto-Polish culture, based on soil cultivation and animal rearing. The old crafts continued to develop but metallurgy (which made use of bog iron ores) and blacksmithing gained in importance, especially in the metallurgical centre in the Świętokrzyskie Mountains. Among the grain crops the role of rye increased, although it was still of less importance than wheat and millet. Trade continued to increase and expand but the economy was, of course, natural. The so-called amber road, with the settlement Calissia (present-day Kalisz in Central Poland), recorded at the beginning of the Christian era, was then of great importance as one of the principal trade routes.

The formation of the proto-Polish culture (the immediate predecessor of the culture which was to be typical of Poland in the Dark and the Middle Ages), took place following the decomposition of the Lusatian culture. The Celts had a very strong impact (especially in the southern part of Poland); and they were more advanced in social development and economically (they were the first people in the Polish lands to use money). It is likely that the fall of the Lusatian culture was at least partly caused by Scythian invasions (which devastated the regions inhabited by the Veletians and thus made them easier to penetrate for the Slavs), and by inter-tribal wars. A dynamic Eastern Pomeranian culture (also known as the Wejherowo-Krotoszyn culture) developed ca. 500 B.C. under the influence of the Saale culture. The Eastern Pomeranian culture, marked by characteristic urns with imitations of human faces, spread over most Polish lands and helped to some extent to revive the collapsing Lusatian culture. A variety of the Eastern Pomeranian culture known as the Bell Grave culture spread westward. The Jastorf culture developed in Western Pomerania up to the Warta and the Noteć. It was brought by the Bastarnae and the Skiroi, Germanic tribes that over one century later moved southwards along the Odra.

Celtic influence was strong; in two centuries it penetrated the Eastern Pomeranian and other cultures contributing to the emergence of the more advanced Cist Grave culture, which had two varieties, the Przeworsk and the Oksywie culture (both named after the localities in which burial places from that period were discovered).

The Roman Age (25 to 500 A.D.) marked a further step toward the cultural uniformity of the Polish lands. The Celtic influence was replaced by that of the expansive Roman Empire. The Slavs were already well known to Greek and Roman authors who have transmitted the earliest written data about them.

The five centuries of the Roman influence in the Polish lands, dominated by the Cist Grave culture, were not a peaceful period for that area.

Ethnic conditions became very complicated. The first 250 years witnessed the southward migrations, from Scandinavia to the lower Vistula basin, of the Germanic Goths and Gepidians, who wanted to gain control of the amber road. At the turn of the 2nd century they moved further east toward the Black Sea and next to the territories belonging to the Roman Empire that was then suffering from invasions by the Visigoths and Ostrogoths. In the mid-3rd century the Gepidians moved to what is now Transsylvania. They were followed by some of the Burgundians, while other Burgundians and the Rugians moved either toward the Danube or westwards. The places left by them were being occupied by the Slavs, who were at the same time also occupying some of the areas previously held by the Balts. In this way, once the Polish lands had been abandoned by the various Germanic tribes and after the Slavs had expanded further westwards, in the mid-3rd century the basins of both the Odra and the Vistula, from the Carpathians to the Baltic (except for Masovia which was still inhabited by the Balts) came to be occupied by the Slavs.

During the last century of the ancient period, the Polish lands suffered much, both directly and indirectly, from the expansion of the Huns, who reached the peak of their power under the rule of the brothers Bleda and Attila (445—53). At this time the Slavs were moving further westwards, in the direction of the Elbe. It has been calculated that in the Iron Age the population in the Polish lands grew from about half a million to some 750,000. But the events which took place in the 5th century (the invasion of the Huns and the migrations of the Slavs to the West and to the South) reduced that population to some 350,000—400,000. An essential increase was to take place only in later centuries.

The reconstructed part of the fortified settlement at Biskupin near Żnin in Great Poland (ca. 500 B.C.)

The head of a figure of a pagan deity, found at Janków in Great Poland

An early mediaeval arrow-head made of iron, with barbs covered with bronze, found at Świętowice near Włocławek

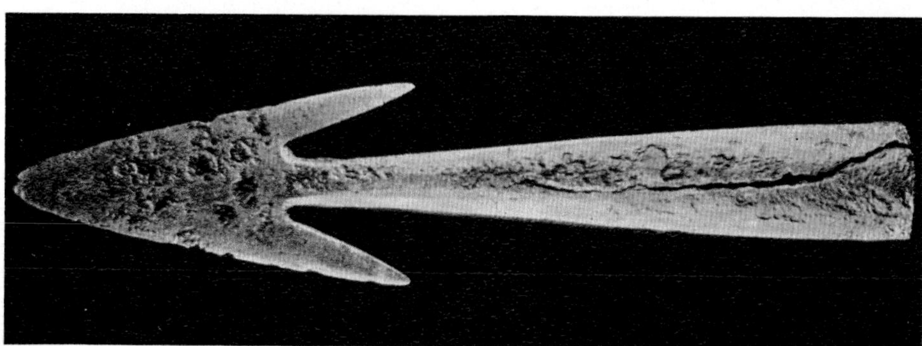

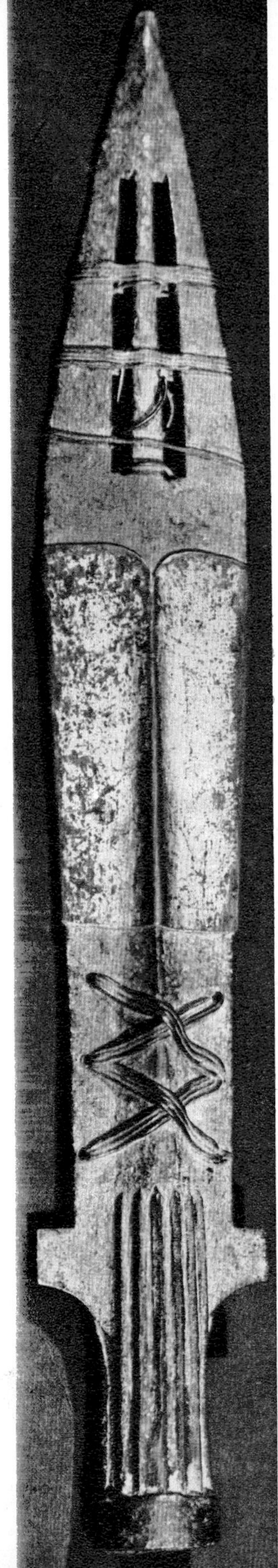

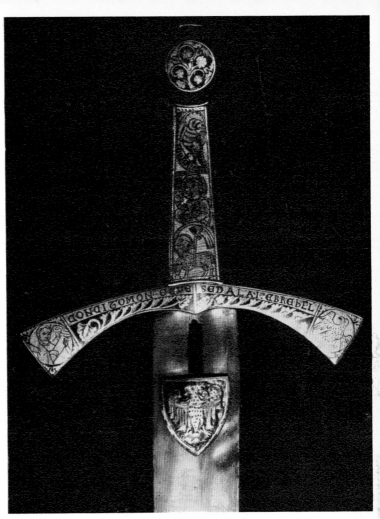

Coronation insignia (regalia) of Polish monarchs: St. Maurice's spear, offered by the Emperor Otto III to Boleslaus the Brave in A.D. 1000, and the coronation sword dating from the 12th or the 13th century

Boleslaus the Brave (reigned 999–1025), the first crowned ruler of Poland (image on the obverse of a denarius)

Part of the bronze door of the Gniezno cathedral (12th cent.), showing the history of St. Adalbert's mission to the pagan Old Prussians

St. Leonard's crypt in Wawel Castle (completed before 1118)

Part of a Romanesque column in Norbertan Sisters' church at Strzelno (ca. 1190)

The monarch on the throne – image found on a paten offered by Prince Conrad of Masovia to the Płock cathedral (mid-13th cent.)

The Romanesque collegiate church at Tum near Łęczyca (ca. 1150)

The Battle of Legnica (1241) as shown in an anonymous oil painting

Chapter II

Polish Territory in the Early Middle Ages. The Beginnings of Poland (from the 6th to the mid-10th century)

1. The breakthrough in the Early Middle Ages

During the several centuries that preceded the rule of Mieszko I the population on Polish territory increased by at least 120 per cent, from ca. 400,000 in the middle of the first millennium A.D. to ca. 1,000,000 in the mid-10th century. This meant that in the 10th century the average density of the population was about four persons per sq. kilometre. The most densely populated areas were those of Great Poland and the western part of Little Poland, while less populated were Masovia and the eastern part of Little Poland. (The terms *Great Poland* and *Little Poland* are traditional and should not be understood as suggesting any expansion from Little Poland into Great Poland. Great Poland roughly corresponds to the region of Poznań, and Little Poland, to the region of Cracow. The mediaeval Latin terms were, correspondingly, *Polonia Maior* and *Polonia Minor — translator's note.*)

That growth of the population was a proof of a fairly long and relatively undisturbed period of economic growth which secured food and better conditions of tillage. The economy provided not only the means that were indispensable for the survival of the direct producers (tillers), but also certain surpluses which could be used by people not directly engaged in producing them. Some labour could also be spent on undertakings which served all the inhabitants, such as the construction of fortified settlements, roads and bridges. This provided opportunities for the emergence of states as the political entities which organized the life of their populations on new principles, but required their material and manual co-operation.

The early Middle Ages marked a breakthrough for just this reason. All the areas occupied by the Slavs witnessed the emergence of states that in turn contributed to breaking up the Slavonic population (originally fairly homogeneous ethnically and linguistically) into the basic groups which from this period became clearly differentiated: the Russian tribes in the East, the Serbian, Croatian, and Bulgarian tribes in the South, and the Bohemian, Moravian, Slovak, Polish and Polabian tribes in the West. The Polabian tribes, sometimes called the Western Slavs, were the only ones not to give rise to a single supratribal state, even though small tribal states did emerge there (for example the Veletian Union).

The Moravians were the most active in this respect among the Western Slavs. The first half of the 9th century saw the rise of so-called Greater Moravia, or the Great Moravian State, which existed for about one hundred years. It subsequently collapsed under the attack of the nomadic Magyars who were then settling in the Danubian basin. The heritage of the Great Moravian State was taken over by the Bohemian State founded by the Premyslids. The strong Bohemo-Moravian political centre expanded in many directions, including northwards. Its sphere of influence covered Little Poland and Silesia, which prevented these highly developed regions from playing any major role in the formation of the Polish state, and at the same time gave rise to the Polish-Bohemian rivalry which was mitigated only by the threat represented by the Eastern German marks at the time of Mieszko I.

The political breakthrough in the form of the emergence of the state as a political organism was connected with far-reaching changes in the economy and in social structure. In agriculture expanded tillage on permanent plots was accompanied by the abandonment of the primitive technique of fertilizing the land by the slash-and-burn method, a technique that required ever new lands to cultivate, and also by the individualization of agriculture in the form of separation of single farms from lands held by communities, and by the stabilization of settlements, that is the formation of permanent open settlements comprising a single household or several households grouped into a small village.

Territorial neighbourhood bonds emerged spontaneously. They linked together fortified settlements with the open settlements around them and also — which process had started in the preceding period — tribes that formed political organizations. The oldest form of Slavic neighbourhood union was called a *żupa*, which originally probably denoted any separate territorial unit. Such a small territory, which was merely a union of neighbours, had a *żupan* as its head. That term, later abbreviated into *pan* and applied to the *castellanei* (literally castle administrators, who were officials of the territorial administration under the Piast dynasty), gave rise to the Polish title *pan*, which means 'lord', 'master', and is now also used as a form of address roughly corresponding to the English *Mr.* Later terms, which developed following the economic growth of the lands and the formation of state administration and denoted territorial neighbourhood unions, were *opole* (which consisted of several *pole* 'field'), in Little Poland called *osada* (which term was due to the Bohemian influence) and *gród,* meaning a 'stronghold town'. In the last-named case we have to do with a transfer of the name of the centre of a neighbourhood union upon the territory of that union.

The social structure and organization of the Early Middle Ages show the development of nuclear forms of the feudal system with its characteristic features — the existence of a privileged stratum (later class) of aristocracy (lords, nobles) and dependent small holders.

In the earliest mediaeval period the lords emerged from the tribal authorities (heads of neighbourhood unions and tribes, members of their families, their advisers, etc.). They used to carve out for themselves ever greater farms as they had at their disposal serfs (mainly those taken prisoner during military expeditions); above all they kept larger numbers of cattle, horses, sheep and pigs. They also began to make dependent upon them many of the local farmers (for instance against the loans advanced to them). The farmers continued to be free, dependent only upon the state, which, however, burdened them with corvée and tributes. The lords, closely connected with the state authorities as administrators and leaders, at first availed themselves indirectly of the charges imposed upon the agricultural population (so that the system of contributions to the state became intertwined with the so-called feudal rent), and later, with the approval of the state authorities, began to collect the rent directly from the farmers.

2. The emergence of the State of Gniezno

Before the 10th century there had been in the Polish lands some 500 to 600 stronghold towns that formed the centres of the neighbouring unions (*żupy, opola, osady, grody* in the sense of territorial units — for the explanation of the terms see above). The average area of such a union was about 300 sq. kilometres. A number of such unions formed what was called a small tribe and a union of these formed a large tribe. The emergence of large tribes, usually by the domination of a dynamic small tribe, marked the first stage in the development of the state. Next was the formation of unions of large tribes, related ethnically and linguistically to each other, and the consolidation and organizational strengthening of such. Before the time of Mieszko I, the Polish lands went through the last stage of statal organization. Small tribes held a territory from 1,000 to 10,000 sq. kilometres each and large tribes, from 10,000 to 30,000 sq. kilometres each.

Detailed information about the number and location of small and large tribes in the Polish lands in the 10th century is given in what was known as *The Geographer of Bavaria*. The tribes then numbered about fifty. The following large tribes were then formed, whose areas were later the main base of the administrative division of the state (and in a sense continue to correspond to that division to this day): the Wiślanie and the Lędzianie in Little Poland, the Mazowszanie in Masovia, the Polanie in Great Poland, the Goplanie in Kujawy, the Ślężanie in Silesia (there were perhaps two large tribes there), and the Pomorzanie in Pomerania. There was also an independent small tribe of the Lubuszanie. Other small tribes existed as a rule within the framework of large tribes. For instance, in Silesia seven small tribes were formed: the Opolanie, the Golęszyce, the Głupczyce (probably), the Ślężanie, the Bobrzanie, the Trzebowianie, and the Dziadoszanie. There were over a dozen small tribes in Pomerania, namely those located at Chełmno, Gdańsk, Łeba, Ujście, Kołobrzeg, Szczecin and Starogard, Pyrzyce, Wolin, Sławno plus a few others in Gdańsk Pomerania. Great Poland was inhabited by the tribes located at Pałuki, Lednica and Gniezno, Giecz, Poznań, Bonikowo and Przemęcz, and on the Orla.

The Polanie, and especially the small tribe at Lednica and Gniezno, formed the centre around which the Polish state developed. The Polanie, whose name derives from cultivated fields (*pole* 'field'), had a comparatively well developed agriculture and nascent crafts connected with metal working. Their tribal territory was fairly densely populated, and the prince of Gniezno monopolized in that locality the profitable trade in salt from Kujawy. He was thus economically superior to the Goplanie, settled around Kruszwica, who had also had a chance of playing an essential role in the formation of the state. But the Goplanie succumbed to the supremacy of the Polanie who, having been successful in integrating the large tribe and subordinating other Polish tribes, felt the need to build a stronghold town that would properly demonstrate their power.

In the late 8th century they planned to build from the very foundations a stronghold town in the place later called Mount Lech. This settlement, surrounded by inland waters and forests, resembled in its situation a nest and so was called Gniezno (*gniezno,* an old Polish form of *gniazdo* 'nest'). The stronghold town was developing rapidly and soon assumed the form of an urban settlement. It gave its name to the political organization which even at the times of Mieszko I used to be called the State of Gniezno. As early as ca. 850 A.D. Gniezno comprised a stronghold, two suburbs inhabited by craftsmen, an open settlement connected with the fortified one and a separate market settlement which later became the centre of the town.

The rivalry between the Polanie and the Goplanie was reflected in the legend about Popiel, the defeated ruler of the Goplanie who, when imprisoned in the Kruszwica tower, was said to have been eaten by mice. The legend in fact mirrored the struggle for power within the Polanie tribe between the dynasty of the Piasts (which held Lednica and Gniezno) and that of Popiel. This was the late 9th century, the time of Siemowit, the first prince of the Piast dynasty to be known by name, and the period in which Gniezno flourished. Siemowit's successor, called Leszek (or Lestek), the grandfather of Mieszko I, incorporated Masovia and the eastern part of Little Poland (the country of the Lędzianie) into the State of Gniezno. Siemomysł, Mieszko's father, was more concerned with administrative problems; it is also supposed that he might have conquered Pomerania.

Silesia and the region of Cracow were then still within the sphere of influence of the Bohemian state. But gradually the rivalry with the Bohemians was ceding place to the defence of the western frontiers — the problem much more essential when viewed in the historical perspective — because the Holy Roman Emipre was engaging through its so-called eastern marks in a direct conflict with the nascent Polish state. The Slavonic barrier which separated the State of Gniezno from the Germans and which still existed in the period of the first Piasts, had a good effect upon the state-forming activity of the Polanie: peace in the West enabled them to get ahead of the Wiślanie and Lędzianie in Little Poland, of the Mazowszanie (who were then involved in conflicts with Baltic tribes and moreover had vast regions to populate) and also of the Pomorzanie (who lagged behind in the development of agriculture) in the process of the formation of the state.

3. Early mediaeval Poland: its economy, society, and culture

As has been mentioned, the economic life was intensifying. Permanent agriculture helped increase the output of oats, wheat, rye, barley, millet, and vegetables. The same applied to animal husbandry, primarily cattle raising, which was the economic foundation of the emerging tribal aristocracy. Land was tilled with furrowing ploughs, and grain was harvested with sickles and grass with short scythes. The crops, undifferentiated before, were replaced by winter crops and spring crops, which enabled rotation and led to the three-field system, so characteristic of the Late Middle Ages (one-third under winter crops, one-third under spring crops, one-third laid fallow, rotated annually). In all, the Polish lands in the early 10th century produced some 200,000 metric tons of grain. The output of iron was some 80 metric tons annually.

The necessary products supplied by craftsmen were mostly turned out on a self-sufficiency basis. Some craftsmen (stone-workers, potters) were largely itinerant. But the process of specialization in crafts had already begun, connected with the development of strongholds and market settlements. The list of the previously specialized crafts, such as metallurgy and blacksmithing (with goldsmithing), was now extended by, for example, pottery, comb-making, amber working and bead-making.

The development of strongholds and market settlements is sometimes regarded as the beginning of the urban revolution on Polish territory which began in the 9th century. For they were in fact the beginnings, even though such settlements as Gniezno, Poznań, Wolin, Wrocław, Kołobrzeg, Gdańsk and Cracow had already made themselves felt in the urban, economic and political life of the country. The further development of the political institutions contributed to an increased intensity of urbanization.

It is interesting to note the commercial contacts between the Polish lands and other territories. In the 6th century they still followed the old pattern: merchants from Western and Southern Europe used to bring primarily ornaments and weapons and exchange them for amber, furs, honey, wax and slaves. This barter was organized by and satisfied the needs of the tribal aristocracy. The 7th and 8th centuries saw considerable disturbance of these trade routes, caused by the arrival of the Avars in the Danubian basin and the migrations of the Longobards to Italy and of the Slavs to Dalmatia and Istria. It was not until the turn of the 8th and 9th centuries that Polish territory began to actively participate in the barter trade primarily with Central, Northern and Eastern Europe. This barter did not cover the basic products. The economy was natural in character and economic activity had as its main incentive satisfaction of daily needs and coping with the burdens imposed by the developing tribal organization. The barter was that of commodity against commodity, although, especially at the end of the period under consideration, it also included the use of so-called object money, for instance in the form of pieces of linen.

As mentioned above, the increased population meant new settlements, at first near rivers and other inland waters. They were mostly single and already individually owned farms, sometimes groups of farms, and only rarely large settlements. Most people still lived in houses that were partly dugouts, but the number of huts constructed on the soil surface was increasing. They were built of logs joined at the corners, or of wooden poles with clay-covered wicker plaitwork between them. Wood and clay were thus the principal building materials.

The living standard was quite high, not inferior to that reached by other rural communities in Europe. The differences at this time were mainly in the sphere of the development of urban life and the extent of the aristocratic culture. But the ways of life were similar, differences being mainly due to the varieties of local products. The diet included groats (made of barley and millet), flour, vegetables, fruit (also wild ones), milk, cream, cheese and eggs. Meat (mainly beef and pork) was eaten stewed, roast, and smoked. Game at this time already played only a supplementary role. Cakes were baked. Bread in its present-day form, made with yeast, did not appear until later (cf. III, 4). Mead and beer were common. The number of kitchen vessels and pieces of furniture was growing. Clothes were made of linen and woollen cloth; footwear, of wood and hides. As the social differences increased, differences in dress were also observed, but that applied mainly to ornaments.

The proto-Polish people knew various musical instruments: guitars, lyres, pipes and drums. There was a well developed sense of beauty, as seen in the forms and ornaments of objects of daily use. Carving was fairly common.

A quite coherent system of religious beliefs had been developed, reflecting a view of the world dominated by the worship of Nature. Magical thinking with related rites was prevalent. The idea of a superior deity, called Swarog or Swarożyc by the Slavs, had emerged. People also believed in lesser deities and in spirits that were either friendly or hostile to man. Hills (such as Ślęża in Silesia), groves and also plain wooden buildings served as the places of worship. Effigies of Swarog used to be carved in stone or wood, often as statues with many faces.

The custom of burning the dead and placing the ashes in urns, usually deposited in small cemeteries, was still common.

Society, which was much more differentiated than in the previous epochs, consisted of the following strata and groups: princes; heads of tribes and *żupy* (and their families); lords (tribal aristocracy); free small holders; a few small holders dependent on the lords; serfs; and craftsmen and traders, living in fortified settlements and suburbs. The strata of priests and warriors also began to emerge. All these, however, were not yet social classes, especially in the Marxist sense of the term.

The formation of the tribes, the process of combination into larger organizations and then the formation of the state resulted in considerable changes in social consciousness. Tribal and supratribal bonds were becoming ever stronger.

Chapter III

The Piast Monarchy: from Mieszko I to Boleslaus Wrymouth. Formation of Mediaeval Poland (963—1138)

1. The characteristic features of the period. The determinants of the progress of civilization

The record made in 963 by Vidukind of Corvey (near Höxter on the Weser) in his *Saxon History,* which mentions Mieszko (*rex Misaca*) for the first time, was, of course, coincidental, but it proves that Mieszko aroused interest in Europe and his nascent state was becoming known to his contemporaries. The historical perspective enables us to take note of what the people of that time did not realize: it was a period of many eminent rulers whose deeds made strong impressions on the history of their respective lands. In Germany it was the epoch of the Ottos: Otto I the Great (936—73), his son Otto II (973—83), and his grandson Otto III (983—1002), friend of Boleslaus the Brave. France was ruled by Hugh Capet (ca. 940—96), the founder of the Capetian dynasty; Rus had as its ruler Vladimir, the prince of Kiev (ca. 980—1015) also called Vladimir the Great; and Spain, occupied by the Arabs, was at the end of the rule of Abd-al-Rahman III (912—61).

The term *Polanie* (*Polanes*), and later *Poles* was more and more commonly used in 10th century Europe to denote the inhabitants of the Polish state, which with an increasing frequency was called *Polska* (*Poland, Polonia* in Latin, *Polan* in Old German, *Polaine* or *Paulenne* in Old French), even though the traditional name of the State of Gniezno (*Civitas Gnesnensis*) was still customarily used. The name of Poland, which etymologically comes from *pole* ('field'), has its analogues in French Champagne (from *champ* 'field') and Italian Campania (from *campo* 'field'). The name *Wielkopolska* has its analogue in the French name Gronterre (Grande Terre), dating from the 13th century. It is to be noted that for a long time the name *Polska* referred only to *Wielkopolska.* As the name *Polska* was becoming increasingly common, the terminological distinction developed which was intended to stress that the territory of the Polanie occupies the most important and the oldest part of Poland and which opposed *Wielkopolska* (*Polonia Maior*) to *Małopolska* (*Polonia Minor*). The most common English renderings, also adopted in this work, are *Great Poland* and *Little Poland,* respectively.

In the period of over 180 years between the time of Mieszko I and Boleslaus Wrymouth the first 60 years proved decisive for the further history of Poland. The initial part of that period of 180 years saw the end of the territorial formation of the state and its internal organization. Poland won recognition from the two principal — and often rival — forces in Europe: the German Empire, which continued the idea of the universal Roman Empire, and the Papacy, which claimed spiritual (and political) leadership. By adopting Christianity in 966 Poland entered into the Latin civilization, in which process the decisive role was played by the Church, which came to Poland as the administrative arm of the Christian religion. The two other great sources of cultural influence in Europe, namely the Byzantine Empire (to which the Kiev Rus was linked much more strongly) and the Moslem world, had only indirect contacts with Poland. This applies in particular to the Arab world (yet it was Arab travellers, among them Ibrahim ibn Yakub, who gave the greatest amount of information about Poland and classed Mieszko I among the most powerful rulers of that time).

While Mieszko I epitomized the unification of the Polish tribal lands, his successor, Boleslaus the Brave, strove for the leading position in the Slavonic world within the cultural hegemony of the Holy Roman Empire. Both operations required a centralized political power, which was more and more threatened by an increasingly self-conscious and ambitious stratum of the lords. This led to a weakening of the state and resulted in difficulties in maintaining Poland's territorial integrity. In such a situation much depended upon the political talents of the rulers and the balance of power in Europe. The 120 years from the death of Boleslaus the Brave were a period of struggle to preserve the territories and the sovereign rights in relation to the Holy Roman Empire. In this struggle Poland had a constant ally in Hungary, whereas the Bohemians, who did not want to reconcile themselves to the fact that Silesia had become part of Poland, usually sided with Poland's adversaries. Poland was also in conflict with the then strong Kiev Rus, primarily over the group of strongholds called Grody Czerwieńskie, incorporated into Poland by Boleslaus the Brave following his great expedition to Rus in 1018, though these two political entities nevertheless strove to maintain good relations. Relations with the Germans were thus the focal issue.

The internal political organization and the political thinking formulated under Mieszko I and Boleslaus the Brave, later observed by successive rulers who took the latter king as their model, must be considered the most important manifestations of the progress achieved by Poland in the 10th and 11th centuries. It was also a period of remarkable advances in technology and administration. There was a rapid development in the art of fortification and the standard of housing, the construction of bridges and erection of stone buildings, dominated by the influence of pre-Romanesque (Carolingian) and Romanesque art. Armed forces were organized, alongside the development of the military art (strategy, tactics, military technology) of the then highest European standards. The size of the army increased, too: the standing army rose from some 3,000 warriors under Mieszko I to some 15,000 under Boleslaus the Brave.

The general development of the political institutions was accompanied by advances in material civilization and intellectual culture in society at large. Intellectual culture at first developed in close connection with the activities of Church and state and was based on the newly adopted Christian ideology. That culture, which included Latin literature, education, and an artistic life following the general lines then prevailing in Europe, was primarily the culture of the ruler's court. In social life the recommendations of the Church came to be observed, but the common people continued for a long time to practice the traditional pagan rites. The inner consolidation of the state began the creation of a supratribal, national consciousness.

2. Poland's struggle for position in the world. The nature of political authority and the frontiers of the state

Mieszko I, by adopting Christianity in 966 in agreement with the Holy Roman Empire and taking as his wife the Bohemian princess Dubrava (Dąbrówka), strove to ensure good relations with his western and southern neighbours. The fact that southern Poland was still under Bohemian influence decided that the first (still missionary) bishopric with Bishop Jordan did not cover Little Poland and Silesia, which were under the influence of the see in Prague. With respect to those regions Mieszko I adopted the tactic of gradually increasing Polish influence there, while with respect to Pomerania in the North he decided to engage in armed conflict with the Germans who strove to dominate that region. The conflict, in which he found support from the Bohemians, ended in the incorporation of Western Pomerania into Poland. In the course of that conflict the Poles defeated the East German margrave Hodo in the Battle of Cedynia in 972. Hodo invaded Poland, as he feared that the Poles would invade the area he wanted to reserve for German expansion.

In 990 Mieszko I succeeded in securing Cracow for his son Boleslaus (the future Boleslaus the Brave), who ruled there while recognizing the Bohemian supremacy in that region. Mieszko I had no time (or no intention) to take further steps towards uniting the Polish lands. The loss of Grody Czerwieńskie (the area bounded by the Bug in the East, the Wieprz in the West, the Bełżec region in the South, and the middle part of the Chełm region in the North, with several dozen stronghold towns), occupied by Vladimir, the prince of Rus, in 981 (cf. III, 1), posed a problem, too.

Boleslaus the Brave (992—1025) completed the unification of the Polish territories and the consolidation of the state, and to put into effect the above-mentioned idea of extending Polish influence upon the neighbouring Slavonic lands he attacked the Polabian (Western) Slavs and intervened in Bohemia and in Rus.

In his foreign policy pride of place went to the German issue. The meeting at Gniezno, the then capital of Poland, where the Emperor Otto III came with a political mission in 1000, is treated as the first attempt at a Polish-German agreement. Otto III accorded to Boleslaus the Brave sovereignty within the Holy Roman Empire, subordinating him as 'a brother and collaborator of the Empire'. But the death of Otto III was soon followed by a change in the Holy Roman Empire's policy toward Poland, which resulted in long Polish-German wars. On the other hand, the decision made at the Gniezno meeting concerning the organization of the Church in Poland, proved durable. Three new bishoprics (Cracow, Wrocław and Kołobrzeg) and the archbishopric in Gniezno were established which cancelled the claims of the archbishopric in Magdeburg, derived from the fact that after the death in 984 of the missionary Bishop Jordan there was practically no Church organization in Poland. Boleslaus the Brave's earlier actions as a Christian ruler included, among other things, his sending a mission to spread the Christian faith among the Old Prussians, a Baltic people who lived in the area between the lower Vistula and the lower Niemen (the Balts included also the Yatvingians and Sudovians, the Lithuanians, and the Latvians). The mission sent in 997 was headed by Adalbert, the bishop of Prague, canonized two years later. The mortal remains of the bishop, who died a martyr's death when on his mission, were worshipped at the meeting of Gniezno, and his cult was later often used for political purposes. His brother Gaudentius became the first Archbishop of Gniezno, while St. Adalbert himself came to be regarded as the patron of the Gniezno cathedral.

The later years of Boleslaus' rule were mainly occupied by his struggle with Henry II, the king and later the emperor (973—1024), for influence in Lusatia and Bohemia. In the spring of 1002 Boleslaus the Brave occupied Lusatia, where the throne was vacant after the murder of Margrave Ekkehard, and married his daughter Regelinda to Herman, the late Margrave's son. The Emperor approved, but Boleslaus' intervention in Bohemia, when he shortly after proclaimed himself duke, exacerbated his relations with Henry II, and led to a war that lasted, with short intervals, from 1002 to 1018, to be concluded in the latter year by the peace treaty of Budziszyn (Bautzen). Poland succeeded in defending its sovereignty and on the strength of the treaty obtained Lower and Upper Lusatia and Moravia, while Boleslaus married Oda, a daughter of Ekkehard. In the meantime, however, Western Pomerania seceded from Poland.

The war confirmed the effectiveness of the tactics of blocking the enemy's advance with fortifications and abatises, making him besiege stronghold towns and at the same time ward off attacks. Irregular warfare tactics was also used successfully. On the whole the war bore testimony to the high level of Polish military art.

Boleslaus the Brave also established links with Kiev Rus by marrying his second daughter to Svetopluk, the son of Prince Vladimir of Kiev. At his son-in-law's request he intervened in Rus to help him ascend the throne, but the success was of short duration, because Svetopluk soon had to leave Kiev. The domination of Bohemia (where Boleslaus ruled for only a year and a half) and Moravia was a short-lived attainment, too. It is true that he held Moravia for over a dozen years, but he probably lost it before the end of his rule; this, however, is not clear from the sources.

Boleslaus' last significant act was his coronation in Gniezno in 1025, which was important for enhancing his prestige with the nobles. It symbolized the integrity of the monarchy and raised the king's status among other contemporary rulers.

The death of Boleslaus the Brave was followed by the hardship-ridden rule of Mieszko II who, for all the adversities, managed to maintain the territorial unity of the state and to consolidate it internally. Lusatia and the Milsko region were lost (as was Moravia, if its loss had not occurred earlier), but Western Pomerania was regained. Mieszko II (1025—34), Boleslaus the Brave's son and successor, continued his father's policy, but Otto and Bezprym, Boleslaus' other sons, who were removed from power, rendered its implementation difficult. Hence after a brief exile in 1031, when power was seized by Bezprym, assisted by Rus, Mieszko II had to accept the hard conditions imposed by the Holy Roman Emperor: in exchange for assistance he renounced the royal dignity and returned to Poland (the coronation regalia had been returned to the Emperor Conrad II earlier by Bezprym, who also sought the Emperor's support).

It was Mieszko II's son, Casimir the Restorer, who succeeded in coping with the centrifugal political forces, with the consequences of the popular uprising in 1037 directed against the Church and the nobles, and the devastating invasion (in 1038 or 1039), led by Bretislas, Prince of Bohemia.

Casimir the Restorer (1034—58) also had at first to flee the country. With the assistance of Yaroslav, the prince of Kiev (whose sister Dobrogneva he married), he defeated Maslav, the noble who ruled Masovia. At the cost of tribute to be paid to the Bohemians he also regained Silesia, which had been occupied by Bretislas.

The devastation by Bretislas of Great Poland (in particular Gniezno and Poznań) made the Restorer move his capital to Cracow.

After Casimir the Restorer's death the rule went to his eldest son Boleslaus called the Bold (1058—79), who manifestly strove to continue the policy initiated by Boleslaus the Brave. His rule saw the confirmation of Poland's international position and of the central authority within the state, which was not accepted by the feudal lords, who represented tendencies to decentralization.

In his striving to make Poland fully independent Boleslaus the Bold ceased paying the tribute to the Bohemians and established contacts with the opponents of the German King Henry IV. For the same reason he supported Pope Gregory VII who claimed full independence of the Church hierarchy from the emperor. Boleslaus the Bold took advantage of the latter conflict to obtain the royal title (1076) and to restore the Church organization in Poland. In 1075 the papal legates re-established the archbishopric in Gniezno, subordinating to it the bishoprics of Poznań, Cracow, and Wrocław, and established a new bishopric in Płock. But the monarchy thus restored proved unstable. The internal opposition, led probably by a noble named Sieciech, offered strong resistance. A conspiracy was made, led by Stanislaus, the Bishop of Cracow, who was later tried for treason. The sentencing of the bishop to death, which the archbishop did not oppose, resulted in a revolt of the nobles and in 1079 Boleslaus the Bold, deprived of power, fled to Hungary.

His brother, Ladislaus Herman (1079—1102), whom the nobles asked to ascend the throne, based his rule mainly on an agreement with the Bohemians and the Germans. Married to Judith, a sister of the emperor, he refrained from having himself crowned and also started again paying to the Bohemians the tribute for Silesia. Dissatisfaction with the excessive influence of the Voivode Sieciech led to internal disorders, and later (1097) to an agreement that provided for the division of the kingdom between Ladislaus' sons, Zbigniew and Boleslaus Wrymouth. After the death of his father, who retained the supreme authority, Boleslaus began to strive for the reunification of the country and for its full sovereignty. After internal conflicts he succeeded in putting his plans into effect thus preventing Poland from disintegrating into provinces. Like Boleslaus the Bold, he established good relations with Hungary and Rus. In 1108 he supported Hungary in its struggle against the invasion by the German King Henry V, which served the latter as a pretext for invading Poland. Henry V, pretending that he wanted to help Zbigniew, who had been deprived of power, amassed some 10,000 knights from various parts of Germany, but the tactics worked out earlier under Boleslaus the Brave proved effective again, and Henry V, at first forced to raise the siege of Głogów, was defeated near Wrocław in open battle.

Boleslaus Wrymouth also strove to incorporate Pomerania into Poland, and ultimately (1122—24) conquered Western Pomerania thus putting an end to predatory invasions by Pomeranian lords in Great Poland. Military operations in Western Pomerania were accompanied by missionary work. Following a mission by Bishop Otto of Bamberg, organized by Boleslaus at great expense, some Pomeranians adopted Christianity in 1124. A bishopric was established at Uznam (later moved to Wolin and Kamień), which replaced that of Kołobrzeg. Moreover, the Church organization in Poland was expanded by the establishment of the bishopric of Lubusz (for the region on the middle Odra) and of Włocławek (for Kujawy and Gdańsk Pomerania).

During the last years of his reign Boleslaus Wrymouth extended his support to Boris, a pretender to the Hungarian throne, who was opposed to the Germans, but that intervention proved unfortunate. Boleslaus was defeated, and his failure abroad was aggravated by his conflict with Polish feudal lords, which culminated in the rebellion of Voivode Skarbimir. Because of the lack of unity in Poland, Boleslaus, summoned by the new Emperor Lothar III, went to Merseburg for a mediation meeting in 1133, following which the emperor confirmed the independence of the Church organization in Poland, and Boleslaus paid feudal homage for Western Pomerania (including the island of Rügge). In 1138 in his last will he divided Poland among his sons, retaining, however, the institution of the senior prince. This led to Poland's disintegration into provinces for some two hundred years, a phenomenon at that time also occurring in other European countries.

3. The state, the economy, and society

The emergence of the state and the satisfaction of its needs were decisive for the whole of economic and social life during the early Piast dynasty. These needs could be met only by a special economic sector, because as a result of the poor development of the market and money economy the income of the state could not be based on taxes in money. This led to a system of burdens imposed upon the agricultural population involving bringing tribute (in cattle or sheep), providing for the ruler and his court, and securing other services (transport, hunting and military operations).

To provide the ruler's court and the local authorities with the various products and specialized services a network of so-called service settlements was established, with craftsmen specializing in some forty trades. The inhabitants were peasants granted land by, and subordinated to, the state (so-called service population), whose duty was to produce shields, arrows, casks, spears, metal objects, etc., to bake bread, to keep horses and other services. They lived in villages the names of which referred unambiguously to the kind of the service contributed. Some of them have survived till our times as Łagiewniki (cask-makers), Szczytniki (shield-makers), Złotniki (goldsmiths), Piekary (bakers), Kobylniki (horse-breeders), Sokolniki (falcon-keepers), Świątniki (people whose duty was to provide services for the local church), Szewce (shoemakers), Kuchary (cooks), etc.

The rulers also drew income from the so-called *regalia,* i.e. monopolies (mills, minting of coins, and the like). That system, known as the ducal law, was based on a network of stronghold towns, which were centres of castellanies, headed by castellans. A number of castellanies formed a province, which as a rule corresponded to the former tribal region. There were seven such provinces in the 12th century: Silesia, Cracow region, Sandomierz region, Masovia, Kujawy, the region of Łęczyca and Sieradz, and Gdańsk Pomerania. The parishes — about one thousand of them in the 12th century — came to play an increasingly important role in the administrative division of the country and replaced the old system of *opole* (settlements). In the parishes, the local church functioned on an increasing scale as the centre of local life, replacing the stronghold town in that respect.

The capital of the state was originally in Gniezno, which later came to share that function with Poznań. In the 11th century, after Great Poland had been devastated by Bretislas, the capital was moved to Cracow. The ruler was systematically visiting the various stronghold towns, and during his absence the capital was administered by the *comes palatinus* (cf. Count Palatine), who, when his function became well established, was called *voivode,* i.e., 'commander of warriors (cf. German *Herzog*).

The decomposition of the ducal law was due to two factors: the development of towns and of the market and money economy, and the rise of large units of landed property. The period from the 10th to the 12th century saw the emergence, near the stronghold towns or at the market places, of many tens of towns (at first with wooden buildings) as the centres of crafts and trade. Only churches and monasteries in larger towns were at that time built of stone and brick. It was not until the 14th and 15th centuries that Poland changed from a country with pit-dwellings, dugouts, and wooden houses, into one with wooden and stone-and-brick buildings (cf. V).

As the principal towns under the early Piast dynasty we have to class Gniezno, Poznań, Kruszwica, Szczecin, Cracow, Wrocław, Opole, Gdańsk, Wolin, Kołobrzeg, and Sandomierz. Wrocław with its suburbs had 5,000—6,000 inhabitants in the 12th century; even earlier Gniezno and Poznań had 2,000—3,000 inhabitants each; Szczecin in the early 12th century had some 3,000 inhabitants, while smaller centres had from 500 to 1,000 inhabitants each. The towns were built-up very densely, for instance in Gdańsk there were nearly 200 buildings on the area of some two hectares (ca. five acres). Various types of buildings would co-exist: dugouts, going about one yard into the ground, with wooden superstructures; wooden buildings with walls of wattle and daub, and the most advanced ones, namely those of wooden logs joined at the corners, with floor space ranging from ten to forty square metres (ca. 100 to ca. 400 square feet). Buildings in the rural areas looked similar, but there was a greater percentage of dugouts with wooden superstructures and pit dwellings.

The towns were centres of local, regional (interprovincial) and long-distance trade. The latter was conducted with almost the whole of Europe. The circulation of money increased, but the bulk of the money was in the hands of the nobles. The Polish monetary system was established in the first half of the 11th century and was based on the Polish mark (as the old measure of gold and silver), which amounted to about one half of the Carolingian pound, and was divided into 240 denarii (367.9 grammes of silver). Foreign coins and silver in ingots were also in circulation, and certain standardized goods (mainly hides) were still used as the so-called object money.

But a self-sufficient natural economy, very loosely connected with the market, was still predominant. Even knights' manors produced mostly goods to be consumed directly by the owner. The manors mainly used as manpower serfs and the growing number of dependent, i.e., indebted peasants, who were granted by the prince together with the land. There was a fair number of the so-called guests, that is new settlers who were obliged to contribute certain services to the owner of the land. The number of free farmers, typical of the previous period (cf. II, 3), was decreasing. On the whole, the 10th to 12th centuries witnessed, on the one hand, the rise of the class of the gentry, and on the other, the formation of the class of dependent feudal peasants (serfs), obliged to contribute services and to provide goods, that is to provide the feudal rent. Among the nobles, Church dignitaries were coming to the fore, because the Church received large grants from the rulers. For instance, the Archbishopric of Gniezno in the early 12th century owned some 150 settlements.

The development of the new system of social relations had its repercussions in the dissatisfaction of the dependent population, which was burdened most with contributions to the state. That dissatisfaction found its most acute manifestation in the uprising ca. 1037 (cf. III, 2) that spread mainly over Great Poland.

4. Culture and society

The development of the state was accompanied by marked advances in the material civilization and intellectual culture of society.

Next to the improvements in house-building, important for every-day life, the former open fireplace in the centre of the room was replaced by the stove, situated at the wall or in the corner of the room. People slept in beds, on benches, or in cases, covered — according to the living standard of a given family — with hides, cloth or rugs. Benches, stools and tree stumps, and gradually also chairs and tabourets were used to sit on. In well-to-do families wardrobes and tables were in use, too. Devices for spinning and weaving were widespread. Pots and dishes used in the kitchen and to serve meals were made of clay or wood. Among the clay vessels those made on the potter's wheel became dominant, while the percentage of those moulded by hand was diminishing. The use of full-rotation querns made it possible to obtain various kinds of flour. Flat cakes were replaced by bread made with leaven, which was to become one of the standard foods of all social strata. Many kinds of groats were known, of vegetables and fruit. Pork was the most common meat, while the consumption of beef was less than previously (cf. II, 3).

The average life expectancy was short, which was due to the great mortality rate (30 to 50 per cent) among the children. The average life span was 30—32 years for women, and 33—36 years for men. Only five to seven per cent lived longer than 50 years.

Dress was very colourful, as shown by the folk costumes that have survived until recent times. The intensity of colours in the churches of those times (wall paintings, tile floors), and of dwelling houses also testifies to the fashion of the time.

Differentiation within society made class differences more visible. The culture of the gentry and of the burghers (cf. IV) was taking shape gradually, while peasant culture remained the most traditional.

The revolution in intellectual culture consisted primarily in Poland being included in the Latin civilization. Penetration of Poland by cultural patterns typical of other countries was made easier by pilgrimages, diplomatic visits, and matrimonial connections among the various courts. It was in this way that the Polish royal court was connected with the courts in Bohemia, Hungary, Russia, Lorraine, Austria, Sweden, Denmark and Germany.

Before the rule of Casimir the Restorer intellectual life was mainly concentrated in Great Poland, later replaced in that respect by Cracow. The Great Poland dialect played an important role in the shaping of the Polish language as spoken by the upper strata, and later of the Polish literary language. Contacts with written culture came very early: the oldest manuscript preserved in Gniezno is dated A.D. 800. After the adoption of Christianity chroniclers kept records of events and described the lives of the saints, the authors being mainly Benedictine monks. Benedictine and other monasteries in Tyniec, Lubin, Święty Krzyż, Ołbin, Czerwińsk, Strzelno, Mogilno, Łęczyca, etc., ranked among the principal centres of intellectual life. The first Polish chronicle was written in 1113—19, probably by a Benedictine monk whose name is not known and who is traditionally referred to as Gallus Anonymus. His work, *Cronicae et gesta ducum sive principuum Polonorum,* testified to the growing historical and patriotic consciousness of the nascent Polish nation.

The schools, connected with the activity of the Church, were developing, too. At first (after ca. 1000) the school attached to the Gniezno cathedral played the principal role, but the number of schools increased gradually. Musical life was very intense: folk music with dances accompanied the inhabitants of Poland throughout their lives. Musical instruments were largely home-made (primitive fiddles have been excavated in Opole and in Gdańsk). Gallus Anonymus mentions zithers as commonly used at that time. Lyres, fifes and pipes of various kinds, horns, and lutes were known, too. The Gregorian chorales reached Poland quite early; the first chorale composed in Poland was the antiphon *Magna vox lauda sonore* in honour of St. Adalbert, written on the occasion of the consecration of the Gniezno cathedral (between 1090 and 1097) or on the occasion of the hanging of the famous door of that cathedral (bronze door with scenes from the life and death of that saint — *translator's note*) during the rule of Boleslaus Wrymouth (ca. 1127).

Pre-Romanesque and Romanesque architecture and sculpture were spreading in Poland from the 10th to the early 12th century. Pre-Romanesque art (the 10th and the early 11th century) imitated ancient forms. The churches were usually round, with semicircular apses, or square or rectangular with a semicircular apse. This type is represented by the churches built in the 10th century on Lednica Ostrów, in Giecz, Cracow (St. Mary's chapel), Przemyśl and probably also in Wiślica, Gniezno, and Poznań. The so-called *palatia,* erected in stronghold towns and connected with sacred buildings, were characteristic of the Piast period. Among the monastic buildings mention is due to those in Poznań, Gniezno, Tum near Łęczyca, Trzemeszno, Lednica Ostrów, and Międzyrzecz.

The ruins of a magnificent palatial building in Lednica have been preserved to this day. A *palatium* with a chapel, a monastery, a small harbour and a bridge of 700 metres were built there in the late 10th century. The construction of a similar residence in Giecz was interrupted by the Bohemian invasion led by Prince Bretislas.

Romanesque art reached Poland in the mid-11th century. A *sui generis* revolution in architecture consisted in an increasing number of stone buildings.

A typical church was built on the plan of the Latin cross, with an expanded choir around the main altar. The prevailing type was that of a basilica with two aisles, the nave being wider and higher than the aisles. Such was the form of the Gniezno cathedral, prepared for the Gniezno meeting in A.D. 1000, rebuilt again after the conflagration in 1018. A similar shape was also given to the Poznań cathedral, built after 968, and to the cathedrals in Płock, Wrocław and Włocławek. The Romanesque churches in Kruszwica, Mogilno and Tyniec were even earlier. St. Andrew's church in Cracow was built after 1086 in the Romanesque style. Among the Romanesque buildings used for secular purposes the early Wawel Castle in Cracow was the most remarkable achievement.

Romanesque architecture gave inspiration to sculpture and numerous artistic crafts. Masterpieces of Romanesque art include the cloister garth in Tyniec, the columns of the churches in Strzelno and Żarnów, the reliefs in the Ołbin abbey, and the tile floor in the crypt of the collegiate church in Wiślica. Polish Romanesque art developed from close contact with various centres in Wallonia, in Western Germany, and in Northern Italy, but it contributed its own values to contemporary artistic life in Europe.

Chapter IV

Poland in the Middle Ages. Disintegration into Provinces (1138—1333)

1. Disintegration into provinces. The main lines of development in the Polish territories

In accordance with the last will of Boleslaus Wrymouth (cf. III, 2) the power in the various provinces went to his sons, who thus initiated the various lines of the Piast dynasty which lived in Silesia, Great Poland, Little Poland, Masovia, and Kujawy. Ladislaus II (1105—59), who received Silesia and Little Poland, with Cracow as the capital of that country, gave rise to the Silesian line of the Piasts, which branched into the Świdnica, Legnica, Głogów, Żagań, Oleśnica, Racibórz and Opole, and Cieszyn and Oświęcim lines.

The genealogical tree of the Piasts who lived in Great Poland was much less complicated, with no more than two lines. This branch descended from another son of Boleslaus, Mieszko, who was later nicknamed the Old (1126—1202).

The Little Poland, Masovia and Kujawy lines of the Piasts originated from Casimir the Just (1138—94), Boleslaus' youngest son. It was not until 1166 that he received his province (part of the Sandomierz region with Wiślica) after the death of yet another son of Boleslaus, Henry, who was also a minor when Boleslaus drew his will, and who died without issue (1127/31—66). Casimir was alloted Masovia only after the death without issue of Leszek, Boleslaus the Curly's (1125—73) son, who had been granted this province in Boleslaus' will.

The division made by Boleslaus Wrymouth initiated the disintegration of the country into smaller and smaller provinces. The process went on for nearly two hundred years, accompanied by constant changes in the kind of possession and in the principles of transmission of power through successive princes. When struggling with one another the princes often tried to win the support of the emperor or the pope, still the two principal powers in mediaeval Europe, which sharpened internal discord and aggravated the danger of external intervention. Personal aspirations were combined in various ways with the emerging idea of the unification of the Polish territories, the aspiration represented (cf. IV, 2) by the various provincial princes. This idea was supported by the nascent Polish nation, and also by the developing economy, especially in terms of trade, for which the internal political divisions meant obstacles of various kinds.

The aspiration to unify the country and the steps taken to fulfil it were for a long time blocked by strong decentralizing tendencies, characteristic of other European countries (e.g., Bohemia, Rus, Hungary, France) as well. But these tendencies, too, had a strong foundation in the development of the stratum of nobles which strove to extend its influence, and in the widely spread socio-political system of feudalism, a system marked by a dispersion of power. Economic development could have consolidated both the centralist and the decentralist tendencies, and it was the latter which were strengthened in the first phase of the process. In the case of smaller provinces the rulers were much more interested in economic problems. They had no longer their separate state sectors (cf. III, 3), from which they could draw their incomes; under the developing market economy their incomes, derived from various sources, depended upon the economic condition of agriculture, handicrafts, and trade. It was only at a later stage that internal centralization and a uniform economic policy became more advantageous. The same applied to foreign policy and the defence of the territory.

The princes who ruled in the period of disintegration usually managed their economic affairs quite well. Like the feudal lords, they tried to make their estates economically productive. As a result of their efforts the incomes of the gentry increased considerably. This was due primarily to an increase in the number of peasant holdings (also through the settling of new farmers on previously unexploited land) and of towns, and also to the great agrarian reform that consisted in introducing — after the Western European pattern — an ordered system of contributions for the benefit of the owner of the land (the rent in money being dominant, but accompanied by considerable tributes in kind) and in a new organization of the rural areas. Its typical representative was now a farmer (with a holding of some 15 hectares), who had to pay rent and was accordingly a member of the already existing class of feudal peasants who were at least partly dependent on the market. That reform is traditionally called the settling of peasants on the principle drawn from German law, because it was connected with German settlers arriving in Poland, encouraged to do so by Polish princes and nobles. These settlers played a positive role in the economic and social changes on Western Slavonic territories in the 12th to 14th centuries. But the adoption of German law cannot be identified with the arrival of settlers from the territories of the former Carolingian Empire. The spreading of German law, also adopted *en masse* by the local population, was of a greater extent than the admission of new settlers from abroad. The Germans settled in the largest number in Silesia, whereas in the territories situated further to the East the prevailing process was that of granting privileges resulting from the German law to the settlements that already existed. Many Germans, especially merchants and craftsmen, also settled in Polish towns (cf. IV, 3) contributing thereby to brisker economic activity, to the development of local government, and to increased commercial contacts between Polish and German towns.

The lack of a strong and unified state had adverse effects upon Poland's position in Europe. First of all, the country was much more exposed to the danger of a German invasion, Germany being in the process of expanding eastwards. Poland had traditionally had good relations with Hungary, nor were there any conflicts with Rus, split internally and subjugated by the Mongols (Tartars). Indeed, the Mongols themselves became a threat. Stopped in 1241 at the Battle of Legnica by Henry the Pious, Prince of Wrocław, who lost his life in that battle, stopped during their later incursions in 1259 and 1287—88, and also weakened by the inner conflicts of the Golden Horde (the Mongol State in the steppes near the Black Sea), they soon ceased to be a major danger, even though they were to harass the Eastern parts of Poland for many centuries to come (cf. VII, 2).

The eastward expansion of Germany, which for economic reasons cannot be identified with the migrations of the German population, was carried out by the so-called marks (in particular the Brandenburg Mark) which developed in the territories occupied by Western Slavs, and by the Order of Teutonic Knights, dominated by the Germans. The Order, which developed from the Order of the Knights of St. Mary's Hospital of the German Nation in 1190 during the Crusades, was invited by Prince Conrad of Masovia in 1226 to settle in Northern Poland and to protect the country against the warlike Old Prussians. In 1237 the Teutonic Knights formed a union with the Order of Chevaliers of the Sword, at that time already settled in Livonia. Western Pomerania, which Mieszko the Old and his son, Ladislaus Spindleshanks, strove to keep for Poland, was lost in 1181—1205, the Danes being additional claimants to that territory. Ultimately, the area was seized in 1231 by the Brandenburgians, who did it with the approval of the Emperor Frederick II; they were thus laying the foundations of what was to become the Prussian State. By driving a wedge between Pomerania and Great Poland the Brandenburgians founded there the so-called New Mark, with the capital in Gorzów, which was granted municipal status in 1257. Despite strenuous efforts on the part of its rulers Great Poland lost Santok, Choszczno, and Drezdenko to the Brandenburgians, while Pomerania lost Drawsko and Świdwin.

The Lubusz region was incorporated into Brandenburg in 1252 through an intermediary, the archbishop of Magdeburg, who bought it from Boleslaus (nicknamed Rogatka 'Strong-headed'), the Prince of Silesia, in 1250. Gdańsk Pomerania, which had its own government and princes who originated from the local feudal lords but had come to be treated on a par with other provincial princes, was more and more exposed to the expansion of the Teutonic Knights who had settled in the region of Chełmno. By 1273 the Teutonic Knights had succeeded in conquering the territories occupied by the Old Prussians and Yatvingians. In 1282 they were granted the region of Gniew by a papal decree and in 1308 they occupied Gdańsk, which had just been taken by the Brandenburgians. The Teutonic Knights pretended to have come to the rescue of the town, which was in fact taken away from the Brandenburgians, but the Order did not return it to Poland. They slaughtered the Polish force that defended the town and began a conquest of the entire region, which soon made it possible to move the headquarters of their Grand Master from Venice to Malbork. Vigorous endeavours made by King Ladislaus the Short (1260/61—1333), who in 1306 occupied Little Poland and the central regions of Poland and also part of Great Poland, in alliance with Lithuania, which was also threatened by the Teutonic Knights, remained unsuccessful. Despite Ladislaus' military victories (the Battle of Płowce in 1331) the Teutonic Order managed to conquer the region of Dobrzyń and Kujawy as well.

The settling of the Teutonic Knights on the northern border of Poland had exceptionally grave effects on the country's political situation. It meant the loss of Pomerania for 155 years and a weakening of the country. This is why Polish historians tend to stress the military activities and the expansionism of the Teutonic Order, whereas German historiographers are inclined to bring out its civilizational and missionary role in the territories it acquired by contract or conquest. The Teutonic Knights arrived in Poland after having been expelled from Hungary in 1225 by King Andrew II, who did not want to have as a remuneration for their assistance in the war with the Polovtsy, an independent political organization in Hungary. The Teutonic Knights succeeded in settling in Poland, in doing which they availed themselves of the assistance of the Emperor Frederick II: the Grand Master Herman von Salza obtained in 1226 the imperial privilege, confirmed by the pope in 1234, which granted to the Order the territories it received from Prince Conrad of Masovia (i.e., a large part of the Chełmno region) and those which it would conquer from the Old Prussians. In 1238 the Teutonic Knights falsified the text of the privilege given to them by Conrad by changing its wording in a manner which suggested that Conrad had renounced the future conquests of the Teutonic Order on its behalf. This gave the Teutonic Knights pretended legal grounds for organizing a state of their own; their territories were to be a fiefdom held directly from the emperor and the pope.

In their territories the Knights settled new people, mainly arrivals from Germany. They founded hundreds of villages and numerous towns, such as Malbork and Królewiec (Königsberg) and expanded existing ones, such as Chełmno and Toruń.

2. Efforts at unification of the Polish territories

The number of the principalities was increasing with every passing year. The process was most advanced in Silesia, while Little Poland and Great Poland to a large extent remained single political entities. In Masovia, split into many provinces, the separate territories were those of Kujawy, the regions of Sieradz, Łęczyca, and Dobrzyń, and later the principalities of Płock, Czersk and Wizna, which were later subdivided into smaller parts.

The establishing by Boleslaus Wrymouth of the function of the senior prince was intended to prevent the disintegration of the state. That disintegration — or, to put it more precisely, the conflict between the seniority principle, represented by more ambitious rulers who were more politically conscious than the others, and the principle of the independence of the provinces (the principalities) — was due to the development of the feudal social and economic structure of the country (cf. IV, 1).

The seniority principle was abandoned in the 12th century, which meant a strengthening of the position of the principalities. The throne of the Grand Duke (this was how Mieszko the Old styled himself) remained vacant, disintegration was progressing, and yet Polish people had an idea of Poland as a state and as an integrated entity. The concept of *gens polonica* (Polish nation) appears in the sources of the times. It was based on the consciousness of a common past, especially the ideas represented by Mieszko I and Boleslaus the Brave, and of a common faith. This concept, especially as referring to a common past, will be seen to grow in importance in a later period, when the Reformation will be shown to result in a greater differentiation of religious denominations (cf. VI, 3).

The Church organization, which was still subject to the only archbishopric in Gniezno, was a unifying factor, and its policy was definitively unity-oriented; the weakening of the state and of the institutions directly subordinated to the state made the Church a fairly independent force. Next to the nobles, whose importance increased, too (hence their frequent rebellions), the Church emerged as a new political factor which the local prince had to take into account. Hence in internal political life there was a constant struggle between the (local) prince, the Church, and the nobles, which in most cases resulted in a weakening of the position of the prince. To win the support of the Church for his aspirations he had to resort to concessions, whether political (renunciation of the right to choose the local bishop) or economic (grants of land, exemption of the Church estates from the burdens resulting from the ducal rights, granting of minting rights, etc.). On the other hand, various concessions were claimed by the nobles, who in practice came to be the decisive factor in electing the local princes. A political idea even developed, which justified a *sui generis* role of society in the election of the ruler, and also defined the duties of the prince and the right to renounce obedience to him on the part of his subjects.

The disintegration of the state brought about the disappearance of the centralized administrative offices (cf. III, 3) and the emergence of local hierarchies of officials. Such a local hierarchy had at its head the voivode (who also wielded some judicial authority); the ducal chancery, and hence also the foreign policy conducted by the prince, was in the charge of the chancellor. The districts which had stronghold towns as their centres were administered by castellans, who handled civilian and police matters, and also had judicial and military functions. It was only Ladislaus the Short who, in the process of reunifying the country, appoined the bailiffs, directly subordinated to the monarch, who ensured a more effective local administration.

The tendencies to reunification were based on various principles. At first, until the 1290's, it was the drive to preserve the seniority principle and to reconstruct the early Piast dynasty. That idea was represented by Mieszko the Old, who originated the Great Poland line of the Piasts, by his son Ladislaus Spindleshanks (1161/7—1231), by Conrad of Masovia (1187—1247), the son of Casimir the Just, the ancestor of the Piasts of Little Poland, Masovia, and Kujawy, and to a lesser extent by Henry the Bearded (1167—1238), the grandson of Ladislaus II, the founder of the line of the Silesian Piasts. Henry the Bearded succeeded in bringing the region of Cracow, Silesia and the southern part of Great Poland under his rule, but he failed in his plans to obtain the crown for himself or for his son, Henry the Pious (the latter subsequently lost his life in the Battle of Legnica — cf. IV, 1).

Other efforts at unification were more in line with the general attitudes of Polish society (to a large extent also of the developing group of burghers) which was opposed to the feudal anarchy. There were clearly defined aspirations, represented also by Cracow burghers, to link Little Poland with Silesia. That was why after the death in 1288 of Leszek the Black from the Kujawy line of the Piast dynasty, the throne in Cracow was offered to the Silesian prince, Henry Probus (ca. 1257—90). He was an outstanding personality and had well formed political ideas based on the concept of a centralized state; he intended to claim the crown, but unfortunately he died in 1290.

The strivings of Przemysł II (1257—96), a grandson of Mieszko the Old, who wanted to reunify the Kingdom of Poland with Great Poland as his base, seemed more likely to succeed. Przemysł II, supported by Jakub Świnka, the Archbishop of Gniezno and an eminent politician and patriot, concluded at Kępno in 1282 an agreement with Mściwój, the childless prince of Gdańsk, on the strength of which after Mściwój's death Gdańsk Pomerania was to come under Przemysł's rule, or in the case of the latter's death, Great Poland was to pass under Mściwój's rule. In 1287, he concluded an alliance with Boguslaus IV, the prince of Western Pomerania. In 1295, after the death of Mściwój, Przemysł II united Gdańsk Pomerania with Great Poland and in the same year was crowned in Gniezno as the king of Poland, but one year later he was assassinated on the orders of the margraves of Brandenburg.

Ladislaus the Short (cf. IV, 1) was the next to try to reunify the Polish territories, and had to strive to do so for over twenty years. After Przemysł's death the people of Great Poland elected Ladislaus their prince. He also assumed power in Gdańsk Pomerania, but, having failed to win the support of the nobles, had to yield to Wenceslas II, the ambitious king of Bohemia, who in 1300 conquered the Polish territories except for Masovia and Silesia and was crowned in Gniezno. Wenceslas II's rule continued until 1305. Wenceslas III, his son and successor, was assassinated in Moravia in 1306. At that point Ladislaus the Short, availing himself of Hungarian help, reconquered Little Poland, Kujawy, and the regions of Sieradz and Łęczyca. When organizing the administration in Gdańsk Pomerania he estranged the noble family of Święca, who entered into a conspiracy with the Brandenburgians, which resulted in the loss of that province (cf. IV, 1): Ladislaus the Short, preoccupied with Little Poland, was not in a position to defend it successfully. The successors of the Premyslids, namely John of Luxemburg and Rudolf von Hapsburg, made claims to Polish throne, vacant after Wenceslas III's death. Cracow saw in 1311 the rebellion led by Albert (who held the municipal office called *advocatus,* cf. section 3 below, roughly equivalent to the German *Vogt*), who counted on the support of John of Luxemburg. Having suppressed that rebellion Ladislaus the Short, who in the meantime also had to fight the adherents of Henry of Głogów (1251/60—1309), of the Silesian branch of the Piast dynasty, occupied Great Poland, where he won the support of the population. He entered Poznań in 1314, and during the years that followed had to repel Brandenburgian invasions. When he had a major part of Poland (Little Poland, Great Poland, part of Kujawy, and the regions of Sieradz and Łęczyca) under his sway he was crowned in Cracow in 1320 with the approval of Pope John XXII. In later years Ladislaus the Short had to engage in dire struggles with the Teutonic Knights (cf. IV, 1). He failed to regain Pomerania, despite the advantageous verdict in the legal controversy between Poland and the Teutonic Order in 1320—21, when upon Ladislaus' request the Pope sent arbitrators to settle the dispute. He was also in a very dangerous situation in 1331, when the Teutonic Knights concluded an alliance with John of Luxemburg in their efforts to deprive Ladislaus the Short of power and to partition Poland. In this emergency Ladislaus found support in the aid extended to him by Charles Robert, the King of Hungary, whose actions prevented Ladislaus' enemies from uniting their forces (cf. IV, 1).

3. The great economic reform in the rural areas. Development of towns and trade. The feudal system of social organization

The adoption of the German law (cf. IV, 1) was part of the great European trend which consisted in making new tracts of land arable, on the one hand, and in a new agrarian system, on the other. The German law is merely a matter of certain legal usages, developed in Western Europe and spreading from country to country. For instance, in Spain an analogous phenomenon was known as the adoption of the French law. To put it in general terms, the reorganization was intended to lay economic foundations for the emerging large landed property (the class of the magnates and/or the gentry). The feudal lords lived on their estates and directly managed their small manors, but were at the same time the owners of groups of villages then in process of being formed; they also derived their principal income from rents paid and tributes made by the peasants.

Progress in the clearing of land of forests was accompanied by organization of the agrarian system, and this originated in breakdown of the system based on the ducal law (cf. III, 3). For the landowners every settler was a valuable asset, and this was why new settlers were offered more advantageous terms. At first, in the 12th and the early 13th century, there emerged the category of so-called free guests, which developed still under the local law; the late 13th, the 14th and the 15th centuries saw a more coherent system, called the German law.

Following the development of the market economy and of large landed property the old economic model, with a strong state sector, underwent an evolution, set going primarily by the gentry, who strove to obtain large incomes. But the peasants, who were now in a position to sell their farm produce and to buy commodities produced by the craftsmen (who now acted as specialists rather than as people making various objects for their own household needs), were also interested in increasing agricultural production.

The process was favoured by technological advances in agriculture. The regular three-field system, that is the rotation of crops: spring crops, winter crops, fallowing, became common. The rotation of crops was carried out jointly, and every farmer had his share in it. Fallow land used as pasture was also common, which increased the opportunities for animal husbandry. The adoption of the three-field system was gradually followed by the advent of the plough which, unlike the old furrowing plough, not only loosened the soil, but turned it as well.

Regulation of the peasants' duties, which were usually defined in the so-called location document (i.e., one granting land to new settlers under German law, or extending the principles of that law to the peasants already resident on that land), was — next to the spreading of the three-field system — an essential element of the new agrarian system. These duties included a tribute in grain crops, not more than 15 per cent of the total output of a given farm, the rent in money — on the average 24 to 48 grammes of silver (i.e., from one-eighth to one-fourth of a mark), minor contributions in money and in kind, and certain corvées which were not too burdensome. The peasants, even though serfs, enjoyed more freedom by having their duties defined in terms of rent and tributes.

The new agrarian system and the convergence of the interests of the landowners and direct producers, who strove to meet their growing needs, resulted in increased production, and hence in a greater amount of commodities. Between the 10th and the early 14th century (i.e., between the times of Mieszko I and those of Ladislaus the Short) the production of grain crops nearly doubled, reaching the level of some 500,000 metric tons for Great Poland and Masovia combined. This was about half due to the increase of the areas under crops (by about one-third) and to increased labour productivity (owing to new technology and new principles of organization). The first phase of the period of large-scale forest clearance went on until the end of the 15th century (cf. V, 3).

Growing agricultural production stimulated the development of the towns that were becoming centres of trade and crafts. Formerly expanding trade was served by fairs, some 250 of which were held in the late 12th century. As in the case of the rural areas, the towns developed on the basis of the organization brought to Poland from the West, mainly by settlers from Germany, who formed the most numerous group of aliens in the growing urban population. The communes of these aliens, mainly Germans, were based on a new system that gradually spread into the other parts of the town. Founding a town on 'the raw root', i.e., in an area that had not been inhabited previously and could have been just cleared of a forest, was an exception; in such cases the initiative was that of the prince or a noble. The 'location' of a town, i.e. the granting of the privileges resulting from German law, was combined with a new physical planning of the town. The statutes adopted were usually those of Magdeburg or Lübeck (in the case of Pomerania). Towns, especially the larger ones, were surrounded with walls. This process intensified in the 13th and 14th centuries; for instance, the 13th century saw the founding of some 200 new towns in Silesia alone. This led in turn to the emergence of the burghers as an estate (in the sense of a status group or class).

The location of a town meant its exemption from the ducal law in the sense of burdens and jurisdiction. The exemption was direct in the case of the towns founded on ducal (state-owned) lands; it was indirect (based on an immunity) if the town was founded by a noble on land already exempt from burdens to the benefit of the prince. The owner of the land (a prince or a noble) also agreed — usually step by step — to the formation of the municipal local government, with a municipal council headed by a mayor, while appointing an *advocatus* as his representative. In the rural areas the *advocatus* had his analogue in the *scultetus* (German *Schultheiss*). The feudal lord would cede to the *advocatus* a large part of his prerogatives, mainly the judicial authority, which was exercised by the *advocatus* together with the jury.

The period of disintegration was above all marked by intensification of home trade, although foreign trade did expand, too. Foreign trade had its principal centres in Cracow, Wrocław, Gdańsk and Poznań, and was concentrated along the South-North line, which made the rivers Vistula and Odra and the port towns of Gdańsk and Szczecin acquire special importance. The imports included cloth from Flanders and metal goods from Germany (largely from Nuremberg), while Poland exported forest products, hides, and furs, and also slowly increasing amounts of grain.

The rise in agricultural and craftsmen's output, accompanied by the development of trade and the market economy, had its effect in population growth. At that time there was a very close relationship between the amount of food and the size of population, based on a *sui generis* feed-back principle. It was not so much the mortality rate which worked as the regulator, as the fact that the number of those who were economically able to start families was limited by the number of jobs available in production units in town and country.

Under Ladislaus the Short and Casimir the Great (cf. V, 2) the territory of Poland, including Silesia and Gdańsk Pomerania, was inhabited by some 1,800,000 people, of whom a little more than 10 per cent (ca. 200,000) already lived in towns. Hence the agricultural production, which nearly doubled in the meantime, could very well meet the needs of the population which increased by some 80 per cent.

The peasants formed the main core of the population. The knights (the gentry), with the overlords as their highest stratum, developed ultimately as an estate (status group) in the period of disintegration; their number was quite considerable, though smaller than that of the burghers. The knights gradually began to realize their political strength. The towns were also a force with which the ruler had to reckon, but they did not succeed in playing any major political role. The number of the clergy, especially regular, increased, too.

4. Culture and society

Cultural life intensified considerably during the period of disintegration. The native Slavonic culture, of which the peasants were the principal proponents, came to be influenced more and more strongly by cosmopolitan Latin culture, represented mainly by ducal courts and the Church (cloisters, the clergy). Burgher culture, which drew from both sources, and was also closely linked to the culture of towns in Western Europe, was also evolving. This led to the emergence of a culture which had many native features but was strongly connected with the various strands of European culture in general. The liveliest contacts were those with the neighbouring Slavonic countries, Bohemia and Rus. Polish cultural patterns interacted vigorously with the Hungarian ones; that interaction was stronger than with Italy in view of the comparative proximity of Hungary. Contacts with Western Europe were intensifying through visits, pilgrimages, and various expeditions.

There was an enormous difference in living standards between the ruling class and the broad masses of townspeople and peasants. This found reflection in the diet, which was due to a wider range of plants cultivated at that time. Cakes baked in hot ashes were eaten only in backward regions; most people could eat bread of whole meal flour, ground in water mills or windmills. Ale was made from wheat and barley. Peas were common and began to replace broad beans and lentils; cabbage was the most common vegetable. Turnips were possibly eaten, too. Milk, especially in its sour form, cheese and eggs were important elements in the diet. Much meat was eaten, including some game and considerable amounts of fish. Hunting rights were strictly dependent on one's social status: for instance, the peasants (other that the *sculteti*) were permitted to hunt only hares, partridges, and other wildfowl. Fruit was eaten very readily, and methods of preserving and processing it were already known. Mead (cf. II, 3) was produced as before. Vines came to be cultivated for the needs of the Church. There were two major meals: *prandium* (breakfast), between 9 and 12 a.m., and *cena* (dinner), between 3 and 6 p.m.), and additionally a light evening meal called *collatio* (supper). Feasts were usually held in the evenings.

Kitchen vessels began to include those made of the various metals. Tableware also became diversified.

The rate of increase in food production exceeded the rate of population growth, so that there was more food per person than in the previous period. The danger of famine was thus not imminent, even though the years 1280—82 were disastrous from the point of view of food production.

Dress (cf. III, 4) did not change much. Differentiation was not so much in the cut as in the quality of the fabrics used, colours, accessories, and ornaments: in these respects there were marked differences among the costumes of the feudal lords, the gentry, the burghers, and the peasants. While in the 13th century men's costumes did not differ much from those worn by women, the 14th century saw the advent of the tightly fitted Gothic dresses for women, and those worn by men became much shorter.

Social status was reflected markedly in the types of building and in the equipment of homes. The development of the gentry was followed by an increasing number of knights' mansions, palaces of nobles, and ducal castles. Houses built of brick made their first appearance in towns, but were to become common only in the next period (cf. V, 4). The general trend, observable especially in towns, was to increase the floor space of apartments. Social differentiation was also reflected in the ways the houses were finished and fitted. Resinous chips used to light peasant huts and cabins were replaced in gentry homes by oil lamps (cressets) and candles.

These advances in material civilization were accompanied by an increase in the number of people with growing cultural and artistic needs.

The role of writing grew in everyday life (written documents). Books written by hand on parchment were becoming common; they were collected in monasteries which had their own scriptoria. Intended for monastic use they did not have any wider influence. It was only lay interest in books that led to many initiatives. The oldest known Polish list of books, that of the library at the Cracow chapter, dates from 1110. The number of books must have accordingly increased. But the greatest advances were made in the popularization of education. In the 13th century the network of schools attached to cathedrals was completed by parish schools, which offered opportunities for learning how to read and write to much larger groups, including the burghers. The curriculum was split into the so-called *trivium* (grammar, rhetoric, and dialectic), and *quadrivium* (arithmetic, geometry, astronomy, and music), or else was confined to reading, writing and singing. Higher education was acquired at universities, primarily those in Paris and Padua. Works by Martinus Polonus (ca. 1205/8—78/9), a historian, theologian and lawyer, by Vitelo (ca. 1230—1314), a mathematician and natural scientist, and also others, such as Nicolaus of Poland, the physician of King Leszek the Black, who ranked among the leading scholars of their times, were already known abroad. Martinus Polonus was the author of a chronicle of popes and emperors and a systematic exposition of canon law. Vitelo wrote many works marked by Renaissance-like boldness of thought, his treaty on optics, entitled *Perspectiva,* being the most prominent. Next to Albert the Great and Roger Bacon he was one of the foremost scholars of his epoch.

In historiography pride of place goes to two chronicles. One was written by Vincentius Kadłubek (ca. 1150—1223), appointed the Bishop of Cracow in 1208, a great scholar, and also a lawyer and politician, connected with the court of Casimir the Just. The other, a work by several authors, called *The Great Poland Chronicle,* covered the history of Poland until 1273 and represented the idea of reunification of Poland, with Great Poland serving as the base of the operation. We have also to note hagiographic works (the lives of Bishop Stanislaus Szczepanowski; St. Adalbert; Kunegunda, the princess of Cracow; and St. Hyacinthus).

Architecture in this period was at first still Romanesque in style (cf. IV, 4), and began to adopt the Gothic forms only gradually, beginning in the early 13th century. The development of the Church organization, the spreading of the Christian religion, and the growing riches of the clergy were followed by a great increase in the number of churches in town and country. Among the fairly imposing Romanesque churches we have to mention the collegiate church in Tum near Łęczyca (erected in the second half of the 12th century), the basilica in Opatów, the cathedral in Płock, and the churches in Strzelno, Ołbin and Piasek. In all probability the royal castle was enlarged. St. Wenceslas' Cathedral within the precincts of Wawel Castle, constructed earlier, was consecrated after the death of Boleslaus Wrymouth. A large castle was also erected by Henry the Bearded in Legnica.

The beginnings of Gothic architecture were due to French influence, France being where that style was born. It reached Poland several dozen years later, to become common by the middle of the 13th century. An important role in its propagation in Poland was played by the Cistercians. The new style had pointed arches as its dominant element, which gave the buildings their high pointed character; it was also marked by cross-and-rib vaults, combined with a system of ground and flying buttresses. The development of Gothic art coincided with the growing wealth of the towns, which had sufficient means to finance construction of expensive buildings made of brick, and hence most Gothic buildings were erected in towns. The beginnings of the reconstruction of the cathedrals in Wrocław and Poznań, based on more ornamental architectonic principles, that referred to the French Gothic style, coincided with the beginning of the construction of the cathedral in Beauvais in France, one of the finest Gothic churches. The Gothic style also impressed its mark on town walls. Many Gothic castles, although inspired strongly by influences from the Middle East, were erected by the Teutonic Knights in the 13th century (in 1274 they started building their huge castle in Malbork).

Art historians stress the fact that the art of stone sculpture (portals, tombstones, ornaments) and reliefs in metal flourished in Poland in the late 12th and the 13th century. The peak achievement in this line is to be seen in the bronze door of the Gniezno Cathedral (functioning as such to this day), made probably ca. 1175 and showing in 18 scenes the history of the life and death of St. Adalbert.

Many crafts flourished, too, including goldsmithing, illumination of books, and embroidery. Musical life was also richer than previously (cf. III, 4). It still followed two courses, that of folk music and that of professional music, the latter growing in importance. Their mutual permeation is visible from the end of the 12th century, mainly under the influence of schools. The comparatively high level of musical art is confirmed by a five-string fiddle from the late 12th century, the discovery of which was a revelation on an international scale.

There were many new compositons connected with the worship of saints, and religious processions came to be dramatized in the form of miracle-plays. Polish religious songs developed, this being an important element in the national consciousness, especially in towns with German settlers. The Polish language was also penetrating Church liturgy on an increasing scale.

Chapter V

Poland in the Late Middle Ages. The Estates (1333—1501)

1. Poland among the European powers

The reunification of Poland by Ladislaus the Short (cf. IV, 2) initiated a period of almost three centuries (until the early 16th century) during which Poland played an important part in international affairs and at the same time underwent uninterrupted economic development. The one and a half centuries between the death of Ladislaus the Short and what is traditionally considered the end of the Middle Ages saw in Poland the rule of three outstanding monarchs who proved equal to the tasks of the developing state, society, and nation, namely Casimir the Great (reigned 1333—70), Ladislaus Jagiello (reigned 1386—1434) and Casimir Jagiellonian (reigned 1447—92). They secured continuity in political thinking, consolidated the state and stabilized the royal authority.

In brief, Casimir the Great completed the reunification of Poland and consolidated the country internally, Ladislaus Jagiello crushed the power of the Teutonic Knights, and Casimir the Jagiellonian dealt them the final blow by reconquering Gdańsk Pomerania.

Against this background the reigns of Louis of Hungary (1370—82), of Jadwiga (Hedvige), who eventually married Ladislaus Jagiello and who reigned in her own right in 1384—86, of the young Ladislaus of Varna (1434—44), and of John Albert (1492—1501) must be considered episodes of minor importance. The first of these monarchs is remembered primarily for the Privilege of Kosice (1374), which granted to the gentry the privileges of a recognized estate; the third, for the unfortunate Battle of Varna (1444), and the fourth, for the defeat of the Polish army in Moldavia (1497), which stopped Polish plans for an active struggle against Turkey. The interregna in 1382—84 and 1444—47 were detrimental to the political stabilization of the country as they enabled the feudal lords and the gentry to strengthen their positions.

The decline of the Middle Ages was marked throughout almost the whole of Europe by the emergence of the idea of sovereign national states, free from the universalistic claims of the Empire and the Papacy, which resulted in the weakening of these two powers. The development of the states, which for the centuries to come would determine European politics, began. France, which in the course of the Hundred Years' War (1337—1453) succeeded in driving the English from its territory, consolidated itself. The expansion of the Hapsburgs was to result in the next period (cf. VI, 1) in a long rivalry with France, which was to a great extent to determine the policies of many European states, including Poland. England began to develop internally until in the 16th century it rose as a country of growing international importance.

To the east of Poland, the Russian territories, freed from the Tartar yoke, were united by Muscovite princes into a single state which in its political complexion resembled the Byzantine Empire, and Ivan III (ruled 1462—1505), who married the niece of the last Byzantine emperor, started styling himself 'Emperor' ('Tsar').

He succeeded in conquering numerous territories in the east and in the north, but Lithuania proved a strong rival to Russia.

In its rivalry with Russia Lithuania did not yield, but, threatened also by the ever stronger State of the Teutonic Order, turned toward Poland, also threatened by the Teutonic Knights. The Polish-Lithuanian union offered Poland opportunities for becoming a European power. The Jagiellonian dynasty, founded by the ascension to the Polish throne of Jagiello, the Grand Duke of Lithuania, became the most powerful royal family in Central Europe. Poland under Jagiello (King Ladislaus Jagiello) defeated the Teutonic Knights in the decisive Battle of Grunwald and Tannenberg (1410), and later, after the Thirteen Years' War, regained Gdańsk Pomerania in 1466, while still later Polish kings came to reign in Bohemia and Hungary. Thus at the close of the 15th century the Jagiellonians held the vast territories of Lithuania, Byelorussia, the Ukraine, Poland, Bohemia, Moravia, and Hungary. This could not continue for long, because the expansionist policy of the Jagiellonians was opposed by the Hapsburgs, also growing in power, and the Muscovite State.

These changes in the political status quo in Western, Central, and Eastern Europe were accompanied by Turkish expansion. Having occupied Constantinople (1453) the Turks, an outpost of the vast Muslim world, began to conquer the Balkans, and in the next period (cf. VI, 2) were to become a direct danger to Poland.

Thus the Late Middle Ages brought Poland not only many successes in striving for a powerful position in Europe, but also gave rise to problems that were to become the burden of political life in the period that followed, when Poland had to match her strength and politics against the aspirations of the Hapsburgs, the French, Muscovy, and Turkey.

Hence the political balance sheet was, for late mediaeval Poland, not completely favourable. The fact that Poland failed to regain (except for very small areas) its western and northern territories, lost at the time of disintegration, namely Western Pomerania, the Lubusz region, and Silesia, was certainly worst of all. The eastward expansion, which was to meet resistance on the part of Muscovy, interested in extending its influence over all Russian lands, gave rise to a certain type of political thinking, later to be called the Jagiellonian ideology as opposed to the Piast ideology that was oriented toward the recuperation of all those territories that had been part of Poland under the Piasts and towards making the Poles sensitive to the German danger.

2. Poland, its territory and policies

During the one and half centuries of the monarchy based on the socio-political system of estates Poland extended its frontiers considerably. While Casimir the Great at first ruled over a territory of some 100,000 sq. kilometres, with a population of some 700,000, after the regaining of Gdańsk Pomerania the area of the country tripled, and the population increased to 2.5—3 million. Thus the density of population rose from ca. seven to ca. ten persons per square kilometre, which placed Poland slightly below the European average, but above the Lithuanian and Russian. The number and the density of the population had at least tripled since the times of Boleslaus the Brave.

Casimir the Great, when continuing the process of reunification of Polish territories, focussed his attention on Pomerania and Kujawy, held by the Teutonic Knights, but he was not in a position to engage in an armed conflict with the Teutonic Order, which had an ally in the Luxemburg dynasty then ruling in Bohemia, the more so as he also strove to regain Silesia and the Lubusz region. He accordingly chose the diplomatic path, by concluding a permanent alliance with the Angevins, consolidated by the previous marriage of his sister Elizabeth to King Charles Robert of Hungary in 1320. The alliance with the Angevins was to strengthen Poland's position in the international arena. Further, in exchange for Casimir's acknowledgement of Bohemian sovereignty in Silesia (except for the principality of Świdnica), John of Luxemburg co-operated in the solution of the conflict with the Teutonic Knights, who returned part of Kujawy (with the town of Inowrocław) in 1337 and later, under the pressure of the verdict of the arbitrators appointed by Pope Benedict XII, who met in Warsaw in 1339, returned the rest of Kujawy and the region of Dobrzyń, and acknowledged the Polish sovereignty of Pomerania by agreeing to pay tribute from that territory. All this was confirmed by a treaty of 'eternal' peace (which lasted 67 years), signed in Kalisz in 1343.

In the same year Casimir the Great occupied the region of Wschowa, but he could not expect to regain the whole of Silesia. Charles IV, the powerful successor of John of Luxemburg, King of Bohemia and Germany, and later the Emperor of Germany and King of Bohemia, formally incorporated Silesia in Bohemia, and Casimir had to acquiesce in that by concluding a peace treaty with the Bohemians, signed in Namysłów. The principality of Świdnica was lost shortly after (1356).

Later years saw further revindications. In 1352, the region of Łęczyca was incorporated into Poland when the last local prince died, and one year earlier Masovia constituted itself a fiefdom of Poland, which was in a position to defend it against Lithuanian invasions. In 1368, Casimir the Great received homage from the regions of Santok and Drezdenko, and incorporated the Wałcz district (together with Czaplinek and Drawsko) into Poland. This was connected with his plans for the estuary of the Odra (for Western Pomerania in the meantime succeeded in freeing itself from Brandenburgian domination), inspired by people from Great Poland, who were opposed to conceding the Polish throne to the Angevins after the death of Casimir the Great, as stipulated in the treaty of alliance with Hungary. As early as 1343 he married his daughter Elizabeth to Boguslaus V, prince of Słupsk and Sławno in Western Pomerania, who did not acknowledge the domination of the Emperor, and later prepared his grandson Kaźko (son of the prince of Słupsk) to occupy the Polish throne. This reflected the king's constant aspiration to extend Poland towards the sea.

Casimir's plans also covered the occupation of the Russian territories, which would open the way to the Black Sea and give Poland control of an important trade route. This was made easier by the fact that after the Romanovich dynasty became extinct the boyars (nobles) of Halicz allied themselves with Poland, which had its rivals in the Lithuanians and Hungarians. Casimir, however, emerged victorious and succeeded in conquering almost the whole of the principality of Halicz and Vladimir (Vladimir, Lvov, Halicz, Chełm and Bełz) by 1366.

After his death the throne of Casimir the Great went to King Louis of Hungary, the son of Charles Robert, who enjoyed the support of the Little Poland nobles and the city of Cracow, which was interested in the trade with Hungary. Preoccupied with his long-terms plans in the Balkans, Louis saw no point in continuing Casimir's policy: in 1372 he renounced all claims to Silesia, and also lost Santok and Drezdenko; Masovia, connected with Great Poland whose nobles opposed Louis' policy, denounced feudal subordination, Lithuanian princes occupied the region of Vladimir (in Volhynia), and Louis himself tried to separate Halicz Ruthenia from Poland.

This atmosphere of political unrest exacerbated the centrifugal forces represented by the nobles. Prince Ladislaus the White, from the Kujawy line of the Piasts (cf. IV, 1) strove for six years to win the throne, in pursuit of which he first tried to become the master of Great Poland and Kujawy. But neither he nor Kaźko of Słupsk, a grandson of Casimir the Great, had any chance of success. To consolidate the rule of his dynasty in Poland, Louis of Hungary tried to win over the nobles and the Church. This led to his promulgating at Kosice in 1374 the privilege which exempted the gentry from state taxes (except for two *grossi* per *laneus*), and which in 1381 was extended to cover the clergy as well. The strivings of Kaźko and Ladislaus the White, the actions undertaken by the adherents of the Angevins, and rivalry among the nobles, made easier by a weakening of the central authority (Louis visited Poland but rarely, and he ruled through the intermediary of his mother Elizabeth, viceregents and bailiffs), gave rise to riots and disturbances, especially in Great Poland.

Louis' throne was to go to his daughter Mary and her fiancé, Sigismund of Luxemburg (the son of Charles IV), who ruled in the Mark of Brandenburg. This plan failed to win the approval of the influential nobles, who decided that the throne should go to Jadwiga (Hedvige), Louis' younger daughter. When, after Louis' death, Jadwiga ascended the throne in 1384, the idea arose that she should marry Jagiello, the Grand Duke of Lithuania, which would make it possible to extend Polish influence in the East, lost as a result of the policy of Louis, who linked the Ruthenian lands directly to Hungary. Following the agreement in Krewo in 1385 Jagiello united Lithuania with Poland and became both the King of Poland and the Grand Duke of Lithuania. Baptized, he assumed the name of Ladislaus (and is accordingly known as Ladislaus Jagiello), married Jadwiga and was crowned in 1386.

The emergence, as a result of the union, of a strong Polish-Lithuanian state meant an upheaval in the political situation in Europe. The fact that Lithuania was administered by Witold (Vitautas), Ladislaus' brother, to which Ladislaus was forced to agree, did not weaken the consolidating bonds and the political unity of the state. Poland was now in a position to regain the Ruthenian territories by expelling the Hungarian troops therefrom, and to take back the fiefdoms held by Ladislaus of Opole, an adherent of Louis of Hungary, who planned a joint action against Poland by Sigismund of Luxemburg (who became the King of Hungary in 1387) and the Teutonic Knights. These had in the meantime bought from Sigismund the region called Neumark (New Mark) (cf. IV, 2), which Great Poland had also tried to buy, and obtained Drezdenko as a fiefdom. The Teutonic Knights were also a mortal danger to Lithuania. An uprising broke out — not without the participation of Witold — against the Teutonic Knights in Samogitia, which they had held after 1398. The controversy over Samogitia, which was adjudged the property of the Teutonic Knights by Venceslas of Luxemburg, the King of Bohemia, who had been asked to act as the arbitrator, was a prelude to a war, preparations for which started in 1409.

The Polish army of 29,000 men (including 11,000 Lithuanian troops) met the Teutonic Knights' army of 21,000 men on the plain between the villages of Grunwald, Łodwigowo, and Stębark (Tannenberg). The battle (called the Battle of Grunwald by Polish historians, and the Battle of Tannenberg by German historiographers), fought on 15 July 1410, was one of the biggest battles in the Middle Ages. It ended in a Polish victory, of which, unfortunately, the Poles failed to make adequate use: Malbork was not captured and not all the castles that had been taken from the Teutonic Order were kept in Polish hands. Only the region of Dobrzyń and Samogitia were regained on the strength of the Peace of Toruń in 1411. The Teutonic Knights planned a new attack, but they were defeated again at Koronowo by Polish troops led by Sędziwoj Ostroróg, the Voivode of Poznań.

Polish diplomacy tried to counteract the anti-Polish propaganda spread by the Teutonic Knights and Sigismund of Luxemburg, presenting the Poles and the Lithuanians as heathens, and the Teutonic Knights as the defenders of Christendom. The culminating point of their endeavours was at the Council of Constance (1414—18), where, however, the Poles were successful in impressing on European public opinion the real facts of the conflict. Paweł Włodkowic, Rector of Cracow University (cf. V, 4), had pride of place in presenting the Polish arguments and advancing progressive views on the settling of international relations. He opposed the mediaeval idea of the Crusades that justified recourse to force in converting non-Christians to Christianity, and he thereby undermined the very *raison d'être* of the Teutonic Order.

1. The War with the Teutonic Order in 1410

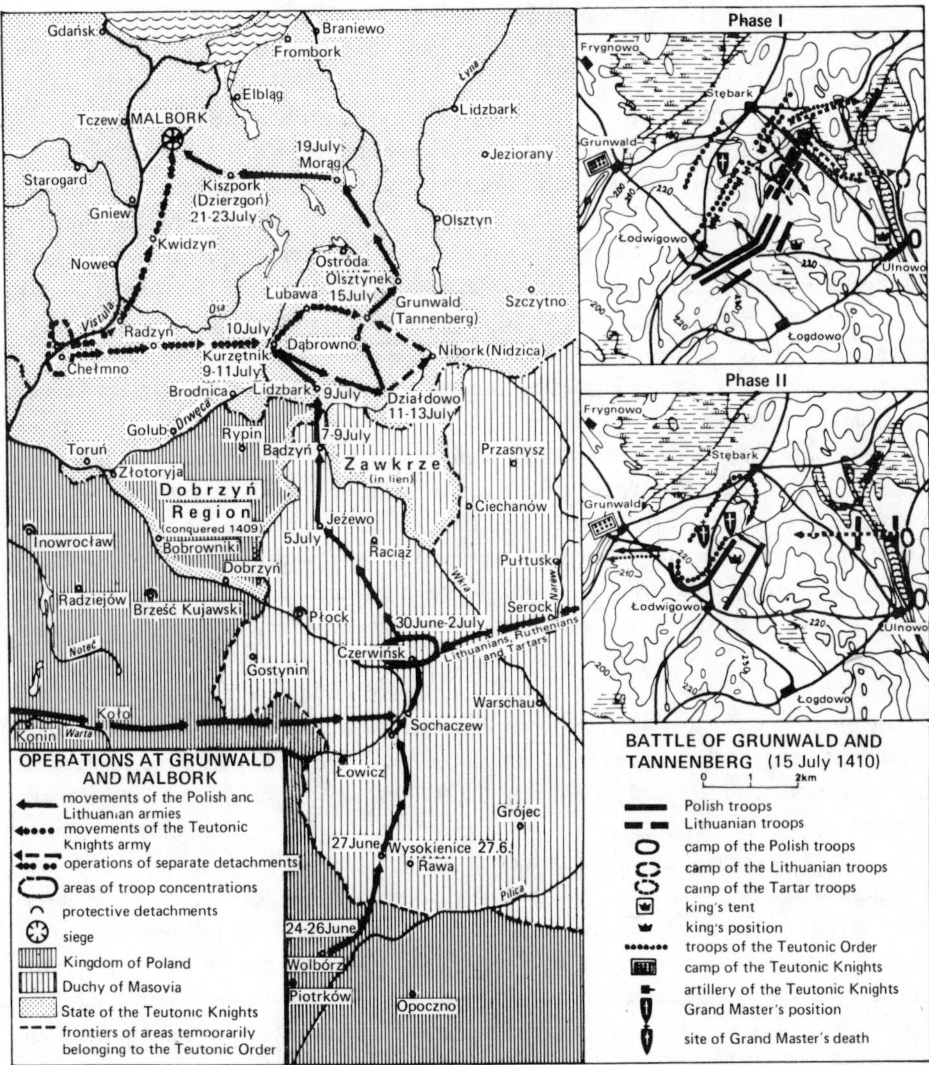

The war with the Teutonic Knights did not end with the Battle of Grunwald. The hostilities continued until 1435 (the treaty of Brześć in Kujawy), and Poland failed to regain Pomerania and the region of Chełmno. But at that time Ladislaus Jagiello was preoccupied with other problems. He had been offered the Bohemian throne after the outbreak of the Hussite uprising in Bohemia (which had strong anti-German implications). Although Ladislaus refused the offer because he did not want to be accused of supporting heretics, friendly contacts with the Hussite movement continued, and the Bohemians helped Poland in its campaign against the Teutonic Order.

Ladislaus Jagiello died in 1434, after a rule in Poland of nearly fifty years. When his son, Ladislaus III (later called Ladislaus of Varna) ascended the throne he was only ten years old, and the country was ruled in his name by Little Poland nobles, who continued Ladislaus Jagiello's policy. After the death in 1437 of Sigismund of Luxemburg succession to the Bohemian throne again became an open issue, and the throne was eventually offered to Casimir Jagiellonian, Ladislaus Jagiello's younger son, but the failure of the Polish expedition to Bohemia cancelled those plans. On the other hand, after the death in 1439 of Albert von Hapsburg the Poles accepted the Hungarian proposal and succeeded in placing Ladislaus III on the Hungarian throne in 1440, which meant a revival of the personal union of Hungary and Poland. This involved Ladislaus III directly in a war with the Turks who were a threat to Hungary; in 1444 he lost his life in the Battle of Varna (whence he has been known as Ladislaus of Varna or, in the Latinized version, Ladislaus Varnensis), and the union with Hungary was broken.

The Polish throne went to Casimir Jagiellonian, who was crowned in 1447. He tried to maintain strong royal rule, but his position was difficult in view of the increased importance of the gentry, who became active both economically and politically. He was accordingly forced to grant the gentry various new political and economic privileges, including the right of provincial diets to decide about calling the *levée en masse* and the imposition of new taxes (the so-called Nieszawa Statutes of 1454).

Casimir Jagiellonian's principal political success was the regaining of Gdańsk Pomerania after a war of thirteen years. He had the full support of the Pomeranians, who strove to free themselves from the rule of the Teutonic Knights and to strengthen their ties with Poland. The year 1440 saw the formation of the Prussian Union, or a confederation of the local gentry and burghers, principally those of Toruń and Chełmno. The Union, which in its conflict with the Teutonic Order failed to obtain a just decision from the Emperor Frederick III (of the Hapsburg dynasty), who acted as the arbitrator, turned to Poland for help. The incorporation into Poland of all the Polish territories held by the Teutonic Knights (6 June 1454) coincided with the outbreak of an uprising in Prussia, directed against the Teutonic Order. War was declared on the Teutonic Knights; it was terminated by the Peace of Toruń on 19 October 1466. Poland regained Gdańsk Pomerania, the region of Chełmno, and Warmia, which became an autonomous *dominium* of the bishops of Warmia. The Teutonic Order retained the eastern part of Old Prussia, which was to be Poland's fiefdom. This enabled a powerful Kingdom of Prussia to emerge two and a half centuries later.

Casimir Jagiellonian continued the Bohemian and Hungarian policy of his predecessors. In 1471, after the death of the Bohemian king, George of Podebrad, the throne went to Ladislaus, Casimir's oldest son, who later, after the death of King Mathias Corvinus, extended his rule to Hungary as well. When John Albert ascended the Polish throne in 1492, and his younger borther Alexander became the Grand Duke of Lithuania, Bohemia, Hungary, Poland, and Lithuania had three sons of Casimir Jagiellonian as their rulers. Jadwiga, daughter of Casimir Jagiellonian and Elizabeth of Austria, married George the Rich, the Prince of Bavaria; the anniversary of their wedding at Landshut in 1475 has been celebrated there to this day, a folk festival being held every third year.

The rule of the Jagiellonian dynasty in many European countries, which depended on the international situation, did not last long (cf. VI, 1), and it is not the spread of the Jagiellonian rule which must be considered the most important fact in Poland's history in that period. Much more important were the regaining of Pomerania, the union with Lithuania, and the internal changes, which taken together led to the emergence of a strong and consolidated state called the Kingdom of Poland, or, a little later, the Crown (Lithuania being the other part of the kingdom). The political system of the state was that of a monarchy with the social structure based on estates (status groups, German *Stände*). The king's position was strong, not threatened by excessive influence of gentry or the Church, and the towns played an active political role. The peasants, serfs as they were, were not so completely dominated by the gentry and not forced, as they were to be in the next period (cf. VI, 4), to provide labour dues. The social structure was marked by the co-existence of the estates that were typical of a feudal society: the gentry, the burghers, the peasants, and the clergy. This equilibrium was to be disturbed only in the period that followed, when the gentry became the dominant force, which was due to a relatively weaker development of the town in Poland as compared with Western Europe.

The machinery of the state was made much more efficient. The bailiffs, who appeared earlier, during the reign of Ladislaus the Short (cf. IV, 2), were the main local representatives of the king; they came to replace the castellans in that function. The scope of their authority was very broad and covered jurisdiction, the army, policing duties, and some economic matters. The law, previously based on customary norms, was replaced by legislation, the pride of place going to the Statutes of Casimir the Great, who also established the supreme court (with the seat in the Cracow castle) for cases covered by the German law, which restricted appeals to German courts. Military and financial administration was also introduced, the treasury being supervised by the official called Royal (or Crown) Treasurer.

But the structure gradually began to crack under the influence of the cumulative privileges of the gentry. Originally they covered only the election of the king (*de facto,* though not yet *de jure,* after the death of Casimir the Great), and later, after the Privilege of Kosice (1374), also the approval of the taxes. These were needed most by the kings, because their income was reduced by the grants made of royal estates. The existing system of the *levée en masse* made the king dependent upon the gentry in that respect, too. The Czerwińsk Privilege of 1422 protected the gentry against excessive interference on the part of the bailiffs, and the Nieszawa Privileges (1454) mentioned above made the calling of the *levée en masse* and the imposition of new taxes dependent upon the approval of the provincial diets of the gentry. The provincial diets continued to increase their prerogatives in the 15th century, largely restricting thereby the authority of the bailiffs. The same period saw the emergence of the Royal Council, consisting of the highest officials of the state. The combination of the Council, which came to be called the Senate, with the institution of assemblies of the gentry resulted in the late 15th century in the emergence of a Diet (the Seym) consisting of two chambers, which was sanctioned by the law passed by the Seym in Piotrków in 1496. It had its infrastructure in the form of the provincial diets, which came to elect deputies to the central diet (Seym) and to solve local problems. The emergence of the Seym, dominated by the gentry, meant the collapse of the monarchy based on estates. At the same time the gentry restricted the possibility of the peasants to leave their villages (*glebae adscriptio*) and prohibited the purchase by the burghers and other plebeians of landed estates.

3. Economic life and social structure

The development of the state and of the estates typical of feudal society went hand in hand with the economic development of the country. Agricultural production and the output of the various goods by craftsmen was increasing, as was also home and foreign trade. The number of the towns and their population were on the rise, accompanied by the development of municipal self-government, which had a good effect on the situation of the burghers. In the late 15th century Gdańsk had 30,000 to 35,000 inhabitants, while Wrocław and Cracow some 20,000 inhabitants each. Other towns had from 2,000 to 6,000 inhabitants. The importance of Poznań and Toruń increased. Warsaw began to develop, too, and soon came ahead of Czersk, previously the most important town in Masovia. In the 14th and 15th centuries municipal rights were granted to some 330 towns, out of the total of ca. 500 at the end of the 15th century.

The growing needs of all the classes and groups were linked to the general advances in standards of civilization, and this in turn stimulated economic activity. Unlike Western Europe, Poland was not affected by the plague (the black death), which decimated the population of many countries in the second half of the 14th century.

The owners of landed estates still tried to attract settlers; the peasants also settled in new territories on their own initiative. It was in the 14th and 15th centuries that deforestation yielded the agricultural landscape we know today. New settlements were particularly numerous in the big forests which separated the various provinces from one another, in the Subcarpathian regions, in Masovia, in the region of Lublin, in Podlasie, and in Old Prussia, left to the Teutonic Knights, where several hundred villages were founded by the arrivals from Masovia (the inhabitants of Masovia being called *Mazury*, the areas settled by them came to be known as *Masuria*). Large numbers of minor gentry also settled in the newly acquired Ruthenian lands.

The scythe became common in agriculture, while the furrowing plough continued to be used along with the asymmetric plough (a wooden mouldboard plough). Harrows were improved, and horses came to be used in land tilling next to the oxen, which had been used earlier. The same plants were being cultivated as before (cf. IV, 3), while gardening and animal breeding increased markedly.

Small peasant holdings were the dominant units in agriculture. A typical holding was one of some 15 hectares (one *laneus*, some 30—35 acres), which produced grain crops and other plants and had a fairly large number of animals kept on its area. In the 15th century, the average per one holding was 3—4 horses, 2—3 oxen, 2—3 cows, 15 sheep, 5—6 goats, 7 pigs. The holdings of the *sculteti* (village administrators) were two to three times larger. The so-called reserves held directly by the lords had two to four *lanei* (30 to 60 hectares) each, and they were tilled by the peasants who were obliged to provide labour dues (corvée) for several days per holding per year. It was also usual to hire those peasants who held small holdings (of two to three hectares each) and who were called cottagers. The owner of the land (a nobleman or a member of the gentry) had his income based on fixed rents collected from the peasants, the value of which was falling as a result of the devaluation of money and the rise of prices. This caused the envy with which the landlords watched how the *sculteti* were growing rich. By availing themselves of their influence upon the decisions made by the kings they made the monarchs issue a number of edicts aimed at the *sculteti*, the most important one being that promulgated in Warka in 1423, which made it possible for the landlords to buy out the holdings of the *sculteti* on a compulsory basis. They were thus ridding themselves of competitors and acquiring land with which to expand their so-called reserves, i.e., manors. The land bought from the *sculteti*, combined with uncultivated tracts, which were quite numerous in almost every village (because some peasants were moving to the expanding towns), gave rise to the lords' demesnes based on corvée. Demesne formation was characteristic only of the 16th century (cf. VI, 4), but it began one century earlier. The process was accompanied by the intensification of corvée which increased from several days per year to one day per week per *laneus* on the average.

The growth of agricultural production was followed by increased extraction of mineral products and the expansion of crafts and early forms of industry. The 14th century saw a rise in the production of gold in Silesia. The lead ore deposits near Olkusz were gaining in importance, and the technique of extracting iron ores was improved: next to bog iron ore deep deposits of iron ore came to be exploited, too. At the time of Casimir the Great the consumption of iron per one inhabitant was several times higher than it had been at the time of Boleslaus the Brave. The technique of iron smelting was still rather primitive, but furnaces with blast obtained by hand or foot operated devices were being replaced by those with blasting devices powered by water or horse power.

The crafts continued to diversify, and the number of guilds in towns was on the increase. This was accompanied by the emergence of regions characterized by the development of early industries. Metal working was developing, and the work of goldsmiths was marked by very good craftsmanship. There was also a growing demand for their products, especially on the part of rich burghers and well-to-do gentry. The production of arms developed, for they were quite commonly kept, even by many peasants. Swords, mail armour, and helmets continued to be the principal elements of military equipment; cutlasses and crossbows appeared. Specialists claim that the large number of projectile weapons made Polish infantry of that time more efficient than that in Western Europe, where the number of archers and crossbowmen usually did not exceed 15 per cent of the whole. Artillery is first mentioned by Janko of Czarnków in his chronicle (1383); its use decreased the disproportion between the advanced techniques for defending strongholds and castles and the low effectiveness of the techniques for laying siege, which was shown during the Thirteen Years' War (cf. V, 2).

Among the kinds of production, other than metal working and the crafts connected with the equipment of the army, the first place was held by the textile industry, based on home-produced raw materials (wool, flax, hemp). There were marked advances in weaving techniques; the so-called horizontal looms, popular until recent times, were common at least from the 13th century on. The spread of water-operated fulling mills and of bleaching techniques was also important. Cloth-making developed in Silesia, Masovia, in the eastern part of Great Poland, and in Little Poland; the 15th century saw the growth of the cloth-making industry in Great Poland in general, even though that region still lagged behind Silesia, and also had to face the competition of imported cloth. Poland was a large-scale importer of Western European cloth (mainly from Flanders), and was also an important trade route by which cloth went to Russia, Hungary, and other countries.

Demand for furs promoted the development of related crafts. There was a large market for shoes and other products made of leather. The production of paper increased rapidly from the early 15th century on. Building crafts were also in demand as a result of more intensive building being in progress.

Home trade intensified as it was based on the rent economy, the feudal rent being primarily rent in money. It consisted mainly in the exchange of goods between town and country. Poland started exporting grain in the 15th century, through the intermediary of Gdańsk merchants who bought grain from the gentry, who were expanding their manors, and also bought grain from the peasants to resell it for export. This form of trade, however, was to develop on a large scale only in the period that followed (cf. VI, 4).

While grain and timber were exported to the West, other goods carried over large distances went through Poland in transit. Oxen were driven to the West from the Ukraine, silk came from China, cloth was carried from Western Europe, and wines and copper from Slovakia and Hungary in the South. A dense network of markets and fairs began to develop, and some towns (Poznań, Gniezno, Lublin, Gdańsk, etc.) specialized in international trade.

The needs of home and foreign trade induced Casimir the Great to carry out a monetary reform, based on the introduction of thick coins (*nummi grossi,* German *Groschen*), common in Western Europe. The perennial shortfall in actual money, due to the rapid growth of economic life, accounted for its gradual devaluation, i.e., the decrease of the amount of silver in the coins.

All this shows that Poland in the feudal period (that of monarchy based on the system of estates) was marked by intensive and many-sided productive work. The rate of economic growth was higher than in many other countries.

4. Culture and society. Education and science. Art

The development of economic life and achievements in politics were followed by a remarkable improvement in living standards and by a broad participation of society as a whole in cultural matters, although the domination of the gentry that came to be felt toward the close of the period was in the future (cf. VI, 6) adversely to affect the participation of the peasants in national culture. Later occurred the separation of 'high' culture, represented by the gentry and the Church, from folk culture. But for the time being the circle of those who were connected with the culture of Latin Christendom, which became the intellectual basis of the emerging nation, continued to broaden. This applied primarily to the burghers. It was not until the turn of the 18th century that motifs of folk culture with elements that went back to the pre-Christian period, came to enrich national culture.

Higher living standards were observable in everyday life. Food was further diversified. New kinds of groats, made of millet and buck-wheat, came into use, and herrings became a fairly common food of the various groups and classes. Food now marked the social status to a greater extent than earlier. The difference between the upper and the lower strata consisted mainly in the amount and quality of the meat consumed. Mainly pork, beef, and poultry were eaten, game being the choice food. The culture of eating became more refined, which is borne out by the commonly known poem *O zachowaniu się przy stole* (Table Manners), ascribed to Słota, the burgrave of Poznań (early 15th cent.) Eating from separate plates was not yet common, except in the richest families.

The development of the estates (status groups, *Stände*) was reflected in the kinds of dress: the peasants, the burghers, the gentry and the lords began to dress in their own distinctive ways. In that respect the 14th century witnessed notable modifications: loose dresses (tunics) worn by men and women, typical of the earlier centuries, were being replaced by tighter ones, more closely fitted (blouse, trousers, belt), which made human figures look slimmer. Men's dress was now shorter and different from that worn by women. At that time it was still varied, but later it was only women's dress that was diversified. This was due to a change in the role of women and their social status: in mediaeval Poland that status was high not only in the legal sense, but also because women participated in social occasions.

The number of people who had, at least elementary, knowledge of reading and writing increased considerably. The importance of writing, documents, and handwritten books was now much greater, which was due to a remarkable development in education. The basis of this was constituted by the parish schools (both in town and country), which at the turn of the 15th century numbered at least 3,000. Thus several tens of thousands of boys, including many sons of peasants, were leaving these schools annually. There were also other schools, with more ambitious curricula — those attached to cathedrals and those run by monks. A university was founded in Cracow in 1364 by Casimir the Great; it was the second university in Central Europe (the first being that in Prague); it was a year later that the university in Vienna was founded, while many other famous European universities (including that of Heidelberg) were still younger.

Cracow University ceased to function in the period of political confusion (the rule of Louis of Hungary — cf. V, 2), but it was re-opened in 1400 by Ladislaus Jagiello, who also secured its material existence, to which a large contribution was made by Queen Jadwiga (Hedvige). In the 15th century, the university had some 8,000 to 10,000 students, including many young men from outside Poland: Germany, Bohemia, Hungary, Switzerland, Scandinavia, Spain, Silesia and the State of the Teutonic Order (i.e., up to 1466, Pomerania, Warmia, and Masuria). The latter tried in the late 15th century to open its own university in Chełmno. About half of the students were of the burgher origin, and there was also a considerable percentage of peasants' sons.

The role of the nobles as promoters of culture was still very important. Many eminent scholarly works owed their origin to the inspiration of the royal court, the Church, and the nobles (the Szamotulski, Odrowąż, Tarnowski, Oleśnicki, and Melsztyński families). Jan Stobner, a burgher from Cracow, founded (1405) the Chair of Mathematics and Astronomy at the University of Cracow, at that time the only one of its kind in Central Europe.

The disseminations of education and culture was promoted by an increase in the number of the reading public, and the second half of the 15th century saw the advent of the printing press, which revolutionized the production of books. It is assumed that the oldest book known to be printed in Poland dates from ca. 1473 (a calendar for the year 1474), but large numbers of printed books had been brought from abroad before that date.

The 15th century saw the development of science in Poland, Polish scientists and scholars being gathered mainly around the new university. The most advanced

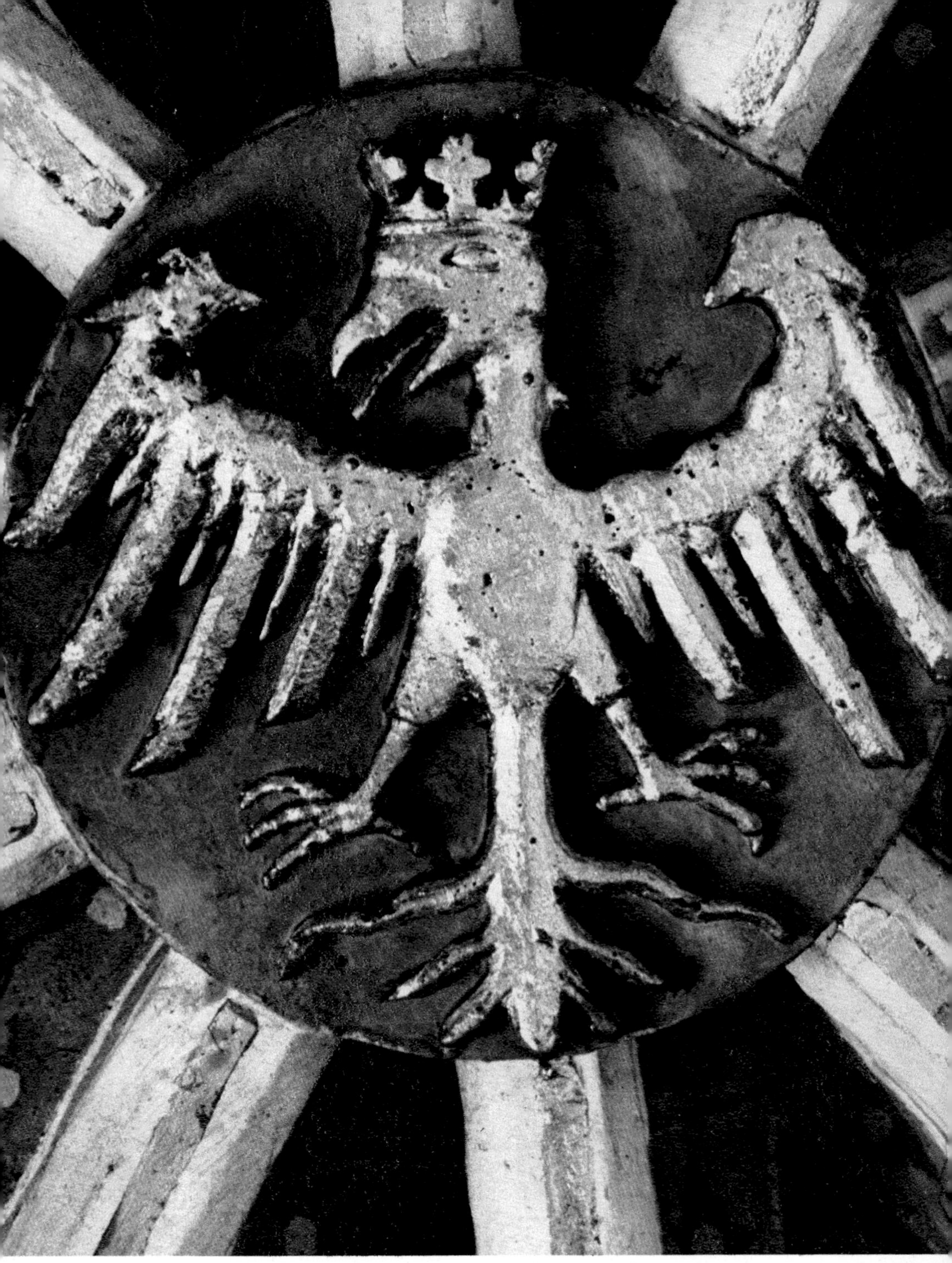

The eagle of the Piast dynasty as shown on a keystone in the chapel of Silesian princes in the Franciscan church in Opole (mid-14th cent.)

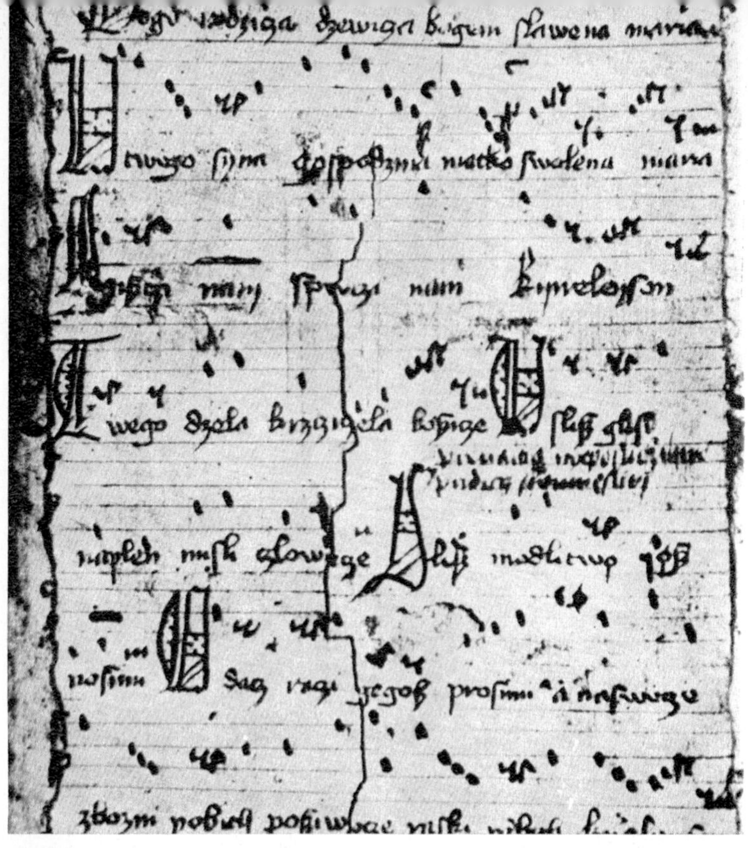

The text of *Bogurodzica* (The Mother of God), the oldest extant Polish song, sung by the Polish knights before battles, as recorded in a manuscript (ca. 1407)

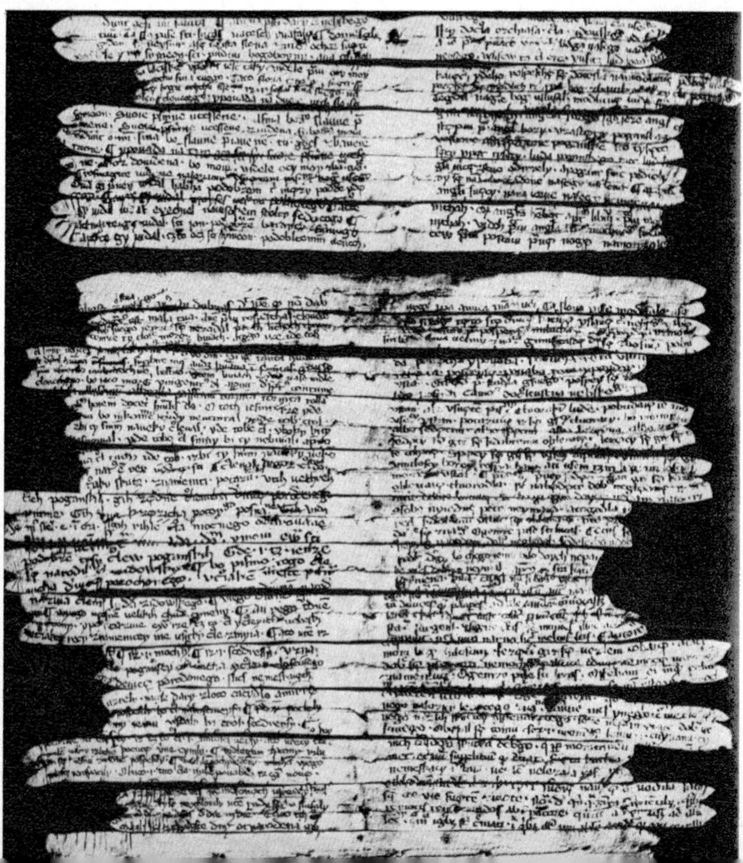

A page from the *Kazania świętokrzyskie* (The Holy Cross Sermons), the oldest monument of Polish prose, dating from the 13th or the 14th century

King Casimir the Great (reigned 1333–70) as shown in his *sigillum maiestatis*

The ruins of the Late Gothic castle at Ogrodzieniec (mid-14th cent.)

Queen Jadwiga (Hedvige) (queen 1384–99) as shown by the sculpture on her sarcophagus in the Wawel cathedral

King Ladislaus Jagiello (reigned 1386–1434) as shown by the sculpture on his sarcophagus in the Wawel cathedral

The Battle of Tannenberg (1410) as shown in a detail of the painting by Jan Matejko, the greatest Polish historical painter of the 19th century

A heavy arbalest used by infantry in the 15th century

The nave of the Gothic cathedral in Poznań (14th cent.)

disciplines included mathematics and astronomy, theology with philosophy, jurisprudence with elements of political science, and ethics. The most eminent astronomers and mathematicians were Benedict Hesse (d. 1456), Martin Król of Żurawica (ca. 1426—60), Nicolaus Wodka of Kwidzyn (ca. 1442—92), Adalbert of Brudzewo (ca. 1445—95) and Martin Bylica of Olkusz (1433—93). That school of astronomy which was held in great esteem in Europe, produced Nicolaus Copernicus, admitted to the Jagiellonian University of Cracow in the autumn of 1491.

Prominent theologians, who also represented philosophy, jurisprudence, and political science (at that time those disciplines were closely interconnected) included Andreas of Kokorzyn, Andreas Wężyk, Jacobus of Paradyż, Stanislaus of Skalbmierz, Paul of Worczyn, John of Ludzisko, and Matthias of Cracow (1345—1410), the last being one of the most eminent theologians of his times and also organizer and rector of Heidelberg University. They advanced progressive and novel ideas and concepts, namely those of equality of nations, just war, reforms of the Church in a democratic spirit, and human dignity. The new ideas, which soon gained support, facilitated the reception of the ideas of humanism which found in Poland a well-prepared ground in the form of native work in science and culture. The ideas of humanism were spread in Poland by the Italian Filippo Buonaccorsi, called Callimachus (1437—96), who found a protector in Gregory of Sanok (ca. 1407—77), the Archbishop of Lvov and an outstanding connoisseur of ancient culture.

Special mention is due to historiography in late mediaeval Poland, pride of place going to the *Chronicle* of Janko of Czarnków, Vice-Chancellor under Casimir the Great, which covers the period from 1370 to 1384, and the *Annals* of Jan Długosz (1415—80), describing the history of Poland from legendary times to 1480. The latter work ranks among the most outstanding achievements of European historiography of the period, as it testifies to the birth of the critical method and the generic interpretation of historical facts.

Many works of literature dating from late mediaeval Poland have been preserved. In the 15th century Polish became the literary language after Latin. Religious songs, later sung by the faithful during religious ceremonies, were recorded in Polish (polyphonic singing was at first propagated by Franciscan monks, and the 15th century witnessed the activity of the eminent composer Nicolaus of Radom). Narrative poetry appeared, which sometimes registered current events, as did *Pieśń o zamordowaniu Jędrzeja Tęczyńskiego* (The Song of the Murder of Andreas Tęczyński, 1461), carried moral teachings, discussed manners, as in *Pieśń o chlebowym stole* (The Song of Bread-laden Table, ca. 1410), and included satirical elements, as did *Rozmowa mistrza ze śmiercią* (Dialogue Between the Master and Death), a medieval Polish poem of over 300 lines. Polish artistic prose was represented by *Kazania świętokrzyskie* (Sermons of the Holy Cross Mountains), dating probably from the late 13th century, and *Kazania gnieźnieńskie* (Sermons of Gniezno), the most important work in that field being, however, *Rozmyślania przemyskie* (Meditations of Przemyśl), which describes the life of Jesus and the Virgin Mary. Quasi-dramatic forms are represented by *Skarga umierającego* (A Dying Man's Complaint).

The vitality of cultural life was also revealed in the music. As previously (cf. IV, 4) all special occasions in the family life of the burghers, especially the patricians, included music and dances by goliards and minstrels, and also by resident musicians, whose number was increasing. Under the rule of Louis of Hungary (1370—82) the custom of the bugle-call from St. Mary's church in Cracow was established (and has survived to this day). The organ and the art of organ playing became popular, but monodic songs were still typical of Church music in town and country. Religious songs, carols (15th cent.), and lay songs, popularized mainly by young scholars, and court music continued to develop.

Polish artistic culture in the late Middle Ages was dominated by Gothic art in architecture, sculpture, painting, and crafts. The expansion of Gothic architecture was reflected in the erection of numerous buildings made of stone and brick, although wooden houses still predominated in the rural areas. The principal Gothic monuments of Polish art of the period include St. Mary's church in Gdańsk, the rebuilt cathedrals in Gniezno and Poznań, St. Mary's church in Cracow, the cathedral within the premises of Wawel Castle in Cracow, St. Elizabeth's church and St. Mary's church in Wrocław, and St. Elizabeth's church in Świdnica. Churches were founded by kings, nobles, prelates, and burghers. Some regions, such as Silesia, Pomerania, and Great Poland, developed their own varieties of Gothic art. The Gothic style affected not only churches, but also castles, dwelling houses, public buildings (such as cloth halls), and town walls.

The castles held by the nobles and the churches they founded testified to the importance and wealth of their owners and founders, which was demonstrated in ornamentation in the form of sculptures and paintings. Sculptures were carved in stone (tombstones, etc.) and in wood (statues of Our Lady, altars, stalls, etc.). The most outstanding works of art in the European context include the wooden triptych (folding altar) in St. Mary's church in Cracow, carved by Wit Stwosz (fl. 1477—89), a Nuremberger who settled in Cracow, and the Madonna of Krużlowa dating from ca. 1400—10.

Intensification of cultural, scientific, and artistic life would not have been possible without permanent and lively contacts with neighbouring countries. New manifestations of culture were coming from Eastern Germany, brought in by German settlers, and later through permanent contacts with other parts of Germany; there were lively contacts with Bohemia, where many Poles studied and taught at the University of Prague; influences were also felt from Hungary, Italy, France, and from the Baltic region via Pomerania (at first held by the Teutonic Knights, and regained by Poland in 1466).

Poland and its people were thus entering the modern age, heralded by the discovery of America in 1492, which greatly broadened the concept of the world in the minds of Europeans, resulting in remarkable achievements.

Chapter VI

Poland under the Renaissance and the 'Democracy of the Gentry' (1501—1618)

1. General features

The 16th century, called by historians 'the golden age' when earlier centuries were regarded in too gloomy a way, was in fact the continuation of Polish political, economic and cultural attainments from the previous period. The achievements of 'the golden age' held the seeds of the difficulties to be encountered later in the development of the country. The hampering, at the close of the 16th century, of the development which had continued for centuries, was primarily due to the domination by the gentry of political, economic, and social life. The gentry blocked the economic enterprise and the participation in culture of the peasants and burghers thus preventing the fulfilment of the creative forces of the entire nation. The consequences of this came to light when the magnates (the most powerful members of the gentry) eliminated the middle gentry (still very active in the 16th century) from political life (cf. VII, 3).

But the 16th century can rightly be called the golden age of Polish culture. Poland became one of the leading centres of the broadly conceived culture of the Renaissance, developing processes of which had originated in earlier periods. Nicolaus Copernicus (1473—1543), whose discovery is associated with the greatest revolution in the history of science (followed by Galileo and Newton), gained his first inspiration in the Cracow school of astronomy, Europe's first Chair of Mathematics and Astronomy established at the Jagiellonian University some hundred years earlier. Jan Kochanowski (1530—84), the founder of Polish as a literary language and one of the most eminent European poets of his time, developed the humanistic elements observable earlier in Polish cultural life. Polish culture reached many countries, primarily Lithuania, Russia, Moldavia and Vallachia, Siebenburgen (Transsylvania) and Ducal Prussia, and in these countries Polish was the diplomatic language. The progressive philosophy of the Polish Brethren (Socinians or Arians) contributed to the development of the ideas that marked the early period of the Age of Reason. The union of Poland with Lithuania also largely reflected the strong influence of Polish political, enonomic and social institutions and the attractiveness of Polish culture.

The wide spreading of print encouraged the development of reading (some four million copies of books were printed in Poland in the 16th century); the educational system continued to develop, and a university was founded in Vilna.

Changes in political and social thinking were revealed in the works of Andrzej Frycz Modrzewski (ca. 1503—73) who was the only contemporary European writer to advance in his works (*De Republica Emendanda*) the principle that all citizens should be equal in law.

Sixteenth century Poland was a large and populous country and after the union with Lithuania its area was second only to that of Russia. After 1569 (the Union of Lublin) and the incorporation of Livonia (cf. VI, 2), Poland (consisting of the Crown and the Grand Duchy of Lithuania), had an area of 815,000 sq. kilometres,

Lithuania contributing some 65 per cent (550,000 sq. kilometres). The population amounted to six million, some 40 per cent of which lived in Lithuania. The ethnically Polish territories were being united. The regions of Lębork and Bytów were incorporated in Poland as fiefdoms in 1526 but the same measure — despite the proposals advanced in 1513—18 by Prince Boguslaus — failed with respect to Western Pomerania, at that time already strongly Germanized. Masovia was incorporated in the Crown in 1529 and Podlasie in 1569. This meant incorporation in the Crown of Ukrainian territories, which offered magnates living in the Crown an opportunity to acquire estates in this region. On the other hand, originally Ruthenian magnates, such as the Wiśniowieckis, the Koreckis, and the Ostrogskis, began to rise in political importance. Livonia was held jointly by the Crown and Lithuania.

Agricultural production was flourishing and surpluses were easily sold abroad. This increase in output was at least partly due to the expansion of demesnes based on corvée, which to a large extent used untilled land. The demesnes limited the production capacity of peasant farms but their impact on economic life in general was to prove detrimental only in the period that followed. The towns on the whole were still expanding and growing rich as can be seen from the new Renaissance-style buildings.

Sixteenth century Poland was marked by high political culture, in a sense exceptional in Europe. There were neither persecution of religious dissenters nor political crimes; it it was 'a state without stakes'. One of its most striking manifestations was the development in Poland of the idea of religious tolerance and the separation (rare in contemporary Europe) of religion from politics. It is true that the gentry held power more and more strongly, but considering the fact that it constituted some ten per cent of the population and that all its members had equal political rights, it was a remarkable phenomenon. The 'democracy of the gentry' thus meant democracy for a much larger percentage of the population than was the case after the electoral reforms in the 19th century. In Britain in 1867, after the Second Reform Bill had been passed, the number of people with electoral rights hardly exceeded three per cent and the corresponding figure for France in 1831—48 was only about one per cent. Of course, in the case of the Polish gentry, the political barriers were based on the system of estates (status groups), while in Western Europe in the 19th century, political rights were associated with property ownership.

Poland was ruled by the Jagiellonians until 1572, the last three kings of that dynasty being Alexander (1501—06), Sigismund the Old (1506—48) and Sigismund Augustus (1548—72). Of special note is Queen Bona, the Italian wife of Sigismund the Old, who lived in Poland in 1518—56 and represented both the strengthening of royal power and the anti-Hapsburg policy. Next came the period of elected kings, the first of whom, Henri de Valois (1573—74), soon left Poland to pursue his plan to ascend the French throne. He was followed by Stephen Báthory of Transsylvania (1577—86), who was in turn preoccupied with his native land, then under the Turkish rule, and Sigismund Vasa (1587—1632) whose vision of Polish problems was blurred by his involvement in internal policies in Sweden. Elections of foreign-born kings confused political actions, because the forces which determined Polish policy were complicated by external factors, only in part in agreement with the Polish policy, and in most cases involving Poland in conflicts detrimental to the development of the country.

Even though an election in itself meant the choice of a definite political course, it did not guarantee the pursuit of that policy by the king. The elections of Henri de Valois, Stephen Báthory and Sigismund Vasa resulted in the supremacy of the anti-Hapsburg movements (which included unwillingness to get involved in a conflict with Turkey and enthusiasm for the formation of an alliance with France) but actual policies were determined by a clash of the political ideology (represented by a given king) with the representations of the gentry and groups of magnates.

As in other European countries, national consciousness linked to the development of historical consciousness, was intensifying in Poland. At this time a community of language meant less than it would do several centuries later. Non-Polish groups of the gentry were becoming Polonized as a result of being citizens of the Polish state. This also applied to those urban patricians who had come to Poland from Germany in the Middle Ages. The Italians, Scots, English and other foreigners who had arrived in Poland in the 16th century were as quickly assimilated. In the eastern territories, the difference in status between the gentry and the peasants was usually intensified by the consciousness of religious difference between the two groups and also by the fact that the gentry felt themselves to be Poles, while the peasants were ethnically Ukrainians, Byelorussians and Lithuanians.

The Renaissance saw a further notable development of the Polish nation, due to achievements in culture and politics. The process was not adversely affected by the religious divisions of the gentry caused by the Reformation (cf. VI, 3). It was only in the towns of western Poland that Lutheranism contributed to the consolidation of the ethnic difference of those burghers of German origin who had not been Polonized.

2. Poland in 'the Golden Age' as seen against the background of Europe

The 16th century saw several important events in the political history of Poland and its people, which were to have grave consequences in the future. These were: the agreement in Vienna in 1515, the so-called Prussian homage in 1525, Polish political activity in the Baltic region and the resulting participation of Poland in the Northern War (1563—70) and the union with Lithuania, concluded in Lublin in 1569. Poland did not participate in the great process of colonial expansion, then prevalent in Europe and represented primarily by England, Spain, and Portugal.

Poland's intensive development was highly influential in the general European political situation. This active position was lost only in the 18th century, when Poland became surrounded by absolute monarchies with greatly increased power (Prussia, Austria, Russia) and the elected kings of foreign extraction introduced political ideologies which were at variance with Poland's interests (cf. VII, 2 and VIII, 2).

In the early 16th century the Jagiellonian dynasty (Sigismund the Old and his brother Ladislaus) reigned over vast areas of Central and Eastern Europe, namely Poland, Lithuania, Bohemia and Hungary, thus becoming a formidable rival to the Hapsburgs who were striving for hegemony in Europe and for the domination of Bohemia and Hungary (cf. V, 1). The Emperor Maximilian I (1486—1519) laid the main foundations of the future power of the Hapsburgs by acquiring — through the marriages of himself and his son — the Netherlands, Spain and Naples, thus paving the way for further acquisitions. He became dangerous to Poland by concluding in 1514 an alliance with Moscow, which from 1507 was engaged in a war with Lithuania (supported in turn by Sigismund the Old), and by siding with the Teutonic Knights who disputed the Peace of Toruń of 1466 (cf. V, 2) and even pretended to sovereign rights in Gdańsk and Elbląg. To make matters worse, Vasili III, the Prince of Moscow, established close contacts with Albrecht, of the Hohenzollern family (the Ansbach line), the then Grand Master of the Teutonic Order. This rendered Sigismund's position even more difficult.

He understood the Hapsburg threat completely; for example, he said that 'once the Germans are permitted to take hold of those kingdoms [Bohemia and Hungary], they will never abandon them'. This was why he allied himself with the powerful Hungarian Zapolya family by marrying Barbara Zapolya in 1511 and at the same time tried to neutralize Maximilian I by concluding with him (Vienna 1515) an agreement that Louis, the son of Ladislaus Jagiellonian, and Anna, his daughter, were to marry Maximilian's grandchildren Mary and Ferdinand respectively. This, however, opened for the Hapsburgs a way to ascend the thrones of Bohemia and Hungary. Maximilian was a past master in matrimonial combinations and his plans were successful because Louis was killed in the battle against the Turks at Mohacs in 1526, whereupon Ferdinand (Anna's husband) gained Bohemia and north-western part of Hungary; the Hapsburgs settled firmly in Bohemia, while the remaining part of the Hungarian territory — and later also Moldavia — with which Poland had waged a war for the domination of the region of Pokucie — were occupied by the Turks who left only Transsylvania as a fiefdom.

Sigismund the Old, like many other influential politicians of his time, did not strive for a war with Turkey, particularly as he had to confront the Teutonic Order (ruled by Albrecht von Hohenzollern), which tried to become independent of Poland by disputing Polish sovereignty. Sigismund anticipated the Teutonic Knights' attack by starting military operations against them in 1519 but two years later he was forced to conclude — with the mediation of the Emperor Charles V — an armistice. Neither side saw any point in continuing war, and Albrecht proposed the conversion of that part of Old Prussia which was then still held by the Teutonic Order into a lay state, with Lutheranism as the official religion. This would be a Polish fiefdom. He was supported in this proposal by the German gentry who had settled in these regions and received vast estates from the Teutonic Order. Charles V's victory over the French — who in 1524 became Polish allies — in the battle of Pavia (1525) was also an advantageous event for them. Sigismund the Old therefore accepted Albrecht's proposal despite the advocates of a military campaign against the Teutonic Order, who included Jan Łaski, the primate of Poland and an eminent politician.

All this led to the famous Prussian homage on 10 April 1525. At this time it marked a success for Poland, because it was a manifestation of the modern secular policy of the Polish king; strong pro-Reformation inspirations also began to come from Lutheran Prussia. But the steps made by Sigismund's successors — Sigismund Augustus, Stephen Báthory, and Sigismund III — namely the admission of the Hohenzollerns of Brandenburg, the Electors of the Empire, to succession in Prussia and the grant to them in 1611 of the fief (which they took over only after the death in 1618 of Albrecht's son, the mentally deranged Albrecht Frederick), created a dangerous situation which led directly to the birth of the Brandenburg-Prussian state some 80 years later. The Hohenzollerns simultaneously tried to get hold of Western Pomerania, Silesia, and Livonia (roughly the region of Latvia and Estonia).

Sigismund Augustus' concessions to the Hohenzollerns were associated with his struggle for the domination of the Baltic Sea (*dominium Maris Baltici*), on which the Polish gentry exported grain via Gdańsk and other Baltic ports, including Riga (cf. VI, 3). In this connection the continuing existence in Livonia of the Knights of the Sword (cf. IV, 1) constituted a political problem. Albrecht tried to extend his domination in the Baltic region through the dissolution of this Order, whereas Sigismund Augustus continued his naval policy by trying to subordinate Gdańsk to the royal authority, by building a navy and undertaking other measures. While doings so he also did not want the Order of the Knights of the Sword to become allied with Muscovy. Accordingly, he gave his support to the Archbishop of Riga, who stood for an alliance with Lithuania against the Grand Master of the Knights of the Sword, and made the latter (by the Treaty of Pozvolsk, 1557) change his policy toward Muscovy and Lithuania. This provoked Ivan the Terrible to occupy, in 1558, the town of Narva which gave Muscovy access to the Baltic, and also other towns; under the same circumstances Denmark and Sweden also occupied certain territories. The wars between Sweden and Denmark, and between Lithuania (and hence also Poland) and Muscovy, which took place at the same time, were terminated in 1570 by a peace treaty between Denmark and Sweden, and a truce between Poland and Muscovy. Each party concerned seized part of Livonia. Muscovy retained Narva and Polotsk, which Ivan the Terrible conquered in

1563; Lithuania kept Riga and Pärnu; Denmark, Ösel; Sweden, the northern part of Estonia. Livonia continued to be a *casus belli* in conflicts between Poland and Sweden, Poland and Muscovy, and Muscovy and Sweden. The Order of the Knights of the Sword was dissolved in 1561 and Gotthard Kettler, its last Grand Master, became a vassal of Poland in Courland and Semigalia, while the other territories were incorporated in Lithuania in 1569 as a Lithuanian-Polish condominium.

The conflict with Muscovy had it antecedents (cf. V, 2) resulting from a clash of the Lithuanian expansion with the Muscovite strivings for unification. During the years 1507—08, 1512—22, and 1534—37 a war was waged between Muscovy and Lithuania in which the Crown was involved for the first time. Muscovy was the more active party and succeeded in seizing Smolensk. The war, during which the Grand Duke of Muscovy sought closer ties with the Emperor Maximilian, made Sigismund the Old try (see the Agreement in Vienna of 1515, mentioned above) to win over the Emperor. The truce of 1537 settled the frontier between Lithuania and Muscovy for a quarter of century.

A new situation developed when Poland's union with Lithuania was achieved in 1569 (at a meeting of the Seym in Lublin) and gave birth to a large multinational state, called the Commonwealth (the Polish term *Rzeczpospolita,* which was used at that time, is a calque from the Latin *res publica* in its original sense of 'public concern', and did not imply then the republican form of government; the term *Republic* can hardly be used today in view of its modern associations; this is why *Commonwealth* seems to be best rendering of the old Polish meaning of *Rzeczpospolita — translator's note*) which had one king, one parliament, one diplomatic service and one monetary system, but had separate systems of local, financial and military administration. The direct incorporation into the Crown of Ukrainian territories, which became the area where the magnates acquired new landed estates (cf. VI, 1), gave rise to a new, additional source of conflicts between Poland and Russia, which soon turned into the principal one. Each country wanted to incorporate the Ukrainian territories, while the Ukrainians strove for their own national and political goals. The vast areas in the East, which Poland acquired on the strength of its union with Lithuania and thus became directly involved in the sphere of interests of Muscovy, brought the issue of Polish-Russian relations to the forefront of Polish foreign policy.

Relations with Russia reached another crisis point during the reign of Stephen Báthory, who was induced to start war in order to stop Russian expansion in Livonia, where in 1575—77 Russia occupied the territories up to the river Dvina, except for Riga and Tallin. The interests of the gentry which was growing poorer and sought material profits in a war and the joint Polish and Lithuanian desire to be established firmly on the Baltic were also important factors in this respect. Finally Báthory wanted to win favour with the Holy See and make it start the anti-Turkish crusade.

The war was financed by Gdańsk (200,000 Polish zlotys) and by Prince Georg Frederick Hohenzollern of Ansbach (200,000 guilders), in consideration of the guardianship of the mentally deranged Prince Albrecht Frederick, the son of Albrecht (who died in 1568). Stephen Báthory wanted to impose his will upon Gdańsk whose burghers refused to accept Báthory's election (three days before his election the magnates declared themselves for Maximilian II, who was, however, forced by the gentry, ill-disposed toward the Hapsburgs, to resign). They did not want to share the harbour dues with the treasury and did not want the privileged position of Gdańsk to be threatened. The king partly succeeded in his plans, since Gdańsk did contribute to the war.

In three successive expeditions Báthory's troops occupied Polotsk (1579), Velikiye Luki, Kholm, and Voronets (1580) and started to besiege Pskov. In 1582 a truce was concluded in Yam Zapolsky; this resulted from the strivings of the papal diplomacy, which expected a union with the Orthodox Church, the unwillingness of the middle gentry to engage in a long war, and the Swedish expansion in Northern Livonia. But before that date (in 1581) Poland had unilaterally incorporated part of Livonia (up to Panava and Dorpat) into the Crown, and the Polotsk region in Lithuania. This meant that the first stage of the struggle among Poland, Sweden and Russia for the domination of the Baltic ended with the greatest success ever recorded in Polish history.

The second stage of the struggle, which followed the arrival in Poland of Sigismund Vasa, also began with Poland's successes in its conflict with Sweden. Sigismund Vasa, also known as Sigismund III and elected the king of Poland in 1587, strove for a personal union with Sweden after his father's (John III's) death in 1592. Formally that union, constantly threatened by Lutheran opposition, lasted until 1598, when Sigismund III was dethroned by the Swedish parliament after his failed expedition to Sweden. As a countermeasure the Polish Seym incorporated in 1600 the northern part of Estonia, earlier occupied by the Swedes. This caused the outbreak of war. When Riga was besieged by the Swedish troops, Hetman Jan Karol Chodkiewicz crushed the Swedish army in the Battle of Kircholm in 1605, and in 1606 Jan Wejher, the Bailiff of Puck, defeated the Swedes in a naval battle near the peninsula of Hel, which rendered Swedish diversion there impossible. The hostilities slowly died out since both belligerents were engaged in a war with Russia, their common enemy.

Sigismund III, looking for compensation for his failure in Sweden, involved Poland in a war with Russia, detrimental to both the state and the nation. He did so making use of the interests of the large numbers of the gentry which was growing poorer and of the enthusiasm of the magnates for the acquisition of new estates in the east. The outbreak of the war ruled out the chances of a permanent understanding, initiated in 1600 by the conclusion of a twenty years' truce. The Polish intervention used as a pretext the claims of Dmitri ('the false Demetrius'), an impostor who pretended to be the brother of Tsar Fiodor who had died without issue and whose brother was believed to have been murdered. The throne was seized by Boris Godunov and the Polish intervention was facilitated by internal troubles in Muscovy. Against the advice of the majority of the gentry and the warnings of politicians (including Jan Zamoyski, Stanisław Żółkiewski, and Jan Karol Chodkiewicz), Sigismund III gave unofficial support to the adventurous magnates from the province of Kiev, Konstanty and Adam Wiśniowiecki and Jerzy Mniszech, the Voivode of Sandomierz, who planned an expedition to Moscow in defence of the 'rights' of the Impostor. The expedition in fact ended in raising Dmitri to the throne in 1605. Also against the advice of the gentry, who wanted to avoid a war, Sigismund III engaged officially in a war with Muscovy in 1609, when after the temporary success of Dmitri (who was eventually killed in 1606), popular riots broke out in Moscow and the boyars raised Vasili Shuysky to the tsar's throne (also in 1606). After Stanisław Żółkiewski's victory in the Battle of Kłuszyn (1610), Shuysky was dethroned and Prince Ladislaus (later King Ladislaus IV), the son of Sigismund III, became the candidate for the Russian throne. But Sigismund III failed to avail himself of the chance to terminate the conflict and on the contrary, caused an intensification of anti-Polish feelings in Russia due to the Polish intervention there. The Polish troops in the Kremlin were forced to capitulate and the Sobor (the Russian parliament) elected Mikhail Romanov as tsar in 1613. Mikhail thus founded the Romanov dynasty which reigned until 1762; their name was later assumed by the Oldenburg family which in turn reigned in Russia until 1917. Despite vigorous protests by the gentry who considered the Moscow war 'a detriment and a disgrace to the Polish nation', Sigismund III organized in 1617—18 a new expedition intended to win the tsarist throne for Prince Ladislaus. This expedition, in which Stanisław Żółkiewski, the victor of Kłuszyn, refused to participate, ended in failure, followed by a truce at Deulino (early 1619) which was to last until 1633. Poland acquired the rights to the region of Smolensk, Chernikhov and Sever (altogether ca. 75,000 sq. kilometres) but the truce meant the collapse of the Polish intervention in Russia and marked the turning point in Polish expansion in the East. The terms of the truce dismissed Ladislaus' claims to the Russian throne. The same applied to the Treaty of Polanowo (1634) which gave both countries several decades of peace, to be disturbed only by the Ukrainian issue (cf. VII, 2). There were also unsuccessful endeavours to expand in the direction of Moldavia and Vallachia, interrupted by the occupation of those territories by the Turks in 1616.

3. Struggle for power. Evolution of the political system. The Reformation and its collapse in Poland

Poland's activities in the international arena would have been impossible without the efficient functioning of the machinery of the state. The Polish state in the 16th century did function efficiently, even though there were some problems. Considerable successes were achieved in centralizing the administration, as is evidenced by the promulgation, in 1506, of the collection of laws (the so-called Łaski Statute, named after Jan Łaski, the chancellor of Poland and later the archbishop of Gniezno), the introduction of the Polish law in the principalities of Oświęcim and Zator in 1564, the adoption of the Crown laws by Masovia and Gdańsk Pomerania and the assimilation of the Lithuanian law into the Polish law, especially in the so-called Third Lithuanian Statute of 1588. The concept of the Crown (*Corona Regni Poloniae*), which appeared during the period of the feudal division of the country to denote the historical links among the provinces, the links which were symbolized by the royal crown, became common after the conclusion of the union with Lithuania.

The monetary union of Royal Prussia and Ducal Prussia with Poland took place in 1528, and the monetary systems of Poland and Lithuania were unified in 1569. The zloty replaced the mark and became the new common monetary unit (divided into 30 *groschen*). The so-called gross (large) coins, namely the thalers (made of silver) and florins (made of gold), were also introduced.

Power was wielded primarily by the king and the middle gentry, then economically strong. This gentry was active in economics and politics and was seen as such within Europe. Indeed the whole of Europe was experiencing the growing importance of the various groups of gentry: the landed gentry (in the strict sense of the term) in England, the *hidalgos* and *caballeros* in Spain, the *dvoryane* in Russia, the *noblesse de robe* and the *gentilhommes campagnards* in France, etc. (The Polish term *szlachta* is derived from Old German *slahta,* now *Geschlecht* 'family, clan, race'). The Polish gentry succeeded in restricting the influence of the aristocracy (the Privilege of Mielnik of 1501, which passed the authority into the hands of the Senate, remained a dead letter) and managed to obtain many privileges for itself. The most important of these was the Nihil Novi Act, stating that henceforth 'nothing new' (*nihil novi*) in matters of essential significance for the state and society would be decided without the approval of the Chamber of Deputies. This meant the emergence of the Seym, which consisted of the Chamber of Deputies, the Senate, and 'the King in the Seym', treated as 'a separate factor'. After the union with Lithuania the Chamber of Deputies had 170 members (of whom 48 came from Lithuania), elected at some 70 provincial diets which could be attended by all the members of the gentry from a given province. The principle of unanimity in the Chamber of Deputies was established, because the deputies were treated as representatives of their electoral districts and not as independent members of the Chamber, but it was not observed rigorously. It was only in the period that followed (cf. VII, 3), that when the magnates tried to use the Chamber of Deputies for their own purposes the notorious *liberum veto* ('the free veto') became a common phenomenon.

The striving for political rights was combined by the gentry with the programme of constitutional reforms, called the struggle for the execution (in the sense of enforcement) of the laws, evaded by the feudal lords (who from the 16th century were commonly called magnates). One element was the limitation of the rights of the Church. The gentry, which was ill-disposed toward the aristocracy, was also opposed to the endeavours to strengthen the royal power. As a result of this, the conflict among the gentry, the king assisted by his advisers, and the magnates made the success of any party involved apparent rather than real, despite the claim of each party that it was striving to improve the functioning of some aspect of political life. Disintegration was increased by the decline of the role of the *levée en masse*, accompanied by the emergence of the authority of the hetman as the military commander (from German *Hauptmann* 'chief, captain') who was largely independent of the king.

The successive stages of the gentry's striving for privileges and reforms were marked by the rebellion of 1537, the Seym in 1562—63, the interregna in 1572—73, and 1574—75, confirmation of the Henrician Articles and of the Pacta Conventa, the establishment of the Tribunal of the Crown in 1578, and Zebrzydowski's rebellion in 1606—09.

The gentry gathered in 1537 and led by Mikołaj Taszycki and Walenty Dembiński forced Sigismund the Old to declare that he would observe the Nihil Novi Act. The further stage of striving for the enforcement of the laws, under the rule of Sigismund Augustus and Stephen Báthory, was associated with the increased political maturity of the gentry and the appearance of such experienced leaders as Walenty Dembiński (mentioned above), Mikołaj Sienicki, Hieronim Ossoliński, Rafał Leszczyński, Andrzej Frycz Modrzewski (the theorist of the movement for improvements in political life and author of the *De Republica Emendanda,* mentioned above), and Jan Zamoyski, the Chancellor and Grand Hetman of the Crown. Like the rebellion of 1537, the meeting of the Seym in 1562—63 marked the submission of the king to the demands of the gentry. At the earlier meetings of the Seym (including that of 1550, when the king arranged the coronation of his beloved wife Barbara, née Radziwiłł, whom he had married despite the opposition of the gentry, afraid of increased influence of Lithuanian magnates), Sigismund Augustus was sẗll dominant; in 1562—63 he attended the meeting of the Seym dressed like a member of the gentry and co-operated in the passing of the acts on the return of the estates granted by the kings after 1504 and on the abolition of the duty of the enforcement by secular authorities of the decisions passed by the clerical courts.

At the same time, appointments to high offices were modified in order to avoid their accumulation (the principle of the incompatibility of certain offices, which the gentry began forcing through as early as the beginning of the 16th century) and a standing army was organized; it was paid by one-fourth of the incomes of the royal estates, which acquired the character of state-owned estates, the needs of the royal court being henceforth covered from the estates set apart especially for that purpose (and traditionally called 'economies' in the Greek sense of the word). The Polish gentry was the least taxed gentry in Europe: the principal tax, called the ordinary *laneus* tax, collected from the time of Louis of Hungary (cf. V, 3) and the extraordinary *laneus* tax (30 *groschen,* which was tantamount to the price of one to two Polish bushels of grain) were in practice collected from the peasants. The king also had to maintain the troops stationed in the Ukraine (some 3,000 strong); at the time of Stephen Báthory special infantry troops (some 2,000) consisting of men drafted from among the peasants working on the royal estates were organized. The taxes also had to cover (after the union with Lithuania) the upkeep and pay of the mercenary troops consisting of Cossacks (who were in the service of the Commonwealth), and the regular navy, formed in 1561. The development of the Polish naval force was supervised by the Naval Commission, established in 1568, but it was hampered by the resistance of the Gdańsk burghers and the fears of the gentry lest the king should become too powerful.

The interregna also saw the adoption of the principle of the free, or *viritim*, election of the kings. This assumed that every member of the gentry had both the right and the duty personally to take part in the election. This principle, as also that of the unanimity of opinion in the Seym, was soon to be used by the magnates. That period was also marked by the decomposition of the group of political reformers: many eminent leaders of the gentry, such as Jan Zamoyski, the Ossolińskis and the Leszczyńskis, had grown rich and now took the side of the aristocracy (magnates).

The magnates were those who in the last analysis derived advantages from the so-called Henrician Articles, that is, the principles by which the king had to abide. First presented in 1573 to Henri de Valois (who shortly after secretly left Poland to become the king of France for a brief period), they summed up the privileges thus far won by the gentry, including religious freedom, but they increased the restrictions on the prerogatives of the king. Significantly enough, they provided for the possibility of renouncing obedience to the king on the part of the gentry (*articulus de non praestanda oboedientia*). But the gentry by depriving the king of strong power had to face alone the growing power of the magnates (cf. VII, 3). The establishment of the Tribunal of the Crown, that is the supreme court (which before that time was a prerogative of the king), and passing it into the hands of representatives of the gentry elected at special provincial diets, still marked the implementation of the principle of enforcement of the laws and the tendency to modernize the machinery of the state but Zebrzydowski's rebellion already meant that the middle gentry had lost their influence in the Seym and sought a new slogan: no longer the enforcement of the laws, but the defence of 'the golden freedom' through action outside of the Seym. The rebels' programme was to oppose the strivings of the royal party to strengthen the prerogatives of the king, to oppose the movement to establish closer links with the Hapsburgs, the Papacy and the Jesuits, and hence also to oppose the Counter-Reformation. The rebellion demonstrated that both the gentry and the magnates, who henceforward started to use the slogan of 'the golden freedom', were against the strengthening of the royal power but also that the magnates were unable to set forth a common positive programme. The routing of the rebels in the Battle of Guzów (1607) meant the victory of the magnates and of the Counter-Reformation and also the abandonment by the king of his endeavours to consolidate his authority.

The stormy struggle for power and for influence in the state, briefly outlined above, was very closely associated with the powerful movements represented by the Reformation and the Counter-Reformation. The Reformation, which had its roots in earlier criticism of the Church (such as the Hussite movement) and was formally originated by Martin Luther's declaration in Wittenberg in 1517, spread in Poland in the 16th century among some of the Pomeranian gentry and burghers.

The Reformation movement represented by the Polish gentry was rather superficial in character: it was used mainly as a pretext for criticising the Church and its growing riches. When the incomes of the gentry were in danger, the Reformation movement provided an excellent excuse for not paying tithes. Since, however, there was comparative plenty of land there were no strong demands (as in Western Europe) that the Church be deprived of its estates.

The intellectually liberal atmosphere in the royal court and in the residences of the magnates and even bishops favoured the adoption of the Reformation 'novelties' and a gradual spreading of new denominations independent of the Church of Rome. Thus assimilation of the new ideas meant in those groups, and later among the gentry in general, receptiveness to new thought. Not always did this lead to a breach with the Church for it was often merely a manifestation of the internal criticism of the Church and its policies and wealth. It was otherwise in the case of the urban and rural population, especially its poor strata, for whom declaring themselves on the side of the Reformation was often a form of a social protest. Such was the nature of the Gdańsk rebellion in 1525—26 and the peasant uprising in Sambia (part of Old Prussia held by the Teutonic Order) in 1525, which was crushed ruthlessly by the patricians and the gentry, regardless of their religious beliefs. This emphasizes the instrumental treatment of the religious issues by the upper strata of the population.

Poland offered a safe shelter to Anabaptists, Dutch townspeople who were versed in reclaiming land. The same applied to the Bohemian Brethren; expelled by the Emperor Ferdinand after the riots in Prague, marked by a great bloodshed, they moved to Poland in large numbers in 1548—51 and settled primarily in Great Poland, where they won many supporters and adherents. Poland was at that time a *sui generis* asylum for people who suffered from persecution elsewhere. Calvinism was the most widespread non-Catholic denomination in the mid-16th century; it was adopted mainly by the gentry in Little Poland, much less so in Great Poland. Lutheranism was adopted earlier than Calvinism in Silesia, Great Poland, and Pomerania, finding there adherents in rich families, such as the Górkas, the Leszczyńskis, and the Ostrorógs.

The Reformation had its greatest success in Poland in the emergence of the local denomination called the Polish Brethren (also termed the Arians and the Socinians), whose doctrine directly contributed to the formation of the philosophy and the social thought of the Age of Reason (cf. VIII, 5). Their doctrine, next to the rejection, on the theological plane, of the dogma of the Trinity, stressed the dignity and freedom of man. This was at variance with the feudal ideas and also led to radical conclusions in the social sphere (pacifism, nuclei of the idea of equality). They stood for religious tolerance and for restricting the interference of the state in religious matters.

The Roman Catholic Church soon started to oppose the Reformation; to do so it carried out reforms which made its organization more cohesive. An important role in controlling the spiritual life of societies was to be played by monastic orders, subject to the direct supervision of the Papal Curia; of particular importance in this were the Jesuits (the Society of Jesus), active from 1540. The Jesuits were introduced to Poland by Stanislaus Cardinal Hosius, Bishop of Warmia; nine years after the establishment of the order there were already some 450 Jesuits in Poland. In the 16th century they organized in Poland over a dozen so-called colleges, that is secondary schools, and gradually acquired an increasing influence on education.

The non-Catholics were becoming increasingly active even though their number was dwindling. Their defence against the pressure of the Roman Catholic Church was given strength in 1570 in the form of the so-called Sandomierz agreement which linked the Lutherans, Calvinists and Bohemian Brethren and was consequently admired by the Protestant-dominated part of Europe. The Warsaw Confederation, passed by the Seym in 1573, guaranteed an unconditional and permanent peace among representatives of the various Christian denominations and also ensured that the non-Catholics (including the Polish Brethren) would be protected by the state. This obligation came to be treated very seriously by the authorities: even after the expulsion, almost one century later, of the Polish Brethren, who were too radical for the gentry, the Polish kings used to show interest in their fortunes abroad.

4. Economic and social conditions

The 16th century saw further development of agriculture based on feudal demesnes using corvée (cf. VI, 1). This was due to increased economic activity among the gentry, counteracting the reduction of incomes from cash rents. Living standards in general were rising, especially those of the gentry whose incomes from demesnes increased. The position of the peasants was deteriorating systematically under those conditions, and the amount of the corvée required from them was also increasing gradually. In 1520 the Seym adopted the principle of the minimum burden of one day per week per farm of one *laneus* (ca. 15 hectares, that is 37 acres), which meant two days per week per farm of one *semilaneus,* which was then the prevailing size of peasant holding. By the turn of the 16th century the amount

The Royal Castle on Wawel Hill in Cracow

King Casimir the Jagiellonian (reigned 1447–92) as shown by the sculpture made by Wit Stwosz in 1492 and placed on the king's tombstone in the Wawel cathedral

Detail of King Casimir the Jagiellonian's tombstone

King Casimir the Jagiellonian receiving the Prussian envoys, as shown by a miniature in the gradual kept in the treasury of the Wawel cathedral (dated 1496)

Wawel Hill with Wawel Castle in the Jagiellonian period as seen from Cracow (engraving by Matthias Merian Sr., ca. 1620)

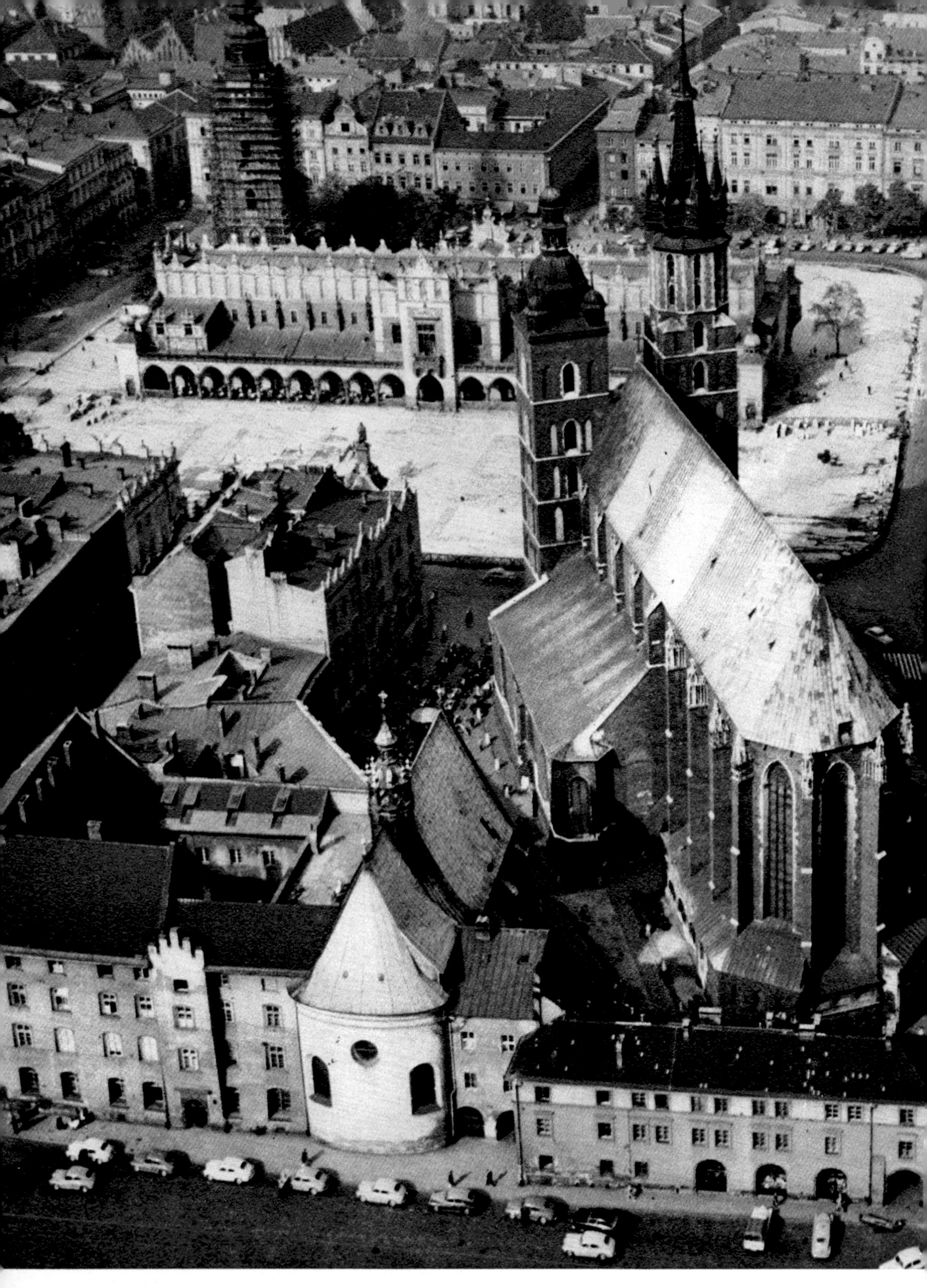

St. Mary's Church in Cracow (15th cent.), the Clothhall in the Gothic and Renaissance styles, and the tower of the townhall that no longer exists

The crane in Gdańsk: a Gothic gate with two towers with a built-in wooden crane (15th cent.)

The topmost part of the façade of the townhall in Wrocław (15th or 16th cent.)

The Late Gothic high altar in St. Mary's Church in Cracow, carved in wood by Wit Stwosz in 1477–89

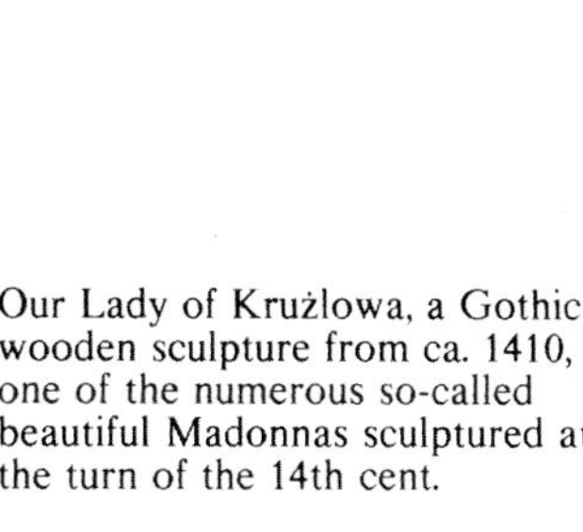

Our Lady of Krużlowa, a Gothic wooden sculpture from ca. 1410, one of the numerous so-called beautiful Madonnas sculptured at the turn of the 14th cent.

A polychrome painting in the Late Gothic parish church at Dębno (1500)

Fragment of an anonymous painting which shows the battle of Orsza (fought in 1514)

The cathedral on Wawel Hill in Cracow; its crypts hold graves of Polish kings

The dome of the Sigismund Chapel on Wawel Hill in Cracow, with ornamental sculptures by Bartolomeo Berrecci and Giovanni Cini (ca. 1525)

Part of the Sigismund Chapel with tombstones of King Sigismund the Old (reigned 1505–48) by Bartolomeo Berrecci (ca. 1530) and King Sigismund Augustus (reigned 1548–72) by Gian Maria Padovano (ca. 1574)

The Chamber of Deputies, in Wawel Castle in Cracow, adorned with Brussels arrases ordered by Sigismund Augustus, with a painted frieze from 1532 and with a coffered ceiling

The museum of the Wieliczka salt mines: a treadmill from the 17th century used to bring out the extracted salt

Extraction and processing of salt in the Wieliczka mine (from an engraving by J. Nilson based on a drawing by J. G. Borlach)

Metallurgists at work (16th cent.), an illustration from Georgius Agricola's *De Re Metallica Libri XII*

Part of the frieze of the gate section of the castle of Piast princes at Brzeg, with busts of the Piasts

A Renaissance miniature by Stanisław Samostrzelnik (ca. 1485–1541) from his *Żywoty arcybiskupów gnieźnieńskich* (The Lives of Gniezno Archbishops) (ca. 1534)

The courtyard of the Collegium Maius of Cracow university (15th cent.)

Nicolaus Copernicus (1473–1543), astronomer, mathematician, economist, physician, founder of the heliocentric theory of the world (a portrait dating from the 16th century)

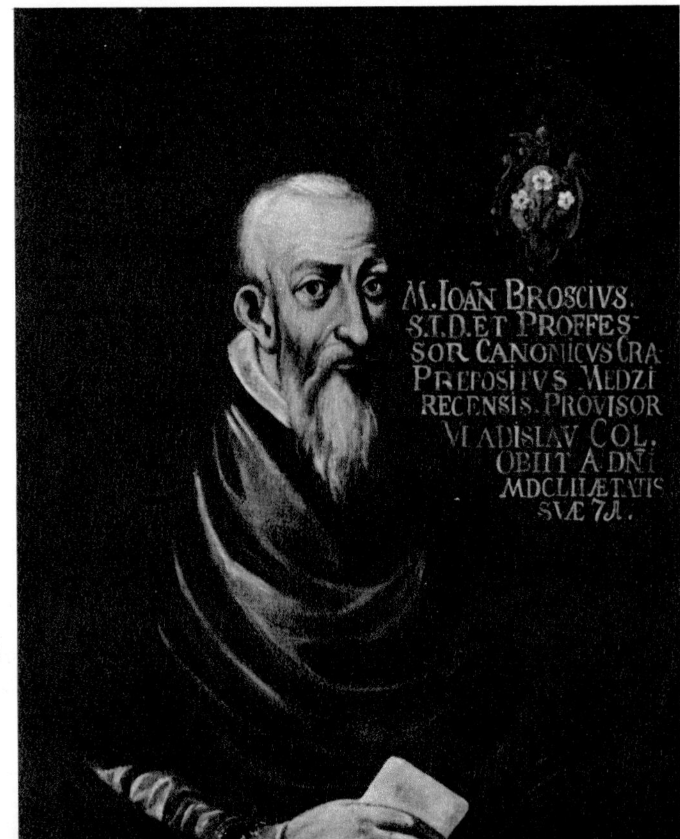

M. IOAÑ BROSCIVS.
S.T.D. ET PROFFES-
SOR CANONICVS CRA-
PREPOSITVS MEDZI
RECENSIS. PROVISOR
VLADISLAV COL.
OBIIT A DNI
MDCLII ÆTATIS

Jan Brożek (1585–1652), mathematician, astronomer, the first historian of science in Poland (an anonymous oil painting)

The vault in St. Mary's Church in Gdańsk (from the 15th or the 16th century)

Pictures from the life of the burghers: the workshop of a sword-maker and bell-founders (miniatures from the Balthasar Behem's Code from 1505, an illuminated manuscript containing texts of the laws and privileges of Cracow guilds)

The Renaissance townhall in Poznań, rebuilt by Gianbattista Quadro (16th cent.)

The bust of Jan Kochanowski (1530–84), the founder of the Polish literary language and the most eminent Polish Renaissance poet (from his tomb at Zwoleń)

Mikołaj Rej (1505–69), called the father of Polish literature (an anonymous woodcut)

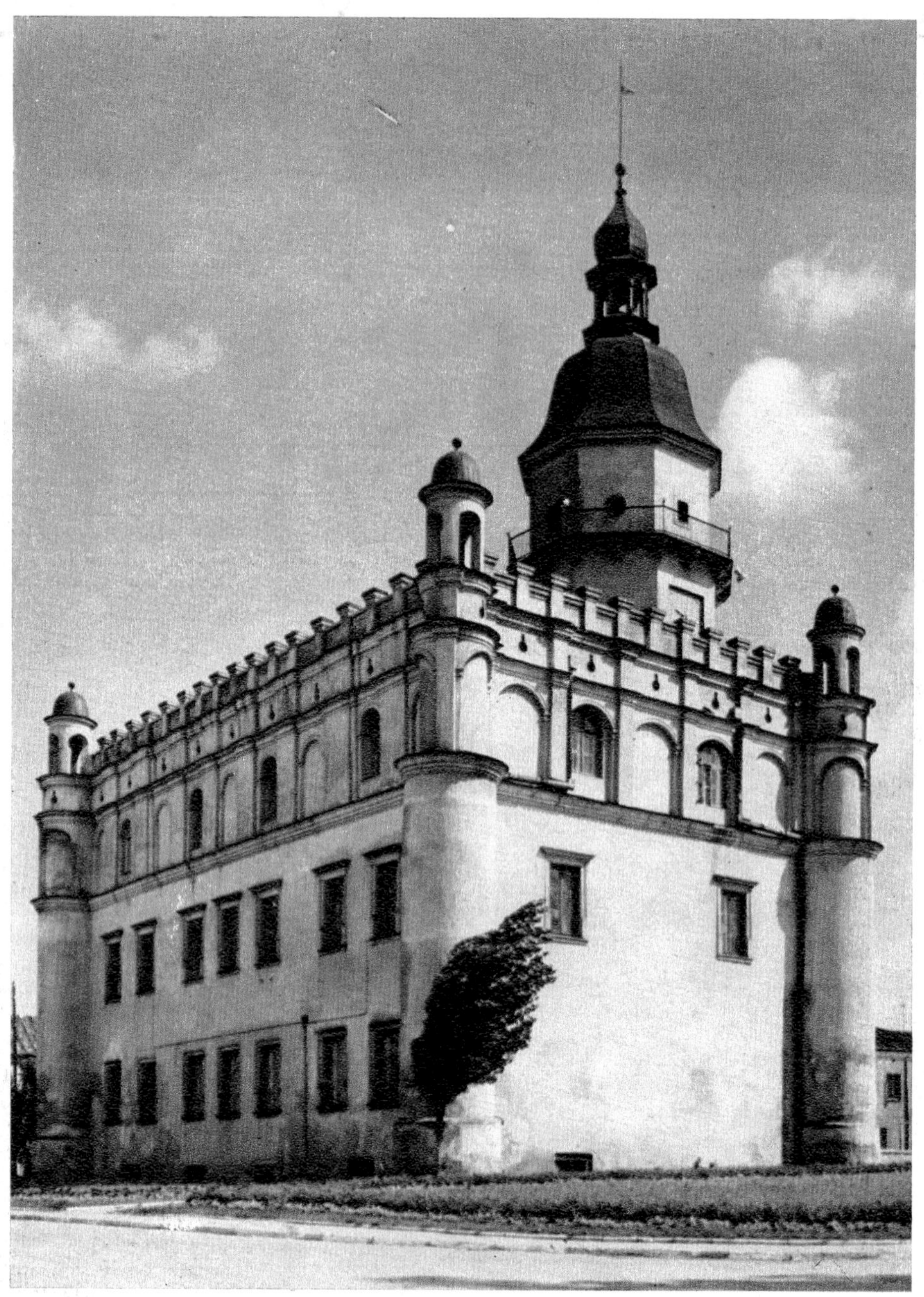

The Renaissance townhall in Szydłowiec

of corvée increased by some 200 per cent, thus reaching, on average, three days per week per *laneus.* Well-to-do peasants were often in a position to hire poor peasants, who held little or no land, to work on the demesnes for them. But the development of the demesnes was accompanied by a marked decrease of the number of peasant farms which produced marketable surplus of grain.

The demesne system with its principle of labour dues provided by peasants resulted in the break-down of independent peasant farms, typical of the Middle Ages, and in intensified forms of serfdom. The peasants' right to leave their villages was already restricted in the statutes issued by Casimir the Great but it was not observed in practice, and in the 15th century peasants used fairly freely to leave villages for the then developing towns. This process was convenient for the gentry who willingly absorbed the abandoned land into their demesnes. These so-called vacancies, which in the early 16th century accounted for over 10 per cent of the entire arable land, became, next to the land held by the *sculteti* (cf. V, 3), the principal reserve of land for the expanding demesnes. In the 16th and the early 17th centuries the demesnes held some 20 to 25 per cent of rural land and the peasants, whose labour was needed, again became attached to the land (*glebae adscripti*). This is why historians often refer to the second serfdom of peasants in the 16th and 17th centuries. The laws which opposed desertions by peasants had already been passed in the second half of the 15th century and gradually all decisions concerning peasants were made the prerogative of the gentry with no appeal to the Seym.

The existing conditions made it possible for the gentry to increase their incomes through the organization of demesnes. First agricultural products were needed by the developing towns and the foreign demand for grain increased considerably, too. The choice of labour-consuming production, namely the cultivation of grain crops, was made possible in Poland by the survival of serfdom which, unlike in Western Europe, did not come to an end in the Middle Ages. The gentry took advantage of its political domination in the state and demanded unpaid labour from the peasants. The natural conditions, such as the soil, the climate and the configuration of the terrain, favoured the production of grain crops. An additional stimulus was found in the constant rise, in 16th century, of the prices of agricultural produce as compared with those of manufactured goods. At the end of the 16th century the prices of agricultural produce were nearly double those of the goods produced by craftsmen and imported from abroad.

Two principal forms of demesne developed, according to the destination of the products. The 'expansive' type was geared to the export of grain via the Baltic ports, primarily Gdańsk, and flourished mainly along navigable rivers. The 'autonomous' type was characteristic of such territories as Great Poland where there were no good conditions for floating the goods and was consequently oriented towards the home market.

The system of feudal demesnes based on corvée also developed in the Grand Duchy of Lithuania. Of particular interest are the agrarian reforms initiated by

Sigismund the Old and his wife Bona Sforza and carried out in the estates held by the Polish king *qua* the Grand Duke of Lithuania. These reforms were continued on a vast scale by Sigismund Augustus and provided a model for private landowners. One *mansus* (slightly more than one *laneus*) was adopted as the unit of the area of arable land, and the rural areas were organized after the Polish model. Despite far-reaching schemes, demesnes used to develop only in those regions where there were favourable conditions for the sale of agricultural produce. The majority of the peasants had to pay both rent in cash and tributes in kind. The incomes of the Grand Duke's treasury increased eightfold as a result of the reforms.

The development of demesnes, made possible by the use of untilled and hence unexhausted land, brought about a 15 per cent increase in the output of grain in the 16th century. But on the other hand, following the limited possibilities of using the formerly untilled land as pastures, and the necessity of keeping additional draught animals for work on demesne land, the number of the animals bred was reduced and the structure of animal breeding changed unfavourably. At the end of the 16th century Poland (the Grand Duchy of Lithuania excluded) produced some 1.5 million metric tons of grain annually. This meant an increase of 100 per cent, as compared with the mid-14th century (cf. V, 3). The fact that the cattle population amounted to some 2.5 million heads (not counting the calves), which meant some 70 heads of cattle per 100 hectares of arable land, proves that it was principally oxen which were used in farm work.

The gentry strove to monopolize the grain trade, agreeing in practice only to the participation of such ports as Gdańsk, but did not cease to complain at exploitation by those unwanted sharers of profits. Participation in the grain trade became a worthy occupation for a member of the gentry, although commercial occupations were held to be unworthy of the gentry in the classical doctrine of gentryhood. Grain was exported mainly to the Netherlands (80 per cent); France, England, Italy, and Spain used to buy Polish grain sporadically, while the Netherlands and Sweden were the regular customers. The exports of grain from Poland increased rapidly in the late 16th and the early 17th century, namely from some 80,000 metric tons to 130,000—150,000 metric tons annually. This amounted to from seven to ten per cent of all the grain produced.

In addition to its considerable share in the European grain trade, Poland played an increasingly important role in trade between Eastern and Western Europe. There was a fairly dense network of international fairs (Gniezno, Poznań, Toruń, Lublin, Gdańsk) for Russian furs and hides and for Western European (and also Polish) cloth. Separate fairs were held for trade in cattle. Poland exported much timber for shipbuilding and production of casks and barrels, potash, wool, dresses of various kinds, goods made of furs and hides. The imports included, next to cloth of better qualities, primarily metal goods (mainly sickles and scythes), weapons, iron and steel. The balance of trade was positive, above all owing to the exports of grain. The technique of transportation did not change considerably, except for the increase in the iron used in construction of the carts. Large boats of various types were still used in river transport. Navigation in the Baltic saw, in the late 16th century, the advent of caravels (sailing ships with three masts and usually one deck). Postal service was started in 1558 and was connected with the European postal network.

The development of towns favoured that of crafts. In metallurgy increased production was accompanied by a larger number and size of forges. The first blast furnaces were built. Production of fire arms and bullets, guns and gun powder began. In pottery, the much more productive technique based on the use of the potter's wheel was widely applied. In the 16th and 17th centuries Gdańsk was noted for the production of cloth but on the whole cloth-making was most developed in Great Poland. Tanning and other forms of hide processing as well as furriery continued to develop, too, in response to the demands of the market.

In the organization of crafts, the characteristic phenomenon was that of the guilds becoming closed groups. This limited the increase in the number of workshops. In turn, outsiders, who were not guild members but were protected by the gentry and the clergy in the areas beyond the reach of urban jurisdiction, began to flourish. The gentry also tried to control the prices of the craftsmen's goods by locating the production of such goods in villages. The guild system did not cover forest products (charcoal, tar, potash) and the new crafts (production of new kinds of weapons, the printing trade); metallurgy, glass-making, shipbuilding (developed especially in Elbląg) and the building trade also remained outside this system and were marked by the emergence of modern enterprises. Manufactories were established. These were enterprises employing up to 40 workers and based on the division of labour, although still using craftsmen's techniques.

Salt mining was flourishing, the mines in Bochnia and Wieliczka producing up to 30,000 metric tons of salt annually. On the whole industry, crafts and mining in the 16th century accounted for some 20 per cent of the national income, which roughly corresponded to the percentage of the urban population.

At the turn of the 16th century the number of towns was ca. 1,000, some 100 of which had over 3,000 inhabitants each. The increased number of towns testified to a growth of the market, without which the demesne system could not develop. In Western Europe, too, the majority of towns had no more than 3,000 inhabitants each; in Germany in the early 16th century only five per cent of the 3,000 towns had a larger population.

5. Economic differentiation of society

The process which began in the 15th century resulted in the emergence, within the gentry (*szlachta*) in general, of the middle gentry (the term gentry being used here somewhat conventionally in view of the fact that the Polish *szlachta* had its privileged hereditary legal status, formally independent of the *de facto* proprietary status — *translator's note*), which was economically strong and conscious of its purpose. It had its approximate analogues in the English landed gentry, the French *noblesse de robe* and the Russian *dvoryane.*

The financial status of the gentry (except for the minor gentry) reflected considerable territorial differentiation. At one extreme there was Great Poland with the overwhelming majority of the middle gentry, one family owning one village, and at the other, the south-eastern territories with genuine 'principalities' of the magnates, one family owning hundreds of villages (those magnates were often called *królewięta,* which might be rendered by 'kinglings' or 'kinglets').

The turn of the 16th and 17th centuries saw the formation of the enormous estates held by the Zamoyskis, the Lubomirskis, the Potockis, the Ossolińskis, the Sapiehas, the Ostrorógs and others (cf. VII, 3). The minor gentry which did not own serfs inhabited chiefly Masovia and Podlasie. In the recent literature of the subject, Polish society at the end of the 16th century is usually divided into eight financial strata:

(i) the super-rich, who as a rule included the Roman Catholic bishops in the Crown and in Lithuania;

(ii) the rich, who included the secular members of the Senate, the ministers of the state, the abbots, the *vladykas* of the Orthodox Church, and those who held the principal posts in the economic life of the country;

(iii) the upper middle stratum, consisting of prelates, those members of the gentry who held several villages each, the officers of the state at the bailiff level and rich merchants and entrepreneurs in towns;

(iv) the middle stratum, which included the middle clergy (canons), the middle gentry (with one village per family), holders of local offices, rich burghers and experts in technology and mining;

(v) the lower middle stratum, with the parish clergy, the so-called split-village gentry (one family holding only a part of a village), craftsmen and small merchants;

(vi) the lower stratum including vicars, the minor gentry, hired labourers, farm hands, journeymen;

(vii) the poor, who included servants of various kinds and the majority of peasants;

(viii) the poorest people, i.e. the village and town poor and apprentices.

The peasants were also strongly differentiated in their financial status. Peasant holdings can be classed as the self-supporting (of at least one *semilaneus* each) and non-self-supporting held by cottagers of various kinds. The number of craftsmen in the rural areas was growing, too. The changes in the social structure of the local serf population were controlled by the landlord, who adjusted them to his advantage by grants of grain, money and farm animals.

6. Culture and science in 'the Golden Age'

The 16th century was marked by the development of gentry culture and the nascence of the culture of the magnates. Folk culture was developing in traditional forms. Vernacular culture, especially in larger towns, also advanced considerably; it derived certain specific features from the arrivals from other countries, in particular the Scots, the Greeks, the Germans, the Armenians and also the Jews (who on a large scale cultivated their own customs linked to Judaism).

The dominant role was played by gentry culture, which was a *sui generis* pattern for other groups, especially the burghers, even though that culture itself revealed remarkable ability to assimilate alien elements; it was attractive to Russian, Lithuanian, and Byelorussian gentry and also to burghers of Armenian, Scottish and German origin.

Houses in towns were rebuilt in the new style of the Renaissance and early Baroque; the newly erected ones were larger and adapted to new functions (for exmaple, that of housing shops). The various urban districts became differentiated in character. The increased prosperity of the gentry and the gradual emergence of the stratum of the magnates was accompanied by a growing number of residences of the magnates and mansions in towns. Houses in small towns and those in the suburbs of large towns were still built of wood, and those of the minor gentry did not differ much from peasant huts and cabins. The mansions newly erected at the turn of the 16th century were built after the Italian model; the same applied to residences of the magnates (including those in Zamość, Nieśwież and Łańcut).

Renaissance-style furniture, often brought in from Gdańsk or imported from Italy, was typical of the residences of the magnates. The gentry and burghers as a rule used furniture of local manufacture. This included chests of various kinds, tables, benches, chairs, stools, and wardrobes. The style and the finish depended on the prosperity of the owners. The same applied to the interior decoration (the fabrics used to cover the walls, rugs of various kinds, etc.), bedclothes, silver vessels and other objects such as musical instruments, clocks, paintings, and books. Houses were heated with wood burning stoves. Glass windows in the form of small plates set in lead or wood became common from the 16th century.

The level of material civilization was comparatively very high both among the gentry and the burghers and reflected both the tendency to live after the Renaissance pattern and the attitude of status seekers.

The new way of life was most clearly reflected in dress. In the 16th century Polish dress was influenced both by fashions coming from Western Europe (primarily Italy, Spain, and Germany) and the Orient (through the intermediary of Hungary). Typical features were tight doublets, over which loose cloaks lined with furs were worn. The national dress (that of the gentry) was taking shape gradually, resulting from the combined influence of Hungarian, Ruthenian, Lithuanian and Oriental fashion but it would develop fully in the period that followed (cf. VII, 3). Doublets over which fur-lined cloaks of various types were worn continued to be the typical dress, furs sometimes replacing the cloaks as the status symbol. Hose and high colourful boots were becoming common, as were also dolmans of the short type. Women's dress was less diversified. Renaissance fashion replaced the slim-looking silhoutte typical of the Gothic period by a puffy one, which made the woman look shorter, particularly as the headwear was flat. The outer garments of women did not differ much from those worn by men. The peasant dress was marked by a great difference between what was worn on workdays (dress made of natural linen or of home-spun fabrics) and on holidays; the latter dress imitated that of the burghers and the gentry, but the fabrics were cheaper and more economically used. Dresses were increasingly made for the anonymous buyer, although those made to order still predominated.

In food the demarcation lines between the various status groups were blurred, although there was, of course, an abysmal difference between the food consumed by the magnates and that of the peasants. The number of products increased, following the development of trade, but there were no fundamental changes as compared with the previous period. Whole-meal rye bread was still most common and wheaten bread, eaten only by the rich, was a rarity. The consumption of cakes of various kinds increased. The same applied to fish, especially carp, kept in numerous artificial ponds. Vegetables that had been unknown earlier included radish, asparagus, lettuce, cauliflower and kale. Fruit included mainly pears, apples, plums, cherries and various imports from the South. Vodka made of rye, wheat and plums, already known, became common in the early 16th century. Beer was also more in evidence. The brand of vodka distilled in Gdańsk was the most valued. Much attention was paid to table-ware and the way the table was set: it was supposed to express hospitality and to promote social contacts. Peasants used to eat with wooden spoons from wooden or clay bowls placed on bench-like tables. Burghers (except the poor ones) and gentry sat at tables covered with cloth. The number of vessels and the amount of table-ware was growing; for instance, in the case of burghers' homes it increased by about one-third in the second half of the 16th century.

Hygienic conditions improved, although the dependence of good health on cleanliness was still little understood. Epidemics of plague were quite frequent (1526, 1572—73, 1591, 1599—1602) and the appearance of venereal diseases was also causing alarm.

Scholarly and literary achievements reached the public mainly through books. The Renaissance witnessed a considerable development in Poland of the printing trade (the process having begun earlier), accompanied by the production of paper and trade in books. The paper-mill at Prądnik near Cracow, put into operation ca. 1493, was one of the oldest. In all, in the second half of the 16th and the first half of the 17th century Poland had some 100 paper-mills. The best known printing shops were those of Jan Haller (1505—25), Florian Ungler and his widow (1510—56) and Matthias Szarfenberg (1521—47) in Cracow and that of the

Wolrabs in Poznań. In the first half of the 17th century there were nine printing shops in Cracow and five in Vilna. Many printing shops were organized and run by the Jesuits to print Counter-Reformation publications (the Socinian texts were printed mainly in Raków, while the Bohemian Brethren had their printing shop in Leszno). Censorship by state and Church authorities accounted for a certain decrease in the number of printing shops in the 17th century. In all, over 4,000 books with the total impression of some four million copies were printed in Poland in the 16th century.

The number of parish schools continued to grow. In the 16th century, nearly every parish had its school. This meant that the total of the schools in the country had doubled or even trebled to reach 3,000 or 4,000, including both Roman Catholic schools and those run by dissenters (though the number of the latter was declining during the Counter-Reformation period). Schools approaching secondary level included that in Pińczów (founded 1551), run first by the Calvinists and later by the Socinians; the Socinians' school in Raków (1602); those of the Bohemian Brethren in Leszno and Koźminek; those run by the Calvinists in Cracow, Łańcut, and Secymin; the municipal school in Toruń, and the Roman Catholic schools in Chełmno, Bojanów, Wschowa, and Elbląg. The so-called academic school in Poznań, founded by Bishop Jan Lubrański in 1519, and that in Gdańsk, founded in 1558, could be regarded as institutions of higher education; both were active centres of humanistic thought. The year 1578 saw the foundation of Vilna University, run by the Jesuits, which in its first year admitted 600 students. In the 16th century still some 50 per cent of university students were the sons of burghers and even peasants. Sons of rich families used to study abroad, particularly in Italy (Padua, Bologna) and Germany (Leipzig, Wittenberg). The Zamość Academy was founded by Jan Zamoyski in 1600.

The development of the schools and the spreading of education reflected the growing respect enjoyed by knowledge and science. Scientific achievements in 16th century Poland would have been unthinkable without the creative changes which took place in the Polish scholarly milieu in all the traditional spheres of philosophy (including theology) and natural science. This consisted in laying stress upon secular activities, in teaching people how to live and behave, in dismissing pure speculation, in emphasizing the role of practical disciplines, such as ethics, politics and economics, in encouraging *devotio moderna* in theology, and in the Aristotelian revival of engagement in observation of the world.

The principal personality in this movement was Nicolaus Copernicus, a true man of the Renaissance: he was not only a brilliant astronomer but also a mathematician, economist, physician and also a political leader and promoter of economic activities. His heliocentric theory of the solar system, formulated in *De Revolutionibus Orbium Coelestium* (1543), not only refuted the opinion that the Earth is the central motionless body in the Universe but also meant a methodological revolution in science and revolution in the *Weltanschauung,* which dismissed the authority of the Bible.

Next to mathematics and astronomy physics developed. Copernicus' discovery paved the way — through the intermediary of Galileo and Huyghens — for Newton's interpretation of gravitation. Alchemy led to the beginnings of chemistry (Michał Sędziwój), while medicine (Józef Struś) and botany (Szymon Syreniusz) advanced. First publications on technology, including military science, appeared. There was notable progress in geography and cartography (Jan of Stobnica, Maciej of Miechów, Bernard Wapowski).

The Renaissance brought a number of outstanding historical works: by the aforementioned Maciej of Miechów, Stanisław Orzechowski (better known as a political writer), Marcin Kromer (author of the widely read history of Poland *De Origine et Rebus Gestis Polonorum,* 1555), Reinhold Heidenstein, Krzysztof Warszewicki and Marcin Bielski. Works concerned with the history of the various regions of Poland and outlines of Polish and general history were published. There were also general reflections on the methods of historiography (Stanisław Iłowski). The development of historical thinking and education was becoming an important and indispensable element in the formation of national consciousness.

Advances in historiography were accompanied by those in classical philology, exemplified by the translation of the Bible by Jakub Wujek (1599), which for a long time was practically the standard Polish version. An important role was played by jurisprudence and political science, without which the various codifications (cf. section 1 above) would not have been possible. In the sphere of political writings pride of place goes to those of Andrzej Frycz Modrzewski, who was also concerned with the theory of law (see the division *De Legibus* in his *De Republica Emendanda*) and of Stanisław Orzechowski. Modrzewski outlined a programme for the organization of the perfect state, which had numerous elements of Utopia, so typical of contemporary political thought. He opposed the pressure of the gentry to limit the rights of the burghers and the peasants and advocated a lay system of education and a democratic organization and the national sovereignty of the Church.

The new movement found its most visible expression in architecture and visual arts where Italian influence was particularly strong. Polish architecture was marked by stressing the horizontal shaping of the body of the building (instead of the earlier Gothic emphasis on its vertical shaping), the use of hemicycles instead of ogives, Neo-Romanesque comb-like ornaments of gables and parapets. The most remarkable architectural undertaking in that period was the re-construction of Wawel Castle (1507—36), for which Sigismund Augustus ordered in Brussels nearly 200 pieces of magnificent tapestry. The project also included the construction of Sigismund's Chapel (1517—33) in Cracow Cathedral (within the precincts of Wawel Castle). This chapel ranks as one of the finest examples of Renaissance architecture.

Giovanni Trevano (d. after 1641), who had Sigismund III as his patron, directed a new re-construction of Wawel Castle; in all probability it was also he who designed the Royal Castle in Warsaw (ca. 1588 to 1611) and the royal residence at Ujazdów near Warsaw (1606—19), now practically in the central part of the city.

Building activity was sponsored by the magnates and gentry. The largest and the most modern undertaking in this field was the town of Zamość, designed by Bernardo Morando, the first town built by a nobleman (Jan Zamoyski) almost from the beginning. The re-construction of Wawel Castle influenced the design of the castles of Stanisław Szafraniec at Pieskowa Skała and the Leszczyńskis in Baranów. Outstanding urban projects included the re-construction of the town hall in Poznań (directed by Gian-Battista Quadro of Lugano, 1550—60) and the Cloth Hall in Cracow (1555). Not many churches were built but Renaissance-style elements (chapels, tombs, plaques, sculptures) appeared in existing ones. The supporters of the Counter-Reformation advanced mannerism and later Baroque art, as their artistic programme: the varied and contorted figures characteristic of these styles were intended to appeal to human emotions. This programme was sponsored with particular vigour by the Jesuits. Mannerism was widely adopted in towns, especially Gdańsk, Cracow and Lvov. The change in style was visible also in sculpture and painting, secular themes being represented along with religious ones. Polychrome wall-paintings developed. The period also witnessed the production of such magnificent miniatures, as those included in *Behem Codex* and showing workshops of Cracow craftsmen.

In many respects the Renaissance marked a turning point in literature. Great interest in antiquity, in particular in the writings of ancient authors, promoted humanistic literature in Latin (Klemens Janicki, Jan Dantyszek, Andrzej Krzycki) but discussions on political and religious issues were conducted in Polish in order to attract a wide readership and the Polish language thus came to play an increasing role in the shaping of national consciousness. It was a period of very fine polite literature in Polish, opened by the work of Biernat (ca. 1465 to after 1520), a burgher from Lublin, and Mikołaj Rey (1505—69). The greatest literary achievement of this age is universally recognized in the work of Jan Kochanowski (1530—84), a laudator of the world, humanity and free thought. The humanist values of his works far surpassed the usual models of the period. He wrote lyric and epic poetry, epigrams and a play. He also influenced the emergence in German literature of a specific Silesian group of poets, who translated his works into German.

The role of music in everyday life intensified. Petrycy of Pilzno (1554—1626) wrote that 'music is needed in the training of young people as it makes recreation honest and renews tired minds'. Bands of musicians appeared in the residences of the magnates and not only in the royal court, as was the case in the earlier period. Cracow was the principal centre of music, and attracted students of that art from the various parts of the country. The most eminent Polish composers of the Renaissance included Jerzy Liban of Legnica (ca. 1464 to after 1564), Sebastian of Felsztyn (ca. 1485 to after 1536), Jan of Lublin (first half of the 16th cent., composer of the famous *Tabulature* for the organ, one of the finest monuments of old Polish music), Mikołaj of Cracow (first half of the 16th cent., who was under the influence of Netherlandish composers), Wacław of Szamotuły (ca. 1526 to ca. 1560, attached to the court of Sigismund Augustus, one of the greatest Polish composers), and Mikołaj Gomółka (ca. 1539 to after 1591), composer of *Melodies for the Polish Psalter,* which was the crowning achievement in the song-writing of the time. The lute became a common instrument and compositions for the organ became much more numerous. The peasants used folk instruments (bag-pipe, viol) and music was played to mark family occasions and meetings in inns. In the Renaissance entertainment became a regular feature of life. Dances and games (cards, dice, draughts, skittles) were popular with people of all classes, while knights' tournaments and large-scale hunting were gradually declining.

Chapter VII

The Baroque and the Dominance of the Magnates (1618—1733)

1. General features. The principal developmental trends in the state and the nation

In Europe, the Baroque was a period of many mutually contradictory developments. While the West saw the development of a capitalist economy, the central and the eastern parts of the continent witnessed a process of refeudalization (development of the system of demesnes based on labour dues, or corvée, and the serfdom of the peasants). Contradictions were also accumulating between the Roman Catholic and the Protestant countries, between the new and the old ideas. On the one hand, it was a continuation of the Renaissance, and on the other, a preparation for the essential intellectual change to be brought about by the Age of Reason. This resembles the situation in the 15th century, when the Middle Ages were coming to an end and the foundations were being laid for the Renaissance. While mention is made here of the period of the Baroque as applied to the whole of Europe, in fact that concept is to be limited to Roman Catholic countries and at the same times those in which — as in Poland — the aristocracy became both important and influential.

The 17th and the early 18th century were marked by the exacerbation and spreading of conflicts that had begun previously. The conflict between the Hapsburgs and France, and to some extent that in the region of the Baltic (where differences of religion were combined with political struggles) resulted in the outbreak of the Thirty Years' War (1618—48), following which France won political hegemony in Western Europe, and Austria shifted its interests to Central Europe, a process that eventually proved disastrous for Poland. The situation changed further in the 18th century: after the War of the Spanish Succession (1701—13), waged also in the colonies, England became a world power, and the Hapsburgs had to resign the Spanish throne. Sweden eliminated Poland from the competition for the *dominium maris Baltici* (the domination of the Baltic), and restricted Polish influence in that region, to succumb in turn to Russia. When Peter I defeated Charles XII at Poltava in 1709 Russia joined the group of the powers that determined the course of European politics. This also meant a weakening of the position of Turkey, and a strengthening of that of Austria, interested — together with Russia — in defeating Turkey. The position of Prussia, the country that emerged from the linking of Brandenburg with former so-called Ducal Prussia (cf. VI, 2), was consolidating in the 18th century. In 1701, Frederick III, of the Hohenzollern family, the elector of Brandenburg, was crowned in Königsberg as Frederick I.

In the 17th century, Poland was still one of the largest and most populous countries in Europe. After the truce of Deulino in 1619 (cf. VI, 2) the Polish frontiers were extended as they had never been before: they reached from Pärnu and Dorpat in the North to Kołomyja and Kamieniec Podolski in the South, and from the Lębork — Żywiec line in the West to the region of Vyazma and the Dnester rapids in the East, the total area of the country being 990,000 sq. kilometres. Ethnic Poles formed only 40 per cent of the population which amounted then to some

10 million people, the majority being the Byelorussians and Ukrainians, with some Latvians, Lithuanians (in the ethnic sense of the term), Germans (in the western regions of Poland), Italians, and Scots; the Jews, who retained their distinct religion and culture, amounted to some five per cent of the population. In Europe, Poland was second only to Russia in area, and sixth in the size of the population. In the 17th century Poland lost to Russia an area of some 160,000 sq. kilometres (cf. section 2 below), which left it still an area of some 730,000 sq. kilometres. The number of the population was growing until the middle of the 17th century, to decrease later to some six million as a result of wars and ensuing epidemics. The making up of the losses was interrupted by the devastations of military operations in the early 18th century.

The internal weakening of the state proved fatal for the future of Poland in view of the fact that its neighbours were gaining in power under strong absolute rule. That weakening was caused by the transformation of the fairly efficient system of the so-called democracy of the gentry into an oligarchy of the magnates. Formally, the political system remained unchanged, but the magnates succeeded in creating certain mechanisms which enabled them to acquire power at the cost of weakening and decentralizing the system. The political struggle was now going on, on the one hand, between the king, who strove to extend his power, and the magnates who used the slogan of 'the golden freedom' and thus succeeded in winning popularity among part of the gentry, and on the other, among the various coteries of magnates. Under the Vasas: Sigismund III (1587—1632), Ladislaus IV (1632—48), and John Casimir (1648—68), the position of the king was still quite strong as it was secured by the continuity of the dynasty, but later the domination of the aristocratic coteries became indisputable.

The means by which the magnates wielded actual power were both social and institutional. They took advantage directly — offering rewards of various kinds — of the votes of the minor gentry, who had full political rights, and also pretended to defend the freedom of the gentry and their rights. In the sphere of the political institutions the manipulations of the magnates consisted in gradually reducing the efficiency of the Seym in favour of increasing the importance of the provincial parliaments and in availing themselves of the principle of the free election of kings. The deputies to the Seym had to observe the instructions formulated for them by the provincial diets, which resulted in the gradual adoption of the principle of unanimity (the *liberum veto*), which made it possible for a single deputy to break the debates. As the Papal Nuncio H. Visconti wrote in 1636, 'The deputies, who largely come from plain, and often even poor, gentry, are tools in the hands of senators, powerful people who thus enable the deputies to live tolerably.'

The situation called for reforms, the more so as the progressing decentralization of the fiscal administration directly affected the condition of the army, so badly needed in a period of continuing wars and dangers originating from various sources. The reform plans came both from the gentry, voiced at meetings of the Seym and in publications, and from the kings and their adherents. The former were primarily concerned with fiscal and military matters, and less frequently with political reforms; the latter advocated the strengthening of royal power and securing better financial foundations for it. It is to be noted that these two trends went hand in hand only on exceptional occasions.

Ladislaus IV failed in his striving for a strengthening of the royal prerogatives. John Casimir was even more strenuous in his efforts to that effect, in which he was assisted by an ambitious wife, Marie Louise, the widow of Ladislaus IV. His plans provided for the election of kings *vivente rege,* i.e. the election of the successor while a given king was still alive; abolition of the principle of the *liberum veto;* appointment of an advisory council that would work between the meetings of the Seym; and regular taxes. But even the shock of the Swedish invasion in 1655 (cf. section 2 below) did not bring the royalist and the anti-royalist group closer to one another on the issue of reform. For instance John Sobieski, who was later to be elected king, linked himself to the royalist group. But some aristocratic families, especially the Lubomirskis and the Leszczyńskis, who had long been ill-disposed toward the king and his French wife, and hence toward connections with France, became very active politically and succeeded in winning over large groups of the gentry and the army which had long been without pay. All this resulted in a civil war known as the Lubomirski rebellion (1665—66), which came to an end after the Battle of Mątwy (1666), where both sides suffered severe losses. In the agreement concluded at Łęgonice (1666) the king abandoned his plans of *vivente rege* elections. Marie Louise died in 1667, and John Casimir abdicated in 1668 and moved to France, where he died in 1672. Four years later his body was transferred to the royal tombs in Wawel Castle, where the mortal remains of Michael Korybut Wiśniowiecki, who had been the king of Poland in 1669—73, were deposited at the same time. Wiśniowiecki's election (he was called by his supporters a 'Piast', not in the strictly dynastic sense, because the Piast dynasty had become extinct by that time, but as a king of Polish extraction) manifested the idea of national independence and the dislike of the magnates' practice of linking Poland's interests to those of foreign courts. The same idea was even more strongly represented by John Sobieski (1674—96). Both he and Stanislaus Leszczyński, elected king in 1704 and in 1733, but unable to assume power (cf. section 2 below), combined the idea of independence with that of internal reforms.

A different political ideology was represented by Augustus II (1697—1733), who opened the 67 years' rule of the Wettin dynasty in Poland. His objective was to use the Polish crown as a means of strengthening his power and obtaining Livonia for himself, and thereby to improve the position of the Wettin family in the German Reich (cf. section 2 below). The Polish-Saxon union, while purely personal in nature, intensified Polish-German cultural contacts. It could also have played a positive role, not only in the field of culture, for Poland's future history, if Augustus II and his ministers had shaped their political ideology so as to take into account the political interests of Poland. Augustus II's striving for absolute power, which resulted in his bringing Saxon troops to Poland, met with firm resistance on the part of the gentry. The year 1715 saw the formation in Tarnogród of an anti-Saxon confederation, headed by Stanisław Ledóchowski, an able political leader of the gentry, whose original intention was to negotiate with the king, but plundering by the Saxon troops provoked a spontaneous resistance in the country. The confederates had a natural ally in the Tsar Peter I of Russia, who did not want the royal power in Poland to be consolidated. As a result of his mediation, and also under the pressure of Russian troops, which came to Poland following the wish of Augustus II, a treaty between the king and the confederates was concluded in 1716; it was ratified by the meeting of the Seym which has been termed the Silent Seym, because Ledóchowski, as the speaker of the Seym, prevented the provisions of the treaty from being discussed in public. Following that treaty the Saxon troops left Poland, and the Polish-Saxon union had its personal character restored, which meant that the links between Poland and Saxony were extremely loose. In 1717 the Seym passed a number of reforms which meant the search for a compromise between Saxon absolutism and Polish 'golden freedom' but with a marked bias towards the demands of the gentry. Even though the political system remained unchanged in its essential features, the decisions of the 1717 meeting of the Seym were the first step toward the reforms to be adopted by that body; further steps were taken only some fifty years later.

The most important decisions included the imposition of new taxes (the poll-tax in the Crown and the chimney tax in Lithuania) to be spent on the upkeep of an army of 24,000 men (that number was not reached in practice), and a limitation of the prerogatives of the hetmans.

The decisions of the Silent Seym were due to exceptional contacts between the royalists' and the gentry's moves toward reforms. The gentry was only beginning to feel the need of essential political changes, although critical opinions had been voiced since the times of Modrzewski (cf. VI, 3). In this connection mention is due to two authors of critical studies, namely Stanisław Szczuka (1654—1710), Deputy Chancellor of Lithuania, and Stanisław Dunin-Karwicki (1640—1724), Subcamerarius (Chamberlain) of Sandomierz. Szczuka's work appeared in 1709. Karwicki, whose *De Ordinanda Republica seu de Corrigendis Defectibus in Statu Reipublicae Poloniae* did not appear in print until 1871, called not only for fiscal and military reforms, but also for a greater efficiency in Seym debates.

The 17th and the early 18th century saw a further consolidation of national consciousness in Poland. The process was speeded up by the nationwide resistance to the Swedish invasion (cf. section 2 below), in which many peasants also took part; by the development of historical consciousness in all strata of society; and also by the phenomenon called the Polonization of Roman Catholicism, which meant that the Roman Catholic faith came to be more strongly associated with folk culture and peasant mentality.

2. Foreign policy. The Swedish invasion and other wars. Relations with Russia

In the 17th century and in the first decades of the 18th Polish foreign policy was dominated by three issues: the Turkish, the Baltic (Swedish), and the Russo-Ukrainian. The problems of eventually regaining Silesia and subordinating Ducal Prussia more strongly were also never shelved. The first issue was linked to the northward expansion of the Turks and to the links between Poland and Hapsburgian Austria; Poland was involved in the second by the policy of the kings from the Vasa dynasty, who wanted to retain their influence in Sweden; and the third was a result of the eastward expansion of the Polish magnates, and gentry.

The connections established by Sigismund III with the Hapsburgs during the Thirty Years' War worsened Poland's relations with Turkey, which had already been far from cordial. Cossacks from the Zaporozhe (literally 'the region beyond the Dneper rapids') used to pillage Turkish territories, and moreover Turkey eyed Polish interest in Moldavia and Vallachia with suspicion. Turkey even intervened in 1617 by sending troops in the direction of the Polish frontier and forced Poland, by the treaty of Bush, to renounce operations in those regions.

Wars with Turkey went on until the end of the 17th century. In 1620—21 Poland suffered a defeat in the Battle of Cecora (1620), in which Hetman Stanisław Żółkiewski lost his life, and the troops led by Jan Karol Chodkiewicz defended the country in the Battle of Chocim (Hotin) in 1621. The peace treaty that followed these inconclusive military operations failed to put an end to conflicts, the more so as the Turks did not abandon their plans for territorial expansion. Ladislaus IV two years after ascending the throne repelled successfully a Turkish invasion, undertaken by Mahmud Bazi Pasha without approval from Istanbul, which contributed to the crystallization of the Polish king's plans to engage in a preventive war with Turkey. He wanted thus to put an end to devastating incursions by Crimean Tartars (in Western Ukraine alone Poland lost some 300,000 people in the first half of the 17th century), but death frustrated these plans.

In the decades that followed Poland was absorbed mainly by the Ukrainian issue and the Swedish invasion and linked itself to France rather than to the Hapsburgs who were the principal enemy of Turkey.

The conflict with Sweden had been caused by the policy of Sigismund III. Sweden, threatened by the Hapsburgs in its striving to dominate the Baltic, first attacked Gdańsk Pomerania (1626) in order later to intervene in Germany, where Stralsund was in danger. Gustavus Adolphus also succeeded in gaining the major part of Livonia, including Riga, even earlier (1621), when Poland was engaged in a war with Turkey. Poland retained Courland with Mitau and the south-eastern part of Livonia with Dyneburg and Rzeżyca. The attack on Gdańsk Pomerania opened the period of Poland's involvement in the Thirty Years' War, which continued until 1629. The Poles had some successes in their war with Sweden (the vic-

2. The National War against the Swedes (1655—60)

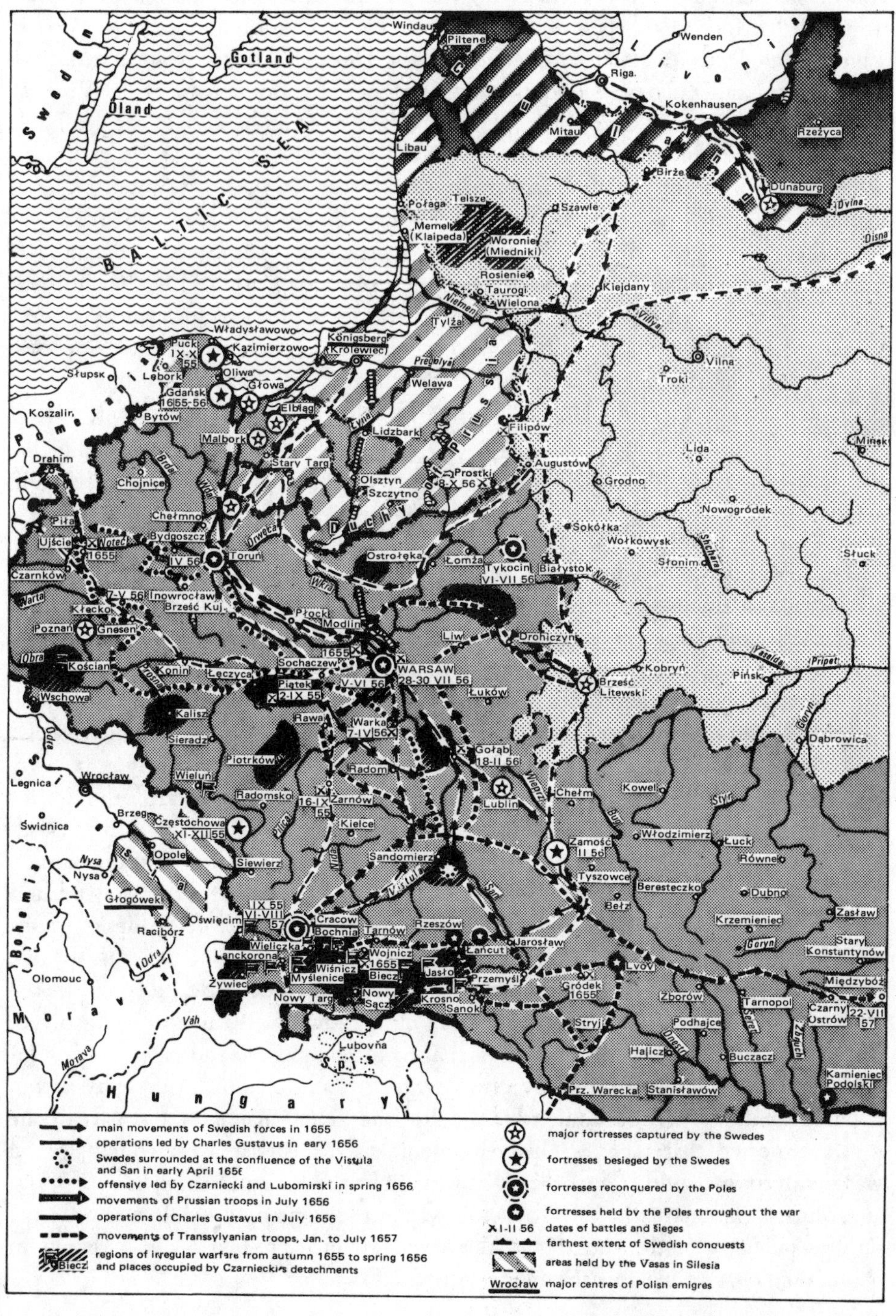

tory in the naval battle at Oliwa in 1627, the Battle of Trzciana in 1629), but the truce concluded in Stary Targ in 1629 was not advantageous for Poland: Sweden acquired the right to collect a duty of 3.5 per cent in Gdańsk and kept the ports in Livonia and Prussia; in exchange for these the Duke of Prussia sequestrated Malbork, Sztum and Żuławy (the fertile alluvial region near the estuary of the Vistula). Ladislaus IV, who was much interested in the Baltic region because of the profitable trade via Baltic ports and at the same time did not cease to think about eventually winning the Swedish crown, concluded with Sweden the truce of Sztumska Wieś (Stumsdorf), which restored the situation that prevailed before 1626; the truce was concluded in 1635 and was supposed to last 26 years. The Swedes, defeated in Germany, were inclined to negotiate, and the Polish magnates did not want a war either. The truce, which cancelled the king's plans for a direct conflict with Sweden, weakened his activity in maritime and naval matters. His best move was to form a Polish commercial fleet, which carried Polish goods to western Europe, and to build a naval port at the Hel Peninsula. He also founded a settlement, named Władysławowo after him (*Władysław* being the Polish form of his first name, the Latinized form of which is *Ladislaus*), which was supposed to develop into a port town. Financial difficulties and the resistance of the Gdańsk burghers prevented further progress in that direction.

The peace with Sweden lasted only 21 years, until 1655. Charles Gustavus, who strove to dominate the Baltic basin, had to cope with two obstacles, Poland and Russia. Although the truce concluded at Sztumska Wieś had not yet expired, in 1655 he started military operations against Poland. The task of driving Russia out of the competition was undertaken some fifty years later by Charles X.

John Casimir, who ascended the Polish throne in 1648 (as mentioned earlier in section 1, he was to abdicate in 1668), realized what the strengthening of Sweden (which as a result of the Treaty of Westphalia that concluded the Thirty Years' War acquired Vorderpommern, the western part of Pomerania from Stralsund to Szczecin) meant for Poland and unsuccessfully tried to ward off the danger. The Swedish army of 40,000 men attacked at the same time Great Poland and Lithuania. The Polish *levée en masse,* led by Voivode Krzysztof Opaliński, capitulated at Ujście putting Great Poland under Swedish protection, and in Lithuania Janusz Radziwiłł, the Grand Hetman of Lithuania, and Bogusław Radziwiłł linked themselves to the Swedes and declared the Polish-Lithuanian Union to be dissolved. The rapidity with which the Swedes managed to conquer Poland (the Swedish invasion often being termed 'the Swedish deluge' in traditional historiography and in popular literature) was facilitated by the fact that some magnates and part of the gentry expected that Charles Gustavus would attack Russia, with which Poland was involved in a conflict over the Ukraine, and joined his ranks. In their eyes it was an ordinary change of the ruler, actually within the same dynasty. It was only the ruthless pillaging of the country by the Swedes which brought about a change in public opinion and led to nationwide resistance.

That resistance movement came to be headed by Stefan Czarniecki, a military commander, who adopted irregular war tactics. Fighting broke out in Great Poland, in Little Poland, and in Podlasie. In November 1655, John Casimir, who had sought refuge in Głogówek (in Opole Silesia) which was the property of the Vasas, issued a proclamation in which he exhorted all the Poles to fight the Swedes. At the same time the successful defence of Częstochowa (situated near the Silesian border), led by Father Augustyn Kordecki, the Paulite prior, also played a certain psychological role, although — owing to the propaganda of the Church — it was only later to become a symbol of defence of the Roman Catholic faith. The fact that the fighting was against 'Lutheran dissenters' facilitated the spreading of the idea of the Counter-Reformation and strengthened the position of the Church. It was also to contribute to the processes that shaped the formation of the Polish nation.

In December 1655, Stanislaus Potocki and Stanislaus Lubomirski, Hetmans of the Crown, formed a confederacy at Tyszowce, which after King John Casimir's return to Poland changed into a so-called general confederacy, formed in Łańcut [A general confederacy was an institution intended to support the king under special circumstances; it made decision-making in the matters of state more effective as the principle of the *liberum veto* was suspended — *translator's note*]. The year that followed was more successful since large parts of the country were liberated. A truce was concluded with Russia at Niemieża, which interrupted the conflict over the Ukraine and made Russia join the system of defence against the Swedish expansion, which modified the general situation of Poland. On the other hand, however, adverse effects came to be felt from the policy of Frederick Wilhelm, the elector of Brandenburg (known as the Great Elector, who ruled 1640—88) who had just introduced his absolute rule in Brandenburg and Ducal Prussia. He joined the Swedish camp, invaded Great Poland, and helped the Swedes recapture Warsaw which had been liberated by Czarniecki in 1656. He even made plans — in co-operation with George Rakocsy, the Prince of Transsylvania, the Cossack leader Bohdan Khmelnitski, and Bogusław Radziwiłł — to partition Poland. But the resistance of the people of Great Poland, who expelled Brandenburgian troops and threatened Frankfurt-on-the-Oder and even Berlin, the defeat of Rakocsy and Austria's and Denmark's coming out against Sweden made the Great Elector change his tactics and seek a rapprochement with Poland.

King John Casimir, in trying to win the support of the Hapsburgs and to improve Poland's position in an expected conflict with Russia agreed in the Treaty of Welawa (1657), confirmed by the alliance concluded in Bydgoszcz, to dissolve the feudal relationship with Ducal Prussia (with the clause of *eventuale homagium* if the Hohenzollern family became extinct).

The war with Sweden was terminated by the peace treaty in Oliwa (1660), which restored the *status quo ante bellum,* but Poland emerged from it incapacitated as a great power (devastation of towns, reduction of the population by about 40 per cent), and lost the Prussian fiefdom. In 1669 the Polish throne went to Michael

Korybut Wiśniowiecki, whose marriage (1670) to Archduchess Eleonora Maria von Hapsburg brought him closer to Austria thus worsening the dissention between the French and Austrian camps. As a result the danger of a Turkish invasion increased. The invasion came in 1672, thus opening a period of wars with Turkey which lasted over thirty years and in which the possession of Kamieniec Podolski was a *sui generis* criterion of success. The Turks occupied Kamieniec in 1672 and, having entered southern territories of Poland, enforced in the treaty of Buczacz (which was called 'disgraceful' and which the Seym refused to ratify) the ceding of the major part of the Ukraine. One year later, following Sobieski's victory at Chocim, they lost what they had gained but succeeded in keeping Kamieniec. The victory at Chocim gave Sobieski the Polish crown and with it a new political ideology for Poland. It was dominated by the striving to regain Ducal Prussia in alliance with France and Sweden and to increase interest in the Baltic region, which required an improvement of relations with Turkey, the more so as the conflict over the Ukraine prevented Poland from concluding an anti-Turkish alliance with Russia. The truce at Żurawno (1678), which was intended by Sobieski to initiate a peaceful settlement of the conflict with Turkey, did not bring the expected results because of the expansionist policy of the Ottoman Empire. This made the Polish policy-makers at the royal court consider an alliance with Russia, but that country itself concluded a peace treaty with Turkey (Bakhchiseray, 1681). In view of this Sobieski renewed his attempts to form an anti-Turkish coalition, which he initiated by concluding in 1683 an alliance with Austria, threatened by the Turkish drive toward Vienna. The alliance saved Austria, because Sobieski's army of 25,000 men defeated the Turks at the Battle of Vienna (12 September 1683) and pushed them back, thus initiating the large-scale European campaign (also joined by Russia) of liberating European territories from Turkish occupation. The war was concluded by the Karlovci Treaty (1699) as a result of which Poland returned to the situation that preceded the Treaty of Buczacz.

Reconstruction after the Swedish invasion proved extremely difficult under the system of demesnes based on corvée. Poland had to wait until the 20th century to regain the territory of former Ducal Prussia. King John Sobieski tried to make up for the erroneous political decision made by John Casimir in the treaty of Welawa by promoting his Baltic policy. Having won the support of Louis XIV of France and in alliance with Sweden, with whom he concluded secret treaties — with France at Jaworów in 1675 and with Sweden in Gdańsk in 1677 — he wanted to regain Ducal Prussia and possibly Silesia as well, to strengthen the Sobieski family by turning Prussia into its hereditary principality, and to carry out internal reforms that would abolish the free election (based on the *viritim* system) and the *liberum veto.* But the opposition at home, mainly on the part of the magnates, and a change in relations between Louis XIV and Frederick Wilhelm cancelled his ambitious plans. When addressing the Senate in 1688 he said that 'posterity will wonder why after such successes and triumphs, renowned throughout the world, we now face eternal

3. The Relief of Vienna in 1683

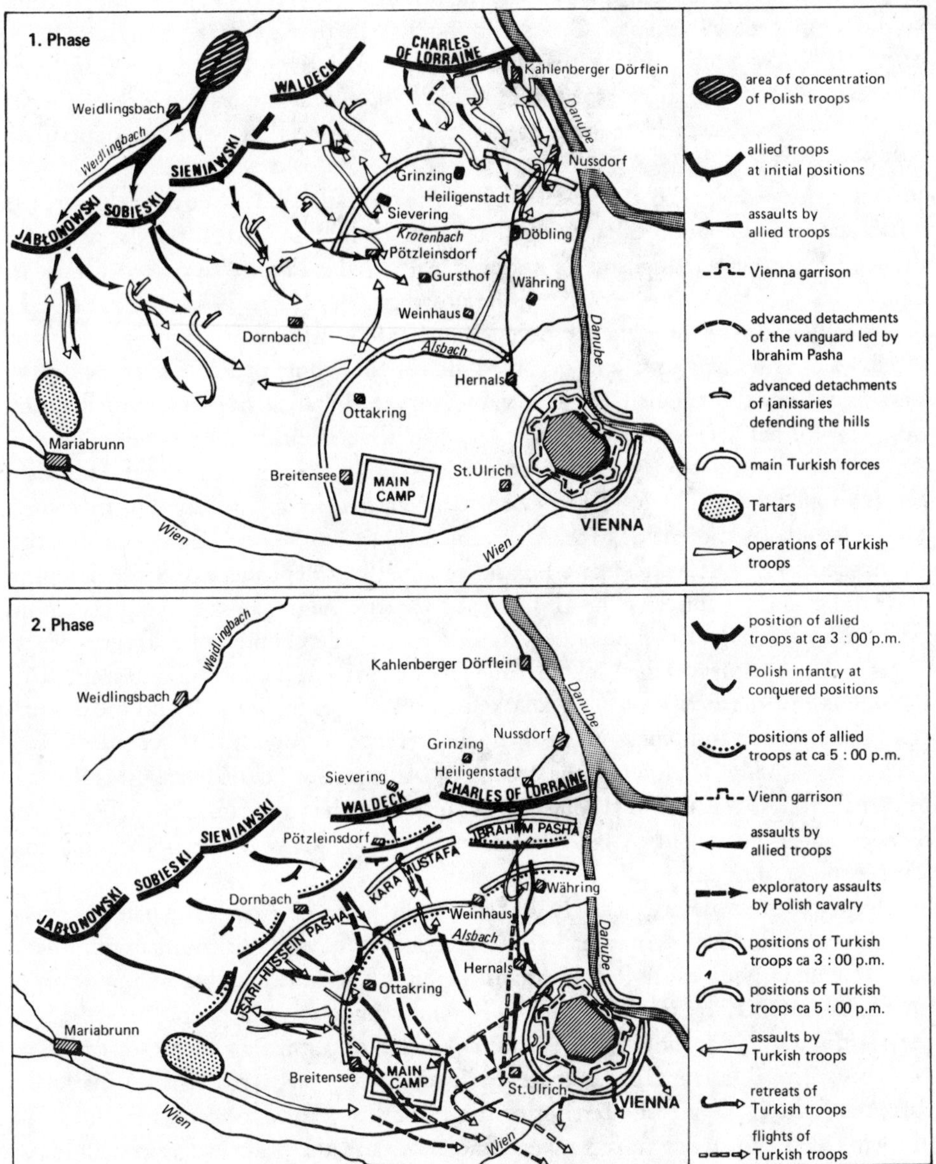

disgrace and irreparable losses as we see ourselves resourceless and almost helpless and incapable of making decisions'. This reflected well the contradiction between Poland's successes in foreign policy and its internal weakness.

It was probably even more difficult to regain Silesia, still inhabited by a large number of Poles. Poland failed to annex it during the Thirty Years' War, and it was only in 1645—66 that the kings of Poland held the principality of Opole and Racibórz as a fief. The last lines of the Silesian Piasts (cf. IV, 1) became extinct in the 17th century: that of Cieszyn in 1625 and that of Brzeg and Legnica in 1675. It is also worth noting that James, the son of King John Sobieski, married to a daughter of the Elector of the Palatinate, stayed in the principality of Oława in 1691—1737, which he held as a pledge in connection with the nuptial endowment of his wife.

When Augustus, who as the Elector of Saxony attacked Sweden in Livonia in 1700 with the intention of winning that territory for the Wettin family, ascended the Polish throne as Augustus II (after defeating the French-supported candidate Conti), his policy involved Poland in the Northern War (1700—21). Charles XII, the young and valiant king of Sweden, defeated Augustus' army at Riga and the Russian army at Narva and occupied almost the whole of Poland. In 1704 Poland and Russia concluded the treaty of Narva, aimed at Sweden, which meant Poland's formal accession to the war. At that time Polish public opinion was divided: part of the gentry (mainly those of Great Poland) supported Stanislaus Leszczyński, whom Charles XII caused to be elected king. Leszczyński, then only 26 years old, promoted ideas that resembled those of Western European dynasts. He unsuccessfully strove to make Poland reasonably independent of Sweden and to unite the country politically; he also warned Charles XII against moving his troops into Russia instead of winning the war in Saxony, the country of Augustus II.

As half a century earlier, plunderings by the Swedish army and disregard of the opinion of the Polish people provoked resistance to the Swedes, and the confederacy formed in Sandomierz in 1704 in the defence of Augustus II scored military successes. Although following the treaty of Altranstädt (1706) Augustus II was forced to resign the Polish throne, he regained it when the Russians defeated the Swedes at Poltava (1709), and he started making plans to strengthen his rule (cf. section 1 above).

The Swedish issue was closely linked to the state of Polish-Russian relations, which were becoming internationalized (cf. section 1 above). This conflict with Russia had as its underlying cause Polish expansion in the Ukraine, initiated by the incorporation of Ukrainian territories following Poland's union with Lithuania in 1569, and the shifting of the frontier of the Grand Duchy of Lithuania in the direction of Moscow. The disadvantageous truce in Deulino in 1619 (cf. VII, 2) made the Russians fight to regain the territories they had lost. They took to arms in 1632 in their failed endeavour to reconquer Smolensk, and the peace treaty concluded at Polanowo in 1634 did not change anything, the only point being that Ladislaus IV renounced his claims to the Russian throne and to the title of tsar.

In the meantime there was growing dissatisfaction among the Cossacks, free peasants who lived in Zaporozhe (i.e. in the region beyond the rapids of the Dneper) and who formed there a *sui generis* military organization with a view to defending themselves against the Tartars and the Turks, and also to making incursions into territories held by their Moslem enemies. Already Sigismund Augustus had hired several hundred Cossacks as mercenaries (by putting them on the so-called register). The number of registered Cossacks tended to grow, but constant changes of that number caused conflicts between the Cossacks and Poland. The increasing number of the registered Cossacks who, having grown rich (on the booty acquired in their incursions against the Tartars and the Turks), aspired to the status of the gentry, was eyed with suspicion by those Polish magnates who had their estates in the Ukraine and wanted to exploit the local peasants on the most advantageous terms. The Cossack uprisings which broke out in 1630, 1637 and 1638 were all suppressed, and moreover a fortress was built at Kudak to control Zaporozhe.

An apparent peace (called the golden peace) lasted ten years, until the time when Ladislaus IV, who planned a large-scale campaign against Turkey (already mentioned), stirred the hopes and ambitions of the Cossacks who were supposed to take part in the operations. The collapse of the king's plans accelerated the outbreak of the next uprising, which this time had a vast scope. It was led by Bohdan Khmelnitski, one of the Cossacks grown rich, an outstanding commander and politician, who had his own grudges against the Poles (Daniel Czapliński, an administrator of the estates of the Polish magnate Aleksander Koniecpolski, confiscated Khmelnitski's estate and abducted his wife).

The uprising, in which Ukrainian peasants also took part, broke out at the moment when the formation of the Ukrainian nation was already advanced, religious conflicts between the Roman Catholic Poles and the Orthodox Ruthenians were gaining in strength, and the opposition, based on class differences — between the Ukrainian peasants and the Cossacks, on the one hand, the Polish magnates and gentry, on the other — was making itself felt. The union, concluded at the synod of Brest-Litovsk in 1596, between the Church of Rome and the Orthodox Church provided for the subordination of the latter to the former and, accordingly, for linking the Ukrainian and the Byelorussian population more closely to the Polish Commonwealth. Hence the union made the religious and the national issues to be more acutely felt.

The Khmelnitski uprising, which led to the emergence of an independent Ukrainian state, with an area of some 200,000 sq. kilometres, governed by Cossack elders led by a hetman, experienced varying fortunes. After the initial defeats of the Polish troops in the battles of Żółte Wody, Korsuń, and Pilavtse (1648) an agreement was concluded in Zborów (1649) following which Khmelnitski became the hetman of the Cossack troops, whose register was increased to 40,000 men. But the Poles succeeded in defeating the Ukrainian army in the battle of Beresteczko (1651), after which an agreement was arrived at in Biała Cerkiew (Byelaya Tserkov); it was not observed by the Cossacks who again defeated the Polish army that tried to prevent a Cossack intervention in Moldavia. The agreement of Żwaniec (Zhvanets) repeated the terms of that of Zborów.

The situation changed radically in 1654, when Khmelnitski concluded the Pereyaslav agreement with Russia, subordinating the then liberated Ukrainian territories to that country. This brought about a war between Poland and Russia, interrupted by the danger of the Swedish invasion. Khmelnitski sought an agreement with the Swedes, because the Pereyaslav agreement had lost its importance for him. That agreement was denounced in 1657 by Jan Wyhowski, Khmelnitski's successor as hetman, who concluded with Poland the union of Hadziacz (1658) that made the Ukraine an equal member of the Polish-Lithuanian-Ukrainian federation. His programme, however, was rejected by the Cossacks and the Ukrainian people, who again linked the Ukraine to Russia. Further military operations, from which Poland emerged victorious, led to the conclusion in 1667 of the truce in Andruszew, which was unfortunate for the Ukraine as it divided it between Poland and Russia. On the strength of that truce Russia obtained, next to the regions of Smolensk, Tshernikhov, and Sever, the territories beyond the Dneper (Zadnieprze) including Kiev. In view of the Turkish danger the truce was changed in 1686 into a 'perpetual' peace (the so-called Grzymułtowski treaty).

These decisions intensified the social unrest of the Cossacks instead of appeasing or stopping it. A large-scale uprising led by Samosin and Paley broke out in 1704, caused by the abolition of the Cossack army by the Polish Seym in 1699. The uprising was the last endeavour to put Khmelnitski's ideas into effect. The Cossack hetman Mazepa strove to become totally independent of Russia by allying himself to Charles XII of Sweden, but his plans collapsed when the Russians defeated the Swedes at Poltava. A *sui generis* Cossack republic under the Russian protectorate survived on the left bank of the Dneper until 1764.

The increased importance of Russia, Austria and the State of Brandenburg and Prussia affected the international position of Poland. Its neighbours would henceforth try to prevent all attempts at the strengthening of Poland as a political entity, when the Polish gentry developed the tendency to carry out internal reforms. At the same time the slogan became common which claimed that 'Poland survives owing to its internal disorder', which expressed the belief that the best way to protect Poland against possible hostile actions by its neighbours was not to introduce any reforms (and thus to keep Poland weak and unable to threaten any other country).

The support extended by the gentry after the death of Augustus II to the French protégé Stanislaus Leszczyński, whose daughter Maria was queen of France (as the wife of Louis XV), was a visible manifestation of the reformist trend. On the other hand, the striving of Poland's neighbours to control the country took the form of forcing through (under the pressure of Russian troops called in by some dissatisfied magnates) the election of Frederick Augustus III, the son of Augustus II, who reigned in Poland as Augustus III. It was in 1732 that Austria, Russia and Prussia concluded the Loewenwold treaty, intended to impose upon Poland their candidate to the Polish throne. Even earlier, in 1720, Prussia and Russia agreed to preserve in Poland the principle of free election of kings. Despite the support of the gentry, the Gdańsk burghers, and even the peasants (at that time rarely active politically), Leszczyński had to resign, which postponed major political reforms in Poland for several decades. It was under the impact of those events of 1733, which showed that Poland's independence was crumbling, that the gentry formed the Dzików confederacy, and appealed to the peoples of Russia and Saxony to help Poland retain its sovereignty.

3. Economy and society

The period 1618—1733 was not good for Poland's economy. Agriculture, based on the system of manorial serf farms, was prosperous at first, and then came to face considerable difficulties. During the first decades stagnation was not so visible as in the later part of the period, but the economic prosperity of the gentry was over. Beginning in the 1620's the grain prices were falling gradually, while agriculture was developing in western Europe to the point of being competitive. Further, Russian grain also found its way to western European markets. All this did not prevent the Polish gentry from advancing just at that time the idea that Polish grain was indispensable to western Europe (the so-called granary concept of Poland), which hampered any tentative reforms in the national economy. The exports continued to expand, to reach, in the first half of the 17th century, an average of ca. 140,000 metric tons of grain annually. The figure for the second half of the century was ca. 80,000 tons, which meant a decline, but if we consider the enormous devastations of the country during the Swedish invasion we have to conclude that Poland's economy was still quite brisk. The exports did not bring such profits as before, so the gentry, without decreasing the exports, tried to avail themselves of the opportunities offered by the home market, also by the sale of alcoholic beverages produced in breweries and distilleries kept in the demesnes.

If we take the nominal prices of agricultural produce in Poland in 1649—50 as 100, the indicators for the successive decades in the second half of the 17th centuries are 101, 110, 121, 140, 202, the indicators for the imported goods in the same periods being 118, 156, 190, 244, 272. This meant that the exports of grain were less and less profitable. Greater profits could be derived from trade in livestock (mainly oxen), but production of that kind (and exports to Silesia and Saxony) developed primarily in Podolia, Volhynia, and the Ukraine, that is in the area dominated by the latifunds of the magnates.

The exports of grain continued to fall in the early 18th century. If the exports via Gdańsk and Elbląg in 1605—15 and 1625 are taken as 100, then the indicator is 53 for 1685, 1695 and 1705, and 33 for 1715, 1725 and 1735. This was, however, the period of coping with the destructive consequences of the Northern

War (1700—21), which made the population of the country fall by about a quarter.

The decline of agricultural and industrial production that had begun before the Swedish invasion of 1655 was greatly aggravated by the devastations caused by that invasion. Immediately after the expulsion of the Swedes the output of grain did not exceed 40 per cent of the pre-1655 level. The number of the towns and villages that came to be completely destroyed varied, according to the region of the country, from ten to 30 per cent. Lower yields were due to the barrenness of the soil, disadvantageous changes in its structure, and defects in tillage. Under the three-field system, when manuring was insufficient, it was not possible to control the fertility of the soil. Laying the soil fallow for one year, during which it was nevertheless used as pasture ground, obviously did not suffice. The farming technique did not change, nor did the implements used (the wooden plough with an iron share, the wooden furrowing plough with a wooden coulter, the wooden harrow). The peasants who had to work, using their own implements, on the demesnes under the labour dues system lacked incentives for work, and were on an increasing scale treating their own farms as the so-called feeding plots (source of food, but not of any marketable products). While in the 16th century the crops on the demesnes were the fivefold of the grain used for seed, they were only its fourfold in the 17th century, and its threefold in the first half of the 18th century.

All this was a direct threat to the incomes of the gentry. The larger the estate was the less the consequences of the new situation were felt, which accounted for the economic domination of the magnates and large numbers of poor gentry dependent upon them.

Isolated opinions on the necessity of promoting industry were voiced (e.g., by Andrzej Maksymilian Fredro), but the dominant opinions were those of naive beliefs that it would be possible to increase the incomes of the gentry by manipulating the currency. For instance, one of the ideas was to lower the rate of exchange of the so-called thick coins (i.e., the silver thalers and the golden florins), used to pay foreign merchants for their goods. The gentry imagined that they would thus obtain more thalers and/or florins for the copper *groschen* coins. Between 1580 and 1650 the price of the thaler in terms of *groschen* rose by 160 per cent, and that of the florin, by 220 per cent. The amounts of gold and silver were dwindling in the country that had to spend so much money on its army and on military operations, and leasing the mints to foreign minters resulted in the country being flooded by coins of a low value. They were mainly the so-called *tymfs* or *tynfs,* struck in very large numbers in 1663—67 by one such minter, Andreas Tymf, whose surname was later used only with reference to other small coins. This led to the home economy becoming more 'natural' as a result of a decreased use of money. The sphere of credit and money was not yet separated from the rest of the national economy, even though the role of credit in towns was quite considerable.

Poland's international trade dwindled markedly, which was also due to a lessening of the importance of the land routes passing through Poland. Handicrafts became a more local undertaking than they used to be earlier. The few exceptions included metal smelting in the so-called Old Polish Industrial Region (near Kielce) and cloth-making in Great Poland, both revealing some features of early industrialization. Great Poland had a more vigorous economic life (cf. VI, 4) which consisted in the development of the food processing industry and the sale of grain products to Silesia, in sheep breeding, and in an intensive use of new tracts of land for cultivation.

After the devastations caused by the Northern War we observe, especially in the western regions of Poland, a striving to change the traditional manorial serf farms so as to increase incomes. Less and less productive labour dues were being replaced by rent in money. For instance, the municipal authorities of Poznań, which town owned a number of villages devastated during the war, started bringing in, beginning from 1719, settlers from the region of Bamberg in Germany. The turn of the 17th century saw the beginnings in Great Poland and Pomerania of an intensive bringing in of settlers, who were free people, partly Germans and partly Poles (they were called 'the Dutch' after the settlers from the Netherlands who first came to Pomerania as early as in the 16th century). Several dozen such settlements came into existence in the early 18th century.

The settling of free people, combined with the replacement of serf labour by rents, began to change the traditional structure of society as fixed in the period of the feudal demesnes (cf. VI, 4), although the scope of those changes was still limited. Since the fall in the population made obtaining a sufficient amount of labour dues difficult there was a temporary increase in the use of hired labour, but the main trend was that of intensifying the exploitation of the peasants by augmenting their burdens in the form of the labour dues they had to provide. This in turn led to a rise in the number of small, not self-sufficient peasant holdings (cf. VI, 4) and also in the number of the landless population.

This threat to the position of the relatively well-to-do peasants and the worsened situation of the peasant population as a whole made the peasants intensify their struggle to improve their situation. Desertion, i.e. abandoning one's plot and looking for better conditions elsewhere, was a regular form of peasant resistance. It was made possible by the fact that, manpower being in short supply, new settlers were usually a valuable acquisition for the owners of landed estates. It is reasonable to suppose that some 10 per cent of all peasants were continually in search for new places to settle, which largely prevented the gentry from intensifying the exploitation of those peasants who were available to them as manpower.

More overt forms of struggle materialized as rebellions of serfs, sabotage of work to be done on demesne estates, and finally armed uprisings, ruthlessly suppressed by the gentry. These took place in the Subcarpathian region of Podhale, in Podlasie, in Great Poland, and in the Kurpie region in Masovia. When the gentry was preoccupied with fighting Khmelnitski (cf. section 2 above), a peasant uprising led by

Aleksander Kostka Napierski and Stanisław Łętowski broke out in Podhale in 1651. Peasants in the central part of Great Poland rose up at the same time.

Those peasants who were 'humbly' submitting supplications or were lodging complaints against tenants of the estates owned by the king with special courts supposed to handle such cases did not prosper, either.

The pauperization of peasants was accompanied by another undesirable change in the social structure, namely by the deterioration of the position of the burghers *qua* an estate (status group, *Stand*). Many of them, especially the richest families, managed to make fortunes, but they had no possibility of making investments. Gdańsk and some towns in Great Poland and Pomerania continued to develop, but the prevailing situation was that of stagnation. Many towns were marked by strong national and religious antagonisms. This applied both to the major towns in Gdańsk Pomerania (such as Gdańsk, Elbląg, Toruń), where the German language was used by the upper and middle strata of the burghers, and to towns in the Ruthenian territories (such as Lvov, Kiev, and Kamieniec Podolski), where there was a marked split among the Poles, the Ruthenians, and the Armenians who had settled there in fairly large numbers. This must have made those burghers feel themselves distinct from the basically Polish burghers of Cracow, Lublin, Poznań, and other Polish towns. The Jews had in towns organizations of their own, and their representatives to the Seym (called *Standländer*) were particularly interested in matters in which the Jewish communities had concern.

The values which developed later, when the sense of nationality was fully fledged, cannot be projected upon conditions earlier than the 19th century. For people living in the period now under consideration membership in a political entity, in a religious community, and in a status group (estate) were much more important. National consciousness was to develop gradually on the basis of supra-estate and supra-denominational bonds, which together with the consciousness of being citizens of the same state would yield the final effect in the form of general multilevel bonds. That was why, for instance, the inhabitants of Gdańsk often viewed the problems of the Commonwealth (in the sense of that term as applied to Poland of that time) in the light of their own interests although, like the burghers in other towns of Royal Prussia, by participating in the political life of their region and by having commercial and cultural contacts with the Polish gentry they felt themselves to be linked more strongly to the Polish people than to that of Brandenburg, despite the fact that many of them shared with the latter the same language and the same creed. When the integrity of the Commonwealth was in danger Gdańsk used actively to demonstrate its loyalty to it: such was the case during the Swedish invasion (1655—60), during Leszczyński's election (1733—34), and later (cf. VIII, 2), during the partitions.

The gentry was undergoing simultaneously two processes, namely that of pauperization of the minor gentry and deterioration of the position of the middle gentry, and that of aristocratization, i.e. growing importance of rich gentry and the magnates. This was accompanied by a marked concentration of the ownership of land. The number of estates of twenty or more villages, which could rank as fortunes, was growing. The offices of senators and state dignitaries usually went to members of magnate families, although the latter group included also members of non-senatorial families (about one-third in the Saxon period). There were constant shiftings in the group of the leading gentry families, some of which were entering the category of the magnates and thus acquiring increased importance. A considerable part in that process was played by royal support and by marriages. The second half of the 16th and the early 17th century witness the extinction or decline of the Tęczyński, Górka, Tarnowski, Kurozwęcki, Szafraniec, Kmita, and Odrowąż families, and the rise of the Leszczyński, Zamoyski, Potocki, Lubomirski, Gembicki, Przyjemski, Ossoliński, Grudziński, Lanckoroński, Koniecpolski, Wiśniowiecki, Mniszech, and Sieniawski families. Later we note the rise of the Czartoryski, Poniatowski, Moszyński, Branicki and many other families, in many cases as a result of well-calculated marriages. Jerzy Mniszech's marriage with a Brühl was important for his career in the 18th century; likewise, marriage to a Countess Cosel by a member of the family contributed to the rise of the Moszyńskis. The Saxon period saw the further advancement of the Szembek, Rzewuski, Poniatowski, Jabłonowski, Sapieha, Tyszkiewicz, Potocki, Lubomirski, and Sułkowski families, followed by the Zamoyskis, the Mniszechs, and their antagonists, the Czartoryskis. The families that declined included the Gembickis, the Leszczyńskis (as a result of the sale of the family estates by King Stanislaus Leszczyński after his settling in France), the Opalińskis, and the Firlejs.

4. Baroque culture and intellectual life in the epoch of wars and the Counter-Reformation

The 17th and the early 18th centuries saw the emergence of at least four basic models of culture, namely those of the magnates, the gentry, the burghers, and the peasants, the magnates' pattern of life being the novelty of that period. This was accompanied by an increase in the number of poor people who either were fitted within the framework of feudal society or remained outside the estate system (called 'loose' or 'drifting' people), who hired themselves out for various jobs. The magnates, desirous of stressing their importance, imitated the royal court and had imposing residences built for themselves. The finest ones included the Lubomirskis' palace in Wiśnicz Nowy (erected in 1621 by the Italian architect Matteo Trapola), Bishop Jakub Zadzik's residence in Kielce (1637—41), Stanisław Koniecpolski's palace in Podhorce (1635—40), and Krzyżtopór Castle in Ujazd (1626—44) owned by Krzysztof Ossoliński. Ladislaus IV expanded the royal castle in Warsaw and erected near it a column to commemorate his father, Sigismund

III (the column was erected in 1643—44 by Constantino Tencalla). Magnificent palatial buildings included the Krasińskis' palace in Warsaw (1675—1700) and the Warsaw residence of the Lubomirskis, expanded (ca. 1694) from the former palace of the Ossolińskis, both the work of the architect Tilman van Gameren. A special mention is due to Wilanów Palace, designed in the style of an Italian villa by Agostino Locci with the personal participation of King John Sobieski, expanded until the 1730's.

The traditions of the Renaissance were still lively among the magnates in the first half of the 17th century; importance was attached to education in foreign universities and to travel abroad, primarily to Germany, Italy, the Netherlands, and France. Their attitude toward European culture was not merely receptive, but innovative.

Marriages were concluded mainly within one's social circle, and mésalliances were rare, even in the case of the poorer gentry. A magnate's court usually had many courtiers (for instance there were some 50 of them at the court of Jeremi Wiśniowiecki). The magnates maintained their own armies, and covered the expenses of the diplomatic missions they headed. In the 17th century, the owner of a major latifund had an average annual income of 200,000 Polish zlotys (one zloty being then equivalent to 30 *groschen);* for comparison it may be added that the annual pay of a hussar (member of the élite heavy cavalry) varied from 160 to 320 Polish zlotys.

The mentality of the gentry, set on preserving the status they had acquired, was less open and marked by a number of dogmas, like the belief that Poland was the granary of Europe (cf. section 3 above), the conviction that 'golden freedom' was the essence of the gentry's existence, and the opinion that Poland was 'the bulwark of Christendom'. That complex of dogmas which emphasized the alleged superiority of gentry-rule Poland with its laws and manners, and ascribed to Poland a special protection of God (and in particular of the Virgin Mary as the *Regina Regni Poloniae,* 'the Queen of the Kingdom of Poland'), came to be termed Sarmatianism by those who criticized that state of affairs in the Age of Reason (the term was due to the gentry's belief that they stemmed from the Sarmatians, a people of Iranian origin who lived in Eastern Europe from ca. 500 B.C. to ca. A.D. 500).

The fact that the Sarmatianist ideology was 'closed' had its effect in a dislike of aliens and their influence. The gentry reacted to their frustrations due to the growing and observable distance between Poland and economically more and more advanced Western Europe, by concentrating their attention on home life. They saw a pattern in the magnates' model of culture, but its inaccessibility only served to consolidate the Sarmatian attitudes. While the gentry began gradually to advance ideas about the necessity of reform, that trend would be supported by some magnate families or groups of families (who thus hoped to promote their own interests) in the period that followed (cf. VIII). The magnates treated the gentry haughtily and tried to subordinate them by resorting to demagogy and by making them economically dependent (thus swelling the numbers of their clients in the ancient sense of the term).

While the dislike of western influence was strong, no objections were felt against imitating the East, in which connection the gentry's dress came to be influenced by Hungarian, Turkish, Tartar, and even Persian fashions. The *kontusz* (a kind of caftan worn by men as the outer garment) became common in the Baroque period, as the main element of the national attire of the Polish gentry. Sashes, some of them imported from Turkey, were fashionable. Regional differences could also be observed: while the gentry in Great Poland was fond of long dress, much shorter coats, cut like those worn in the army, were in daily use in the eastern parts of the country.

The burghers were willing to imitate the gentry in the way they dressed, although on the whole they represented a different mode of life, namely one more focussed on direct economic activity. Their upper strata (the patricians) also succumbed to the dogmatization of thinking that tended to preserve the *status quo*.

There were no major changes in material civilization as compared with the preceding period (cf. VI, 6), but differences in the living standards of the various groups of the burghers became noticeable. The same applied to the peasants; the general pauperization lowered their living standards and at the same time increased the contrast between the few rich peasants and the rest of the rural population.

Hard living conditions, incessant wars and plagues made large numbers of the population live at the minimum subsistence level: poor people ate no more than ten kilogrammes of meat and drank some 120 litres of milk per person annually. As in the preceding period (cf. VI, 6) the food of the rich was spicy, heavy, and sweet, while that of the poor was sour.

Polish culture in the 17th and the early 18th century was largely determined, rather than by the magnates and the gentry, by the Church which was very active in the Counter-Reformation. The number of monastic orders was rising as was also that of the monks (some 15,000 in the 17th century). Their influence upon society was quite strong. The Church's successes in consolidating Roman Catholicism in Poland, both in the sphere of the Church organization and incomes, and in that of the ideology and mentality of the people, were due to the fact that the gentry saw in the Church the bulwark of Sarmatianist stabilization and the guarantor of the existing socio-political system. Frustrations caused by economic difficulties in towns often found vent in actions aimed at the Protestants and the Jews. But it must be emphasized that the Counter-Reformation followed in Poland a course of its own, because it assumed the principle of religious tolerance that was sometimes undermined but never abolished. The Church was officially against tolerance, although it was more and more becoming a tolerance interpreted not as equality but as toleration. The freedom of worship in Gdańsk Pomerania, where there were many Lutherans in most towns, guaranteed by Sigismund Augustus in 1557—58, was confirmed. Many Protestants settled in Great Poland being brought there by the local gentry who needed manpower. At the same time (1633) Ladislaus IV recognized the existence of the Orthodox Church, which from the Union of Brest-Litovsk on (cf. section 2 above) had been functioning illegally.

The situation changed somewhat after the Swedish invasion, when dissenters (Protestant Swedes) came to be identified with traitors to the national cause. This led to certain restrictions imposed upon the Protestants, the most drastic measure having been the expulsion of the Arians in 1658, which cannot, however, be compared to the expulsion of the Huguenots from France in 1685. In the case of Poland, the Arians were never persecuted when they came to visit their families, and the Polish kings considered it their duty to act as their protectors abroad.

Poland remained a country of relative religious freedom in spite of the growing influence of the Church upon the mentality of the faithful and the expansion of the schools run by the Jesuits, with the resulting quite frequent manifestations of fanaticism and a narrowing of the intellectual horizon of the gentry. It was only in 1717 that the erection of new Protestant churches was prohibited, in a situation where there were at least 150 such churches in existence. The notorious Toruń case of 1724, when Protestants, reacting to provocation, destroyed a Roman Catholic church and a college run by the Jesuits, for which act the mayor and nine burghers were sentenced to death, was a demonstration on the part of Augustus II: he wanted the executions to take place because he wanted to prove to royal courts in Europe that only an absolute rule could stop fanaticism in Poland. It was one of the first cases when the issue of the dissenters was used against Poland, this time by Prussian propaganda.

The army was another factor which, in a period of numerous wars, had a strong impact upon attitudes and ways of life. As in other European countries, the basic military formation consisted of mercenary troops recruited in the name of the king (i.e. of the state), whereas the mercenary troops typical still during the Thirty Years' War were formed by commanders who offered their services to kings on the contract basis. The *levée en masse* was losing its importance, even though it was still called in 1621, 1649, 1651, 1655—57, 1672. In addition to the army of the state there were various non-state formations: regional and provincial troops, which during the interregna acted as the police force; small detachments kept by towns; troops kept by magnates; and the private troops of the king (the royal guards). In the early 17th century there were still no standing armies in Europe, greater military efforts being provoked only by wars. Poland had its nucleus of a standing army in the form of a small number of soldiers paid from the income from the royal estates. Unwillingness to make financial efforts and the gentry's fear of the absolute rule did not favour a numerical increase in the army's strength, and approval by the Seym was required in the case of extraordinary recruitments of mercenary troops. In the battle of Pilavtse, where the Polish army had some 30,000 men, the majority consisted of private troops. Later on mercenary troops became domi-

The mannerist interior of the townhall in the principal part of the city of Gdańsk, with a *plafond* by Isaac van den Blocke, symbolizing Gdańsk's links with Poland (1608)

Burghers' houses in Kazimierz Dolny on the Vistula (the décor of the façade dates from 1615)

King Stephen Báthory (reigned 1576–86) (a painting by Martin Kober)

The Renaissance courtyard of the castle at Baranów Sandomierski (built by Santi Gucci between 1591 and 1606)

King Sigismund III of the Vasa dynasty (reigned 1587–1632) (a portrait on a silver thaler)

The Polish Diet (an engraving by J. Lauri from 1622)

Stefan Czarniecki (1599–1665), a Polish commander at the time of the Swedish invasion (as shown on a votive plaque)

The early Baroque palace of bishops in Kielce (17th cent.)

King John III Sobieski at Vienna: a painting by an anonymous artist from the end of the 17th century showing the relief of Vienna in 1683

The armour of a hussar with brass ornaments and with wings (17th cent.)

Marie Sobieski, the wife of King John Sobieski, on horseback (by an anonymous painter)

The palace at Wilanów near Warsaw, residence of King John III Sobieski (built by Agostino Locci in the 17th century)

A view of Warsaw in 1656
(drawn by Eric Dahlberg)

F L U V I U S

The palace of the Ostrogski family in Warsaw (built by Tylman van Gameren in the 17th century)

The wooden church in Rabka (the turn of the 17th cent.)

Part of the Long Market in Gdańsk (15th to 17th cent.)

nant. In the second half of the 17th century, the strength of the Polish army (the Crown and Lithuania together) amounted to ca. 15,000 soldiers, the analogous figures being 200,000 for France, and some 30,000 for Brandenburg. The Turkish army in the operations against Austria in 1683 amounted to some 150,000 men.

Despite the numerical weakness of their army the Poles succeeded in introducing many modern forms of operations. It was after the example of Poland that Gustavus Adolphus reformed the tactics of his cavalry by making it charge in gallop using side arms, which came in turn to be imitated by the Imperial Army. Except for France, only Poland had special units of infantry and dragoons for protecting the artillery during marches and in battles. The military art was developing. Although the principal formations in the Polish army consisted of heavy (the hussars) and light cavalry (with medium-armed cavalry being introduced later), the proportion of cavalry and infantry were gradually becoming equal. But the army, when irregularly paid, was often a plague to the civilian population because it used to plunder villages and towns. Both during the Swedish invasion and the Northern War the civilians often suffered from both foreign and their own troops.

The schools — another element of consciousness formation — were more and more under the influence of the Church of Rome, which meant restrictions on schools run by dissenters and a gradual domination of Jesuit ones. In the initial period of their activity the Jesuits kept the educational standard at a comparatively high level. The number of secondary schools was growing, and the fairly dense network of parish schools was maintained. In the first half of the 17th century the better known secondary schools (colleges) included Nowodworski College in Cracow; the secondary school in Poznań; the Arian school in Raków (closed down by the decision of the Seym in 1638); the school run by the Bohemian Brethren in Leszno (which flourished until 1656, when the town was burned at the time of the Swedish invasion), which had as its headmaster Jan Amos Komenský (1592—1670), the famous Bohemian scholar, founder of modern pedagogy, who stayed in Leszno for many years, and which also had as one of the teachers the polyhistor John Jonston (active there 1625—56); and the secondary school founded by Krzysztof Opaliński in Sieraków. In the second half of the 17th century the secondary schools in Pomerania (Toruń, Elbląg, Gdańsk) continued to function, and their scholarly ambitions came to be manifested in the 18th century. The secondary school in Chełmno was reopened in 1692. Polish schools flourished in Silesia (Byczyna, Kluczbork, Wrocław). The universities experienced much less favourable conditions than during the Renaissance. The magnates gave preference to foreign universities and/or to the system of private tutors.

The gentry and the burghers drew much information from books, more than in the preceding period. In the early 18th century some 70 per cent of the gentry and some 60 per cent of the burghers were literate, the analogous figures for the minor gentry, the peasants, and the poor urban population being from five to ten per cent.

These were no small percentages, comparatively speaking. The reading public increased in the Baroque period, which was due to the appearance of publications of new kinds, intended for broad masses of readers, in particular printed calendars with much miscellaneous information, often uncritically repeated. *Merkuryusz Polski Ordynaryjny,* the first Polish printed newspaper, started appearing in Cracow in 1661; Jan Cenkier, a Polish printer, published *Poczta Królewiecka* in Królewiec (Germ. Königsberg, now Kaliningrad) in 1718—20, and the newspaper *Kurier Polski* started appearing in Warsaw in 1730.

People were increasingly eager to learn about the world, their curiosity being incited by the earlier geographical discoveries. A group of Poles arrived in America, where they formed one of the first settlements on the New Continent. Memoir-writing was common owing to intensified consciousness of the history of one's country and the past of one's family. Epistolography flourished, letters often performing the function of newspapers in transmitting the news. Private records from meetings of the Seym, family chronicles, etc., were kept. In the literature of this type special mention is due to the memoirs written by Jan Chryzostom Pasek (ca. 1636 —ca. 1701) and the letters written by Krzysztof Opaliński (1609—55) to his brother Łukasz (1612—62).

In science pride of place went to astronomy, mathematics, history, and classical philology. Political and economic thought was closely linked to the general situation of the country (cf. section 2 above). Among the eminent astronomers and mathematicians mention is due to Jan Brożek (1585—1652), Johannes Hevelius of Gdańsk (1611—87), who had King John Sobieski as his patron, the Jesuits Adam Kochański (1631—1700), and Bartłomiej Nataniel Wąsowski (1617—87), and Michał Sędziwój (1566—1636), who was one of the most famous alchemists of his times. The development of historical writing is borne out by the works of Szymon Starowolski (1588—1656), Kasper Niesiecki (1687—1744) whose genealogy of gentry families, *Korona Polska* (The Polish Crown), met the highest standards of his times, Bartłomiej Keckermann, the author of *De Natura et Proprietatibus Historiae* (1610), who engaged in polemics with Jean Bodin, and Joachim Pastorius (1610—82), who studied modern historiography with G. J. Voss of Leyden, at that time the principal methodologist of history writing.

Those *belles lettres* which tackled topical issues came close to historiography, geographical and historical descriptions, and memoirs. More general in nature was the poetry of Maciej Kazimierz Sarbiewski (1595—1640), who was called the 'Christian Horace' and whose poems written in Latin were being read throughout Europe. They reflected the two aspects of Baroque literature: disruption of the classicial patterns intended to facilitate grasping human nature and human actions, and faithfulness to religion. This found expression in the versions of God encountered in that literature: that of God who is severe, and that of God who understands man's need of earthly happiness. The same can be seen in the works of Jan Andrzej Morsztyn (ca. 1620—93), the poet of the royal court. More Sarmatianist in nature was the poetry of Wacław Potocki (1621—96) and that of Wespazjan Hieronim Kochowski (1633—1700), who extolled 'golden freedom'. More critical elements can be found in the epic poetry of Samuel Twardowski (b. between 1595 and 1606, d. 1661). Plebeian literature formed a separate trend. In Silesia, it included the works of Protestant pastors of Polish nationality, Jerzy Bock of Oleśnica (1621—90) and Adam Gdatius of Kluczbork (1615—88), who realistically described the life of burghers and peasants and criticized the gentry. More liberal ideas in printed texts were suppressed by Church censorship.

In Baroque culture, which attached much importance to external effects, an important role was played by the theatre. The most popular performances were those of a religious nature. The theatres were mainly attached to the royal court and courts of the magnates, and to schools, especially those run by the Jesuits. Molière's *Bourgeois Gentilhomme* was published and staged in Leszno as early as in 1687.

Next to the theatre, the Baroque added signally to European music, in which Poland — commonly recognized as a country of remarkable musical culture — had its share. The original Polish composers of that period included Bartłomiej Pękiel (d. 1670), Jacek Różycki (d. after 1697), and Marcin Kretzner (1631—96). During the Counter-Reformation the Church was particularly anxious to enrich religious ceremonies with music and songs. It was in this connection that organ playing developed.

Courts of the magnates were also centres of musical activity. During the reign of Ladislaus IV the royal theatre staged 12 operas and three ballets. It was during the Baroque period that folk music developed many forms that later became typical of it (for instance the rhythm of the mazur dance) and also influenced European music (e.g., the sonatas of the German composer Georg Philipp Telemann).

The Baroque style, with its tendency to replace straight lines by curved and polygonal ones and to use many embellishments, made the strongest impact upon architecture and the visual arts. In Poland it developed its local characteristics even though it drew from both the Renaissance tradition and the Italian and Spanish patterns. The Dutch influence in art was still visible, though this applied primarily to towns; in architecture it was manifested in the form of palaces, monasteries, and churches. The interiors of the churches were usually adjusted to the requirements of the Baroque style mainly by the use of sculptures, including magnificent tombs. Many new churches were built by Tilman van Gameren, mentioned above. The finest Baroque churches erected at that time include the Jesuit church in Poznań (in the style of the Roman Baroque) designed by Bartłomiej Wąsowski and completed by Giovanni Catenaci in 1698—1701. The famous architects Kacper Bażanka (ca. 1680—1726) and Pompeo Ferrari (ca. 1660—1736) also erected their buildings in the Baroque style.

Architectural knowledge was spreading among the gentry and the burghers: Stanisław Solski's *Architekt Polski* (The Polish Architect) was published in 1690, and the status of the architect changed from a guild craftsman to a forerunner of the engineering profession. The number of people engaged in the building trade, construction of 'engines' and military engineering was growing.

The style of the gentry manor-house was finally established as a wooden building having ground floor only, on a symmetrical axial plan, easy to expand, with strongly accentuated porches, alcoves, and roofs. Two types of stone-and-brick houses developed in towns: the Little Poland type (Kazimierz, Lublin), with enormous parapets, and the Pomerania and Great Poland type (Gdańsk, Toruń, Elbląg, Poznań, Warsaw), with elaborate front elevations.

In painting we have to note outstanding works produced in the Pomerania and Great Poland milieu (Herman Han, Bartholomeus Strobel) and in Cracow (Tomasso Dolabella, a Venetian who lived in Cracow until his death in 1650). There was a growing interest in portraits and in paintings concerned with historical subjects and showing battle scenes. The specifically Polish form was that of sexagonal coffin portraits, painted on the head end of the coffin.

Polish culture and science in the Baroque period, while drawing upon the general European achievements and tradition, in turn made its own contributions to them. Polish culture may be said to have affected many countries. Polish was used as the diplomatic language in South-Eastern Europe. Ukrainians, Moldavians and others published their works in Polish, as did the prominent Moldavian historian Miron Costin (1633—91), who also took Polish historical writings (for instance those of Maciej Stryjkowski) as his model. Many cultural attainments (including also the sphere of material civilization) found its way from Western to Eastern Europe through the intermediary of Poland which also had its share in bringing 17th century Sweden closer into the sphere of continental intellectual tradition. But, when viewed in the historical perspective, the most signal Polish contribution to modern thought was that made by the Polish Arians (Socinians, Polish Brethren — cf. VI, 3). Their ideas concerning the freedom of thought considerably influenced the philosophy of the Age of Reason by linking the ideas current during the Reformation with the beginnings of the Enlightenment. In 1668—69, expelled from Poland, the Arians founded in Amsterdam the famous Bibliotheca Fratrum Polonorum (Library of Polish Brethren) series, which included works by Johann Crell, Samuel Przypkowski, Jonah Schlichting, Faustus Socinus, and Ludwig Wolzogen. The fact that even in the liberally-minded Netherlands the Bibliotheca was banned from circulation (together with such works as Hobbes' *Leviathan* and Spinoza's *Tractatus Theologico-politicus*) shows how novel these ideas must have been at that time. The impact made by the Socinians upon the new ways of thinking was admitted by such people as Pierre Bayle, one of the forerunners of the Age of Reason, and Voltaire.

Chapter VIII

The Age of Reason and the Age of Reforms. The Partitions (1733—95)

1. The causes of change

Carrying out such reforms as would enable an efficient functioning of the state (cf. VII, 1—2) was the most important issue for the future of Poland. Such reforms would also mean the removal of the discrepancy between the considerable achievements in culture and the political consciousness of the gentry, on the one hand, and the weakening of the state and the reduction of Poland's role in the international arena, on the other. The task of strengthening the state was made even more urgent by the fact that the neighbouring states, which were eyeing with suspicion any possible consolidation of Poland as a political entity that could threaten the *status quo* were growing in strength.

The problem was extremely difficult to solve not only because of the community of interests of Russia, Prussia, and Austria (or sometimes, on the contrary, because of the particular interests of each of these states), but also, and primarily, because of Poland's socio-political structure being exceptionally incapable of reforms. While, for example, in France the sequence of reforms effected in the 18th century and culminated in the revolution of 1789 opened with a rebellion of the aristocracy which was ever better educated and wanted to have a direct share in the government, in Poland the aristocracy (the magnates) could not complain of the absolutism of royal rule. The magnates derived the greatest economic advantages from the existing state of affairs: the very size of their estates ensured them increased incomes. What a magnate could afford (for instance, the long process of transporting the grain to Gdańsk), could not be done by the middle gentry who were thus automatically eliminated as competitors. This was why most magnates did not want any change and declared themselves in favour of the opinion that Poland could survive primarily owing to its internal disorder and weakness; this meant abstention from any reforms that could alarm the powerful neighbours. Incidentally, it must be said that the aristocracy's struggle against the royal power in France was much more comprehensible than striving to limit one's own influence in the state (in the case of Poland). Those who were going to the extreme were ready to transform Poland into a federation of small states, each ruled by a magnate, which would accelerate the trend toward refeudalization, already manifested in intensifying serfdom.

Those reactionary opinions, at variance with the anti-feudal ideas typical of the Age of Reason that called for an improvement of the political system and admission of broader strata to power, were opposed by some groups of the aristocracy, mainly those gathered around the Czartoryski family, in a sense the first organized political party in Poland (and traditionally called 'the Family' in Polish historiography). They wanted to wield power in a state that would be better governed; actual rule would still be in the hands of the aristocracy, no strong royal power being envisaged in that political programme.

It was only on some points that this programme coincided with the ideas advanced by the middle gentry, who were again becoming more active. They perceived with increasing frequency that a week state, with a small army, offered little opportunity for them. Hence fewer and fewer references were being made to 'golden freedom', and more and more, to the need of an efficient system of government. At the same time the middle gentry were increasingly interested in economic issues because a rise in incomes, which were falling as a result of the low productivity of labour in a system based on serfdom, was vital for them. Their programme was aimed at the magnates as they saw advantages in strengthening the royal prerogatives. But like the overwhelming majority of the aristocracy they did not want any change in the social conditions, nor any improvement in the position of the peasants, because that would require a change in the system of landed estate management. On many points that programme was supported by the burghers, more active in the 18th century but unable to present any political programme of their own.

Next to these two programmes mention is due to the programme of reforms advanced by the kings, namely Stanislaus Leszczyński (at the time when he ruled Lorraine) and Stanislaus Augustus Poniatowski (reigned 1764—95).

There was also a growing trend towards reforms represented by comparatively radical social thinkers, such as Stanisław Konarski (1700—73), Stanisław Staszic (1755—1826), and Hugo Kołłątaj (1750—1812). For tactical reasons they linked themselves to enlightened magnates, the gentry, the burghers, or the king, but they kept their own opinions, which were far ahead of the actual measures and the slogans connected with them. For instance, Kołłątaj was perfectly well aware of the narrow scope of any reforms that had real chances of being put into effect, but he claimed that posterity would comprehend the gap between the political consciousness of the élite of reformers and the proposals which could in practice be advanced. The opposition of the magnates, weak burghers, large numbers of obscurantist gentry who exploited the peasants and were particularly ill-disposed toward any changes in the status of the peasants, and finally the gaps between the various programmes left little chance for successful reforms. Moreover, the neighbouring countries, interested in keeping Poland weak, watched closely what was going on in Poland, which hampered the freedom of movement of the patriots. The advocates of reform had to study the international situation very keenly — this applied in particular to the mutual relations among Russia, Austria and Prussia — to take advantage of the minutest contradictions in the relations between these three powers. This was why Poland's foreign policy in that period was focussed on the issue of reforms. As a result internal problems became so closely intertwined with external ones that they cannot be treated separately.

In view of the conditions outlined above the historic importance of what was achieved in Poland in the second half of the 18th century must be emphasized. Suffice it to mention the Commission for National Education (founded 1773), which was the first ministry of education in Europe, and the renowned Constitution of the Third of May (1791), which was also the first constitution in Europe to base (though not quite consistently) political prerogatives on property, and not on birth.

In general history it is treated as one of the three most important contemporary revolutions in the world, next to those in France and in America. The label revolution is justified by the scope of the reforms, even though the process took place without bloodshed.

All this would not have been possible without gradual changes in mentality and without a broadening of the group of those who thought in terms of the state, and not merely in those of an estate, a social group, or a region. The concept which identified the nation with the gentry was becoming increasingly obsolete; growing numbers of people, other than the gentry, considered themselves members of the Polish nation and citizens of the Polish state, linked together by a common past and a common present. The group solidarity of the burghers was consolidating: as townspeople they felt engaged in striving for civic and political rights, so far monopolized by the gentry. This striving resulted in a rapprochement between the gentry and the burghers, which was to intensify later. The peasants, too, felt to be more and more strongly linked to the state; the more enlightened among them were closely watching the struggle for the reforms, and sent petitions to 'the Honourable Estates in the Seym' as they expected an improvement in their conditions not only from their respective demesne lords, but also from the state authorities.

Now this state which was undergoing advantageous political reforms, and its developing nation, a vigorus centre of culture, had to face the tragedy of the partitions. Under the circumstances they were very painfully felt and strongly condemned by European public opinion. The partitions poisoned the political morality of the partitioning powers which faced an impossible task: the partitions could not be justified, and programmes of denationalizing the Poles and/or absorbing the Polish territories culturally all ended in signal failures. The liberation struggle, later continued throughout the 19th century, began at once with the process of imposing the partitions, initiated by the Kościuszko Insurrection of 1794. Developing Poland was an inviting prey for the income-greedy and militarist neighbouring powers under absolutist rule. Suffice it to say that the fiscal revenues of Prussia increased by some 90 per cent after the first partition of Poland. Ethnic considerations were at that time still out of the question; they were only later added by chauvinist historiography. In 1772, Frederick II himself wrote to Friedrich von Domhardt, president of the Gdańsk Chamber, that 'the (local) inhabitants, especially in Pomerania..., are mainly of the Polish nationality'.

2. The problem of reforms and the international situation up to the first partition of Poland

The death in 1733 of Augustus II raised the issue of the next occupant of the Polish throne. At first everything seemed to indicate that Stanislaus Leszczyński, supported by France (father-in-law of Louis XV from 1725) would become the next Polish king. He was accordingly elected king by 13,000 gentry who gathered in the Wola suburb of Warsaw (the large number of the electors was a proof of the political activeness of the gentry). Russia for its part, acting in co-operation with Austria, advanced the candidacy of Frederick Augustus, the Elector of Saxony. Under the protection of the Russian troops, which in the meantime reached the Vistula, Frederick Augustus was elected King of Poland (as Augustus III); the election took place not on the traditional election site at Wola, but at Kamień, on the right bank of the Vistula, and the number of the electors was about one-tenth the number of the gentry who had elected Leszczyński. Leszczyński withdrew to Gdańsk, but even the army of 23,000 men, recruited by the Gdańsk authorities, failed to secure him the throne. After a siege of several month Gdańsk was taken by the Russians, and Leszczyński had to flee the country. By a treaty concluded in Vienna in 1735 he renounced his claims to the Polish throne, and received instead the Duchy of Lorraine, where he won an excellent reputation as the wise 'benefactor king'.

Augustus III (reigned 1733—63) stayed mainly in Dresden and let Poland be governed by his officials and the rival groups of the magnates. This led to the emergence of the doctrine of *sui generis* republicanism, sponsored by the magnates, that is a system in which the king would perform purely ceremonial functions. The scattering of the state authority had its most glaring manifestation in the fact that the meetings of the Seym were being disrupted as a rule: the only one which did not suffer that fate was the so-called pacification meeting of the Seym (1736), which passed an amnesty for the adherents of Leszczyński who took part in the Dzików Confederacy.

When seen against this background, the programme of the Czartoryski family (cf. section 1 above) had its distinct and different features. The wealth of this family had its source in the marriage concluded by August Aleksander Czartoryski, the Voivode of Ruthenia, with Maria Zofia Denhoff, née Sieniawska, whose dowry included vast estates. There were also family ties between the Czartoryskis and Stanisław Poniatowski, the father of the future king of Poland and the closest collaborator of Stanislaus Leszczyński, author of the renowned *List ziemianina do pewnego przyjaciela z innego województwa* (Letter of a Landowner to a Friend of His in Another Province; 1744), in which he outlined a programme for the consolidation of the state.

Leszczyński influenced the Załuski brothers, eminent representatives of the early period of the Age of Reason in Poland; one of them, Andrzej Stanisław (1695—1758), Chancellor of the Crown in 1735—46 and the Bishop of Cracow, was an advocate of political, economic and fiscal reforms; the other, Józef Andrzej (1702—74), the Bishop of Kiev, was a patron of science and literature. They both founded the famous Załuski Library in Warsaw, at that time one of the largest in Europe. Feliks Oraczewski (1739—99), one of the initiators of the formation of the Commission for National Education and an advocate of the programme for the improvement of the position of the peasants, had been educated at the Military Academy founded by Leszczyński in Lunéville. Stefan Garczyński (ca. 1690—1755), Voivode of Poznań and author of *Anatomia Rzeczypospolitej* (Anatomy of the Commonwealth), published in 1751, which advanced ideas of economic development and the demographic expansion of the country, also had been influenced by Leszczyński. His ideas were linked to those of the cameralists, who stressed the involvement of the state in economic matters and associated national prosperity with the growth of the population. The texts mentioned above, together with *Głos wolny wolność ubezpieczający* (Free Voice in Defence of Freedom), written by Leszczyński himself (1749), stimulated the political and economic thinking of the emergent progressive intellectual élite. They served as a background for the works of Stanisław Konarski (1700—73), the principal advocate of Leszczyński and his programme, and also the main ideologist of the Czartoryski faction in the late period of the Saxon dynasty's rule in Poland. His work *O skutecznym rad sposobie* (On Effective Counsels) showed a distinct influence of that programme. Konarski criticized the existing political system and suggested reforms, concerned mainly with the Seym (he advocated the abolition of the principle of the *liberum veto*).

Russia and Austria were alarmed by the strengthening of Prussia under the rule of Frederick II (reigned 1740—86): in 1740—45 Prussia occupied Silesia which had been in Austrian possession, leaving only the principalities of Opava-Karnov and Cieszyn in the hands of Austria. They accordingly supported the Czartoryski faction, which in the period between 1738 and 1752 was submitting to the Seym bills that provided for fiscal and military reforms. This was opposed by the 'republicans' (see above), led by the Potockis (primarily by Józef Potocki, the Hetman of the Crown, and Teodor Potocki, the Primate of Poland) and supported by Prussia and France (which at that time was allied with Prussia). The taking over of Silesia by Prussia worsened the situation of the local Polish population, which was numerically dominant in Upper Silesia.

Poland did not participate in the Seven Years' War (1756—63) in which Austria unsuccessfully tried to recover Silesia, but was not in a position (this applied to the Silesian campaigns of 1740—45 as well) to prevent the passage of foreign troops, with the accompanying plundering of Polish territories. Requisitions, recruitment of soldiers and circulation of forged money, made at the instigation of Frederick II, were especially acutely felt. Frederick II had an already well-defined political ideology, which planned an economic exploitation of Poland (Great Poland in particular) and stripping it of the various territories in the same way as an artichoke is stripped of its leaves (as he put it in his political testament).

In the Seven Years' War Prussia was also opposed by Russia, and it was only the death in 1762 of the Empress Elizabeth and the ascension to the Russian throne of Peter III, of the German family of Holstein, a fanatical admirer of Frederick II, which saved Prussia from a partition by its enemies. The new Russian Emperor concluded a peace treaty with Prussia in 1762, and in the following year, a treaty of alliance which envisaged co-operation in connection with the approaching election of a new king of Poland. The war left Europe divided into two hostile blocs: the Southern system, which comprised France, Austria, Spain, and Turkey, and the Northern system, consisting of Russia, Prussia, England and Denmark, in which Russia openly strove for hegemony. This meant a dissolution of the alliance of imperial courts. At the same time Russia became interested in a strengthening of Poland as a possible ally in the threatening war with Turkey.

The death in 1763 of Augustus III intensified the fear that a new war of Polish succession would break out. The Czartoryski faction accordingly sought Russian support in its striving to secure the Polish throne for August Aleksander Czartoryski, the Voivode of Ruthenia, already mentioned above, or for his son, Adam Kazimierz Czartoryski (1734—1823). Russia opposed the plans, supported by some 'republicans', of passing the throne to Charles, the son of Augustus III, but did not declare itself in favour of the Czartoryskis either: it secured the election of Stanislaus Augustus Poniatowski. As the Empress Catherine wrote to her diplomatic representatives in Poland, 'It is indispensable for us to place on the Polish throne a Piast [a conventional term for a person of Polish origin — *translator's note*], who would be convenient for us, would be useful for our real interests, in a word, a man who would owe his rise to us only. The person of Count Poniatowski, the Master of the Pantry of Lithuania, meets all the conditions that suit us and we have accordingly decided to elevate him to the Polish throne.'

But facts proved much more intricate. Poniatowski was a talented man, a very clever and sober politician, and knew how to win over and choose people with whom to work. A person of considerable knowledge and vast cultural interests, he rendered enormous services in promoting the various fields of intellectual and cultural life. He was an adherent of the ideas of the Age of Reason and an enemy of Sarmatianism (cf. VII, 4). His impact upon all spheres of life (the political system, public administration, diplomacy, the fiscal system, the national economy, the army, the school system, the theatre and other branches of art) was so strong that his rule came to be traditionally referred to as the Stanislaus period. When ascending the throne he had a well-conceived and constantly developing programme that envisaged the making of a new, modernized Poland, the opposite to what it was under the Saxon rule. 'I myself and all Polish citizens,' he wrote, 'are, and should be, friends of Russia, and that just for patriotic reasons,' but if 'that goal is to be attained we must make our constitution better, our army stronger, and our revenues larger.' He inspired various reformist undertakings, and was gradually building up an ever increasing number of his supporters, joined by his former enemies who had become convinced that Poniatowski's reforms were good. He wanted to be neither a pawn moved by the Czartoryskis, nor a puppet whose strings would be pulled by the imperial court in St. Petersburg, even though he was scorned as such by the 'republicans', who sought alliance with the Southern system, were hostile to all reforms, and could not suffer the fact that the throne went to a 'Master of the Pantry', i.e. to a person who had held a minor office.

The royal programme coincided with the ever stronger and increasingly radical reformist trend, which fact consolidated the position of the king.

It thus turned out that the courts in St. Petersburg and Berlin were unable to control the situation in Poland through the intermediary of the king. Both the king himself, and the nation at large, growing more active politically and surpassing in that respect the peoples of Prussia and Russia, suppressed under absolutist rule, proved to be obstacles on that path. Russia and Prussia had therefore to resort to other means. Between 1764 and 1772 these two countries interfered with Poland's internal affairs by defending religious dissenters, torpedoing the reforms through supporting the opposition of the magnates, and making plans — advanced mainly by Frederick II — of partitioning Poland by annexing some Polish territories, which would weaken Poland and at the same time mean great advantages for the partitioning powers.

Between 1764 and 1772 the Czartoryskis acted in favour of reforms, but they did not support the royal plan of strengthening Poland as an ally of Russia within the Northern system, because they still hoped they could seize power. On the other hand, the plans of the 'republicans' envisaged liberation of the country from royal 'tyranny' by Russian troops and restoration of the domination of the magnates.

The 1764 meeting of the Seym, animated by the famous speech of Andrzej Zamoyski (1716—92), Chancellor of the Crown and the principal legal adviser of the Czartoryski faction, brought a number of essential economic and administrative reforms. The appointment of the Commission for the Army curbed the power of the hetmans, whose offices were as a rule held by magnates, and the appointment of the Commission for Fiscal Matters, one for the Crown and later another for Lithuania, made the administration of the country more efficient. The matters submitted to the Seym by the Commission for Fiscal Matters were to be decided by a majority of votes (i.e. unanimity was not required), and the deputies were forbidden to take an oath on the instructions formulated by the provincial diets. The king set up an unofficial professional advisory body, the so-called Royal Cabinet, and started organizing the Polish diplomatic service. The postal reform of 1764 gave Poland one of the most efficient postal systems in Europe.

Faced with the situation in which projects of reforms were growing in number, the court in Berlin was sending protests to that in St. Petersburg. Russia's attitude toward King Stanislaus Augustus changed: endeavours were at first made to isolate him from the Czartoryskis, who were also warned against far-reaching reforms, the more so as Russia feared that Poniatowski could ask Austria and Turkey for help. Prussia and Russia availed themselves of the hostile attitude of the 'republicans' toward the king and of the issue of religious dissenters. Certain limitations of the rights of non-Roman Catholics to participate in political life (much milder than in many other countries) were used as a pretext (which was clearly stated by

Frederick II) for interfering with Poland's internal affairs in the name of defending the rights of the dissenters. Russia decided to force through (by using for that purpose Repnin, the Russian envoy in Warsaw) the principle of equal rights for the dissenters. When the Seym at its meeting in 1767 did not comply with the Russian and Prussian demands, Repnin activated the magnates who were opposing the king and made them set up a confederation, i.e. a legal rebellion against the king, led by Karol Radziwiłł, the notorious representative of the bad traditions of Sarmatianism (Radom, June 1767). Repnin rested satisfied with a demonstration, but the confederates, supported by some of the gentry who were attracted by the slogans of the defence of the true faith against the confederations set up by the dissenters (and also inspired by Repnin) strove to dethrone the king and to seize power.

When Repnin's intricate intrigues were laid bare, the anti-Russian attitudes intensified, and the various groups combined in the defence of their religion and their 'freedom' (from the king and from Russia). The gentry, still imbued with the old ideas, let themselves be manipulated by the magnates who were advancing various catchy slogans, but at the same time were trained in political tactics. When the Seym at its sessions in 1767 and 1768 again refused to comply with the demands concerning the dissenters and passed new reforms, Repnin resorted to a measure which was to have very grave consequences: he let several prominent deputies to the Seym (representatives of the Radom confederation) be interned in Kaluga in Russia, where they stayed for nearly five years. This greatly intensified the anti-Russian feeling, of which the magnates who still strove to depose the king and to bar reforms succeeded in taking advantage; they set up (in the town of Bar in Podolia) a confederation aimed at the king, the reforms, and Russia; the confederation was led by Józef Pułaski (1704—69), the father of Kazimierz (Casimir) Pułaski (1747—79), and Adam and Michał Krasiński. Casimir Pułaski after the defeat of the confederates emigrated abroad, and in 1777 went to America where as a general in the American army he became famous by his victory in the battle of Charleston. He lost his life on 11 October 1779, during the siege of Savannah.

The Bar confederation, whose military operations shook the country for several years (1768—72), created a new situation which Russia had not expected when it intrigued against Poniatowski and the Czartoryskis, the more so as the confederates proclaimed the dethronement of the Polish king in the autumn of 1770. Poniatowski, however, did not accept the Russian proposal to crush the confederates by using Russian troops for that purpose.

The situation in Poland favoured a further rapprochement between Russia and Prussia, which made plans for snatching some of the Polish territories. As early as 1770 Frederick occupied a large part of Great Poland under the pretext of protection against plague (the *cordon sanitaire* principle) and engaged in lively diplomatic activity intended to persuade Austria and Russia to partition Poland. The international situation also provided suitable pretexts: Austria became alarmed by the Russian victory over Turkey in the Balkans in 1774 (these operations having also been inspired by the Bar confederation); Austria was also interested in Silesia and sought a rapprochement with Prussia, which was skilfully stimulated by Frederick II; Russia in turn was afraid of that rapprochement. This made it easier for Frederick II to obtain the approval of Russia (which had earlier not advanced any proposals for a partition of Poland) and Austria to the seizure by these three states of part of the Polish territories, which meant a failure of the Russian policy and a strengthening of the position of Prussia and Austria. A treaty between Russia and Prussia was signed first (17 February 1772), to be followed by a tripartite treaty of 5 August 1772. The territorial issues were finally settled in 1776, because Prussia and Austria resorted to usurpations in snatching territories other than those specified in the treaty. The economically most valuable territories (Gdańsk Pomerania without Gdańsk and Toruń, and the northern part of Great Poland with Kujawy — in all 36,000 sq. km. and 580,000 people) went to Prussia; Austria took the part of Little Poland situated to the east of the Vistula and the San, nearly the entire provinces of Ruthenia and Bełz, and parts of the provinces of Podolia and Volhynia — in all 83,000 sq. km. and 2,650,000 people, while Russia incorporated the eastern part of Byelorussia, i.e., the province of Livonia, the northern part of the province of Polotsk, nearly the whole of the province of Vitebsk, the province of Mstislav, and the south-eastern part of the province of Minsk — in all 92,000 sq. km. with 1,300,000 people. The losses to Prussia and in part those to Austria concerned the ethnically Polish lands. Moreover, Prussia, by settling on the Vistula, gained control of the Polish foreign trade. The old Piast towns, at one time capitals of the country — namely Cracow, Poznań, and Gniezno (and also Sandomierz), became border towns. Moreover, in 1775 Prussia imposed upon Poland a very disadvantageous commercial treaty, intended primarily to increase the Prussian revenues from custom duties.

The balance of power in Europe was changed: the Northern and the Southern systems collapsed to be replaced by the alliance of the three partitioning powers.

3. Between the first and the second partition. The great national effort. The Third of May Constitution

After having annexed the territories specified above the partitioning powers demanded that the Seym formally ratify those measures (1773—75). Under the military pressure of the three powers the Seym was forced to approve the partition and also the commercial treaties, of which that with Prussia concerning the custom duties was particularly disadvantageous. Stanislaus Augustus engaged in diplomatic and propaganda activity to draw the attention of European public opinion to this act of violence, but this had a purely moral significance. By supporting some of the reforms Russia confirmed that it would strive to include Poland in its sphere of influence if Poland renounced — as Otto von Stackelberg, the new Russian ambassador in Warsaw put it — its 'fancies about independence', represented in his opinion primarily by Stanislaus Augustus. The first point accordingly was to restrict the royal power. That was to be achieved through the establishment of a Permanent Council; while the idea was advanced by a group of politicians who were ill-disposed toward the king (they were headed by August Sułkowski), it nevertheless to some extent complied with the king's interests as it curbed the self-will of unruly magnates. The Permanent Council had 36 members appointed by the Seym, and was divided into five departments, concerned respectively with foreign affairs, home affairs, the army, administration of justice, and fiscal matters. The legislative measures were, however, inconsistent, because the commissions established in 1764 (cf. section 2 above) were maintained; this applied also to the Commission for the Army, which after 1775 proved to be a tool in the hands of the hetmans who traditionally came from magnate families. On the other hand, the Commission for National Education (cf. section 1 above) was totally subordinated to the king. Also established was a Commission for Hospitals, which was the first ministry of health and social welfare in the country. Some fiscal and economic reforms were passed (including the Act on Bills of Exchange). The position of the peasants was much discussed, and it was suggested that their duties be made uniform throughout the country, but on the whole the subject matter was taboo for the gentry, who did not want the state to interfere with the relations between the landowners and the serfs.

The plan to restrict the royal power through the intermediacy of the Permanent Council thus failed, because the king subordinated the Council to himself through people who were devoted to him, and moreover exercised power through his chancelleries. In 1776 the Seym abolished the Commission for the Army (and thus curbed the power of the hetmans) and let the appointments in the army be made by the king and his military chancellery.

Many decisions transformed the Permanent Council into a modern executive branch of the state. Andrzej Zamoyski was commissioned to prepare a code that would systematize the laws in force in Poland, but his proposal was not accepted in 1780. The proposal provided for a certain extension of the rights of the burghers and an improvement of the position of the peasants, and also covered certain matters concerned with the Church. This resulted in an attack upon the proposal on the part of a coalition consisting of the 'republican' magnates, the obscurantist gentry, von Stackelberg, and the Papal Nuncio Archetti. This fact showed what were the limits of reforms that were then likely to be carried out by a regular parliamentary procedure. But the striving for reforms was spreading. Next to the determined policy of the king, it was another factor which Poland's neighbours failed to estimate properly. Von Stackelberg tried to take advantage of the political contradictions within the gentry and among the magnates, but he was not in a position to oppose the growing social forces that were in favour of reform and the consolidation of the state.

The state began to function more effectively. It was supposed (this applies, for instance, to Vergennes, the French minister for foreign affairs) that Poland would soon again become a European power. The numbers of the adherents of the king were growing both in the Senate and in the Chamber of Deputies.

Endeavours were made, mainly on the part of the king, to take advantage of all divergences between the partitioning powers; it was expected that a war might break out between Prussia and Austria in 1778, which was in fact a likely event. Poland tried to take an active part in international politics by offering its assistance to Russia in that country's war with Turkey, which would bring Poland into the Russo-Austrian bloc, but the meeting between the Empress Catherine and Stanislaus Augustus in Kaniov (1787) failed to yield the desired results. The proposal was ultimately rejected under the pretext that Prussia protested against the negotiations between Poland and Russia.

The debates of the Seym in Warsaw, which came to be known in historiography as the Great Seym or the Four Year Seym (1788—92) constituted another important event. Its speakers were Stanisław Małachowski and Kazimierz Nestor Sapieha. It was a period of revolutionary tide on the continent. While the Seym in Warsaw was passing its successive reforms, the French revolution was in full swing from 1789 and contributed to increased political activeness on the part of broad masses of the gentry and the burghers. Four months after the destruction of the Bastille the so-called black procession took place in Warsaw (November 1789): representatives of 141 Polish towns, led by Jan Dekert, the Mayor of Warsaw, submitted their demands to the king and to the Seym. Stanislaus Augustus had as his adherents the powerful patriotic party with Ignacy and Stanisław Potocki, Adam Kazimierz Czartoryski, Stanisław Małachowski, the Italian Scipione Piattoli, and Hugo Kołłątaj, who was the ideological leader of that group. That group, inspired by the king and in accordance with his proposals, worked out a Constitution Bill, which was passed on 3 May 1791. The passing of the Constitution had many features of a *coup d'état*: only about one-third of the deputies were present because of the Easter recess, and these were largely bound by an earlier oath to keep the secret; the part of the city adjacent to the Royal Castle, where the debates were held, was full of troops, Varsovians were in the streets, many burghers watched the debates.

The adoption of the Constitution was preceded by legislative measures concerned with an improvement in the local administration, abolition of the Permanent Council, increase in the number of the troops up to 100,000, imposition of taxes on estates (10 per cent of the incomes in the case of those held by the gentry, and 20 per cent in the case of those held by the Church and the clergy), adoption of the Provincial Diets Act of 24 March 1791 (which excluded the landless gentry from participation in the provincial diets), and the Towns Act of 18 April 1791, later included in the Constitution, which met the demands submitted by 'the black procession'. Burghers in the royal towns (those owned by the magnates were not covered by the Act) were assured personal inviolability, the right of purchasing estates, access to many offices and ranks in the army, and participation in the Seym (with the decisive vote in matters concerned with towns and trade). The Constitution itself paved the way for the organization of a modern state and modern society. It also introduced a hereditary monarchy: Stanislaus Augustus was to be succeeded by the Saxon dynasty. The Seym, which would pass decisions on the majority vote, was to be the principal legislative body, while the executive power was to be placed in the hands of a body called the Guardians of the Law (*Straż Praw*), consisting of the king, the primate, and five ministers. Responsibility of the members of the government to the Seym was adopted as a principle (for the first time in the political and legal history of the world). The Guardians of the Law took over supervision of all the offices and agencies through the intermediary of the major commissions (those for the army, fiscal affairs, the police, i.e. public administration, and national education). While the federal (Polish-Lithuanian) character of the state was preserved the dualism of offices, the fiscal affairs and the army was abolished. In the social structure the most important decision was the rejection of the principle that the state would not interfere with the situation of the peasants: Article 4 of the Constitution stated that 'the agrarian people... are granted the protection of the law and of the national government'. Settlers arriving in Poland were guaranteed personal freedom.

Work on the reform which yielded the Third of May Constitution was facilitated by a favourable international situation. Russia, as has been said, was engaged in a war with Turkey, and Russian successes alarmed Prussia and England which considered armed intervention. The partiotic party advocated accordingly the conclusion with Prussia of an alliance which that country offered to Poland: the alliance was in fact concluded on 29 March 1790, and the patriotic party expected it would strengthen Poland's position as a full-fledged member of the pro-Russian camp. But the patriots erred in disregarding the earlier established Prussian political ideology, which determined Prussia's attitude toward the Polish territories. If this ideology had been analyzed in greater detail, it would be clear that all Prussian declarations about the integrity of the Polish territory were insincere. The alliance soon became valueless because several months after its conclusion Prussia reached an agreement with Austria (the motive being the Austrian commitment to a war with revolutionary France), and in the next year Vorontsov, the Russian ambassador in London, succeeded in averting the military action against Russia which had been planned by William Pitt. This changed Poland's international position radically, and Prussia and Russia were to take revenge for Poland's non-observance of the principle of abstaining from political reforms.

Groups which were in favour of a second partition of Poland gained the upper hand in Russia, and the Empress Catherine II came to share their opinion after a long hesitation. Vorontsov said then that a new partition of Poland would bring 'nothing else than our eternal disgrace, and [become] a source of belated regrets. I would like to believe,' he said, 'that for the time being we do not think about that partition, but intrigue-prone Prussia knows perfectly well how to bring that about and to drag us in like blind people.'

And it did happen as he had predicted. As soon as the opposition of the magnates (led by Franciszek Ksawery Branicki, Szczęsny Potocki, and Wacław Rzewuski), intent on destroying the work done by the Four Year Seym, set up, in collusion with the Russian court, a confederation in Targowica (April 1792), thereby provoking a counter-revolutionary campaign on Russia's part, Prussia disclaimed all obligations resulting from the alliance. Together with Austria, it considered intervention in Poland, infected by the spirit of democracy and revolution, to be legitimate. Stanislaus Augustus, expecting an alliance with Russia and a possibility of reducing the scope of reactionary measures, joined the Targowica Confederation himself, afraid that in the case of a defeat he would be deposed from the throne and his plans would collapse utterly. He was followed in that step by other members of the government. The king did not believe that an armed struggle had any chance of success, but he underestimated the attitude of the masses, which were ready for war.

This war, waged in the defence of the new Constitution, showed the new qualities of the reorganized army, which fought bravely and won victories at Zieleńce and at Dubienka (where it was led by Thaddeus Kościuszko).

Prussia, engaged in a war with revolutionary France, clamoured for 'compensation' in Poland, while Austria, which expected it could acquire Bavaria, declared no intention to participate in the next partition of Poland. In the meantime, a new meeting of the Seym was being prepared, which was to approve changes and to agree to a new partition of the country. It was convened not in Warsaw, which was too radical in the attitude of its population, but in Grodno (1793), where new principles of the political system — a compromise between the traditional system and the achievements of the Four Year Seym — were worked out. Even though the deputies were specially selected for the purpose, several dozens of them protested openly, and the Seym ratified in silence the new partition treaties, that with Russia on 22 July 1793, and that with Prussia on 25 September of the same year. As Sievers, the Russian envoy, reported to the Empress Catherine, the partition treaty 'was passed by violence, to which I considered it necessary to resort'.

In the second partition of Poland Prussia took the provinces of Poznań, Gniezno, Kalisz, Sieradz, Łęczyca, Inowrocław, Brześć Kujawski, and Płock, the region of Dobrzyń, parts of the province of Rawa and Masovia, and the towns of Gdańsk and Toruń — in all 57,100 sq. km. with one million inhabitants. While these areas were being occupied by the Prussians, Great Poland and Gdańsk offered armed resistance. Russia took vast territories in Byelorussia, the Ukraine, and Lithuania, namely 250,000 sq. km. with three million people. They were the rest of Polotsk province, a small part of Vilna province, eastern parts of the provinces of Minsk, Volhynia, Brest Litovsk, and Nowogródek, the whole provinces of Kiev, Bratslav, and Podolia. The frontier ran from Druia to Pinsk to the Zbruch.

4. Economy and society. From economic regression to economic growth. Social conflicts

Work on political and social reforms was accompanied by processes which increased Poland's economic strength. The 18th century was marked in Poland, as in the whole of Europe, by increased economic activity. The population after the first partition reached some nine million, which gave Poland third place in Europe. Economic expansion was favoured by the gradually growing home market, although the general conditions were not conducive to the process. The devastations suffered during the Northern War were followed by those due to the Seven Years' War and the Bar Confederation (cf. section 2 above) and by the blow which the first partition meant to the country's economic life. It suffices to say that Prussia, after having imposed upon Poland the commercial treaty of 1775, received some five million zlotys from the tariffs paid by Polish merchants, which meant some 15 per cent of the fiscal revenues of Prussia, while Austria, having snatched the salt-mines in Little Poland, exported salt to Poland for some 12 million zlotys. For comparison note that the annual state expenditures at the time of the Four Year Seym amounted to some 30,000,000 zlotys. The partitioning powers availed themselves of the links between the territories they had acquired and the rest of Poland and tried to make their advantages as great as possible. For instance, Prussia, in view of the fact that Poland had to export its grain by sea, set up five tariff houses along the Vistula between the new (i.e. post-partition) Polish-Prussian frontier and Gdańsk. The Prussian authorities resorted to various chicaneries to hamper trade, which reduced the volume of trade and undermined the economic position of Gdańsk. This led to the increased importance of exports via Elbląg, Królewiec and Riga to the Baltic and also via Kherson on the Black Sea, where Prot Potocki, a magnate fascinated by economic activity, organized a special commercial company for the purpose.

In all, trade brought out the links among the various regions of Poland, including the territories lost as a result of the first partition, and also Silesia and to some extent Western Pomerania as well. For instance, commercial contacts especially between Great Poland and Szczecin were clearly intensifying.

It was also Great Poland which was developing most dynamically of all regions. This was borne out by a continued expansion of new settlements (cf. VII, 3); between 1750 and 1772 alone over 200 new villages with some 3,000 farmsteads were founded there. The process was even more vigorous in the case of free settlers (cf. VII, 3), who mainly paid a rent; some 40 per cent of them were German peasants, attracted by landowners. The upward business trend in agriculture was also linked to advances in early industrialization. As a contemporary author wrote, in Great Poland towns full of opulent manufacturers would instantly buy all products. These products were mainly textiles, primarily cloth (some two million metres of textiles annually, which was about 70 per cent of the whole output of textile products in Poland). Every eighth or tenth family had its basic, or major, source of earnings in the production of textiles, and nearly as many families were connected with the food industry.

Little Poland was, next to Great Poland, also an important centre of the textile industry. In the Subcarpathian region there were hundreds of villages, with the business centre situated in Andrychów, which were engaged in linen weaving. The then strongest centre of the metallurgical industry was in the vicinity of Kielce (the so-called Old Polish Industrial Basin) and in the western part of the Cracow-Częstochowa Upland. The Old Polish Industrial Basin had 70 per cent of all smelting furnaces in Poland (about the same amount as Silesia had at that time).

Crafts developed throughout the country as a result of the growth of the home market. They were ever invading the rural areas in the form of cottage industries, connected with a growing number of manufactories (338 of them recorded in the 18th century). Many new manufactories were set up by the magnates on their estates, treated by them as a manifestation of progressive economic activity. Their manufactories produced mainly luxury goods, such as ornamental belts, chinaware, faience goods, glass objects, weapons, coaches, etc. (the best known manufactories being at Urzecze, Naliboki, Korzec). Special mention is due in this connection to Antoni Tyzenhaus (1733—85), Court Treasurer of Lithuania, who administered the royal estates in Lithuania (in the vicinity of Grodno). Manufactories on the estates of the magnates, based on serf labour, were usually short lived, unlike those run by burghers, which, however, had to cope with many difficulties (shortage of man-power, due to the still surviving serfdom system).

Urbanization processes were observable even before the partitions. In addition to the growth of Warsaw, the number of whose inhabitants rose from some 20,000 in the mid-18th century to over 100,000 at the turn of that century, and other larger towns, such as Poznań, new towns were being founded; they were either completely new, or set up near already existing settlements.

In agricultural production the crops were still meagre: about three or four grains gathered per one grain sown. The three-field system, with one field lying fallow and two fields under grain crops, was the dominant method of land cultivation, but the concept of so-called new agriculture (the use of crops, such as clover, which improved the structure of the soil and facilitated animal breeding, and also the use of improved implements) was spreading under Western European influence. It was still rather a tendency toward change than change itself, but nevertheless the second half of the 18th century saw the appearance in Poland of over one hundred works on agriculture. Although the volume of agricultural production increased, the level of the late 16th century was not yet reached at the turn of the 18th century. Poland continued to be a country with a backward economic structure, due to the persevering system of demesnes based on corvée. That sphere of economic life was then not yet covered by progressive trends. It may be assumed, by way of estimate, that in the 18th century the rate of growth of the total production (agricultural and industrial) was about 0.3 to 0.4 per cent annually, which meant a growth from 30 to 40 per cent for the century. The average for Europe was at that time from 0.35 to 0.7 per cent annually.

Regulation of the monetary system was indispensable for the development of the national economy, the more so as much harm had been done by the flooding of Poland with false coins, which was a policy pursued by Frederick II. The Polish authorities even in the Saxon dynasty period tried to debase Polish coins, which, however, resulted in disturbances on the home market and caused dissatisfaction. Reforms of the tariff system were also tried but these were frustrated by opposition on the part of the neighbouring powers.

Stanislaus Augustus stood for honest money, following which the Polish florin in 1766 was second in its standard only to the Hungarian one. Sixty-eight florins were minted from the Köln mark of 233.8 grammes of gold, one florin being equal to 16.75 zlotys. One thaler was to amount to eight zlotys, 80 thalers being minted from a mark of silver. But Prussian coins continued to penetrate Poland, bringing about a loss of 6.7 grammes of silver on each thaler and Poland in all lost some 40 million zlotys. It was only in 1786 that one florin was made to equal 18 zlotys and the amount of silver in one thaler was reduced to 22.4 grammes. The mint started bringing profits, but the Polish standard was still too high as compared with the Prussian. It was adjusted only during the Kościuszko Uprising, when eight to 15 zlotys were minted from one mark of silver. Increased money circulation and the requirements of economic life contributed to the emergence of credit institutions. Burghers started setting up banks (e.g. Tepper in Warsaw). Banks at the Jewish consistories were developing, too, and ideas were advanced of establishing a large central bank (August Sułkowski).

Unification of measures and weights, abolition of private tariffs and tolls, and construction of roads and canals promoted the growth of the home market. The Ogiński Canal, connecting the Niemen with the Dneper, and the Royal Canal, linking the Pripyat with the Bug, were completed in 1784, and construction of a Bydgoszcz canal was planned, too.

Poland was among those countries in which more than 70 per cent of the population was engaged in agriculture. The demesne based on labour dues (those of serf peasants) was still the dominant form in the economic structure of the country, so that the peasants faced serious difficulties in developing their own farms. The rural population was strongly differentiated: owners of self-supporting farms (of at least seven hectares each), which marketed some of its production, formed

20 per cent of that population; small holders, who had to seek additional sources of income (for instance, by working on demesnes), accounted for 62 per cent; 16 per cent were landless people (who mostly lived on other people's farms), while two per cent had other occupations (e.g. inn-keepers). The development of the home market led to a stronger stratification of the rural population, which meant that the structure dictated by the laws of the market was imposed upon that determined by the requirements of the demesnes. This explains the fact that the number of landless people was the greatest in Great Poland (25 per cent), where the home market was developing most briskly. This observation is confirmed by data from other European countries. Stratification was thus accompanied by the pauperization of the peasants, which could be noticed earlier. The characteristic feature, which also facilitated transition from the traditional socio-economic structure to the new one, consisted in the increased role of rent, which on a growing scale was replacing labour dues. This took place in various ways: estate owners, either in order to increase their incomes or to act in accordance with the ideas of the time promoted by Paweł Brzostowski, Joachim Chreptowicz, and Stanisław Poniatowski, a nephew of the king, introduced reforms upon their own initiative; or the rent replaced some performances in kind; or man-power was hired against wages; or new farmers were settled on the rent-paying basis. The so-called paying off labour dues, i.e. making contributions in money to the demesne owner instead of working on his estate, was also quite frequent in both Great and Little Poland. This led to the necessity of using hired labour that would work on the demesnes, which in turn resulted in the concept of obligatory hired labour: the peasants had to work for certain minimum wages, fixed by the estate owner, such wages being only to some extent determined by the market.

Modernization of the relations between the demesne and the peasants was only one of the ways of increasing the incomes of the gentry. Another was to impose additional burdens upon the peasants: fixed targets per one day of corvée per person, obligatory transportation by the peasants of the products turned out on the demesne; also the duty was imposed upon the landless peasants to provide corvée, and the amount of labour to be contributed by one person during one year was increased.

All this had the accompanying phenomena in the age-old forms of class struggle waged by the peasants, such as desertion, sabotage, refusal to contribute corvée. The now more common form was that of writing petitions addressed to the landowners (with complaints against administrators and tenants of the estates) and to public opinion (as was the case of the Torczyn petition of 1768). At the same time resistance was stronger and often led to open conflicts. For instance, re-introduction by Tyzenhaus of labour dues on the royal estates in lieu of the rent paid by the peasants there for nearly a century led in 1769 to a large-scale rebellion that had its centre at Szawle in Lithuania. The anti-feudal peasant rebellion, called Kolishchyzna and ultimately drowned in blood, was the largest of all; it broke out in 1768 in the region of Humań and Śmita and, led by Ivan Gonta and Maxim Zhelezniak, covered the regions from Balta in the south to Charnobyl in the north, and from Cherkasi, Chehryn, and Pereyaslav in the east to Vinnitsa and Zhitomir in the west. Cossacks from the private police forces held by the magnates, and rebel Ukrainian peasants (called haydamaks) carried the idea of Cossack freedom to the Ukraine on the right bank of the Dneper. Peasant uprisings also took place in ethnically Polish territories (e.g. in the Kurpie region in Masovia, where the peasants rose in defence of King Stanislaus Leszczyński), but these were not so violent. It is also to be noted that the right of the demesne lords to sentence peasants to capital punishment was abolished in 1768.

The economic development which took place at that time brought about a certain strengthening of the middle gentry and stopped concentration of land ownership, but these processes did not result in any major changes in the class structure of the gentry. The same applied to the burghers, who were still, especially in smaller towns, dependent upon the landowners. But the early bourgeoisie emerged from among the rich burghers; it included large-scale merchants, bankers, owners of manufactories and large craftsmen's workshops.

The reign of King Stanislaus Augustus also saw the emergence, still in a nuclear form, of the group of professionals (the future Polish intelligentsia), who came mainly from the gentry and educated burghers. The needs of the state administration determined the formation of the group of (professional) officials, while the development of the towns and of the national economy in general led to the rise of professional technologists, such as architects and land surveyors. That group as a whole also included, of course, writers, journalists, scholars and scientists, teachers, artists, physicians, lawyers, and to some extent army officers.

5. Changes in social consciousness. Culture and society

Despite the survival of its old social structure Poland under Stanislaus Augustus was one of the most active centres of the Age of Reason in Europe. The most important phenomenon was certainly that of the gradual disappearance of the traditions of Sarmatianism, vigorously attacked by progressive-minded people as early as during the rule of the Saxon dynasty. The external manifestations of Sarmatianism (e.g. the traditional gentry costume) were with increasing frequency treated as a demonstration of patriotism, but also of conservative views on social issues. The previously uniform pattern of attitudes of the magnates also collapsed at that time. Some magnates (cf. section 1 above) tried to adjust the ideas of the Age of Reason to their own interests under the local conditions. The simplest thing, which did not involve a change in the social system, was to promote education and modernization of schools, to advance science, and to propagate certain modification in the economic sphere. The aristocratic culture in the Age of Reason also included such elements as liberal views in the matter of morals and manners, on the attitude toward the Church, etc. Together with changes in the attitudes of some gentry this was a manifestation of that trend in social consciousness which strove to undermine the traditional thinking in feudal terms. Plebeian consciousness, still in a rudimentary form, emerged too; it was increasingly revolutionary-minded, which became clear later during the Kościuszko Uprising (cf. section 6 below). But, unlike France, Poland did not see the development of a political and social anti-absolutist liberal trend within the aristocracy and the gentry, for the conditions necessary for that process (such as royal tyranny) did not exist in Poland; hence there was no contact between the progressive trends, one represented by the élite and the other by the masses, which would bring about formation of revolutionary consciousness, indispensable for revolutionary action. This was even more obvious in Russia, where the plebeian trend, most strongly manifested in the peasant rebellion led by Pugachov (1773—75), followed its own course.

A low level of urbanization prevented burgher culture from developing vigorously, even though urban life began to be valued more than it had been before. This was due to increased social mobility, although crossing the barrier separating one status group (estate, *Ständ*) from another was far from easy, despite the opinions voiced about the harmfulness of prejudices based on status group membership. A strong influence conducive to changes in the treatment of barriers between status groups was exerted by the famous political club initiated by Hugo Kołłątaj (and traditionally called 'Kołłątaj's Forge' (Kuźnica) in Polish historiography). His group propagated anti-feudal attitudes, tending also to remove, or at least to lower, the barriers between status groups. An outstanding representative of the club, Franciszek Salezy Jezierski (1740—91) wrote: 'In my opinion, the common people should be called the first estate of the nation, or, to put it more plainly, the nation itself.' Such opinions, however, were isolated, and Jezierski himself was not quite consistent on that point.

In the rural areas, the growing share of relations based on the payment of rent and the increasing role of new, personally free, settlers, brought about what might be termed the contract approach, as different from the feudal approach, based on the idea that the gentry had used to impose their own terms upon the peasants (extra-economic co-ercion).

The schools played a considerable role in shaping new social consciousness. The number of Jesuit colleges increased from 58 in 1700 to 104 in 1773, and at the same time — to some extent under the impact of the Jesuits who came from France when the Jesuit colleges were closed down there in 1762 — the schooling became less traditional and less theologically oriented.

In 1740, Stanisław Konarski founded the famous Collegium Nobilium (College of Nobles), with a relatively modern curriculum, and initiated a reform of the schools run by the Piarists. The establishment in 1765 of the Knights' School (a military academy), headed by Adam Czartoryski and August Sułkowski under the supervision of the king, was a further step in the evolution of the school system that paved the way for the great reform connected with the setting up of the Commission for National Education. Sułkowski also founded a school for cadets in his estate at Rydzyna in Great Poland.

Before the first partition of Poland the number of pupils in secondary schools amounted to some 30,000 to 35,000, which meant a triple increase as compared with the early 18th century (similar proportions, in relation to the population, were observed in France). Some 80 secondary and some 1,500 elementary schools functioned at the time of the Four Year Seym.

The Commission for National Education, established in 1773 (cf. section 3 above) combined in its work the ideas of laicization with those of the democratization of the school system; it also stressed linking school education to the requirements of life (which meant putting an end to the Latin-based system of training). A more important role was assigned in the curricula to natural history, the history and geography of Poland, the Polish language, and civic education ('moral teachings'). The school system came to be treated as a public issue and also as a necessary factor in the shaping of the nation. This was forcefully formulated by Father Grzegorz Piramowicz (1735—1801), Secretary of the Commission, in his work *Uwagi o nowym instrukcji publicznej układzie* (Comments on a New System of Public Education; 1776). The active members of the Commission, which was expanding numerically, included its first president Igancy Massalski, Bishop of Vilna; Michał Poniatowski, brother of the king and later the primate of Poland; Ignacy Potocki; August Sułkowski; Joachim Chreptowicz; Adam Czartoryski; Andrzej Zamoyski; Antoni Poniński; Julian Ursyn Niemcewicz; Feliks Oraczewski; Hieronim Stroynowski; and members of the Radziwiłł, Małachowski, and Mniszech families, educated and enlightened people, often pursuing their own scholarly and scientific interests, members of the various foreign academies and learned societies. At that time people were entering active social and political life at a very young age: Kołłątaj was 23 when he started working on the Commission, Piramowicz was 38, and Potocki was 26. That 'magnificent team', as it has been called by Ambroise Jobert, a French scholar concerned with the history of that Commission, worked smoothly, without letting differences of opinion on other issues to be reflected in the functioning of the Commission. The Commission supervised 74 secondary schools and was also in charge of the training of teachers and preparation of handbooks (this through its auxiliary body, the Society for Elementary Books, i.e., primers and school textbooks, which included many eminent scholars as its members). The Commission brought about a reform of the Jagiellonian University in Cracow (then called the Cracow Academy) and the University of Vilna (the Vilna Academy) by working through its plenipotentiaries, namely Hugo Kołłątaj and Marcin Poczobutt, respectively; these two universities were named by the Commission the Central School of the Crown and the Central School of Lithuania, respectively. The reform was important in particular for Vilna University.

Without the work of former pupils of the schools supervised by the Commission neither the reforms carried out by the Four Year Seym nor, later (cf. IX), the activity of the Legions and efficient administration at the time of the Duchy of Warsaw would have been possible. The year 1785 also saw the establishment in Warsaw of the School of Medicine and Surgery, and later two other schools of a similar kind.

Plans were also made for the setting up of an Academy of Sciences (Domenico Merlini even made a project for its building) and an Academy of Fine Arts, but — in face of many other problems — those plans failed to materialize.

Poland actively participated in the general advances of natural history and the humanities in the Age of Reason. These achievements become even more pronounced if we compare them with the intellectual atmosphere under the Saxon dynasty, and also in later times: speculative philosophy, criticism of the work of the most eminent philosophers, such as Descartes, Gassendi, Leibniz, and Newton, in which the Jesuit colleges and the Cracow Academy excelled, religious zealotism, worship of the supernatural, etc. As early as the first half of the 18th century the scholarly milieu in Gdańsk and Toruń differed in that respect from the rest of the country. The Naturforschende Gesellschaft (Society for Natural Science), which grouped renowned European scientists, was founded in Gdańsk in 1742; it enjoyed the protection of the Polish king, and was closed down only under the Nazi regime. The period 1722—55 saw the appearance of the ten volumes of *Geschichte der Preussischen Lände* (A History of Prussian Territories), written by Gottfried Lengnich. The aforementioned learned society in Gdańsk contributed signally to the development of physics, chemistry, and medicine, even though only zoological research was of European standard. There were strong scholarly milieux in Wrocław and in some smaller towns; these included Leszno in Great Poland, greatly interested in the attainments of German science, which also saw the publication in 1749 of a Polish translation of *Der Hausarzt,* a book of 700 pages by Samuel Beimler. The year 1750 saw the appearance of volume I of the medical periodical *Primitiae Physico-medicae*; the next two volumes were published in Sulechów, and the initiative was due to E. J. Meifeld, the court physician of Augustus III and Stanislaus Augustus, B. E. Hermann, district physician in Bojanów, and Laurentius Mitzler de Kolof (1711—78), who arrived in Poland from Leipzig and became the editor and publisher of the first scholarly periodicals in Poland, which included *Acta Litteraria* (1755—56), *Nowe Wiadomości Ekonomiczne i Uczone* (Economic and Learned News; 1758—61), *Patriota Polski* (The Polish Patriot; 1761), and *Monitor* (1765—85) — founded upon the initiative of Stanislaus Augustus — which rendered great services in combatting Sarmatianism. *Monitor* can be treated as the principal Polish periodical concerned with social and political issues in the Age of Reason.

In 1752 Franciszek Bohomolec, later one of the editors of *Monitor* (the first was Ignacy Krasicki, the famous author), when watching advances in science could legitimately write that 'We... can cherish the strong hope that our country will soon be not only in a position to equal other nations in scientific pursuits, but will even come ahead of them.' In 1760—63 Józef Aleksander Jabłonowski started his endeavours to have the works of Nicolaus Copernicus struck from the *Index Librorum Prohibitorum*. As in European historiography in general, a critical school of historiography was developing in Poland which stressed collection and publication of the sources. Publications included the collection of all the decrees of the Seym (*Volumina Legum*), the works of Adam Naruszewicz (1733—99), those of Tadeusz Czacki (1765—1813), and those of Feliks Łoyko, who polemicized with the various Prussian historical justifications of the first partition of Poland. There were also studies in mathematics and astronomy (Michał Hube, 1737—1807; Jan Śniadecki, 1756—1830; and Marcin Poczobutt, 1728—1810), chemistry (Jan Jaśkiewicz, 1749—1809; Franciszek Scheidt, 1759—1807), botany and zoology (Krzysztof Kluk, 1739—96), and medicine (Rafał Czerniakowski, 1743—1810, founder of the school of medicine in the Cracow Academy). The reforms were conducive to the development of political writing (Hugo Kołłątaj, 1750—1812; Stanisław Staszic, 1755—1826) and jurisprudence (Teodor Ostrowski, 1750—1802; and Wincenty Skrzetuski, 1745—91). Hugo Kołłątaj was one of the most eminent minds in Poland at the turn of the 18th and 19th centuries. His anonymously published letters to the Speaker of the Seym, *Do Stanisława Małachowskiego... Anonima listów kilka* (A Few Letters to Stanisław Małachowski by an Anonymous Author; 1788—89), completed with *Prawo polityczne narodu polskiego* (The Constitutional Law of the Polish Nation; 1790) defined the programme of a 'mild revolution', based on a compromise between the gentry and the nascent bourgeoisie. Next to Stanislaus Augustus he may be considered the second principal promoter of that reform. A similar role must be accorded to Stanisław Staszic, the son of a Mayor of Piła, author of *Uwagi nad życiem Jana Zamoyskiego* (Comments on the Life of Jan Zamoyski; 1787) and *Przestrogi dla Polski* (Admonitions for Poland; 1790). It is to be noted in this connection that Polish political and economic thought developed in contacts with ideas advanced at that time in Italy and France. Already some participants in the Bar Confederation (M. Wielhorski and I. Massalski) established contacts with Mably and Rousseau.

In the Age of Reason, political writings, and historiography as well, had much in common with *belles lettres*. Adam Naruszewicz was both a poet and a historian, while Stanisław Trembecki (ca. 1739—1812) and Ignacy Krasicki (1735—1801) in their poetry gave expression to rationalist and liberal ideas. Trembecki commented on the ideas advanced by the king, while Krasicki criticized social vice, myths, obscurantism, and bigotry. In his *Mikołaja Doświadczyńskiego przypadki* (The Adventures of Mikołaj Doświadczyński; 1776) he outlined an Utopian vision of society, drew attention to the national tradition and stigmatized an uncritical adoption of foreign ways.

Polite literature, next to its rationalist trend, had a sentimentalist trend as well, represented by the poets Franciszek Dionizy Kniaźnin (1750—1807) and Franciszek Karpiński (1741—1825). Revolutionary elements were found in the works of Jakub Jasiński (1759—94). The leading names in playwrighting were those of Franciszek Bohomolec, Franciszek Zabłocki, Julian Ursyn Niemcewicz (1758—1841), Wojciech Bogusławski (1757—1821), and Adam Kazimierz Czartoryski. The role of the theatre increased in Poland at that time, as it did in many other European countries, because the theatre was treated as the nationwide school of social teachings, and at the same time the audiences grew in numbers. Teatr Narodowy (the National Theatre) was founded in Warsaw in 1765 as the first permanent and professional theatre in Poland, and under the reign of Stanislaus Augustus some twenty buildings were adapted to serve as public theatres.

The king used to give his famous Thursday dinner parties, to which eminent thinkers, authors and artists were invited. Music was developing, too, and the desire for musical education was manifested in the setting up of numerous schools of music. Music was then being permeated by national elements, much inspiration also being drawn from folklore. The opera was the most representative form of music in that period. First Polish operas appeared simultaneously at the royal court in Warsaw and in the residences of musically talented magnates, the Radziwiłłs in Nieśwież and the Ogińskis in Słonim. The theatre in Słonim was founded by Michał Kazimierz Ogiński, Grand Hetman of Lithuania (1728—1800), an amateur poet and musician. In 1771 he staged his own opera *Filozof odmieniony* (The Philosopher Reformed); seven years later Warsaw saw the first night of the opera *Nędza uszczęśliwiona* (Poverty Made Happy) by Maciej Kamieński, based on a comedy by Bohomolec. Adam Kazimierz Czartoryski founded a theatre on the family estate in Puławy, and employed in this connection Wincenty Lessel (1750—ca. 1825), of Bohemian origin, composer of many operas and other works. Poland at the time in general attracted many prominent artists. The most popular opera of that period, frequently staged to this day, was *Krakowiacy i Górale* (Cracovians and Highlanders), composed by Jan Stefani to the libretto by Wojciech Bogusławski. Its first night (1 March 1794) had lively political repercussions.

Symphonic music was played and composed in the residences of the magnates and in major towns, the principal names in this connection being those of Jan Wański (1762—1840), Wojciech Dankowski (b. ca. 1760), and Feliks Janiewicz (1762—1848).

The visual arts under the reigns of Augustus III and Stanislaus Augustus saw, next to the still cultivated Baroque style, the appearance of quieter forms, even though in the transition period these did not abstain from the embellishments typical of the Rococo. In course of time, all the arts assumed Polish national features, regardless of the style in vogue. In painting this can be seen in the works of Marcello Bacciarelli (1731—1818), Jan Piotr Norblin (1748—1830), Franciszek Smuglewicz (1745—1807), and Aleksander Orłowski (1777—1832). Applied art national in character also made itself manifest (ornamental belts, glassware, furniture), and was now accessible to somewhat broader circles of buyers than it had been earlier.

In the sphere of architecture, construction of palaces and churches was the dominant feature of the period. Special mention is due in this connection to the extension of the Royal Castle in Warsaw (1747—63), in which such renowned architects as Jakub Fontana and Efraim Szreger were engaged, extension of palaces in Białystok, Puławy, and Kock, extension of Ossoliński Palace and Brühl Palace (Heinrich von Brühl (1700—63), was the all-powerful minister of Augustus III), construction of palaces in Krystynopol (1756—61), Radzyń Podlaski (1758—60), Opole Lubelskie (1766—72), Szczekociny (completed in 1777), and also of Karaś Palace in Warsaw (1764—72). A fairly dense network of palaces came into being in Great Poland, which, while inhabited mainly by middle gentry, had a high level of income due to its advanced economy (cf. section 4 above). Palaces there were already classicist in style; this applies, for instance, to the palace of Poznań Bishops in Ciążeń (1760—68), Józef Mycielski's palace in Pępów (after 1760), that of Kazimierz Raczyński in Rogalin (after 1768), that of Maksymilian Mielżyński in Pawłowice (after 1776), and that of Jan Lipski in Czerniejewo (ca. 1771—75). The 1780's saw the reconstruction, under the supervision of Ignacy Graff, of the famous castle in Rydzyna, held by the Sułkowskis (previously by the Leszczyńskis), one of the finest in Europe.

The palace of Kujawy Bishops in Wolborz (1768—73) and the royal summer palace, called Łazienki (The Baths), in Warsaw (after 1775), with statues sculptured by Andreas Le Brun (1737—1811) were erected in the same period.

Church building was even more intensive; the churches were at first in the Baroque and the Rococo style, and later in the Classicist style (often with elements of the Polish Baroque). Special mention is due here to the Dominican church in Warsaw (1760—71), the church of Regular Canons in Trzemeszno (1782—91), the Bernardine church in Koło (1773—81), the parish church in Podhorce (1752—60), and St. Anne's church (1786—88) and the Protestant church (1777—79), both in Warsaw. Urban housing and construction of public buildings expanded, too. In Warsaw, the large merchant house of Rezler and Hurtig (1784), the banking house of Tepper (1784), and the Hotel at the White Eagle were new elements of the townscape. The typical feature now was placing the palaces of the magnates in the front line of the street or the side of the market place (instead of localizing them as buildings standing separately), as was the case of Działyński Palace in Poznań (1773—87).

6. The Kościuszko Insurrection. The third partition of Poland

The Kościuszko Insurrection (1794) was one of the major turning points in the history of the Polish people and the Polish state. It opened the period of national uprisings and struggle for independence in Polish history. The Kościuszko Insurrection was a direct reaction to the rule by members of the Targowica Confederation and a manifestation of the growing resentment of foreign oppression. The preparations were made in May 1793, that is even before the Grodno session of the Seym (cf. section 3 above), but even earlier, in February 1793, the masses in Warsaw prevented the arsenal from being seized by tsarist troops. The conspiracy was initiated by Ignacy Działyński (1754—97) and Andreas Kapostas, an ennobled banker of Hungarian extraction, who settled in Warsaw ca. 1780. This co-operation between a member of the gentry and a *de facto* burgher sheds light upon the process of a nascent alliance between the gentry and the burghers, which marked a new factor in the social condition in the country. Particularly active were those young Polish officers who under the rule of the founders of the Targowica Confederation had been deprived of their higher ranks obtained during the war of 1792 and of the Virtuti Militari orders awarded to them at that time.

The insurrection was triggered by the demonstration of a cavalry detachment of 1,200 men, led by Antoni Józef Madaliński, who marched in the direction of Cracow to protest against the reduction of the Polish army, which Yosif Igelström, the Russian ambassador in Warsaw, forced through with the Permanent Council, restored after the second partition. Then events followed one another in a rapid succession. In accordance with the plans of the conspirators, Tadeusz Kościuszko (1746—1817), an eminent military commander and expert in military engineering, was appointed the commander of the insurrection, which was formally proclaimed in Cracow on 24 March 1794. Kościuszko was already known in Europe and in America, where he fought for the independence of the United States (as the chief engineer of the Northern Army from 1777 and of the Southern Army from 1780).

Kościuszko, a friend of Thomas Jefferson, one of the most democratic among the then American leaders, was one of three foreigners who were members of the Society of the Cincinnati (1783), which grouped those who had rendered the greatest services in the War of Independence. In 1789, he became general in the Polish army, expanded following a decision of the Four Year Seym, and in 1792, as second only to Prince Józef Poniatowski, was awarded the Virtuti Militari order. When the members of the Targowica Confederation seized power he emigrated to France, where he was granted honorary citizenship. Immediately before the outbreak of the uprising — after having met representatives of its organizers in Leipzig — he clandestinely arrived in Cracow, where he helped prepare the insurrection. His eight years' stay in America during the War of Independence added immensely to his military experience, in particular in the sphere of organization of a national war with the participation of society at large, and developed his republican and democratic attitude. The Act of Insurrection of Citizens, Inhabitants of the Province of Cracow, of 24 March 1794, transferred to Poland the ideas of the American Revolution by pointing to the strength inherent in the masses struggling for freedom and independence.

On his way from Cracow to Warsaw Kościuszko defeated the Russian troops led by General Tormasov, which were in the pursuit of Madaliński's detachment. The battle, which took place at Racławice on 4 April 1794, is marked for the engagement in it of peasant troops, armed with scythes specially adapted for that purpose, led by Kościuszko himself and very skilfully used by him in the battle.

In the meantime, in Warsaw, where Tomasz Maruszewski was active as Kościuszko's emissary, the insurgents — among whom the decisive role was played by the people of Warsaw, led by Jan Kiliński, a shoemaker by vocation — succeeded in driving out Igelström's regiment on 17 and 18 April 1794. Ignacy Wyssogota Zakrzewski, appointed Mayor of Warsaw by the king, joined the Cracow Uprising and ordered the elections of a Provisional Substitutive Council. The uprising was spreading rapidly, and on 22 and 23 April Colonel Jakub Jasiński, who headed a group of radically-oriented conspirators, got hold of Vilna after having disarmed the local Russian garrison.

The masses were rapidly turning radical in their attitude; this applied both to the towns (especially Warsaw) and to the rural areas. An important role in that process was played by the so-called Polish Jacobins (also termed Hugonists), who mostly came from the group formerly connected with Kołłątaj's Kuźnica (J. Jasiński, T. Maruszewski, A. Orchoński, J. Zajączek, Father J. Mejer, F. Jelski, J. Dembowski). They advanced a programme of full rights for the burghers, abolition of serfdom and corvée, adoption of the republican system of government, and brotherhood of nations (this was addressed to the Russians and the Germans). The political club they formed on 24 April 1794, was termed by them the Association of Citizens Who Offer Assistance and Services to National Magistratures for the Good of the Country. In order to exert pressure upon the not very radical Provisional Substitutive Council they organized a demonstration of the Warsaw populace (9 May 1794) who demanded the punishment of the traitors who set up the Targowica Confederation. In view of these demands the Council extended the prerogatives of the criminal court, who sentenced Hetmans Ożarowski and Zabiełło, Ankwicz, Speaker of the Permanent Council, and Bishop Kossakowski to death. At the same time Hetman Szymon Kossakowski was hanged in Vilna. The Provisional Substitutive Council was replaced by the Supreme National Council, dominated by representatives of moderate opinions. But the Jacobins remained active, and the new plebeian demonstrations (28 June) became even more radical. Members of the Targowica Confederation were being dragged from prisons by force and hanged without trial.

Kościuszko, who was already in Warsaw, sharply opposed those acts of terror, and in his intention of keeping the unity of the nation in the struggle for independence he opposed an excessive radicalization of the uprising. During his march to Warsaw, in his camp at Połaniec he published (7 May) a proclamation, resentfully received by the gentry, which granted personal liberty to the peasants, reduced the legal amount of corvée, and adopted the principle that peasants could not be expelled from the land they tilled.

Invasion by the Prussian army made the military situation of the insurgents much worse. Unable to equal the combined Prussian and Russian forces Kościuszko was defeated at Szczekociny (6 June). This was followed by the defeat at Chełm three days later, and the capitulation of Cracow on 15 June 1794. In July the Russians and the Prussians began to besiege Warsaw, and its defence by Kościuszko, which required a great talent in the sphere of military engineering, can be treated as the greatest military success of the insurrection.

The spontaneous uprising which broke out in Great Poland (20 to 30 August) forced the Prussian troops to retreat from Warsaw. To support it Kościuszko sent there in September Jan Henryk Dąbrowski, a capable and experienced commander, who stormed Bydgoszcz on 2 October and managed to disorganize Prussian administration in Great Poland, Silesia and Pomerania. But the uprising was nevertheless declining. Prussia withdrew from the coalition against revolutionary France to be in a better position to attack the insurgents, and Russia sent Alexander Suvorov, its eminent commander, to lead the troops engaged in suppressing the insurrection. Dąbrowski had to retreat from Great Poland. Kościuszko was defeated in the battle of Maciejowice (10 October 1794) and, wounded, was taken prisoner by the Russians. Tomasz Wawrzecki became the new leader of the uprising, and the Jacobins set up a new political club (the Association for the Preservation of the Revolution and of the Act of Cracow) and proclaimed the idea of a radical appeal to the populace in the defence of the uprising. But by that time the insurrection was without a chance. Suvorov stormed Praga, the right-bank part of Warsaw, on 4 November 1794, where many civilians lost their lives (the massacre in Praga). Left-bank Warsaw also fell soon after that.

The opponents of the uprising wanted to revert to the ideas advanced by the Targowica Confederation and at the meeting of the Seym in Grodno, but the Empress Catherine II was determined to eliminate 'the focus of the Jacobin infection on the Vistula'. An agreement between Austria, Prussia, and Russia resulted in the third partition of Poland (1795). The frontier between the territories seized by the partitioning powers went along the Bug, the Vistula, and the middle course of the Pilica. Warsaw fell to the Prussians, and Cracow to the Austrians. Poland ceased to exist as an independent state.

The election of Stanislaus Augustus Poniatowski as shown in an 18th century painting by Bernardo Belotto called Canaletto

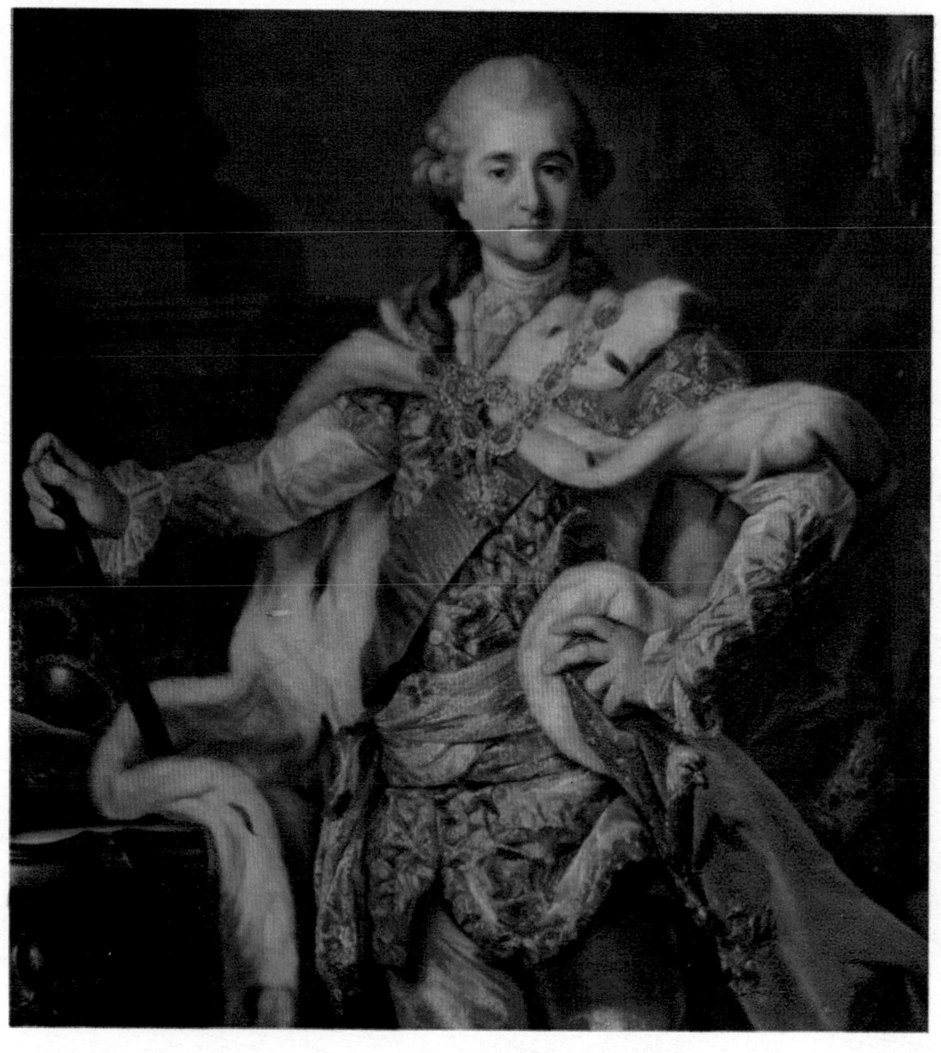

Stanislaus Augustus Poniatowski, the last king of Poland (reigned 1764–95), portrayed in his coronation robes by Marcello Bacciarelli

The classical Water Palace in Łazienki Park in Warsaw, rebuilt for King Stanislaus Augustus by Domenico Merlini in the 18th century

The Grand Theatre in Warsaw, built by Antonio Corazzi in 1826–33 (after an engraving by Friedrich Christopher Dietrich)

Wojciech Bogusławski (1757–1829), called the father of the Polish theatre (engraved by James Hopwood after a drawing by Antoni Brodowski)

The adoption of the Constitution on 3 May 1791 (engraved by Józef Łęski after a drawing by Jan Piotr Norblin)

Hugo Kołłątaj (1750–1812), philosopher, author, politician and ideologist in the Age of Reason in Poland, member of the Committee on National Education, co-author of the 1791 Constitution (painted by Józef Peszka)

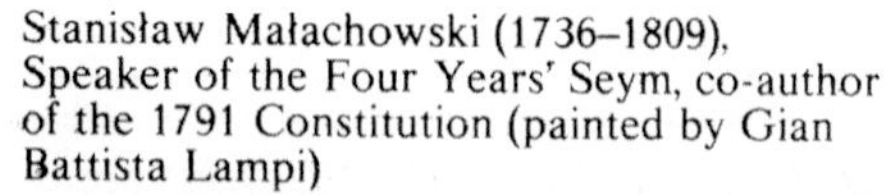

Stanisław Małachowski (1736–1809), Speaker of the Four Years' Seym, co-author of the 1791 Constitution (painted by Gian Battista Lampi)

Staszic House in Warsaw, built by Antonio Corazzi in 1821 to serve as the seat of the Society of Friends of Science

Stanisław Staszic (1755–1826), scientist and philosopher, political writer, advocate of social reforms at the time of the Four Years' Seym (engraved by Józef Cholewiński after a painting of an unknown artist)

Ignacy Krasicki (1735–1801), Bishop of Warmia, the most eminent Polish author in the Age of Reason (a lithograph by Chodkiewicz after a drawing by Walenty Śliwicki)

The Castle Square in Warsaw as seen from Krakowskie Przedmieście Street (painted by Jan Seydlitz)

Chapter IX

The Beginning of Foreign Rule. Napoleon I and Poland. The Duchy of Warsaw (1795—1815)

1. The attitude of the partitioning powers toward the Polish territories and the Polish nation

The annexation by Prussia, Austria, and Russia of the Polish territories removed the Polish state from the world map. The various parts of the country found themselves within alien states and became objects of different economic, social, and cultural policy. The state factor thus came to play a negative role in the formation of the Polish nation: it split the so far uniform territory into several parts, ruled out the conditions that were conducive to the emergence of a single and uniform market and to integrated economic development. There was another factor which came to the fore in the historical development of Poland, namely the all-national struggle for the regaining of independence that united all the Poles, irrespective of the partition zone they lived in although changes in social structure were accompanied by increasing differences of opinion as to the methods of that struggle and the principles on which a future free state would be organized. These differences were already observable during the Kościuszko Insurrection, which advanced the watchwords of Freedom, Equality and Independence. The principle of equality (which could be interpreted in various ways, as it was advanced by both Kościuszko and the Polish Jacobins) could not be put into effect in view of the still surviving feudal structure of Polish society.

But the partitioning powers began to organize Polish territories in 1772, and they strove to do so in accordance with their assumptions, which included the belief that the partition was a durable phenomenon. This was accompanied by two interconnected processes: the emergence in international politics of the so-called Polish issue, and the incessant struggle of the Poles for their political liberation. As early as 1792 Ignacy Potocki claimed that 'the revolutionary movement does not stop in Poland, and the Poles are merely waiting for a suitable occasion to cast off the yoke that has been imposed upon them'. The realities of Polish life were thus the resultant of the strivings of the partitioning powers, which on the whole acted in co-operation with one another, the changing events in the internatioanl arena, and the actions undertaken by the Poles themselves. In the period to be discussed now international politics first of all reflected the steps taken by Napoleon in his desire to change the map of Europe.

The territories seized as a result of the first partition found themselves within absolutist monarchies with a well developed bureaucracy and an advanced fiscal system, which was particularly resented by a gentry which traditionally opposed all state interference. The whole population, except for the gentry, was subject to compulsory military service. In the Prussian-occupied territories the gentry were deprived of their offices in the local administration and barred from military careers. The taxes were raised and endeavours were made to win over the aristocracy.

Gdańsk Pomerania, seized by Prussia, was re-named Western Pomerania, while Warmia was included in the former Ducal Prussia, now re-named Eastern Prussia, and the annexed northern part of Great Poland was now officially called the Noteć Region. A new division into administrative, fiscal, and court districts was introduced. German became the official language. The landed estates held by the Church were confiscated.

The region seized by Austria as a result of the first partition was re-named the Kingdom of Galicia and Lodomeria, with the Duchies of Zator and Oświęcim. The gentry, divided into two strata, the upper and the lower, were deprived of the right to make decisions concerning the peasants. The latter in turn, being needed as recruits in the army, were guaranteed irremovability from their farms, the upper limit of labour dues was fixed, and state officials were delegated to the estates of the gentry. Monasteries, which numbered ca. 150, were closed. The territory was divided into 18 districts (1782).

In the territories seized by Russia the Roman Catholic Church organization was subordinated to a special bishopric in St. Petersburg, the point being to separate the local Roman Catholics from contacts with Poland through Church institutions. Two provinces (Mohylev and Polotsk, the latter later moved to Vitebsk) were formed with districts as their territorial subdivisions.

The territories seized by Prussia in 1793 were officially termed Southern Prussia and divided anew into administrative and court districts. The principal measure consisted in establishing in Poznań a special agency, called the *Kammer* (Chamber), which was the main administrative authority for that region. Posts in public administration and the administration of justice went to people brought in from Germany, and the newly occupied areas were covered by the measures, started after the first partition, intended to bring in German settlers. The clergy this time were not deprived of their estates, but these were charged with a tax which amounted to 50 per cent of the income. Local government in towns was restricted through the appointment of mayors and clerks who functioned as paid officials. The process of putting all these measures into effect was interrupted by the Kościuszko Insurrection.

In the areas annexed by Russia the principles adopted in connection with the previous partitions were applied. Two new provinces, those of Izaslav and Bratslav, were organized.

After the third partition, Prussia was enlarged by so-called New Eastern Prussia, which formed a separate province together with Western Prussia and Southern Prussia. They were recognized as sovereign territories of the kings of Prussia, not included in the German Reich. Southern Prussia was divided into the departments of Poznań, Kalisz, and Warsaw (the latter also being the capital of the province), while New Eastern Prussia was organized in two departments, Płock and Białystok.

The areas annexed by Austria in 1795 were termed New (or Western) Galicia; in 1803 they were combined with those annexed previously into a single province (and a single administrative region), subdivided into districts; the administrative authorities of the province had their seat in Lvov.

The territories annexed by Russia in 1795 were divided into the provinces of

Vilna, Kowno and Grodno. A new administrative and judicial system was introduced on all these territories.

The partitioning powers were keen to obliterate Poland from the memory of European public opinion, and hence nowhere did they refer to Poland as it existed before partition. After the third partition they made it a point to punish the insurgents by resorting to such measures as confiscation of estates, imprisonment, exile (to the eastern parts of the Empire in the case of Russia), assignment of compulsory place of residence. The rights of the gentry in public life were considerably limited and completely abolished in the case of Prussia. By selling the former royal estates and those confiscated from the former insurgents the Prussian and Austrian authorities started creating in the Polish ethnic territories large estates owned by non-Poles (in practice Germans). Military service was accessible to the gentry, but on the condition of a fixed minimum of property owned and of the knowledge of the German language. In the territories annexed by Russia the Polish language continued to be used in public life.

The economic position of the peasants underwent no major changes, but in conformity with the principles valid in absolutist monarchies their legal status in the areas annexed by Prussia and Austria was improved. This did not apply to the towns and the burghers: on the contrary, the administrative system in force in the partitioning powers was imposed upon the towns. The breaking of the unity of the Polish territories had an adverse effect upon their economic situation, for in addition to all other changes very high taxes were imposed. The rights of the Jewish population were restricted in the areas annexed by Prussia and Austria, military garrisons were assigned to towns where the settling of ethnically German population was encouraged.

The situation of the schools deteriorated, and the number of the schools and the teachers diminished, except for the Russian-occupied part of the country: there the Vilna Academy was transformed into Vilna University, with the secondary schools subordinated to it, and Adam Czartoryski was appointed curator of the school district.

In Warsaw, at that time occupied by the Prussians, endeavours were made to promote cultural and scientific life, including collection (e.g. the Czartoryskis in Puławy) of objects connected with the nation's history. The Warsaw Society of Friends of Science was founded in 1800 (cf. section 2 below).

2. Endeavours to regain independence. The Polish Legions

Conspiracies with a view to restoring a *de facto* independent Poland began even before the final partition of the country in 1795, namely during the rule of the Targowica Confederation, and they resulted in the outbreak of the Kościuszko Insurrection. For eight months the country was engaged in the uprising, troops were formed, arms were produced, food supplies were organized, and the appropriate financial policy was pursued. Altogether some 300,000 people were directly involved in military operations.

When the uprising collapsed, activities concerned with restoring the independence of Poland were conducted in various forms, which covered consolidation of the economic foundations of the country, promotion of intellectual pursuits, political conspiracies both in Poland and abroad, often intensifying after the failure of other forms of actions, and official formation of Polish military units abroad.

Long-term activities concerned with economic and educational development, which in a sense preceded 'organic work' (cf. X, 1), found expression in the establishment, in 1800, in Prussian-held Warsaw, of the Warsaw Society of Friends of Science, at the opening of which Stanisław Staszic said that 'even a great nation may fall, but only a base one decays of its own accord'.

Conspiracies at home took the form of clubs, which united representatives of various status groups. They could most easily work in Galicia (i.e., the Austrian-held part of Poland), where the Kościuszko Insurrection had the weakest manifestations, and hence the centre of the movement came to be localized in Lvov in the form of the Lvov club, called the Centralizacja (Central Assembly; 1796—97), with 150 members headed by Ignacy Potocki, Stanisław Sołtyk, and Wiktoryn Walerian Dzieduszycki, a local aristocrat. A club led by Colonel Erazm Mycielski was active in Poznań. The hopes that Austria would be defeated by Napoleon I were dashed when a truce between Austria and France was signed in Leoben in 1797; the Central Assembly was discovered by the Austrian authorities, and its leaders arrested. The endeavour to organize an uprising, undertaken by Colonel Joachim Makosiej Denisko, who grouped in Moldavia several hundred ex-soldiers who had fought under Kościuszko, also ended in failure. A somewhat Utopian conspiracy, organized in Podlasie by Franciszek Gorzkowski (1760—1839), one of the Polish Jacobins, within the framework of the Central Assembly, was exposed in the spring of 1797; it was the only conspiracy which planned to win over the peasants who would fight for the abolition of serfdom and the system of corvée. In Gdańsk, Gottfried Bartholdy strove to organize a movement of Polish and German youth under the slogans of the French Revolution, in the defence of social equality and in opposition to Prussian rule. Its exposure was, as usual, followed by arrests and reprisals. There were also demonstrations by the Polish population in Silesia, which had sided with the rest of the country during the Kościuszko Insurrection.

The clandestine Society of Polish Republicans, to which Kościuszko himself acceded, set up by former Polish Jacobins in Warsaw in 1798, was more to the left than the Central Assembly. The Society stood for the republican form of government and for abolition of barriers between status groups (estates), but failed to make any clear declaration about granting to the peasants the land they tilled. It also propagated the formation of Polish units abroad.

Among Polish emigré circles in France radical demands were advanced by the so-called Deputation, which had its roots in the Jacobin movement, whereas more moderate people, who did not include social issues in the programme of the liberation struggle and were less committed to conspiracies in Poland, were grouped around the so-called Agency and the person of Franciszek Barss (Polish representative in France during the Kościuszko Insurrection), who was joined also by Józef Wybicki (1747—1822) and Jan Henryk Dąbrowski (1755—1818). The last-named planned taking the rest of the troops — after the collapse of the Kościuszko Insurrection — to France. His plan failed, but as early as the autumn of 1796 Dąbrowski, summoned by Wybicki, arrived in Paris, where in 1797 he started organizing the Polish Legions as an auxiliary corps attached to the army of the newly established Lombard Republic. He had in that the approval of Napoleon Bonaparte, who did not want to support the radical Deputation and the even more revolutionary plans advanced by Józef Sułkowski. The Polish Danube Legion, commanded by General Karol Kniaziewicz, was organized at the Rhine Army in 1799. While Bonaparte condemned the unjustice which the partition of Poland was and promised his support for the Polish cause, the aforementioned armistice in Leoben, followed by the peace treaty of Campo Formio, which spared Austria, did not improve the situation of the Poles. In the meantime, the Polish Legions were consolidating, and in the summer of 1797 they amounted to two regiments of infantry (ca. 7,000 men), one regiment of cavalry, and one artillery unit. At that time also Wybicki, who arrived in Italy, wrote *The Song of the Polish Legions in Italy* beginning with the words *Jeszcze Polska nie zginęła, póki my żyjemy...* (Poland is not yet lost as long as we are alive...), which was to become the Polish national anthem.

The next blow to the Polish cause took the form of the secret clause of the treaty concluded by Bonaparte with Austria and Russia in Lunéville (1801), on the strength of which Napoleon renounced the support of the Polish cause in exchange for a similar renunciation by the other two countries of their support for the French royalists abroad. This made the Polish Legions an awkward asset turned liability from Bonaparte's point of view; the regiments were accordingly dispersed: some 6,000 were sent (1802—03) to San Domingo (Haiti) to fight insurgents there, while some 5,000, led by Dąbrowski, remained in the Cisalpine Republic in Italy.

In the meantime (1800) a pamphlet inspired by Kościuszko and written by Józef Pawlikowski, *Czy Polacy mogą się wybić na niepodległość?* (Can the Poles Achieve Independence?), which attacked the pro-French orientation and the idea of the Polish Legions abroad, advanced a plan for a popular uprising without counting upon external help. This clear abandonment by Kościuszko of his moral support for the struggle for independence in alliance with France and his adoption of the maximalist programme was due to his disenchantment with Bonaparte's policy, in particular his abolition of the Directory, the last government of the French Republic, as a result of the famous *coup d'état* of the 18th Brumaire (9 November) 1799. Kościuszko called Bonaparte 'the grave-digger of the Republic'; he had, incidentally, even earlier warned the Directory against such a course of events.

The crisis in the pro-French orientation in the Polish independence movement attracted attention to the idea of establishing connections with Russia (then under the rule of Alexander I, who reigned 1801—25, advanced by Adam Jerzy Czartoryski, minister and friend of the tsar, who was then beginning his long career in politics. Czartoryski planned a restoration of Poland that would consist of the territories seized by Prussia and Austria and some of those seized by Russia, and would be closely linked to Russia within a federation. He suggested to the tsar that Russia should occupy the Polish territories seized by Prussia before the new (third) coalition would engage in a war with Napoleon. His plan collapsed quickly, because, first, Prussia afraid of its position joined the coalition, and next, Napoleon (who became the emperor in 1804) crushed the Austrians in the battle of Ulm (1805) and later defeated the troops of the three allied emperors in the battle of Austerlitz (2 December 1805). He also was victorious in his war with the fourth coalition (Britain, Russia, Prussia, and Sweden) by defeating Prussia in the battles of Jena and Auerstädt (14 October 1806). Upon entering Berlin Bonaparte summoned Dąbrowski and Wybicki to discuss with them Polish operations against Prussia. The collapse of the pro-Russian orientation and the victories of the French army instilled new life in the pro-French orientation in Poland.

3. The uprising of 1806. The Duchy of Warsaw and its role in Polish history

Bonaparte was primarily concerned with the total defeat of Prussia, which he wanted to achieve with the assistance of newly organized Polish forces. Vague hopes that the Polish cause would be settled favourably sufficed to bring about a general Polish uprising in Prussia. Polish public administration was organized immediately, and expenses were not spared to put up a Polish army. By the spring of 1807 the Polish troops amounted to 30,000 men in three legions, led by Jan Henryk Dąbrowski, Józef Zajączek (1752—1826), and Józef Poniatowski (1763—1813). Even earlier, in January 1807, a Governing Commission was set up in Warsaw with its authority extending over 'the Polish territories reconquered from the King of Prussia'. It was headed by Stanisław Małachowski (1736—1809) and included, except for Wybicki, members of the richest Polish families. This showed that Bonaparte succeeded in winning over the liberal and patriotic aristocracy, which was at first ill-disposed towards him, by resorting to political blackmail: he threatened to appeal to the masses, which were ready to take up a plebeian struggle against the partitioning powers. The magnates connected previously with the Targowica Confederation were discredited enough to be ready to co-operate. The Commission, whose composition suggested the continuity of the legal national authority, while dependent upon the French, succeeded in functioning as an efficient centre of public administration. Detachments formed in Great Poland liberated Gdańsk Pomerania and Western Pomerania. The activeness of the Poles, combined with Bonaparte's victory in the war of 1806—07 (especially after the defeat of the Russians in the battle of Friedland on 14 June 1807, in which Dąbrowski took part having arrived in time from Gdańsk) made the Polish cause loom large in the French-Russian treaty of Tilsit of 7/8 July 1807. The compromise reached there led to the formation of a rather small state (104,000 sq. km. with 2.6 million inhabitants) under the protection of Napoleon I, called the Duchy of Warsaw. It covered the territories seized by Prussia during the second and the third partition of Poland (without the Białystok region, which now went to Russia) and the southern part of the areas seized by Prussia during the first partition, that is territories comparatively well developed economically. Gdańsk Pomerania, however, was not included in the Duchy, Gdańsk being transformed into a free city. The fact that King Frederick Augustus was to be the Duke of Warsaw referred to the idea of the Four Year Seym to invite the Saxon dynasty to the Polish throne.

The Governing Commission wanted to restore the Third of May Constitution, but Napoleon I granted the Duchy a more radical constitution together with the civil code (the Napoleonic *Code Civil*). This opened the way to the development of the capitalist social structure and a modern state based on a strong civil service. All the citizens were made equal before the law, which involved the abolition of serfdom (and the judicial authority of the lord of the demesne over the local peasants), but, on the other hand, by a decree of 21 December 1807, the gentry were recognized to be full owners of the land tilled by the peasants, which in turn offered them the opportunity of removing the peasants from the land (of which the gentry did avail themselves on various occasions). Political rights were given to those who had adequate property, but all the places in the Senate and three-fifths of the places in the Chamber of Deputies were reserved for the gentry. This preserved the supremacy of the gentry (with the domination of the aristocracy), but not in so complete a form as before. In 1809, representatives of social estates other than the gentry held 21 per cent of the places in the Chamber of Deputies, but in 1811 the figure was merely 17 per cent. The gentry did not find it difficult to preserve their supremacy because the burghers, still weak, to such an extent failed to aspire to participation in political life that in 1807 members of the gentry were elected the mayor and the deputy mayor of Warsaw. A strong executive power was assured by the fact that it was concentrated (together with the legislative initiative) in the hands of the Duke, who exercised it together with the Council of State, the Council of Ministers, which had Stanisław Kostka Potocki (1755—1821) as its president, the ministers and the civil service of some 9,000 persons. The prerogatives of the Seym were very limited in the sphere of the fiscal, civil, and criminal law.

While the authorities strove to cover by their administrative action all the matters of the Duchy and its inhabitants, in view of the place which the Duchy of Warsaw held in Napoleon's plans most attention was focussed on military matters. Des-

4. Duchy of Warsaw (1807—15)

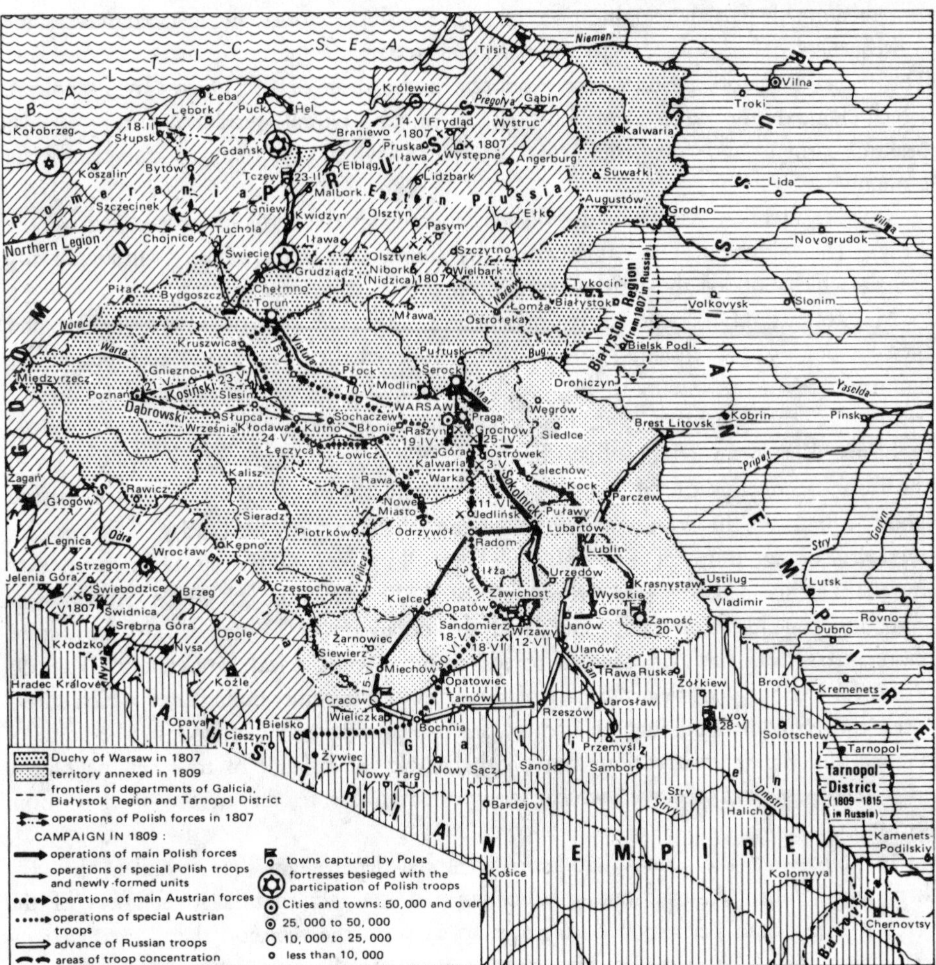

pite the fact that the national army of 30,000 men — which the Duchy was bound to put up — was subordinated to French command, its very existence was of extreme importance. Some 200,000 young men (in 1812 as many as 115,000 were called to arms) who served in the army came in touch with the modern way of thinking that abolished the prejudices resulting from differences between status groups, with democratic ideas and with the traditions of the Polish Legions abroad. Poles served also in the regiment of the light cavalry (*chevaux légers*) led by Wincenty Krasiński and in the Vistula Legion, formed from the remnants of the former Polish Legions and of the cavalry of the Danube Legion and commanded by Józef Chłopicki.

Despite the difficult conditions prevailing during the Napoleonic period the united Polish territories (though not all the territories of former Poland) became for a short time an arena of economic development.

The most important positive factor which stimulated economic growth was the aforementioned partial re-unification of the Polish territories, which removed some consequences of the split due to the partitions and made the home market quite brisk. The negative factors included the economic exploitation of the Duchy by Napoleon, which limited the investment possibilities of agricultural producers (in particular peasant farms), and the continental blockade, which disorganized the European economy.

Separate mention is due to the financial burden in the form of expenditure on the army. The situation was aggravated by monetary chaos, caused primarily by Prussia which flooded the Duchy with cheap copper coins.

Maintenance of a large army, marches of large numbers of French troops and their stationing for months; the burdens imposed by Napoleon; distribution by him of state-owned estates to his protégés, who did not contribute anything to the treasury of the Duchy — all this gave rise to numerous economic and financial problems. But it turned out that the fall in the price of agricultural produce (with the resulting decline of the exports of grain) and the rise in the prices of imported goods stimulated the economic activity of the inhabitants of the Duchy. Cloth-making was developing in Great Poland, while the Old Polish Industrial District, annexed by the Duchy in 1809 (see below) increased the output of its goods. Abolition of compulsory guild membership stimulated the expansion of handicrafts. In agriculture, more stress was laid on animal breeding and technological innovations. The demand for various goods on the part of the army was an important factor which stimulated the economy, although it had its adverse accompanying effects in the form of French and Saxon competition. But on the whole the balance of trade in the Duchy in 1810—11 was positive, which was primarily due to the export of cloth from Great Poland.

In 1810—11 the Duchy had more territorial departments than it had at the very beginning. When Austria, taking advantage of the fact that large numbers of the French troops had been moved to Spain to suppress the rebellion there, tried to conquer the Duchy, it was defeated in the war of 1809, and the departments of Cracow, Radom, Siedlce and Lublin were added to those of Poznań, Bydgoszcz, Kalisz, Warsaw, Płock, and Łomża. The area of the Duchy increased to 155,430 sq. km. and the number of the inhabitants, to 4.4 million, which of course resulted in greater financial and military activity for Napoleon's benefit. During the hostilities in 1809 the Polish army of 12,000 men, skilfully commanded by Prince Józef Poniatowski, defended the Duchy successfully, and ultimately defeated the Austrians in the battle of Raszyn (19 April 1809). The territorial expansion of the Duchy was recognized by Austria in the peace treaty concluded after Napoleon's victory in the battle of Wagram (5—6 July 1809).

The short-lived Duchy helped further to promote science, now focussed around schools of university standing. The Chamber of Education, which referred to the Commission for National Education, was established in 1807, and Polish schools, closed down by the Prussians, were re-opened. The schools were made secular in character and were instructed to admit girls, too. In view of the immense needs of modernized public administration a School of Law was opened in Warsaw in 1808, changed in 1811 into the School of Law and Administrative Sciences; together with the School of Medicine, founded in 1809, it was treated as the nucleus of the future university. The School of Law had eminent lawyers and economists (Jan Wincenty Bandtkie, Wawrzyniec Surowiecki, Dominik Krysiński, and others) as professors, Bogumił Linde continued his work on the dictionary of the Polish language, while Feliks Bentkowski wrote his history of Polish literature. There was a lively interest in historical studies; historiography was represented by Stanisław Staszic, who also worked on geological maps of Polish territories. The theatre directed by Wojciech Bogusławski was active as before, and had a state-owned school of drama attached to it in 1811. Music, visual arts, and architecture flourished, too.

The existence of the Duchy was terminated by the war in 1812, which ended in Napoleon's retreat from Moscow and his defeat in the battle of Leipzig in October 1813, where Prince Józef Poniatowski lost his life. In January 1813 the Russian troops entered the Duchy. Czartoryski revived his plans for uniting the Polish territories under the Russian rule, but that was blocked by Prussia and Austria. The future of the Polish territories was to be settled at the Congress of Vienna.

Chapter X

National Liberation Struggles of the Polish Nation. Collapse of Feudal Structures (1815—64)

1. The Congress of Vienna. The alliance of governments versus the alliances of peoples. Evolution of the Polish nation

The Congress of Vienna (1815) put an end to that independence which the Poles acquired during the Napoleonic period. The Polish territories were again partitioned among Prussia, Russia, and Austria. The Holy Alliance, initiated by Alexander I and concluded in the same year, was opposed to the ideas advanced by the French revolution, i.e. the ideas of social equality and political democracy. It was an alliance of the partitioning powers, to which other governments were invited to accede and which was intended to stand guard over the inviolability of the *ancient régime* in Europe. This exacerbated the conflict between the growing aspirations of the peoples, on the one hand, and the governments and their social base in the form of the aristocracy and the gentry, on the other. The Holy Alliance in a sense automatically internationalized any struggle waged at home in any country concerned with a view to democratizing the political system. Every action undertaken by the Poles against the partitioning powers thus automatically impaired the order defended by the Holy Alliance and evoked avalanche-like reactions.

In the case of the Poles the struggle for independence and for modernization of social and economic structures became even more difficult. Other peoples which fought for freedom, such as the Greeks, the Italians, the Rumanians, and the Hungarians, had one principal enemy each, and usually also an ally interested to some extent in their struggle. The Poles had three principal enemies, and at the same time they lost their independence in the epoch which saw the birth of the principle that accorded the right of political independence to every people with national consciousness. The Poles, experienced in struggles for independence, became an object of interest to all nations that fought for freedom, which obviously had certain adverse effects in the form of Polonocentrism in Polish political thinking. Direct struggle in the sense of political conspiracies and armed resistance brought more spectacular effects, but the nation's fight for its own survival and development also followed another course and was usually being undertaken by the same people who exchanged tools for weapons, and vice versa. The Romantic and the 'positivist' (in the sense of systematic work, and not in that current later in philosophy and sociology) attitudes cannot be contrasted with one another, because they were not so contrasted by people who lived in that period. As there was no Polish state that would provide employment for civil servants, technologists, and other professionals, thousands of talented Polish engineers, physicians, architects, chemists, businessmen, and artists, made signal and direct contributions to the development of other nations and states.

At the same time the Poles were actively helping other nations that strove for freedom. They took part in the revolutions in France, Italy, and Germany in 1848—49, and also in the Hungarian revolution. They supported the aspirations of the Czechs, Slovaks, Croatians, Serbians, and Bulgarians. The uprising in Poland in November 1830 helped the Belgians to regain independence. Solidarity of the peoples fighting for freedom was propagated by the daily *La Tribune des Peuples,* edited by the Polish poet Adam Mickiewicz in Paris in 1849. All these actions later gave rise to the radical ideas of co-operation of all the revolutionary forces in Europe.

The Congress of Vienna gave Russia the central part of Poland and formed the so-called Kingdom of Poland with the Russian tsar as its king. It had an area of 127,000 sq. km., i.e. less than the former Duchy of Warsaw, with a population of over four million (in 1830). Austria acquired an area of 77,300 sq. km. with a population of 4.2 million (in 1830), and gave that territory the name which had been used earlier by the Austrian authorities, namely that of the Kingdom of Galicia and Lodomeria. Prussia received the western part of the Duchy of Warsaw (Great Poland) as the Grand Duchy of Poznań (29,000 sq. km. with 776,000 inhabitants). Cracow and its vicinity was turned into a (seemingly) free city. That Republic of Cracow (1,150 sq. km. with 88,000 inhabitants) was placed under the supervision of representatives of the partitioning powers. Austria and Prussia tried to liken the political system of the territories annexed on the strength of the Treaty of Vienna to that in their remaining provinces, respectively. Only the Republic of Cracow and the Kingdom of Poland obtained their own political systems; in both cases the Napoleonic Code was retained, and the constitutions of these two political entities referred to the traditions of the Duchy of Warsaw, in particular to the (often fictitious) principle of equality before the law.

Executive power in the Kingdom of Poland was in the hands of the tsar (as the king), but in fact in those of his governor general; that post was occupied until 1826 by General Józef Zajączek (who from a Polish Jacobin became a zealous executor of the instructions given him by the tsar). After his death his prerogatives were transferred to the Administrative Council. The Council of State was preserved and the functions of the government were performed by the Administrative Council consisting of ministers. The legislative power was in the hands of the Seym, with two chambers, which primarily considered the bills submitted by the Council of State. The Senate was appointed by the tsar, and the Chamber of Deputies was elected, but the number of people who had electoral rights was not greater than previously in the Duchy of Warsaw (except for the members of the army). Representatives of status groups other than the gentry held merely 16 to 18 per cent of the seats in the Chamber of Deputies. The system introduced by the Constitution of 1815 was seemingly liberal, but in fact gave the power into the hands of the aristocracy, whose members performed the highest functions.

The Kingdom of Poland, artificially joined to an immense state with 45 million inhabitants, a feudal structure and a reactionary absolutist political system, had no chance of maintaining the relative independence guaranteed by the Constitution and of avoiding the pressure of the tsarist system. The Constitution was regularly violated, the first major action of this kind being the introduction of censorship in 1819. The reactionary trend was growing stronger and stronger. From 1820 Grand Duke Constantine, commander-in-chief of the army of the Kingdom of Poland, received *de facto* unlimited prerogatives in the Kingdom of Poland; his conduct was in fact extremely authoritarian. He was in turn under the strong influence of Senator Nikolai Novosiltsov, who acted as the plenipotentiary of the tsar, which function was not provided for by the Constitution.

In the Prussian-occupied part of Poland, where Antoni Radziwiłł, married to Luisa Hohenzollern, was appointed governor general, executive power was wielded by a Generalpräsident. In 1823—24, like the other Prussian provinces, the region was granted a Diet with very limited prerogatives, its members being elected as representatives of the various status groups (*Stände*). More or less the same held for Galicia, where a Diet dominated by landowners was restored by the emperor in 1817.

These vestigial state institutions could not replace for the Poles a state of their own. Hence, unlike in normal circumstances, the state could not provide conditions for the formation of the nation. On the contrary, the partitioning powers deliberately tried to hinder that process by gradually intensifying Germanizing and Russifying measures. But the Polish nation was developing nevertheless, and its national consciousness intensified.

A nation is an extremely intricate social structure, and the national bonds constitute a very strong, historically evolved type of social bonds. When sufficiently developed they are stronger than social bonds of other kinds (e.g., religious, class, professional, etc., bonds). In Poland these bonds, which had their manifestation in national consciousness, were developing rapidly despite the fact that the Poles had no state of their own. The factors which in the case of Poland were decisive for that process were as follows:

(i) Development of an all-national culture (both in the spatial sense, regardless of the partition of the territory among the three powers, and in the social sense, through participation in culture of various social classes and groups) and of thinking about culture, and hence politics, too, in terms of the entire nation. This led to a gradual integration of society as to its consciousness, and accordingly to the emergence of a subjective sense of national bonds.

(ii) Modernization of the economic and social structure consisting in the gradual abolition of structures based on feudal principles and divisions into estates (status groups, *Stände*), which contributed — but only in connection with the general changes in consciousness that was growing more and more nation-embracing — to the development of thinking in terms of the entire economy and entire society.

(iii) Struggle for an independent Polish state (the uprising of 1830—31, 1846, 1848, 1863). That struggle cemented society and promoted political culture and thinking in political terms. The state — as an idea which should be made to materialize — contributed integratively to the shaping of the nation (the more so as

An allegory of the first partition of Poland (1772) (after à contemporaneous copperplate by Noël Lemire)

Tadeusz Kościuszko (1746–1817), fighter for the independence of Poland and the United States, commander-in-chief during the 1794 uprising (painted by K.G. Schwekert)

Kazimierz Pułaski (1747–79), member of the Bar Confederacy, fighter for the independence of the United States (an oil painting from the early 19th century after a steel engraving by Antoni Oleszczyński)

General Henryk Dąbrowski at the head of Polish Legions organized in Italy in 1797 (painted by Juliusz Kossak)

The Battle of Racławice, fought successfully during the Kościuszko Uprising in 1794 (drawn by Aleksander Orłowski)

Prince Józef Poniatowski (1763–1813), the Minister of War and Commander-in-Chief in the Duchy of Warsaw, a nephew of King Stanislaus Augustus Poniatowski; created marshal by Napoleon I (a lithograph by Grevedon)

The arrival of the troops of the Duchy of Warsaw in Cracow on 15 July 1809, when part of the Austrian partition zone was incorporated into the Duchy of Warsaw (drawn by Jan Kurowski)

Soldiers of the 4th regiment of line infantry and of the 3rd regiment of mounted riflemen in 1831 (a lithograph by C.A. Simon)

The taking of the Arsenal in Warsaw during the Uprising of 1830–31 (painted by Marcin Zaleski)

Joachim Lelewel (1786–1861), historian, national leader, member of the National Government during the Uprising of 1830–31 (a contemporary lithograph)

Jan Śniadecki (1756–1830), mathematician, astronomer, philosopher, popularizer of science in Poland, Rector of Vilna University (a contemporary lithograph)

Jędrzej Śniadecki (1768–1838), brother of Jan, chemist, physician, biologist, philosopher, originator of the concept of metabolism (a contemporary lithograph)

Adam Mickiewicz (1798–1855), reputed to be the greatest Polish poet, romanticist, spiritual leader of the Polish émigrés in Paris (painted by Walenty Wańkowicz)

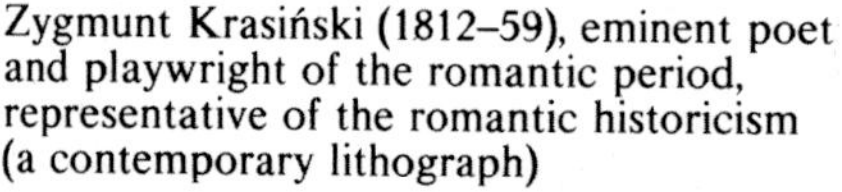

Zygmunt Krasiński (1812–59), eminent poet and playwright of the romantic period, representative of the romantic historicism (a contemporary lithograph)

Juliusz Słowacki (1809–49), reputed to be the national poet second only to Mickiewicz, originator of the Polish romantic drama (drawn by Jan Kurowski)

Cyprian Kamil Norwid (1821–83), a poet and artist, since 1849 in exile in Paris. His precursory writing constitutes the development of Romanticism. Photo

during the uprisings Polish state-like institutions were being set up). This laid foundations for a rapid development of political ideologies.

It is obvious that intellectual ideas and behaviour patterns, also in the sphere of politics, were those that crossed the frontiers the easiest between the various parts of partitioned Poland. The partition of the country split and deformed its economic life, which hampered the emergence of economic thinking in national terms. This was why the economic and social development, while objectively conducive to a strengthening of national bonds, carried the risk that the differences between the various parts of the country would become more strongly marked. The struggle for national survival and the related development of spiritual culture (including science and art) accounted for the fact that the Polish nation and Polish national consciousness were developing firmly in ethnically Polish territories, despite the long perseverance of the feudal social and economic structure. But the hindering effect of that structure and of those social forces which stood behind it (the aristocracy, the gentry) upon the shaping of a modern nation must be understood. The peasants, handicapped and exploited, when their class consciousness grew demanded primarily an improvement in their conditions, whereas the gentry, while desirous of the political independence of Poland as a state, were not inclined to make concessions easily. Such being the case the agrarian issue rose to the level of the fundamental political problem; it was also used by the partitioning powers to exert pressure upon the Polish people.

2. Development of national culture as the principal factor of the growth of national consciousness

Spiritual culture, which shapes human consciousness and attitudes, was one of the strongest bonds keeping together a nation that was not only deprived of political independence but lived on a territory divided into three alien states. The lack of political independence made its impression on literature and art, while the policy of the partitioning powers restricted the possibilities of research and the spreading of centres of Polish cultural life.

Science developed mainly in the university towns. Cracow University, though not without obstacles raised by the authorities of the partitioning powers, trained young Poles from the Russian- and Prussian-occupied parts of the country. Very fine libraries were founded, which facilitated research in the sphere of the humanities. In 1817, Józef Maksymilian Ossoliński (1748—1826), of an aristocratic Polish family, himself a historian and novelist, founded the library and the publishing house (which exist to this day) currently referred to as the Ossolineum. The prestigious secondary school in Krzemieniec continued to function, and an important role in the development of science was played by Vilna University, which in 1807—15 had the famous astronomer Jan Śniadecki as its rector, and Joachim Lelewel (1786—1861), the most eminent Polish historian in the 19th century, as one of its professors. The Royal Warsaw University (later closed down by the tsarist authorities in 1831) was established in 1816 upon the initiative of Stanisław Kostka Potocki and Stanisław Staszic by the fusion of the School of Law and Administration with the School of Medicine (cf. IX, 3). That university, too, had young Poles from all parts of the country as students. The Warsaw Society of Friends of Science, for which Staszic founded a fine building (existing to this day), with a statue of Nicolaus Copernicus by Bertel Thorvaldsen in front of it, was very active and attracted scholars and scientists from the whole of Poland. The Institute of Singing and Diction, organized in Warsaw by Józef Elsner in 1821 was transformed into the Central Music School in 1826. Schools of agronomy, veterinary science, mining, and civil engineering were also set up in Warsaw.

Stanisław Kostka Potocki was in charge of the Board of National Education, which tried to continue the ideas at one time advanced by the Commission for National Education. Opponent of obscurantism and clericalism, he contributed to the closing down of many monasteries. His satirical poem *Podróż do Ciemnogrodu* (A Visit to Obscurantsville) evoked a strong attack upon him on the part of the episcopate, supported by the tsar, who used this as pretext for removing him from office; he was replaced by Stanisław Grabowski in 1820. Potocki's dismissal symbolized the obstacles raised by the Russian authorities to a free development of Polish culture, and also showed that the struggle for cultural advancement would mean a struggle for national survival. In the parts of Poland annexed to Prussia and to Austria the situation was similar. In Galicia, German and Latin were used in schools, and in Great Poland the German language started to be introduced after 1824. The endeavours to have a university established in Poznań ended in a failure. A particularly strong Germanization campaign was conducted in Silesia and Pomerania, that is, in the former Polish territories that were not incorporated into the Grand Duchy of Poznań.

In spite of the political frontiers cutting Poland into three parts the level of national and historical consciousness continued rising. This was revealed by such events as the building in Cracow, the town which then linked the Poles from all parts of the country, of the Kościuszko Mound (1820—23), dedicated to the memory of that national hero. The growing impact of the authorities of the partitioning powers upon the school system, treated by them as a means of weakening the Polish character of the country, resulted in an immense rise in importance of the ways of shaping national consciousness out of school: patriotic education in the family, polite literature, scholarly books, libraries, dailies and periodicals, museums and exhibitions, the theatre, societies concerned with cultural activities, public lectures, social occasions intended to promote national traditions, etc. Increased demand for publications also helped promote education out of school and to propagate culture. Impressions of books were increasing systematically. In 1819 General Zajączek imposed upon the publishing firms and the printing houses the duty of sending one copy of every printed matter each to the three libraries: that at Warsaw University, that attached to the Council of State, and that run by the Warsaw Society of Friends of Science. This gave rise to the concept of the library as a national treasure-house. Next to the large libraries which also collected manuscripts, such as the Ossolineum library in Lvov and the library founded in Poznań (1829) by Edward Raczyński (1786—1845), private libraries and those attached to offices, guilds, and societies, sometimes quite big, and also libraries set up in the rural areas, were growing in numbers.

The demand for books and the number of printing houses were growing, too. The subscription system, with the participation of representatives of the various social groups, was widely used. Special mention is due to the publishing activity of Jan Konstanty Żupański (who published the works of Joachim Lelewel) in Poznań, Tadeusz Antoni Mostowski in Warsaw, and Józef Zawadzki in Vilna. Polish books in large impressions were also printed, in the early decades of the 19th century, by such publishers abroad as Korn in Wrocław, Friedrich Arnold Brockhaus in Leipzig, and Maurice Wolff in St. Petersburg. The growing numbers of the reading public found reflection in publication of books and periodicals for peasants, which was initiated by the popular historical narrative *Pielgrzym w Dobromilu* (The Pilgrim at Dobromil) by Izabela Czartoryska (1746—1835). Great Poland ranked first in the size of the reading public. This can be easily understood if we note that in the Prussian-occupied part of Poland — where obligatory schooling at the elementary level for children aged from six to 14 was introduced in 1825 — by the mid-19th century some 85 per cent of young people had received elementary education. The corresponding figures for Galicia and the Kingdom of Poland were 28 and 20 per cent. The same phenomenon was also observable in secondary education. This helped promote the national consciousness and political culture of the peasants. The uprisings, the first of which broke out in Great Poland in 1806 (cf. IX, 2), had a wide scope, and the peasants came to feel themselves full-fledged members of the national community.

Among publications of various kinds mention is due to encyclopaedias for the broad public (the first was that which Samuel Orgelbrand (1810—68), a Warsaw bookseller, started publishing in 1859). The spreading of information and its influence upon popular attitudes was revolutionized by the immense development of periodicals, which in the Kingdom of Poland alone in the middle of the 19th century amounted to about one hundred. Clandestine publications were being circulated, too. Out of the long list of those periodicals mention is due to *Izys Polska* (Polish Isis; Warsaw), *Szkoła Polska* (The Polish School; Poznań), *Tygodnik Warszawski* (The Warsaw Weekly), *Dziennik Mód* (Journal of Fashion; Lvov), *Tygodnik Literacki* (The Literary Weekly; Poznań), and *Biblioteka Warszawska* (The Warsaw Library), a popular science periodical which appeared first in 1841 and continued to be published until World War I. The most popular dailies included *Orzeł Biały* (The White Eagle) with 500 subscribers, *Gazeta Warszaw-*

ska (The Warsaw Newspaper) with 1,000 subscribers, *Gazeta Polska* (The Polish Newspaper), and *Kurier Polski* (The Polish Courier).

The spreading and democratization of culture were also promoted by museums, exhibitions, and the theatre. It was a period of avid collection of objects connected with national history. Izabela Czartoryska was one of the pioneers in this field as the founder of a museum in Puławy. The Museum of Fine Arts, which later developed into the National Museum, was established in Warsaw in 1862. Exhibitions were organized by the Society of Friends of Fine Arts in Warsaw, by similar societies in Cracow and Lvov, and by the Polish-German Society for Fine Arts in Poznań.

Interest in the theatre was even more widespread than it had been in the Age of Reason (cf. VIII, 5). There were permanent theatres in Warsaw (two of them from 1829 on), Cracow, Lvov and Vilna. In the provinces performances were staged by both travelling theatres and — in the summer season — the companies of the permanent theatres.

The emerging all-national culture was represented mainly by the aristocracy and the upper strata of the gentry and the nascent bourgeoisie and — proportionately in the greatest degree — by the newly forming class of the intelligentsia. The peasants and the town poor could avail themselves of cultural achievements on a very limited scale only, because of the hindering effect of the backward social and political structure still prevailing in the Polish territories. The Polish terminology concerned with the social structure of Poland at that time is rather difficult to render in English where the various terms refer to different social phenomena. What was called 'the people' comprised the peasants, who lived very modestly or even in poverty, and the growing numbers of the town poor, including the nascent working class. For some uses of those words, 'the people' could be equated with 'the masses' as opposed to 'the classes' in English terminology or rather phraseology. Above 'the people' there was the still small bourgeoisie, the gentry (who were breaking up into various substrata in terms of financial status and ways of life), and the owners of large estates (including the aristocracy) who were running them more and more on capitalist principles (cf. section 3 below). In the case of the masses ('the people') barriers to vertical social mobility at that time must be seen mainly in difficult access to schools of all types — in 1830, at Cracow University only three per cent of the students were of peasant origin — and to what would now be called white-collar jobs.

Non-existence of the Polish state did not favour the growth of the intelligentsia (who roughly corresponded to the intellectuals, the professionals, and the holders of higher clerical jobs taken together with their families). About 1860 that group amounted merely to 0.73 per cent of the population in the case of the Kingdom of Poland, but its role in the life of the nation and in the shaping of new national and social consciousness was incomparably greater.

The two principal attitudes, namely the ideas of Romanticism, which treated the masses as the source of the vital forces of society and — on the political level — often stood for armed struggle for independence, and those of 'organic work' (also called 'positivism', but rather loosely connected with positivism as a trend in philosophical and social thinking in Western Europe), which stressed the defence and development of the nation through systematic work, economic activity, spreading of education, and prudence in political actions, could yield results only if adopted in an active manner by those to whom they were addressed. The masses, when continuing their traditions, did not experience the need for going outside the sphere of their own folk culture, although the latter, when discovered by members of the intelligentsia, contributed to national culture and even — as was the case of the music composed by Frédéric Chopin, who drew largely from the Polish folklore — to world culture in general.

The Philomath Society (1817—23), founded in Lithuania upon the initiative of Tomasz Zan (1796—1855) and the poet Adam Mickiewicz (1798—1855), advanced the idea of national education. (The Society was crushed by Novosiltsov as a result of a trial following which 20 philomaths and philarets — members of a similar Philaret Society — were exiled to Russia.) In the Grand Duchy of Poznań, where organic work, focussed on economy and education, brought the greatest successes, Hipolit Cegielski (1815—68), a teacher turned businessman, wrote in 1849: 'Let us take to real things, organic things, in order to act directly, both morally and materially, upon the common people, to raise their living standards and to promote their national feelings and education.' The Polish League, active in 1849—50, which had its principal workers in the philosopher Karol Libelt (1807—75) and Jan Palacz (d. 1891), a civic and political worker of peasant origin, set up libraries and nursery schools and organized popular lectures. The League referred to what had been done earlier by Karol Marcinkowski (1800—46), who helped establish in 1841 the Society for Educational Assistance, concentrated on offering scholarships to young people.

Among the various disciplines an important role in shaping the opinion of Polish society was played by historiography, Slavonic studies, and ethnography. Great services to the study of Polish history and the Polish language and to the promotion of those sciences which were needed for the economic development of the country were rendered by the already mentioned Society of Friends of Science in Warsaw (1800—32), the Cracow University Scientific Society (from 1816), and the Society of Friends of Science in Poznań (from 1857). All these were, of course, substitutes for genuine scientific institutions. This is why Poles had to seek abroad better conditions for the development of their talents. Their scholarly and engineering activity in other countries often resulted in pioneering discoveries. Ignacy Domeyko (1802—89), an ex-philomath and graduate of Vilna University, mineralogist and geologist, ultimately president of Santiago University, contributed signally to the economic and cultural promotion of Chile, while the study by Paweł Edmund Strzelecki (1797—1873), *New South Wales,* published in London in 1843, was till recent time one of the best geographical works concerned with Australia.

The strong trend for organic work, called work from the very foundations (based on the assumption that an eventual armed struggle for independence required a previous strengthening of the economy and promotion of science and education), was conducive to the development of mathematics and engineering. Adam Mickiewicz, the poet, and other philomaths and philarets were interested in mathematics, and General Ignacy Prądzyński (1792—1850), the Commander-in-chief of the Polish Army during the Uprising of 1830—31, designed in 1822—24 the Augustów Canal, at that time a remarkable achievement of civil engineering.

Description of Polish scholarly achievements between 1815 and 1864 requires mention of the historians Joachim Lelewel, Jędrzej Moraczewski (1802—55), and Karol Szajnocha (1818—68), the literary historian Michał Wiszniewski (1794—1865), Stanisław Kostka Potocki, already mentioned as art historian, and the ethnographer Oskar Kolberg (1814—90).

Philosophical thinking also witnessed considerable development. Such philosophers as August Cieszkowski (1814—94), the first president of the Society of Friends of Science in Poznań; Bronisław Trentowski (1808—69); and Karol Libelt, already mentioned previously as organizer of cultural life, referred — both critically and creatively — to Hegelian philosophy. They emphasized the importance of action, spreading of education, and improvement of individuals, and also the special role of the Polish nation in the changes that were already taking, or were still to take, place in Europe. A different trend was represented by Edward Dembowski (1822—46) and Henryk Kamieński (1813—65). Unlike Cieszkowski and Trentowski, who stood for social solidarity, they propagated the early ideas of socialism, materialism, and dialectics, and advocated a moderate programme for an agrarian revolution, i.e., a revolutionary abolition of still surviving feudalism.

Stanisław Staszic continued his research in geology. In 1852 Ignacy Łukasiewicz (1822—82) invented the petroleum lamp. In medicine the pride of place goes to Tytus Chałubiński (1820—89), Józef Dietl (1804—78), and Józef Majer (1808—99).

Lack of political independence accounted for the special role played by literature; it was one of the important bonds that kept the Polish nation together, contributed to the cultivation of the Polish language, popularized personality patterns, and preserved national tradition. Its most eminent representatives rose to the status of spiritual leaders of the nation. Literature reflected the griefs and aspirations of the Poles.

In the period under consideration Polish literature was dominated by Romanticism, a new intellectual current which abandoned the universalism and the optimistic belief in an inevitable and incessant progress in human history, so typical of the Age of Reason. Romanticism laid stress on the individual features of the various nations, the role of action by eminent individuals, and historical tradition in the creation of reality. The belief in the creative possibilities of human will was a specific heritage of the Napoleonic period, which witnessed how a seemingly stable world crumbled under the blows of a great leader.

In Polish literature, Romanticism was opened by the publication in 1822 of *Ballady i Romanse* (Ballads and Romances) by Adam Mickiewicz, soon followed by parts II and IV of his *Dziady* (Forefathers' Eve). The epoch gave three poets, Adam Mickiewicz, Juliusz Słowacki (1809—49), and Zygmunt Krasiński (1812—59), who not without justification won the names of 'the bards of the nation' (the Polish word *wieszcz* having further-reaching implications than *bard,* because its meaning comes close to Latin *vates*). Their works were mainly concerned with the tragedy of the nation deprived of freedom and the need for struggle for the materialization of the hope by which the Poles lived. They also reflected the social conflicts that were disrupting Polish society (part III of Mickiewicz's *Forefathers' Eve* and Krasiński's *Nie-boska komedia* (Undivine Comedy).

After the November Uprising of 1830—31 (cf. section 4 below) Polish Romantic literature was developing largely abroad, mainly in Paris, Wrocław, Leipzig, Dresden, London, and Brussels. Adam Mickiewicz, Juliusz Słowacki, Zygmunt Krasiński, and Cyprian Kamil Norwid (1821—83), an extremely talented poet, playwright, painter and sculptor, originator of modern intellectual poetry, discovered only in the 20th century, were all active abroad.

Maurycy Mochnacki (1803—34) was the most eminent literary and musical critic and theorist of Polish Romanticism, who attacked the aesthetic principles of the classicist period. His *Powstanie narodu polskiego w r. 1830—1831* (The Uprising of the Polish Nation, 1830—1831), published in 1834, became the model of Romantic prose.

At home, in the period up to 1849, i.e. the collapse of the revolutionary movement that shook continental Europe (and has been traditionally termed 'the Springtime of Nations' in Polish historiography — cf. section 4 below), literary activity was most lively in Great Poland, which had two important periodicals, *Tygodnik Literacki* (The Literary Weekly), progressive and marked by a high standard of scholarship, and *Przyjaciel Ludu* (The Friend of the People), which Jan Poliński started editing in Leszno in 1834. Poznań attracted authors from the remaining parts of Poland; these included Narcyza Żmichowska (1819—76), Teofil Lenartowicz (1822—93), Roman Zmorski (1822—67), and Edward Dembowski. The literary milieu in Galicia was also very active for some time, its most prominent figures being Wincenty Pol (1807—72), extoller of the Sarmatianist tradition, Kornel Ujejski (1823—97), author of the choral *Z dymem pożarów* (With the Smoke of Conflagration), and Józef Korzeniowski (1797—1863), whose novels included elements of the realist trend (*Kollokacja*; The Gentry Village, and *Krewni;* The Relatives). It was there too that the talent of Aleksander Fredro (1793—1876), Napoleon's ex-aide-de-camp, exploded somewhat unexpectedly. His comedies, *Pan Geldhab* (Mr. Geldhab), *Damy i Huzary* (Ladies and Hussars), *Śluby panieńskie* (Maiden Vows), *Zemsta* (Vengeance) etc., in which he referred to traditional gentry culture, are to this day standard items in the repertoire of the Polish theatres. That period also saw the appearance of the first works of Józef

Ignacy Kraszewski (1812—87), whose cycle of historical novels covered nearly the whole of the history of Poland, from legendary times (*Stara baśń;* The Old Tale) to the 18th century (*Saskie Ostatki;* The Saxon Carnival). The historian Karol Szajnocha was also active at that time (1835—1865) as an author of historical dramas.

Music, which together with literature stimulated national consciousness, saw the outburst of the genius of Frédéric Chopin (1810—1849), son of a Frenchman who had settled in Poland and had taken part in the Kościuszko Insurrection. Chopin, who wrote almost exclusively for the piano (58 mazurkas, 17 polonaises, 26 preludes, etc.) excelled in drawing inspiration from elements of Polish folk music. The novel elements in his art as a composer made strong impact on the evolution of music in Europe. Much more limited was the influence of the music composed by Stanisław Moniuszko (1819—72), the father of the Polish national opera; his operas including *Halka* (1848), *Verbum nobile* (1861), *Straszny Dwór* (The Haunted Manor; 1865) referred to national customs and traditions.

Painters also started looking for inspiration in local elements. This applies to Aleksander Orłowski (1777—1832) and Piotr Michałowski (1801—55), whereas classicism was represented by Antoni Brodowski (1784—1832). Up to 1830 the classicist style dominated also in architecture, where it was later replaced for decades by the Neo-Gothic and the Neo-Renaissance style. Polish culture of that period was, on the one hand, imbued with the topical problems of the nation which had to live in three different foreign states, and on the other participated in the development of culture at large. Ever new social groups and strata were covered by the radiation of culture, although its spreading among the town poor and the peasants was very slow in view of the low level of education.

3. Formation of economic and social structures under late feudalism and growing capitalism. The problem of agrarian reforms

Any economic policy intended to satisfy individual, regional, and national needs was rendered difficult by the splitting of the country among the three partitioning powers. The partitions had interrupted the emergence in Poland of a market on a national scale, and inclusion of the various Polish regions into foreign political and economic organisms imparted to them new features varying according to the partitioning powers involved. The development of the money and commodity economy gradually destroyed the feudal structures (feudalism being here used in the sense of a political and economic system in which owners of large estates are the dominant force), even though those structures were supported by a large part of landowners of gentry origin, and early forms of capitalism were emerging in town and country. Industry experienced the technological revolution, from handicrafts to mechanized production, in which process the principal role was played by the spreading of the steam engine. It is to be noted that the Industrial Revolution took place in Poland much later than it had done in Western Europe. There were also some changes in agriculture. The period 1842—48 saw the construction in the Polish territories of the first railway lines, not sufficiently used because of the poorly developed home market.

Inclusion of Great Poland in the Prussian zone undermined the cloth-making industry which had been flourishing there (cf. VIII, 4). Some 10,000 craftsmen moved to the Kingdom of Poland to give rise later to the Łódź industrial region. Their departure was indirectly caused by the Prussian policy of turning the region of Poznań into the granary of the industrial regions of Germany, and also by industrial competition of other German provinces; the immediate cause must be seen in the raising by the Russian authorities of the tariffs which deprived the cloth-makers of Great Poland of the vast markets in the East. On the other hand, favourable conditions of sale in Germany of agricultural produce from Great Poland were conducive to the development of agriculture, which was at first extensive in character: as in the rest of the country, it took place through an increase of the area under crops, and not through an increase in the crops per unit of area.

By about 1860 the percentage of arable land in the Polish territories had increased on the average by 35 to 50 per cent, the rate of increase in Great Poland and the Kingdom of Poland being by about one-fifth higher. That process was being accompanied by a gradual elimination of fallow land and the abandonment of the traditional three-field system. Technological progress was at first visible only in large estates (but not in all of them). The structure of crops was changed, too. Much more potatoes and root crops were cultivated, which was linked to the development of animal breeding. Between 1814 and 1843 all Polish territories witnessed a large increase in the sheep population: 250 per cent as compared with some 50 per cent in the case of other animals. This was an effect of intensified animal breeding after the devastations caused by the Napoleonic wars (cf. IX, 3). Horses came more and more often to replace oxen as draught animals used in field work. Polish indicators of animal breeding were by some 25 per cent higher than those for Prussia, over four times higher than those for Spain, but amounted only to some 40 per cent of those for Britain, and were roughly on a par with those for France and Austria. This fair development of agriculture was interrupted in the mid-19th century. An extremely long period of poor yields in 1846—55 (due, among other factors, to a potato pest) caused disease and starvation, with the resulting increase in mortality rate and a decrease in the population. In the Subcarpathian region alone as many as 200,000 people starved to death or died of epidemic diseases in 1847—48. Between 1840 and 1861 the population of the Polish territories increased by 13 per cent, the analogous figure for Germany being 26 per cent. At that time about one million people starved to death or died of typhus in Ireland. The whole of Europe was shaken by riots caused by starvation.

The Kingdom of Poland witnessed, next to the growth of the textile industry, also the expansion of mining and metallurgy. Remarkable initiative in that field was shown by Prince Franciszek Ksawery Drucki-Lubecki (1779—1846), minister of the treasury, in 1829 also appointed administrator of mines. He worked out a long-term plan for the development of mining and metallurgy and granted financial assistance for its implementation. He acquired the necessary means from the taxes ruthlessly collected from the peasants. The founding of the Agrarian Credit Society (1825) and the Bank of Poland (1828) was also due to his initiative. The bank, being a government-owned institution, was engaged in industrial investments on a large scale; these included the famous Huta Bankowa (Bank's Iron and Steel Works), built in 1834—40 in the village of Dąbrowa, today known as the Dzierżyński Iron and Steel Works. Lubecki continued Staszic's work in that respect, because as early as 1823, when Staszic was in charge of mining and metallurgy, there were nearly 40 government-owned iron ore mines and four coal mines.

Warsaw was becoming an important centre of industry; the city's population grew from 140,000 ca. 1830 to 230,000 in the 1860's. In the same period, the population of Poznań increased from 30,000 to 46,000, that of Cracow from 33,000 to 40,000, and that of Gdańsk from 50,000 to 70,000. Łódź changed from an ordinary village which it was ca. 1830 into a town of several dozen thousand inhabitants. Its growth was due to the inflow of weavers from Great Poland and eastern provinces of Prussia, and also the activity of manufacturers who arrived there from western parts of Germany.

The rate of industrial growth in the Kingdom of Poland increased after 1851, when the tariff barriers between that region and the Russian provinces were abolished. The resulting increased demand contributed largely to the mechanization of existing manufactories, that is, to advances in the industrial revolution. Galicia, however, was not covered by industrialization, nor did the towns develop there.

Successes in the general economic development of the country depended to a lesser degree upon the business trends in trade, the economic policy and developing economic thought (represented, for instance, by Fryderyk Skarbek; 1792—1866); the principal factor must be seen in the increased demand on the home market, that is, in the rural areas, which, however, still required fundamental reforms.

The granting of land to the peasants (i.e. conversion of the possession of the land they tilled into the ownership of that land) under the Prussian system, that is, upon the initiative of the state, took place in the various parts of Poland in different ways, in each case under specific political and social conditions. In the Prussian-held part of the country the appropriate act was passed first, in 1823, having been preceded by various partial regulations. Conversion of possession into ownership was to apply to larger holdings only, namely those of at least 6.4 hectares (under the principles adopted in 1836). In exchange for the ownership of the land the peasant had to cede to the landlord part of his holding or to pay for it in cash or in kind; in the case of his feudal duties he could either buy them out or perform gratuitous work on the landlord's estate. In all, the peasants in Great Poland lost about one-sixth of the land they had held in possession and paid to the gentry considerable sums of money which made it easier for the gentry to switch to a capitalist economy. The process of the regulation of land ownership under the aforementioned act went on for several decades; it was marked by numerous conflicts and the peasants on the whole felt they had been wronged. The processes strengthened the economic position of large estates; among the peasants those who were fairly well-to-do, met the criteria of the act and passed the test of producing themselves for the market became the central figures in their villages. The inhabitants of the rural areas became clearly stratified into owners of self-supporting farms, the rural proletariat, and the small holders, who amounted to about two-thirds of the rural population and often lived in utter poverty. In 1858, the area of an average peasant farm in the Grand Duchy of Poznań amounted to 33 hectares.

The rural areas in Galicia (i.e. the Austrian-held part of Poland) were particularly backward and poor. Most peasants were small holders: in the mid-19th century as many as 44 per cent of holdings had an area of less than three hectares, the average size being five hectares. A strong movement directed against the gentry developed in 1846, when the peasants burnt some 470 manor houses. That movement, led by Jakub Szela (1787—1866), was at first used by the Austrian authorities to prevent the uprising brewing (cf. section 4 below) and was then suppressed by the Austrian army. Two years later, following the pressure of the events connected with the wave of revolutionary movements that swept Continental Europe in 1848 (cf. section 4 below), an agrarian reform was carried out in Galicia. All those peasants who possessed land had their possession converted into ownership, which meant that the reform was more advanced than that in the Prussian-held part of the country, the more so as in Galicia the landowners were indemnified by the state. On the other hand, no land was granted to the small holders.

The gentry in the Kingdom of Poland were the most resistant to all change in the rural areas. The peasants struggled for decades to improve their position, which led to certain partial solutions, confined to state-owned estates. It was only the considerable improvement in the demand for agricultural produce, due to the abolition of tariffs on grain in Britain and increased demand in other countries, which swelled the number of the advocates of conversion of peasant possession into ownership. When the act which granted land to Russian peasants was promulgated in 1861, peasants in the Kingdom of Poland started refusing to perform gratuitous work on the estates of the landlords. In an atmosphere of political tension the tsar's *Ukases* were published in 1861 and 1862, which abolished corvée against the payment of high indemnities and imposed upon the peasants the duty of paying a rent, but were silent on the point of conversion of the possession of land into its ownership. It was only the outbreak of the 1863 Uprising (cf. section 4 below), followed by a decree of the Provisional National Government (i.e. the government set up by the insurgents) of January 1863, which converted the possession of land into its ownership without indemnification and granted plots of three hectares each to those landless peasants who joined the Uprising, that induced the tsarist government to carry out a reform that would weaken the impression of the initiative taken up by the insurgent authorities. The tsarist reform followed exactly in the steps of the decree issued by the Provisional National Government, and the tsarist government promulgated enfranchisement of the peasants on 2 March 1864.

The agrarian reforms brought about an essential change in the structure of Polish society. Abolition of the feudal system in the rural areas (in spite of some of its survivals) turned the gentry into capitalist landowners, and the peasants, into small producers.

All this did not, however, result in the disappearance of the gentry model of life, which — while subjected to the unifying impact of capitalism — still bore heavily upon the mentality of the Polish people as a whole. The developing bourgeois way of life (including that of the grande bourgeoisie) was under the marked influence of the gentry (and aristocratic) pattern and also that of the western bourgeoisie. The former was manifested, for instance, in the tendency to obtain aristocratic titles and to establish family connections with prominent aristocratic families; the latter, in the development of material civilization that drew inspiration from a market which was being better and better supplied.

Dress was made more uniform which meant disappearance of the typical gentry costumes. The *kontusz* of the gentry was replaced by the bourgeois frock-coat which directly led to the present-day business suit. The glaring colours of men's dress were at the same time replaced by dark ones, colourfulness being now the attribute of the women's dress only. The 1840's saw the advent of the crinoline, which had its predecessors in the Spanish dress worn in the 16th century, and in a certain type of petticoat that was fairly common in 18th century Poland.

The standard so far represented by the aristocracy now became that of the rich bourgeoisie, which strove to demonstrate its wealth by possessing palaces (which were often turned into warehouses, shops, apartments). The food was standardized in the case of average town-dwellers, but the number of people whose housing and feeding standards were extremely poor increased as compared with the previous period of the natural economy. Potatoes, a new element of the diet, soon became the staple food of the growing numbers of town-dwellers.

Between 1815 and 1864, the social structure typical of the capitalist system, marked by the emergence of the bourgeoisie and the working class, was being gradually imposed upon that typical of the feudal system with the gentry and the peasants as the two principal groups of the population. In view of the slow and uneven development of industry in the Polish territories the new social structure was taking shape slowly and was constantly affected by the strong remnants of the feudal system that had existed for over eight centuries. Nevertheless, especially in the Kingdom of Poland, the bourgeoisie, the beginnings of which went back to the reign of Stanislaus Augustus, was becoming increasingly strong. It consisted of owners of industrial and transport enterprises, merchants and bankers. The most eminent of them lived in Warsaw and Łódź (e.g. Piotr Steinkeller, Leopold Kronenberg Sr. and Jr., Ksawery Szlenker, Herman Epstein Sr. and Jr.), the less affluent ones, in smaller towns. The Polish bourgeoisie was largely of foreign origin and made it a point to be in good social and economic relations with the aristocracy and the intelligentsia. While less revolutionary than that in the more advanced countries, it did not confine itself to its own circle and was not indifferent to the fortunes (or rather misfortunes) of the Polish nation. For instance, two Epsteins, of the rich banker family, took part in the Uprising of 1863; one of them was killed in action and the other was deported to Siberia. Many members of the bourgeoisie were of Jewish origin, but only some of them merged totally with the Warsaw bourgeoisie, consisting of people of various origins but taking root in Polish society.

The working class, very small at that time, was growing as industry expanded. In the Kingdom of Poland in 1830 industrial workers amounted to merely 2—3 per cent of the population, and their situation was exceptionally bad. There was no labour legislation at all, and they often had to work 16 hours per day for very low wages. Women and children were exploited accordingly. The workers reacted with strikes and riots which were ruthlessly suppressed by the authorities.

4. Struggle for political independence: from the Philomath Society to the 1863 Uprising

The so-called November Uprising of 1830—31 was the first independence struggle on the national scale. It was preceded by earlier conspiratorial activity and an intensifying anti-Polish policy in the Russian zone.

Immediately after the Congress of Vienna, and for decades after, conservative circles (part of the aristocracy and the higher clergy) counted upon an understanding with the partitioning powers and the guaranteeing by them of political autonomy in partition zones. These hopes failed to materialize, nor were they shared by the Polish people as a whole.

There was also a legal opposition within the local representative bodies (the Seym in the Kingdom of Poland, the House of Representatives in the Republic of Cracow, and in the Provincial Diet of the Grand Duchy of Poznań), which fought for national rights and democratic freedoms on the basis of the liberal ideas developing at that time. The firmest opposition was that in the Seym of the Kingdom of Poland, called the Kalisz group (from the region of Kalisz which they represented) and including Alojzy Biernacki, Teofil Morawski, Stanisław Kaczkowski, and Wincenty and Bonawentura Niemojewski.

While the liberal opposition worked legally, the other trend, much broader and influential, led by the so-called gentry democrats, acted in conspiracy. It was linked to the vast movement of the Carbonari, aimed at the Holy Alliance and striving for democracy in political life, for political independence, and often for social reforms as well. The first Polish conspiracies were formed among students. They were the already mentioned Philomath Society, set up in Vilna in 1817, which had social, patriotic and self-educational goals in view; the Union of Friends of Panta Koina, organized in Warsaw; the Polonia Society in Berlin and Wrocław; and the Carbonarist Union of Free Poles, set up in Warsaw in 1820. The conspiracy formed in 1819 and led in the Kingdom of Poland by Major Walerian Łukasiński (represented in the region of Poznań by Ludwik Sczaniecki) was disguised as a semi-legal Freemasons' lodge. Called the National Freemasonry, it was soon transformed — upon the initiative of the secret Union of Scythebearers (the name referred to the peasants armed with scythes who took part in the Kościuszko Insurrection), set up in Great Poland by members of the local lodge — into the secret Patriotic Society that became active in preparing an uprising.

In 1822, the tsar ordered reprisals aimed at secret societies. Łukasiński was arrested and later, in 1830, taken to the fortress of Schlüsselburg, where he remained until his death in 1868; his successor, Colonel Seweryn Krzyżanowski, was arrested, too; in spite of a mild sentence passed by a tribunal established by the Seym, the next tsar, Nicholas I, had him deported to Siberia, where he died in 1839. The Patriotic Society, and even earlier the Philomaths in Vilna, developed even closer co-operation with Polish and Russian progressive circles. On the other hand, the secret organizations that were then springing up in Russia, such as the Northern Association (in St. Petersburg), the Southern Association, and the Association of United Slavs (in the Ukraine), strove to establish contacts with Polish organizations, but before that took place on any considerable scale the attempted Decembrist *coup d'état* in Russia had ended in failure (1825), which resulted in numerous arrests in the Kingdom of Poland as well. In the meantime the younger generation of Polish activists in the independence movement decided to organize a conspiracy in the Infantry Cadets' School in Warsaw, to be led by Piotr Wysocki (1797—1874, i.e. 11 years younger than Łukasiński), who was associated with Lelewel. The conspiracy was joined by members of the intelligentsia and university students. The outbreak of the uprising — 29 November 1830 — was accelerated by the mobilization ordered by the Tsar Nicholas I, who wanted to use the Polish troops to suppress the national uprising in Belgium. The events in Warsaw cancelled the tsar's plans and helped the Belgians to win independence.

The Uprising of 1830—31, the strongest manifestation of gentry revolutionism, disclosed the weakness of that movement which was due to the limitation of its programme of social reforms. The cadets who attacked the Belvedere Palace, residence of Grand Duke Constantine, were supported above all by the people of Warsaw, who thus helped to free Warsaw. But both the Administrative Council, joined by several patriots popular in the country, and later the Provisional Government were dominated by conservatives and tended to negotiate with the Russian authorities. A similar attitude was represented by General Józef Chłopicki

(1771—1854), 'dictator' of the insurrection, which reduced readiness to fight for independence. When Chłopicki resigned and the Patriotic Society, incapacitated by the Provisional Government, was revived, and when also the dethroning of the Romanov dynasty was proclaimed and the memory of the Decembrists honoured, the uprising was joined by conservatives, too. The National Government, headed by Prince Adam Czartoryski, was set up, which meant the reappearance of an independent Polish state. Its survival proved extremely difficult: the National Government depended more on a favourable diplomatic situation (neutrality of Prussia, friendly attitude of Austria, diplomatic assistance of Britain and France) than on internal forces at home. It was only under the pressure of the requirements of the military situation — the defeat at Ostrołęka (26 June 1831) caused by the indecision of General Jan Skrzynecki, the new commander-in-chief, that came after the victories at Stoczek, Wawer, Grochów, Dębe Wielkie, and Iganie — that the insurgent authorities resorted to a *levée en masse.* But the peasant issue was totally disregarded, which limited the participation of peasants in some guerilla operations. The military situation deteriorated, the more so as under the new commander-in-chief, Jan Krukowiecki (1771—1850), the political trend became even more reactionary. The Russian troops led by Marshal Ivan Paskevitch took Warsaw in September 1831, and Modlin and Zamość, the last points of resistance, fell in October.

The collapse of the uprising and participation in it of many Poles from the territories held by Prussia and Austria (in the case of Great Poland the uprising covered the region of Kalisz) were a good pretext for the partitioning powers to intensify their anti-Polish drive. In the Kingdom of Poland the Polish troops were dissolved and young men were covered by military service in the Russian army; Warsaw University and the Society of Friends of Science were closed down; the Russian monetary system and the administrative division of the country into *gubernyas* (largest territorial units in the Russian administrative system) instead of voivodships (provinces in the Polish administrative system) were introduced; the Seym of the Kingdom of Poland was abolished and Russian civil servants were gradually being brought in to replace Poles on the administrative staff. Marshal Paskevitch became the tsar's deputy governor, and participants in the uprising suffered reprisals (numerous confiscations of estates).

In the Prussian-held area the harsh policy toward the Poles was being put into effect by Eduard Flotwell, *Oberpräsident* of the province of Poznań. The office of the deputy governor was abolished, but there were no confiscations of the estates of the participants in the uprising. Endeavours were made, however, to increase the number of the German population in those territories and the share of Germans in public administration and schools. The change (in 1832) of the municipal electoral rules, which introduced electoral qualification based on property owned, automatically increased the influence in towns of well-to-do German inhabitants. Flotwell also attacked the clergy, but his failure added to the authority of the Church. As a result of all that the anti-Polish drive intensified Polish resistance and at the same time stimulated 'organic' work (cf. section 1 above). Poznań became the centre of conspiratorial activities.

Many Germans gave expression to their friendly feelings toward the Poles who were struggling for political independence; some of them participated in the 1830 Uprising as physicians and medical corpsmen. Societies of Friends of Poland were springing up, and those participants in the uprising who left the Kingdom of Poland as political emigrés were greeted enthusiastically.

The last statement is especially applicable to the German territories, especially Saxony, because Poles were treated as representatives of the struggle for freedom. Polonophile feelings were growing throughout Germany; songs, poems, and other works were composed to honour the Poles, and committees were set up to organize aid to the Polish emigrés who were travelling westward. That widely spread phenomenon even acquired a special term, namely that of *Polenbegeisterung* (agitation in favour of Poland). The attitude of the Prussian government contrasted strongly with the almost universally friendly feelings of the German people. Some thousand insurgents had to perform forced labour in the fortresses of Gdańsk, Piława, and Grudziądz for two years before they were permitted to leave Prussia as political emigrés. On the other hand, many Prussian and Austrian officials in other towns facilitated their departure to western Europe.

Now that conspiratorial activity at home was difficult to carry out, the task of organizing the struggle for the political independence of Poland became the task of the people traditionally called the Great Emigration in Polish historiography. It was a group of some 11,000 persons who lived mainly in France, but also in the United States, Britain, and other countries. At that time they formed the intellectual and political élite of the Polish nation and included such prominent personalities as Adam Czartoryski, Maurycy Mochnacki, Frédéric Chopin, Adam Mickiewicz, Juliusz Słowacki, Joachim Lelewel, and Julian Ursyn Niemcewicz.

The first wave of conspiracies was linked to the Carbonari, members of secret revolutionary societies in Western Europe, and had Lelewel as the leader. Conspiratorial activity was at first strongest in Galicia, but arrests at the turn of the 1830's and 1840's incapacitated the secret organization there to a considerable degree. In the Kingdom of Poland, and also in Volhynia and Lithuania, there was a conspiracy organized by Szymon Konarski in 1832. Konarski's arrest was followed by imprisonment of many members of the conspiracy, and Konarski himself was executed.

In the meantime (1832) Western Europe saw the formation of the Polish Democratic Society, with a liberal and democratic programme, which had in view an uprising that would be supported by the whole nation. In order not to estrange the gentry no demands to break up the estates were formulated, but the programme included the enfranchisement of the peasants. It was only the left wing of that society, called Gromady Ludu Polskiego (Communities of the Polish People, also rendered as Communes of the Polish People), which advanced a radical programme in the spirit of Utopian socialism (abolition of private property). Opinions more radical as compared with those of the Democratic Society were also propagated by the Union of Plebeians, organized in Poznań in 1842—43 by Walenty Stefański; the same applies to the views of Edward Dembowski and Henryk Kamieński, and to Father Piotr Ściegienny (1800—90), who called for a social revolution, to be carried out primarily by the peasants.

The conservative camp was represented by adherents of Adam Czartoryski (the group was nicknamed Hôtel Lambert after Czartoryski's Paris residence). It continued to count above all upon 'the courts', that is, upon good configurations of international forces. It was only under the pressure of the opinion prevailing among the emigrés that it included the enfranchisement of the peasants in its programme (the operation was to be carried out under the supervision of the gentry). In the plans of the conservatives Poland was to be a constitutional monarchy, its frontiers being those of 1772.

Conspiratorial activity in the Grand Duchy of Poznań and in Galicia was linked to the emigrés. The Polish Democratic Society had the strongest influence there through the intermediary of the Poznań Committee, set up in 1839, but among the poor strata of the population the Union of Plebeians was more popular. Unfortunately, that union was denounced by Seweryn Mielżyński. The Poznań Committee came soon to be headed by Ludwik Mierosławski (1814—78), an emissary of the Polish Democratic Society, who was to lead the uprising the outbreak of which in all Polish territories was expected to take place in 1846. There was, however, no uprising in that year in the Poznań region, whereas in Cracow, whence the Austrians were expelled, a National Government of the Republic of Cracow, with a very radical social programme, was set up on 22 February 1846, headed by Józef Tyssowski (1817—57). But four days later the troops of the Republic of Cracow were defeated by the Austrians and the Republic collapsed. In their *Communist Manifesto* Karl Marx and Friedrich Engels wrote that the communists supported that party in Poland which 'insists on an agrarian revolution as the prime condition for national emancipation, that party which fomented the insurrection of Cracow in 1846'.

The defeat suffered in 1846 was a blow to conspiratorial activity at home. Two hundred and fifty-four participants in the Polish liberation struggle were tried in Berlin in 1847, which aroused the interest of German public opinion in the Polish issue. The trial must be treated as a factor which stimulated revolutionary attitudes in Europe.

In February 1848, following the revolution that broke out in Paris, a revolutionary wave swept France, Italy, and Austria, to reach Polish territories in March. In the Prussian partition zone hopes were revived for a greater autonomy and a democratization of the political system, but those trends were not supported even by German liberals. This was demonstrated by the notorious debate in the Frankfurt Parliament, which started an intensified Germanization drive that followed the suppression of the uprising in Great Poland. That uprising was led by Ludwik Mierosławski, one of the prisoners held in Berlin after the trial of 1847 and liberated as a result of the revolution. The collapse of the revolution in Prussia, with the authorities gaining the upper hand, led to the defeat of the Polish uprising despite the mass participation of the peasants and the initial victories at Miłosław and Sokołów. It is to be noted that next to the National Committee in Poznań a similar one was formed in Gdańsk Pomerania, which was not part of the Grand Duchy of Poznań.

In Galicia, the revolutionary trend did not develop into an armed uprising. A National Committee was set up in Cracow, and a National Council in Lvov, and endeavours were made to induce the Austrian authorities to restore an independent Polish state. Nothing was gained in that respect. The Austrians suppressed the resistance of the Cracovians and made the National Committee dissolve itself. The same occurred in Lvov, which surrendered to the Austrian troops. The revolution of 1848 brought the enfranchisement of the peasants in Galicia (cf. section 3 above) and stimulated the national Ukrainian movement. The Polish national movement also became more lively in the Cieszyn region of Silesia.

After the failure of the revolution in Poland the Poles fought 'for your freedom and for ours' in Italy (under Giuseppe Garibaldi), in Baden, and in the Hungarian uprising, of which General Józef Bem (1794—1850) was one of the commanders. During the Crimean War endeavours were made to organize Polish troops that would help Turkey. It was in the course of such activities that Adam Mickiewicz died in Istanbul on 26 November 1855.

Conspiracies continued at home, mainly in the Kingdom of Poland, where the peasant issue was still unsolved. Refusal to the Poles of their national rights led to a wave of patriotic sentiments and demonstrations. Such demonstrations occurred in Warsaw at the funeral of the poet Zygmunt Krasiński (1854) and that of Mme Sowińska, the widow of General Józef Sowiński, who lost his life in the defence of Warsaw in 1831, during the final stage of the November Uprising. Demonstrations were also held on the thirtieth anniversary of the outbreak of that uprising. During one of them (27 February 1861) tsarist gendarmes shot five demonstrators, which led in turn to the next mass demonstration at their funeral. Public opinion was moved by the dissolution, ordered by Margrave Aleksander Wielopolski, a politician loyal to the tsar, of the recently formed so-called Municipal Delegation, a *sui generis* representation of Polish people and of the merited Agricultural Society, which was a forum for discussion of many problems. Finally public opinion became alarmed by the conscription to the Russian army, also ordered by Wielopolski and directly intended to foil preparations for a national uprising. Those preparations were being made by the Central National Committee, dominated by the Reds, i.e. the group which wanted to link the uprising to agrarian reforms (conversion of the possession of the land held by the peasants into ownership) and also co-operated with Russian revolutionaries, such as Alexander Herzen, Mikhail Bakunin, and Nikolai Ogarev.

Another secret organization active at that time, that of the Whites, consisted of liberals and advocates of legal activity, who largely came of the bourgeoisie. The latter organization was led by Leopold Kronenberg, the well-known entrepreneur and banker. The Whites propagated the principle of 'organic' work and counted on favourable international constellations and concessions on the part of the Russians. But when the uprising broke out the Whites strove to intercept power. They succeeded to do so only in April 1863, after Stefan Bobrowski (1841—63), chairman of the Executive Commission into which the Central National Committee was transformed, had been killed in a duel, and Zygmunt Padlewski (1835—63), member of the insurgent government, had been executed by the Russians in Płock.

It was the Reds who promulgated the decree on the enfranchisement of the peasants (cf. section 3 above) and strove to put it into effect. They also had to their credit the initial military successes won despite the fact that the number of armed insurgents amounted to only 25,000 to 30,000 people, while the Russian army was increased (1863) from 100,000 to 490,000. The majority of the insurgents were not of gentry origin, but came from the bourgeoisie, the intelligentsia, and the peasants (it was only in Lithuania and Byelorussia that the gentry constituted the majority). There was also a considerable percentage of the urban and rural poor, who came from the Prussian and the Austrian partitions to join the uprising. There were also volunteers from many foreign countries: Italians with Colonel Francesco Nullo, the French under Fraçois Rochebrun, Russians (including Andrei Potebnia, who lost his life in action), Czechs, Slovaks, Serbians, the British, and Germans. Only few Polish aristocrats adhered to the uprising (e.g. Jan Działyński and Ignacy Sapieha). The attitude of the higher clergy was not uniform, and the Papal Curia (as was also in the case of the Uprising of 1830) tended to support the existing order.

The military operations amounted mostly to guerilla warfare, scattered into hundreds of local actions undertaken independently and without any general military plan. The prominent commanders of these guerilla troops included Marian Langiewicz, Michał Heidenreich-Kruk, and Józef Hauke-Bosak.

The supremacy of the Russian troops and intensified reprisals (the power in the Kingdom of Poland was given to ruthless General Fiodor Berg), turned the scales. The endeavours made by Czartoryski's party active in France to secure diplomatic support for the uprising failed, too. Under the circumstances the Reds again gained the upper hand and appointed Romuald Traugutt (1826—64) to be the 'dictator'. He tried to save the cause of the uprising by attracting larger numbers of the peasants, but all that came too late. The tsar, in order to neutralize Traugutt's endeavours to put the insurgents' decree on the agrarian reform into effect, himself promulgated the *Ukase* that enfranchised the peasants (cf. section 3 above). The uprising ended in an utter defeat, to be followed by reprisals on the part of the Russian authorities. Traugutt and four other leaders were hanged in Warsaw. Some 38,000 people were deported to Siberia. Many thousands of the insurgents were killed in action, some 10,000 of them succeeded in emigrating. More than 1500 estates belonging to insurgents were confiscated. Reprisals also took place in the territories held by the Prussians.

Chapter XI

Advances of Capitalism in Poland. Struggle for National Identity. Regaining of Independence (1864—1918)

1. The Polish nation in the post-insurrection period

The defeat of the 1863 Uprising interrupted a half-century long armed struggle for independence. The greatest chances of an ultimate victory were those of the November Uprising of 1830—31. Later the situation was much more difficult. The supremacy of the partitioning powers which strove to co-operate in suppressing Polish endeavours for independence was growing, the Poles had no national army of their own (which was still the case in 1815—30), and other powers were not inclined to commit themselves to the Polish cause.

Increasingly the Poles came to realize that unless the Holy Alliance collapsed (which could occur only as a result of a widely spread international conflict), they would never regain independence. The centre of the revolutionary movement was now neither in Poland nor in Germany: it had shifted to Russia, a country marked by greatest internal contradictions, and hence the Holy Alliance was strongly supported by all the partitioning powers. The hopes connected with the conflict between Prussia and Austria failed to materialize because Prussia quickly gained the upper hand following the Battle of Sadova (1866). France became neutralized by its defeat at Sedan (1870), inflicted by Prussia under Bismarck's iron rule. The meeting of the three emperors on the centenary of the first partition of Poland, i.e., in 1872, confirmed that they were united on the Polish issue.

Once the Polish issue was recognized as an internal concern of the partitioning powers, the most important task for the Polish people was the maintenance and strengthening of national consciousness. This was to be achieved by permanent contact with intellectual and artistic movements and by promotion of 'organic' work that would improve the economic state of the country. The point was that if a situation favourable to reconstruction of the Polish state should develop the nation must have both the motivation and leaders; links with the partitioning powers should be restricted to material concerns rather than political goals. The governments of the partitioning powers, especially those of Prussia and Russia, by intensifying the anti-Polish drive and striving to remove all the specific features of the Polish ethnic territories, stimulated the resistance of the Polish nation, now in a more modern form after the agrarian reforms. The earlier uprisings had played an immense role in raising and maintaining national consciousness; this became one of the principal elements of the historical bonds that kept the Polish people together.

All this was accompanied by a period of a fairly dynamic economic development, due primarily to the agrarian reforms and an increase in the population. The number of the Poles at home nearly doubled between 1870 and 1914, rising from about 10,000,000 to 18,000,000 despite the emigration of many people. Of those 18,000,000, 15,500,000 lived in the areas densely inhabited by the Poles (which might be termed the Polish ethnic areas). Of the remaining 2,500,000, 1,350,000 lived in Eastern Galicia, over one million in western Russian provinces, and some 100,000 in eastern Prussian provinces (regions of Wrocław, Legnica,

Królewiec, Gąbin, Lębork, Bytów and Słupsk). Before World War I, the territories densely inhabited by the Poles — outside the Kingdom of Poland, Galicia, and the Grand Duchy of Poznań — included the Cieszyn region of Silesia (ca. 55 per cent of the population were Poles), the Opole region (ca. 57 per cent), Western Prussia, i.e. Gdańsk Pomerania (ca. 35.5 per cent), and the southern districts of Eastern Prussia. The ethnically Polish territories held by Prussia noted an increase of the number of the Poles despite the Germanization drive, the process known as the *Ostflucht,* i.e., migration of Germans from the agricultural provinces in the East to the industrialized districts in western Germany. That increase did not, of course, balance the large earlier inflow of the Germans to the territories seized by Prussia as a result of the partitions, so that, for instance, in the region of Poznań the percentage of the Germans rose from several per cent in the late 18th century to about 32 per cent in 1910, the analogous figure for the region of Bydgoszcz being about 50 per cent. This process was even stronger in Gdańsk Pomerania.

Since Poland lacked political independence and the various territories were developing economically at a very uneven pace, hundreds of thousands of Poles lacked either satisfactory living conditions or good opportunities for the manifestation of their talents at home. Many migrated to various countries, opening an entirely new chapter in the history of Poles abroad. At the turn of the 19th century, emigrants numbered millions. Over 3,500,000 people left ethnic Polish territories between 1870 and 1914, the figures being 1,250,000 for the Russian zone, 1,200,000 for the Prussian zone, and over one million for the Austrian zone. They went mainly to the United States. In all, the number of the Poles outside the ethnically Polish territories amounted to 4,300,000, of whom about 3,000,000 lived in the United States, some 750,000 in Germany, some 100,000 in Brazil, 45,000 in Canada, and 400,000 in Russia. On the other hand, many Jews were moving to the Polish territories from Russia in search of better living conditions.

The post-1864 period was marked by a great acceleration of changes on an unprecedented scale. This is borne out when we compare the 1863 Uprising, which was still largely a matter of the gentry, with the revolution of 1905—07. In some forty years it became possible to pass from a gentry-led movement to a movement of the working class, with all the deep-reaching changes behind that process, changes which had a strong impact upon economic and social life, culture, and the whole sphere of social consciousness.

2. The economic and social development of the Polish territories

The capitalist system developed in the Polish territories in the second half of the 19th and the early 20th century, but it still included numerous survivals of the former feudal system and moreover was very little resistant to the economic developments in more advanced countries. This was manifested in the penetration of the Polish territories by foreign capital, which took advantage of cheap manpower and a growing market. In 1900 it controlled some 60 per cent of the industrial production in the Kingdom of Poland.

The considerable increase in the number of the population mentioned above was mainly due to the general economic development that secured an adequate number of jobs and also to increased amounts of food, improved hygienic conditions, spreading general education, advances in science and technology and better medical care. The infant mortality rate decreased while the average life span increased. That was fairly common in Europe at that time. These changes were largely due to improved living conditions in towns, where, for example, water mains and sewage systems were built, streets were paved and sanitary care was assured. The growth of the urban population accompanied the development of industry. Urbanization advanced but this process revealed differences according to the various regions. In Great Poland, agrarization of the provinces helped preserve a very dense network of small towns dating back to the pre-partition period but even there the percentage of the population in towns with more than 10,000 inhabitants each doubled in that time (from eight to 16 per cent). That process of urban growth was more dynamic in the Kingdom of Poland, where the percentage of the population of such towns reached 18 per cent. In Upper Silesia the rise was from nine to 36 per cent, while in Galicia it was much lower, namely from six to 13 per cent. Large towns were growing most rapidly: the population of Warsaw increased from 300,000 in 1870 to 850,000 just before World War I, that of Łódź, from 50,000 to 450,000 and that of Poznań, from 50,000 to 150, 000. In Silesia and in Dąbrowa district some villages, for example, Sosnowiec and Zabrze, became populous towns.

While in the 1850's some 80 per cent of the population lived from agriculture, in the early 20th century agriculture provided subsistence for 42 per cent in the Prussian zone (in 1882 that figure was still 55 per cent), the analogous data for the Russian and the Austrian zone being about 65 per cent. Urban population was swelled by peasants who were leaving the rural areas and by many members of the gentry who did not know how to switch to the capitalist mode of production in agriculture, which required rational calculation based on the knowledge of the laws of the market.

In the second half of the 19th century agriculture was at its best in the Prussian zone, since agricultural producers had advantageous markets for the sale of their products in western Germany and in Silesia. In the Austrian zone the Austro-Hungarian market, protected by preventive tariffs, was not an easy place to sell agricultural produce. In the Kingdom of Poland, much grain was exported at first and the exports continued during the early years of the agrarian crisis that swept Europe in 1873—95. But since, unlike in Great Poland, agriculture in the Kingdom of Poland was intensified and mechanized on a minimum scale only, which applied to both large landed estates that still availed themselves of various semi-feudal performances by peasants, and peasant farms, it soon came to face competition of other countries. The process was accompanied by a decline in the prices of agricultural products. The income yield of agriculture diminished and the position of the peasant population deteriorated considerably. The continuance of small holdings stabilized the structure that hampered advances in agriculture. The degree of concentration of land ownership in the Kingdom of Poland was 28 per cent in 1877 and 27 per cent in 1904, while the figure for the Prussian zone was 70 per cent.

The business trend in agriculture improved to any extent only at the turn of the 19th century, when agricultural prices rose by 15 to 20 per cent. Yet the Kingdom of Poland, in view of its remarkable growth of population, and urban population in particular, had to import from Russia some 100,000 metric tons of grain annually. This had an adverse effect upon agricultural progress in the Kingdom of Poland, which could not compete with the low cost of grain production in Russia, then only entering the path of capitalism. For all that, between 1850 and 1880 the agricultural production and the profitability of agriculture in the Kingdom of Poland were increasing, on the average, by three per cent annually. It was only the long agrarian crisis which intensified the difference between the standard of agriculture in the Kingdom of Poland, on the one hand, and in Great Poland and Gdańsk Pomerania, on the other. In the second half of the 19th century the rise in agricultural production was no longer obtained by an increase in the area of arable land, but was effected by intensification of production (three-field system without laying land fallow, rotation of crops). In the 1880's, no land was laid fallow in Silesia, and the figures were small for Pomerania and Great Poland. Mechanization of agriculture and the use of fertilizers were coming from the West. In the Prussian zone in 1907 the majority of farms of more than five hectares used agricultural machines. It was also in Great Poland that a system of loans for agricultural purposes was most widely spread. From 1855 credit-and-loan co-operatives had at their disposal a bank of their own.

The development of the rural areas, decisive for the volume of the commodities that could be sold at home (which factor was in the 1880's the principal driving force in the expansion of industry), had an essential influence upon industrialization. It was only after 1890 that the role of exports to Russia increased: in 1900, industry (mainly textile) in the Kingdom of Poland yielded some 15 per cent of the value of the entire industrial output of the Russian Empire, whereas Galician industry accounted for only four per cent of the output of the Austro-Hungarian Empire. Exports to Russia benefited the bourgeoisie which was growing rich and was favoured by the Russian protective tariffs introduced in 1877. These exports covered mainly textile goods, which amounted to 68 per cent of the value of all exports to Russia. The share of ferrous goods in that year was 7.5 per cent as compared with 17 per cent fifteen years earlier. This decline was due to rapid development in the iron industry in Russia. The growing competition in the Russian home market, as in the case of textile goods, accounted for the fact that industry in the Kingdom of

Poland started again to produce principally for its own internal market, which was advantageous for that region.

The textile industry was concentrated in the region of Łódź and, to a lesser extent, in that of Białystok, and also, in Little Poland near Andrychów and in the town of Bielsko-Biała. Mining had its main centres in Upper Silesia and the Dąbrowa Basin, while the metal industry developed in Warsaw. Silesia witnessed a dynamic development in the mining and the metallurgical industry, even though its share in the total output of the German Empire was falling as a result of the industrial development of western Germany. There were very close connections between Upper Silesia (in the Prussian zone) and the Dąbrowa Basin (in the Russian zone), caused by the flow of manpower across the frontier. The metallurgical and the engineering industry were also developing in some towns in Great Poland and Pomerania, mainly in Poznań and Gdańsk. In Galicia, extraction of petroleum gradually came to the fore in industrial production, but the foreign capital that dominated that branch of industry prevented the construction of a refinery. The output of petroleum in Galicia rose from 1.2 per cent of the world output in 1900 to five per cent in 1909.

As in other countries, industry in the Polish territories was subject to concentration, which meant that small enterprises were driven out of the competition by large ones, which yielded larger profits. This was particularly visible in the region of Łódź (textile industry), and began first in Upper Silesia. Joint stock companies were springing up and cartels and syndicates were being formed.

Industry as a whole witnessed a technological revolution consisting in the mechanization of labour. Electric engines were driving out steam engines on an increasing scale. In the metallurgical industry open-hearth furnaces and Thomas' technology were being used. The extraction of hard coal increased from 4,300 metric tons in 1864 to 62,600 metric tons in 1913, the analogous figures being 163,200 and 1,413,600 metric tons for pig-iron, and 70,400 and 192,400 metric tons for zinc (the initial date for that metal being 1880).

The growth of industry swelled the ranks of the working class, recruited mainly from those peasants who were leaving the rural areas, craftsmen, and to some extent from the poor gentry. In 1913, the Kingdom of Poland had some 350,000 workers as compared with some 150,000 twenty years earlier. In Upper Silesia the proletariat at that time amounted to some 500,000 people. The crafts were still dominant in the Poznań region, while the Galician proletariat numbered some 90,000 persons in 1910; some of them were peasants who worked in the oil industry without abandoning their farms.

The numerical growth of the working class and its connections with large factories, metallurgical works, mines, etc. helped form the class consciousness of its members. Working-class traditions and ways of life were gradually evolving. This had a considerable effect upon the atmosphere of the political life at that time (cf. section

4 below). But the rural areas, too, witnessed significant changes in the consciousness of their inhabitants. The growing social stratification of the rural areas revealed more strongly than before the antagonisms between the well-off and the poor. Differences in financial means were increasing with the lapse of time, and the distance between well-to-do farmers, on the one hand, and poor peasants and farm labourers, on the other, was becoming greater. Owners of latifundia formed the élite of those who owned land and were often connected with big business. The last-named group, which was the bulwark of conservative tendencies, was marked by a strong sense of intra-group solidarity.

The urban population was numerically dominated by the petite bourgeoisie, consisting of craftsmen and small shopkeepers. The bourgeoisie, joined by rich craftsmen and traders who switched to the capitalist system of production, was also growing in numbers. That class had its élite in the industrial and financial oligarchy, its richest group co-operating closely with the aristocracy.

3. Political life. Resistance to denationalization. Visions of a future Poland

The new social structure influenced considerably the political life in the post-1864 period. Two principal factors were closely intertwined: the aspirations of the new groups and classes, more and more conscious of their place in society, namely the workers, the peasants, and the consolidating bourgeoisie and petite bourgeoisie that strove to make their voice heard on national issues, and the struggle against the anti-Polish policies of the partitioning powers. These two areas could not be separated from one another, and hence programmes of social reform were inevitably linked to the national issue.

Until the late 1880's, that is for nearly a quarter of a century, no political group envisaged a situation in which Poland could regain political independence. It seemed that the loyalists (i.e. those who advocated loyalty to the respective partitioning powers) and the conservatives, most numerous in the Austrian partition, were right. It soon turned out that the governments of the partitioning powers took advantage of these conciliatory attitudes. The socialists in the original period of their activity (cf. section 4 below) stressed the struggle against exploitation and believed that a future revolution would put an end to all exploitation, including the national one. They feared that the goals connected with the national issue might come before the social goals of the oppressed classes. But the 1890's witnessed a general change in the prevailing opinion: the vision of political independence — and not only the struggle for the preservation of the Polish national character — began to set the tune for political life. We can thus speak about two essential points in the political programmes in that period: the cause of national self-defence and the vision of a future independent state. This was associated with such problems as the share of the people in political life (electoral law), the attitude toward the Church, promotion of education and science, participation in economic and cultural organizations. In the case of the social issues, which were dominant in political life, the most important ones included the living conditions and the rights of the workers, and the agrarian issue, i.e. the problem of fragmentation of large estates. The emergence of the first political parties, which represented the interests of the bourgeoisie and the landowners, of the working class, and of the peasants, was a characteristic phenomenon.

The struggle for the preservation of national identity was becoming increasingly difficult. In the intensifying Germanization and Russification drives (cf. X, 4) the essential change consisted in the fact that they were joined by fairly large groups of the German and the Russian population, respectively, which adopted the growing chauvinist tendencies. That gave a new dimension to the problems since the governments of the partitioning powers (or at least Germany and Russia) could find fairly wide support for their activities.

After the collapse of the 1863 Uprising the first attack against the Poles in the Prussian partition was the *Kulturkampf* waged by Otto von Bismarck, Prime Minister of Prussia and the first Chancellor of the German Empire, in the period 1871—75. It was all-German in character, and its point was to subordinate the Church to the state, which in the Prussian-held part of Poland meant an anti-Polish drive in view of the role of the Church in the preservation of the Polish national character of those territories. The campaign, which failed to subordinate the clergy to the political authorities, had its Polish hero in the person of Mieczysław Halka-Ledóchowski (1822—1902), Archbishop of Gniezno and Poznań.

But the authorities continued their policy of adopting new anti-Polish measures. The Polish language was being gradually eliminated from the schools; from 1900 on even religious instruction was to be held in Polish only in the two lowest grades, which caused the school strike in Września in 1901 that had repercussions all over Europe. From 1908 discussions at all public meetings had to be held in German. The year 1894 saw the formation of the *Ostmarkenverein* as a *sui generis* pressure group advocating anti-Polish measures and intended to influence both public opinion and the authorities. Even earlier, namely after 1885, some 30,000 Poles who were not Prussian citizens were expelled from the Prussian zone, and in the year that followed a Colonization Committee was set up with a view to bringing German settlers to the land bought from the Poles; from 1908 land could be purchased from Poles as a compulsory measure undertaken under specified circumstances.

In the late 19th century the so-called *Hebungspolitik* (the policy of promoting the Eastern territories from the civilizational point of view) was used by the German authorities to consolidate the German element in the areas seized by Prussia, and to do so more thoroughly and with greater intensity. No means were spared in investments in towns and bringing German settlers to the rural areas. Polish peasants were forbidden to erect new buildings on newly purchased land (to circumvent that prohibition Michał Drzymała lived on his plot in a circus waggon).

The legal forms of defence of Polish rights were used in the Prussian partition (Pomerania and Great Poland, and parts of Silesia) in many different ways. They consisted above all in 'organic' work: organization of economic and cultural institutions, such as the so-called 'agricultural circles' (local organizations of peasants which had mainly mutual assistance in agricultural work in view), headed by Maksymilian Jackowski (1815—1905), the Popular Education Society, the Popular Reading Rooms Society, numerous choirs, and the Sokół (Falcon) Society which promoted physical culture while having also national goals in view. The *Gazeta Grudziądzka* (Grudziądz Daily) was founded in 1894 and had the greatest circulation in the Polish territories, the editors of daily papers exerting generally a very strong influence upon public opinion. Another form of the national self-defence was the participation of Poles in the Polish Group in the Prussian Diet, and later in the Parliament of the North-German Union and the Parliament of the Reich (the *Reichstag*).

Unlike in Prussia, where the constitutional monarchy offered opportunities for legal action, in the Russian zone there were practically no possibilities of open organizational work. The Kingdom of Poland was renamed the Vistulan Region; by 1885 the Polish language was almost completely eliminated from the schools (except for religion classes). The Roman Catholic Church was subordinated to the Roman Catholic College in St. Petersburg, the Uniates were forced to adopt the Orthodox faith. A temporary mitigation of these anti-Polish measures, and the granting of certain democratic rights, such as the right to set up associations and a partial re-Polonization of the schools, which was due to the revolution of 1905—07 (cf. section 4 below), was followed by a return to the previous policy, reflected, for instance, in the dissolution in 1907 of the Polska Macierz Szkolna (the Polish School Organization). Such being the case the continuous clandestine and semi-legal educational work was important for the preservation of the Polish national character of the population. A seemingly paradoxical phenomenon could be observed (also in the Prussian zone): the driving out of the Polish language from the schools was accompanied by a considerable growth of the reading public and increased circulation of Polish-language books, newspapers, and periodicals (see section 5 below).

Activity based on the principle of 'organic' work had its intellectual reflection in the trend named Warsaw positivism. Its representatives, gathered around the periodical *Przegląd Tygodniowy* (The Weekly Review), advocated modernization of the country, and hence its economic and cultural progress. They expressed the aspirations of the liberal bourgeoisie, which for some time was opposed to the traditions of the gentry's ways of life. That attitude found its manifesto in a much publicized article by Aleksander Świętochowski (1849—1938) entitled *My i wy*

(We and You) of 1871. Such eminent novelists as Bolesław Prus (the pen name of Aleksander Głowacki, 1847—1912), Henryk Sienkiewicz (1846—1916), and Eliza Orzeszkowa (1841—1910) ranked among the adherents of that trend, which made the recommending of 'organic' work extremely popular. Work 'from the bottom up' had already had long traditions in Great Poland. Galicia (like all parts of the country) witnessed the emergence of co-operatives of various kinds. For instance, savings and credit co-operatives, which offered assistance to peasants on favourable terms, had their main promoter in Franciszek Stefczyk (1861—1924), supported in his activity by Stanisław Szczepanowski (1846—1900), who called for a programme to end the proverbial 'Galician poverty'.

The most liberal conditions prevailed in the Austrian partition zone, with the only two Polish universities in Cracow and Lvov. When the Austrian monarchy was divided in 1867 into two parts, the Austrian and the Hungarian, the Vienna government made numerous concessions in order to win the support of the Polish landowners in Galicia. The autonomy of Galicia was established in 1873, but with the preservation of the Austrian territorial and police authorities. The Provincial Diet was the highest local authority; its members came mainly from the landed gentry, which was due to the electoral law, conceived so as to secure the great majority of seats for representatives of that class. This was why the conservatives had the strongest influence in Galicia, which meant strong loyalist tendencies, gradually counteracted by the growing political consciousness of broad strata of the population, i.e. the petite bourgeoisie, the peasants, and the workers.

The advent on the political scene of new social classes and strata (cf. section 4 below) which were opposed to stabilization and conservatism was an important factor that led to the resuscitation, in the late 19th century, of the movements which had the political independence of Poland in view and of discussions about the social and political shape of future Poland. The political activity of all social classes and strata intensified, but the growing radicalization of the left wing (cf. section 4 below) resulted in clear rapprochement between the landed gentry and the bourgeoisie. The former, economically strong and referring to the old Polish traditions, was preparing for seizing power in a future Poland.

Conspiratorial movements which had political independence in view began in the 1870's, shortly after the collapse of the 1863 Uprising. Next to clandestine education (conducted in Polish, which was banned from the schools, and covering the Polish language and Polish history and literature) mention is due to self-education in the patriotic spirit, common in the case of secondary-school pupils. The Tomasz Zan Society had a particularly wide scope of activity (Tomasz Zan was a friend of the poet Adam Mickiewicz and one of the organizers of the philomathic and philaretic groups in Vilna; cf. X, 2). But it was only at the end of the 19th century that the emergence occurred of political parties in the modern sense of the word that were to determine political life in Poland not only up to World War I, but also after Poland had regained independence. They were the parties of the bourgeoisie (including the petite bourgeoisie), of the peasants, and of the proletariat.

This led to two different visions of future Poland. The left-wing movement sought the support of the workers and peasants and strove for a free, democratic country where progressive social reforms would be put into effect; the national democrats, who enjoyed the support of the propertied classes, had a vision of a hierarchical state government from the top downwards.

The national democrats evolved from the Romantic tradition of the Polish uprisings, which was still visible in the programme of the Polish League, founded in Switzerland in 1887, to more chauvinistic tendencies that made themselves felt when political workers of the younger generation took power in 1893 and characteristically changed the name of their party into the National League. The Polish League had connections with the Union of Polish Youth, founded by Zygmunt Balicki (1858—1916), while the National League had its principal leader in Roman Dmowski (1864—1939), author of *Myśli nowoczesnego Polaka* (The Thoughts of a Modern Pole; 1903), who gradually rose to that role. The National League gave inspiration to many movements and organizations, it was gaining influence in all the three parts of the country and also among the Poles living abroad. Its leaders founded the National Democratic Party at first in the Kingdom of Poland (1897) and then in Great Poland (1904) and in Galicia (1905).

The peasant movement reflected the growth of the national and class consciousness of the peasants. It played a great role in further shaping that consciousness but in spite of the fact that the peasants accounted for nearly 80 per cent of the Polish population it was not a political force on a national scale. It had its centre in Galicia and was aimed primarily at the landed gentry. In that part of the country the peasants strove for decades to have the situation that followed the enfranchisement brought to order. They claimed rights to forests and pastures. The leaders of the political peasant movement included in the first place Father Stanisław Stojałowski (1841—1911), Maria (1858—1905) and Bolesław (1855—1937) Wysłouch, editors of *Przegląd Społeczny* (The Social Review; 1886—87) and *Przyjaciel Ludu* (The Friend of the People; after 1889), and Jan Stapiński (1867—1946). The Peasant Party was formed at a congress in Rzeszów in 1895, and had among its leaders two peasants, the above-named Jan Stapiński and Jakub Bojko (1857—1944). Its programme was very moderate and did not call for the fragmentation of large estates. In 1903 its name was changed into the Polish Peasant Party, which was intended to stress the tendency to engage in a more vigorous political activity; at the same time its programme was made more radical and not confined to defending the interests of the peasants. It was the programme of a left-wing movement that strove for political independence, even though it was at first still rather a movement 'for the peasants' than 'by the peasants'. The political consciousness of the peasants increased considerably as a result of the revolution of 1905—07 (cf. section 4 below).

4. The working class movement. The revolution of 1905—07 in the Polish territories and its impact upon political life

Before the revolution of 1905—07 there had been in Poland for over forty years no large scale anti-tsarist movement except for that of the working class. This testifies to the emergence in the political and national life of a very active factor connected with a rapid growth of the working class. While the population of the Kingdom of Poland increased between 1880 and 1910 by nearly 70 per cent, the analogous figure for the working class was 350 per cent, the respective figures for the Prussian partition zone being 30 per cent and 70 per cent. The organizational maturation of the working class movement was preceded by its ideological maturation. An important role in that process was played by the Polish political emigrés, who found in Western Europe a situation different from that encountered by those who had left Poland after the 1830 Uprising. The former groups and organizations had by that time lost in importance, and the political movements in Western Europe became on the whole more radical in character. International progressive and revolutionary organizations were springing up and attracted many Poles, who were members of the Central Committee for European Democracy, of the League of Peace and Liberty, and finally of the First International (the International Association of Workers), established on 28 September 1864, at a meeting organized by working class leaders to demonstrate solidarity with the 1863 Uprising in Poland. Karl Marx determinedly stood for the reconstruction of an independent Polish state. The radicalism of the Poles who lived in Western Europe as political emigrés can be gauged by the fact that about 400 of them took part in the Paris Commune. One of them, Jarosław Dąbrowski (1836—71), who was for some time the commander-in-chief of the troops of the Commune, lost his life on the barricades when fighting for a democratic France and for the workers' cause; another Pole, Walery Wróblewski (1836—1908), was also a general of the troops of the Paris Commune.

Socialist ideas were gradually gaining more and more adherents in Poland. Socialist inspirations were coming from both Western Europe and the developing socialist movement in Russia. Polish socialism was thus emerging at the interface of two political cultures of the labour movement, and came to contribute its own values to it. Polish socialist leaders were often active simultaneously in the Polish, the Russian and the German working class movement. Contacts between the Polish and the Ukrainian socialists, among whom Ivan Franko (1856—1916) was an important figure, were established at a comparatively early date.

The working class movement was at first developing spontaneously. The number of workers' demonstrations, mostly economic strikes, increased in the late

The 18th century country manor at Żelazowa Wola, where Frédéric Chopin was born

Frédéric Chopin (1810–49), the greatest Polish composer and an outstanding pianist in his time, since 1831 in exile in Paris (painted by Ary Scheffer)

Stanisław Moniuszko (1819–72), composer, the founder of the Polish national opera and writer of lyric songs

General Jarosław Dąbrowski (1836–71), revolutionary, leader of the 'Reds' during the Polish 1863 Uprising, commander-in-chief of the troops of the Paris Commune

General Józef Bem (1794–1850), artillery commander during the 1830 Uprising, one of the leaders of the revolution in Vienna in 1848, commander of the Hungarian revolutionary troops in 1848–49 (shown here with the Hungarian generals Arthur Görgey and Lajos Kossuth and the Polish general Henryk Dębiński, also one of the commanders of the revolutionary Hungarian troops)

GÉNÉRAUX HONGROIS.

1. GŒRGEI 2. DEMBINSKI 3. KOSSUTH 4. BEM

Romuald Traugutt (1826–64), the last 'dictator' in the 1863 Uprising, later hanged in the Warsaw Citadel

The 1863 Uprising was depicted in a series of drawings entitled *Polonia,* by Artur Grottger (1837–67)

The interior of the weaving mill of the Poznański Co. in Łódź in 1906

Ignacy Łukasiewicz (1822–82), pharmacist, pioneer of the oil industry, inventor of the petroleum lamp

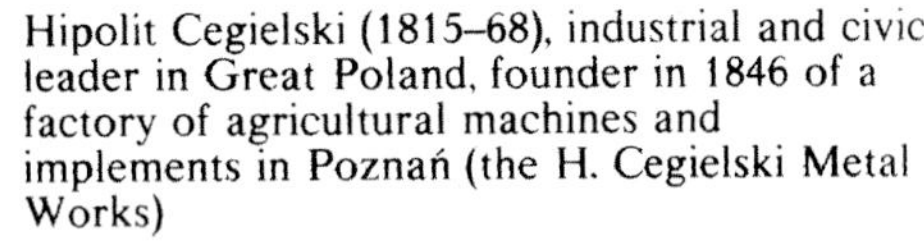

Hipolit Cegielski (1815–68), industrial and civic leader in Great Poland, founder in 1846 of a factory of agricultural machines and implements in Poznań (the H. Cegielski Metal Works)

The panorama of the Huta Królewska (the Royal Iron and Steel Works) in Chorzów in Upper Silesia (an anonymous lithograph from 1870)

Karol Miarka (1825–82), Polish national leader in Upper Silesia, founder of a cultural and educational association in Królewska Huta

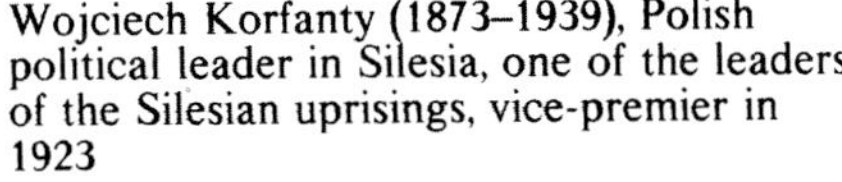

Wojciech Korfanty (1873–1939), Polish political leader in Silesia, one of the leaders of the Silesian uprisings, vice-premier in 1923

School pupils in Września, who took part in a strike in 1901 to protest against the Germanization drive

Polish emigrants on arrival in the United States (the turn of the 19th century was marked by the greatest wave of the Polish emigrants seeking employment in the United States)

The Proletarians – a painting by Felicjan Kowarski showing members of the Great Proletariat, the first Polish worker party (1882–86), founded by Ludwik Waryński

A street in Łódź during the revolution of 1905, with a barricade visible in the background

The Red Regiment of Revolutionary Warsaw, formed in the spring of 1918 as one of the first units of the Red Army (Moscow, 15 May 1918)

1860's. Various organizations were springing up, among them the so-called resistance funds. Socialist ideas came to be propagated by political writers and worked out by such young intellectuals as Stanisław Krusiński (1857—86), Stanisław Mendelson (1858—1913) and Ludwik Krzywicki (1859—1941). Bolesław Limanowski (1835—1935), who called himself an epigone of the Reds from the time of the 1863 Uprising, also won much publicity in that period. His ideas were largely imbued with doctrines of Utopian socialism and ill-disposed toward a revolution.

The first programme of the Polish socialists was formulated in Brussels in 1878, but following police oppression many leaders had to leave Poland. The periodical *Równość* (Equality) followed by *Przedświt* (The Dawn) were founded in Switzerland. In 1881, Limanowski organized the Socialist Association 'The Polish People', and in 1882 Ludwik Waryński (1856—89), on his return to Warsaw from abroad, organized the first Polish socialist party, whose full name was the International Social-Revolutionary Party 'The Proletariat'. 'The Proletariat' laid stress on class issues and criticized the national movement that led to social solidarism; it emphasized above all the internationalist and universalist goals of socialism. The periodical *Walka Klas* (Class Struggle), founded abroad, had among its contributors Friedrich Engels, Karl Kautsky, Wilhelm Liebknecht, and Pyotr Lavrov. 'The Proletariat' met its end after a wave of arrests in 1883—84 and the trial in which six death sentences were passed (two of which were commuted to penal servitude for life). Those executed were Stanisław Kunicki (who headed the party after Waryński's arrest), Michał Ossowski, Jan Pietrusiński, and the Russian Pyotr Bardovsky. Waryński was sentenced to 16 years of penal servitude and died in the Schlüsselburg prison in 1889.

The traditions of 'The Proletariat' were continued by 'The Second Proletariat', headed by Ludwik Kulczycki (1866—1941) and Marcin Kasprzak (1860—1905) and by the Union of Polish Workers with Janusz Tański (1864—99), Julian Marchlewski (1866—1925), and others. The formation of new organizations was accompanied by a growing number of workers' May Day demonstrations and strikes, including the general strike in Łódź in 1892. The international labour movement also entered a new phase of development: 1889 saw the birth of the Second International, founded in Paris at a congress attended, among others, by Stanisław Mendelson and Feliks Daszyński (1863—90). Ideological divergences within the labour movement soon became manifest: there was a split into the moderate wing, which had reforms and parliamentary action in view, and the revolutionary one, which wanted to bring about radical changes by means of an armed struggle. The ultimate goals were similar, namely a socialist system, but the policies differed. The former trend developed into the social-democratic movement to find, decades later, its place on the left wing of the bourgeois parties. The latter, on the contrary, became the nucleus of a later communist movement.

In the case of Poland there were additional differences connected with the national issue. The Polish Socialist Party, founded at a congress in Paris in 1892, advanced as its principal goal the various democratic changes in a state which had first to be restored. That state was to include the eastern territories (ethnically not fully Polish) on the basis of a voluntary federation and the evolution should be toward socialism.

The revolutionary party, founded in 1893 as the Social Democratic Party of the Kingdom of Poland, and in 1900 renamed the Social Democratic Party of the Kingdom of Poland and Lithuania, did not raise the issue of the political independence of Poland as it did not want to oppose the Polish proletariat to the proletariat in the partitioning powers and thus to weaken their social consciousness. That was why many class-minded and revolutionary-minded workers and other adherents of socialism joined the Polish Socialist Party thus making it more revolutionary in character than was envisaged in its programme.

This ultimately led to a split in the Polish Socialist Party. Evolution toward a mass movement based on the class principle, which could, for instance, find manifestation in strikes, did not satisfy the 'old leaders', who advanced as the primary goal the necessity of organizing directly, and through diplomatic action, an armed struggle for political independence, aimed at Russia. The 'old leaders' were headed by Józef Piłsudski (1867—1935), an outstanding activist of the Polish Socialist Party, who was motivated above all by the idea of political independence and considered a political party (in his case the Polish Socialist Party) as an indispensable platform of action. His co-workers included Witold Jodko-Narkiewicz, Stanisław Jędrzejewski, Stanisław Wojciechowski, Aleksander Prystor, and Walery Sławek. They also dominated the Conspiratorial and Military Organization of the Polish Socialist Party, led — from October 1905 — by Józef Piłsudski, who even earlier strove to co-operate with Japan, at that time engaged in a war with Russia. The internal conflicts within the Polish Socialist Party became even more acute during the revolution of 1905—07; the Military and Conspiratorial Division, which was in charge of the said Conspiratorial and Military Organization, was expelled from the Polish Socialist Party, and this resulted in the formation of the Revolutionary Faction of the Polish Socialist Party, subordinated to Piłsudski and having the formation of para-military organizations such as Strzelec (The Rifleman), Związek Walki Czynnej (Union for Active Struggle) and the Polish Legions in view. In the course of their activity intended to restore the political independence of Poland many active members of the Faction, including Piłsudski himself, left the ranks of the Polish Socialist Party. The other party which emerged as a result of the split in the Socialist Party was named the Left Wing of the Polish Socialist Party and was largely engaged in working among the workers *en masse*. Its leaders included Maksymilian Horwitz-Walecki, Feliks Sachs, Feliks Kon, and Maria Koszutska. In December 1918, the Left Wing united with the Social Democratic Party of the Kingdom of Poland and Lithuania to form the Communist Party of Poland, while in 1919 the Faction united with the Polish Socialist Party of Galicia and Cieszyn Silesia and with the Polish Socialist Party active in the Prussian zone to form a single Polish Socialist Party (cf. XII, 1).

The Social Democratic Party of the Kingdom of Poland and Lithuania was founded by the activists of 'The Second Proletariat' Party and the Union of Polish Workers. Its founders included such leaders (also those active in the Social Democratic Party in Germany) as Rosa Luxemburg (1871—1919), Julian Marchlewski, Leon Jogiches-Tyszka (1867—1919), Adolf Warszawski-Warski (1867—1937), and Bronisław Wesołowski (1870—1919). When the activity of the party subsided after the arrests of its many members in 1896—99, it was revived mainly by Feliks Dzierżyński (1877—1926), who had returned from the place of his deportation, Jan Rosoł (1845—1914) and Antoni Rosoł (1882—1902), and Marcin Kasprzak (who, later arrested in Warsaw where he ran a clandestine printing shop, was hanged in 1905). The year 1897 saw the formation of the Bund, also known as the Union of Jewish Workers, but workers of Jewish origin were also members of the Social Democratic Party of the Kingdom of Poland and Lithuania and of the Polish Socialist Party.

The Social Democratic Party of the Kingdom of Poland and Lithuania co-operated with the Social Democratic Party of Russian Workers, which did not prevent controversies between the two. The second congress of the latter party in 1903 witnessed a polemic between the delegation of the Social Democratic Party of the Kingdom of Poland and Lithuania, in particular Rosa Luxemburg, and Vladimir I. Lenin (1870—1924) on the national issue, in which Lenin defended the nations' right to self-determination. This was a continuation of the controversies over the standpoint to be taken by the working class relative to the struggle for the political independence of Poland, controversies in which Karl Kautsky, Wilhelm Liebknecht, Georgyi Plekhanov and Antonio Labriola had voiced their opinions. The theorists supported the principle of Poland's independence, whereas the majority of the leaders of the Second International sided with the views advanced by the Social Democratic Party of the Kingdom of Poland and Lithuania.

The revolution of 1905—07, which radicalized the Polish people, but, on the other hand, led to the union of all those who were against the socialist idea, i.e. the bourgeoisie, the landed gentry, the petite bourgeoisie, and the well-to-do peasants, demonstrated that under the conditions prevailing in Poland it was not possible to separate a socio-political struggle from a national one. Hence the revolution, started by the Russian proletariat which was growing more and more revolutionary in its attitude, in the Polish territories became an open struggle against the tsar and had many features of a national uprising. The Kingdom of Poland became the strongest centre of the revolution: it accounted for 29 per cent of the strikes in 1905 and for 47 per cent of the strikes in 1906 in the whole Russian Empire. The working class acted as the motive power, but hundreds of thousands of members of other social classes and strata took part in the revolution, too. The struggle against tsarist absolutism and for a democratization of political life, including the restoration of many rights to be enjoyed by the Poles, united many people although revolutionary demands had fewer supporters.

The revolution began with the general strike which broke out in the Kingdom of Poland on 22 January 1905. It was followed by other strikes — mainly political in character — and demonstrations, such as the general strike on 1 May 1905, an armed uprising of Łódź workers (22—24 June 1905), which was the first armed action by European workers after the Paris Commune, the third general strike in October and November 1905, and the setting up, in November 1905, of the 'Republic of the Dąbrowa Basin', which meant that power in that region was seized by the workers. As has been calculated, during the first year of that revolution one worker went on strike more than six times on the average. Workers' strikes and demonstrations were accompanied by strikes of farm labourers, and by the struggle of farm owners for the right of using forests and pastures. All this was integrally connected with resistance offered to the tsarist machinery of the state, demands for re-introduction of the Polish language in schools and public offices, formation of a Polish police force and of people's committees, etc. Young people, also very active at that time, were mainly concerned with the restoration of the Polish language in schools. The anti-tsarist campaign was cleverly joined by the national democrats.

The successes were considerable and included the setting up of Polska Macierz Szkolna (The Polish School Organization), which ran 800 schools, of the Union of Societies for Social Self-help, which ran 655 schools, and of the Polish Culture Society, but they proved short-lived (cf. section 3 above). Many attacks on the tsarist police were organized, mainly by the Polish Socialist Party.

The revolution had an immense influence upon the national consciousness of the Poles; it raised their political culture by promoting lay and democratic elements in national life and making people sensitive to social wrongs; it also gave occasion for many theoretical and ideological discussions.

The revolution brought the Social Democratic Party of the Kingdom of Poland and Lithuania still closer to the Social Democratic Party of Russian Workers, in which the Bolsheviks led by Lenin were gaining the upper hand. The Social Democratic Party of the Kingdom of Poland and Lithuania called for a determined struggle with tsarism for a democratic system; the Polish Socialist Party, as mentioned above, was split with the resulting victory of the leftist tendencies; the ideology of the national democrats became more reactionary, which led to a rivalry between the group guided ideologically by Roman Dmowski and Józef Piłsudski who was still a member of the Revolutionary Faction of the Polish Socialist Party. But soon far-reaching changes in the international situation and advances in the social and economic sphere contributed to a further evolution in political life (cf. section 6 below).

5. Dynamism of Polish culture and science

The post-1864 period — despite the fact that the Polish people then lost all hopes of regaining political independence soon — added singally to Polish culture and science. Cultural achievements were at the same time reaching ever broader public.

The level of education was the essential condition in that respect. Next to the regular school education, largely controlled by the authorities of the partitioning powers, an immense role was played, as has been said, by the various forms of out-of-school education: books, libraries, lecture courses, cultural associations, informal schools called popular universities, etc. The western parts of the country, where illiteracy was practically non-existent, were leading in that respect, whereas the percentage of illiterates in the early 20th century was as much as 65 per cent in the Kingdom of Poland and 57 per cent in Galicia, even though by 1914 every Galician village had a school. At the Jagiellonian University in Cracow some 15 per cent of the students at that time were of peasant origin.

In Great Poland even before World War I 70 per cent of the peasants had houses built of brick, the analogous figures being five per cent for Galicia, 11 per cent for the western part of the Kingdom of Poland, and 1.4 per cent for its eastern part. There were also great differences in furniture and dress. On the whole, the rural areas in the period after the enfranchisement of the peasants witnessed two processes: an outburst of folk culture, and the gradual assimilation by the peasants of national culture which was becoming less and less elitist in character.

In science, too, there emerged various forms of private and social sponsorship which replaced the functioning of governmental institutions. Scientific life focussed in the universities in Cracow and Lvov, and also in the Polish National Museum founded in Rapperswil (Switzerland) in 1870. Warsaw University, closed down after the Uprising of 1830 (cf. X, 2), was revived as the Central School in 1863 for a period of seven years. Its students and graduates included such eminent authors and scholars as Henryk Sienkiewicz, Bolesław Prus, Zygmunt Gloger (ethnographer), and Jan Baudouin de Courtenay (linguist). Under the Russification drive the Central School was changed into a Russian university, and re-Polonized in 1915 when Warsaw was taken by German troops. In the transition period former professors of the Central School strove to set up a Polish institution that would promote the advancement of science. In 1881 they organized the Józef Mianowski Fund (named after the Rector of the Central School, who died in 1879), which clandestinely functioned in that capacity. It was only in 1907, after the revolution, that the Warsaw Scientific Society could be made legal. Various vocational schools of university standing were founded, too; a College of Technology was founded in Lvov in 1870, and a similar one in Warsaw in 1898, at first run by the Russian authorities and — like the University — Polonized in 1915. The Warsaw School of Rural Economy was set up in 1918; it had its forerunner in the lecture courses run by the Society for Science Courses in Warsaw, and later in the Courses in Agriculture and Industry sponsored by the Museum of Industry and Agriculture. The Warsaw School of Commerce, originating from a private school founded in 1906, was set up in 1915. There were also agricultural schools at Dublany near Lvov, at Czernichów near Cracow, and at Żabikowo near Poznań (closed down by the Prussian authorities after a few years of functioning). There were also learned societies in Poznań and in Toruń. The Academy of Learning, established in Cracow in 1872 (the forerunner of the Polish Academy of Learning and the Polish Academy of Sciences), exerted an influence upon all ethnically Polish territories. In 1893 it took over the Polish Society for History and Literature in Paris and changed it into its local centre which functions to this day.

There was a growing number of scientific and popular periodicals in the sphere of medicine, law, economics, agriculture, technology, etc., which informed the public about research results. The popular weekly *Wszechświat* (The Universe), which has appeared to the present day, was founded in 1882, while *Poradnik dla samouków* (A Guide for the Self-taught), which could boast the most eminent scholars and scientists as contributors, started appearing in 1897.

Scholarly information was provided by such works as *Słownik geograficzny Królestwa Polskiego* (The Geographical Dictionary of the Kingdom of Poland; 1880—92), *Bibliografia polska* (Bibliography of Polish Publications), compiled by Karol Estreicher (from 1870 on), *Wielka Encyklopedia Powszechna Ilustrowana* (The Great Illustrated Universal Encyclopaedia; from 1892), and various dictionaries.

A considerable intellectualization of life took place in that period. Foreign works were translated into Polish, including three books by Henri Poincaré, *Science et hypothèse* (1908), *La Valeur de la science* (1908), and *Science et méthode* (1911).

Historiography continued to develop briskly and to reflect opinions on the fortunes of the Polish nation. Discussions in particular pertained to the causes of the fall of the 'commonwealth of the gentry'. The dominant social ideas were the conservative ones, which made themselves even more visible after the collapse of the revolution of 1905—07. The most eminent historians included Walerian Kalinka (1826—86), Józef Szujski (1835—83), Michał Bobrzyński (1849—1935), Stanisław Smolka (1854—1924), Tadeusz Korzon (1839—1918), Adolf Pawiński (1840—96), Władysław Smoleński (1851—1926), and Tadeusz Wojciechowski (1838—1919). The early 20th century brought new trends: the renascent ideas which stressed the necessity of political independence found their reflection is historiography. The leading role in that respect was played by the school of Szymon Askenazy (1866—1935), while other outstanding historians included Wacław Tokarz (1873—1937), Marceli Handelsman (1882—1945), Władysław Konopczyński (1880—1952), and the founders of economic history, Franciszek Bujak (1875—1953) and Jan Rutkowski (1886—1949).

Advances were scored in Slavonic linguistics with Jan Karłowicz (1836—1903) and Aleksander Brückner (1856—1939), in ethnography and sociology. The year

1884 saw the publication of the first Polish translation of Karl Marx's *Capital* by Ludwik Krzywicki, the most outstanding Polish sociologist of that period.

Natural history continued to develop, pride of place going to geography (cf. X, 2), zoology with Benedykt Dybowski (1833—1930), palaeontology with Jan Czerski (1845—92) and geology with Aleksander Czekanowski (1833—76).

In technology, many eminent engineers worked outside Poland. This applies to Rudolf Modrzejewski (also known as Ralph Modjeski, the son of Helena Modjeska, an actress of international renown), who constructed many bridges in the United States (1861—1940); Władysław Kluger (1849—84), who contributed much to the development of railway transport in Peru; and Gabriel Narutowicz (1865—1922), an expert in hydrodynamics who worked in Switzerland and was later to become president of Poland (cf. XII, 3).

Biology and medicine could also boast eminent scientists, most of whom worked outside Poland. Mention is due to Kazimierz Funk (1884—1967), co-discoverer of vitamins, and the botanist Leon Cienkowski (1822—87).

Polish achievements in the exact sciences were of great importance for the advancement of science. Zygmunt Wróblewski (1845—88) and Karol Olszewski (1846—1915) were the first to have liquefied oxygen and nitrogen; Marian Smoluchowski (1872—1917) had to his credit remarkable attainments in substantiating the molecular kinetic theory (study of Brownian movements), and Maria Skłodowska-Curie (1867—1934), who worked on radioactivity in France, was twice awarded the Nobel Prize: in physics with husband Pierre in 1903 and in chemistry by herself in 1911.

The ideological currents, political tendencies, and social conflicts of the period found reflection in literature. At first, Positivism in literature was dominated by the novel, represented above all by Eliza Orzeszkowa, Bolesław Prus, and Henryk Sienkiewicz, who campaigned for the implementation of Positivist ideals (including that of 'organic' work). Historical novels were extremely popular, especially those written by Kraszewski (cf. X, 2) and Sienkiewicz, who was awarded the Nobel Prize for *Quo Vadis* in 1905. Poetry was represented by Maria Konopnicka (1842—1910) and Adam Asnyk (1838—97), and the drama by Michał Bałucki (1837—1901).

At the turn of the 19th century Polish literature entered the stage of Naturalism and Neo-Romanticism — the period being called in Polish *Młoda Polska* (Young Poland), apparently coined by analogy to the German term *Junges Deutschland* — which in the visual arts had its analogue in what is termed *Art Nouveau* or *Sezessionstil.* Cracow was the principal, though not the only, centre of the Young Poland style which had its most brilliant and versatile representative in Stanisław Wyspiański (1869—1907), painter, poet, theatre reformer, and playwright, author of many dramas concerned with the Polish national issue, the most renowned being *Wesele* (The Wedding Party, 1901). Much ferments were caused by Stanisław Przybyszewski (1868—1917), poet, essayist and novelist, the idol of the

Young Poland literary circles, who arrived in Cracow from Berlin (via Scandinavia, Paris, and Spain) in 1898 and brought with him the atmosphere and manners of Western European Bohemianism. The most renowned authors of that time were the playwright Gabriela Zapolska (1857—1921) and the novelists Stefan Żeromski (1864—1925) and Władysław Reymont (1867—1925); the latter was awarded the Nobel Prize in 1924 for his novel *Chłopi* (The Peasants).

Among the cabarets, which began to spring up in that period, *Zielony Balonik* (The Green Balloon) in Cracow won the greatest popularity. It was inspired by Tadeusz Żeleński (1874—1941), best known under his pen name Boy, a physician by training, but in practice active as literary and theatre critic and translator of French literature into Polish.

In painting, social and political consciousness was influenced by realistic painters concerned with national and historical topics, mainly Jan Matejko (1838—93), Artur Grottger (1837—67), and Juliusz Kossak (1824—99). Social issues were being taken up by Józef Szermentowski (1833—76), Wojciech Gerson (1831—1901), Józef Chełmoński (1849—1914), and Maksymilian Gierymski (1848—74). Those influenced by impressionism, post-impressionism and *Art Nouveau* included Józef Pankiewicz (1866—1940), Olga Boznańska (1865—1940), Aleksander Gierymski (1850—1901), Jacek Malczewski (1854—1929), Stanisław Wyspiański, and Józef Mehoffer (1869—1946).

In sculpture, mention is due to the epigones of classicism who worked abroad, namely Wiktor Brodzki (1817—1904) and Marceli Guyski (1830—93). Prominent sculptors linked to the new trends in art included Konstanty Laszczka (1865—1956), Jan Raszka (1871—1945), and Xawery Dunikowski (1875—1964).

The part played by the theatre continued to grow (cf. X, 2); this applies in particular to theatres in Cracow and Lvov, because censorship in Galicia was less severe than in the other two partition zones. The outstanding actors included Wincenty Rapacki (1840—1924), Aleksander Zelwerowicz (1877—1955), Ludwik Solski (1855—1954), and Helena Modrzejewska (1840—1909), who later won international renown. The year 1907 saw the appearance of the first Polish films.

In music, the changes in comparison with the preceding period consisted mainly in closer contacts with international trends, contacts initiated by composers connected with Young Poland. Their two well-known predecessors, Władysław Żeleński (1837—1921), the father of Tadeusz Żeleński, and Zygmunt Noskowski (1846—1904), programmatically abstained from all novelties. Noskowski's disciples included Karol Szymanowski (1882—1937) and Ludomir Różycki (1884—1953), who with some others, among them Mieczysław Karłowicz (1876—1909), formed the Young Poland group in music. Considerable successes were scored by Polish violinists, among them Henryk Wieniawski (1835—80), and the conductor Grzegorz Fitelberg (1879—1953).

Ignacy Paderewski (1860—1941) was a composer and pianist of international renown; versatile in his interests, he was also very active in social affairs and as a statesman (cf. XII, 1). Novel elements were brought to Polish music somewhat later by Karol Szymanowski who — like Chopin before him — drew amply from Polish folk sources.

The developing folk culture, from which national culture came to draw on an increasing scale, stimulated ethnographical research, which gradually left the stage of collection of data and artifacts. Special mention in this connection is due to Oskar Kolberg, who worked on the description and explanation of folk culture. Folk culture in Silesia and Pomerania, which was then gaining in vitality, became an object of interest. The year 1863 saw the printing in Wrocław of *Pieśni ludu polskiego na Górnym Śląsku* (Songs of the Polish People in Upper Silesia), compiled by Juliusz Roger. Folk dialects came to be studied by linguists.

Material civilization was also becoming more uniform, although social differences (e.g. as represented by incomes and earnings) were very great. Bourgeois culture, gradually imitated also by the peasants, became the model of life, but it was not uniform, either, housing conditions being a major differentiating factor. Most people had a very low standard of housing because house building did not keep up with the growth of the population.

Next to science, literature, and the visual arts, interest was also aroused by physical culture: the activity of the Polish Gymnastic Society called Sokół (The Falcon), founded in Galicia in 1867, spread to the other partition zones. The ideas of the Scouts Association began to spread in 1910 (the scout movement soon acquired in Poland certain specific local traits). All this had a considerable impact upon evolution toward a modern society and upon national integration.

6. The Polish issue during World War I. The regaining of independence

Multifarious developments in economics, science, culture and political life, with resulting changes in the consciousness of the Poles, proved to have been, when viewed in the historical perspective, the principal factor which preserved in the Polish people the will to regain an independent state of its own; and 'the Polish issue' did not vanish from the scene of international politics. The first breach in the international agreements, which gave a chance of materialization of the Polish national aspirations, consisted in the formation of two camps growing more and more hostile to one another; they were the Triple Alliance of the so-called Central Powers (Germany, Austria-Hungary, and Italy), and the Entente, also known as the *Entente cordiale,* i.e. an agreement between Britain and France, a few years later joined by Russia (and hence sometimes called the Triple Entente). In 1914 the Entente was joined by Serbia, Montenegro, Belgium, Japan, Italy (which had left the Triple

Alliance), Portugal, Rumania, and, in 1917, the United States. On the other hand, the Central Powers were joined by Turkey and Bulgaria. Numerous events, such as the annexation by Austria of Bosnia and Herzegovina (1908) the Moroccan conflict (1911), the Balkan Wars (1912, 1913), and the growing political expansion of Germany, indicated that a major war in Europe was quite likely.

In the meantime, in the Polish territories political activism was focussed in Galicia, where political leaders from the two other partition zones tended to arrive. The dominant orientation was that of Józef Piłsudski and leaders of the Revolutionary Faction of the Polish Socialist Party, which assumed that the Central Powers would emerge victorious from the conflict. In 1908 they formed the already mentioned Union for Active Struggle, which had participation in an armed conflict in view: its leaders also included Kazimierz Sosnkowski (1885—1969), Marian Kukiel (1885—1973), and Władysław Sikorski (1881—1943). In 1910, Piłsudski founded a military organization called Strzelec (The Rifleman), while Władysław Sikorski, active in the independence-oriented Progressive Democratic Party, founded in Lvov, organized the para-military Związek Strzelecki (The Riflemen's Union).

It is worth noting in this connection that at that time Piłsudski and Sikorski began to co-operate, so that Sikorski, next to Edward Rydz-Śmigły (1886—1941) and Kazimierz Sosnkowski found himself in Piłsudski's most intimate political orbit. Sikorski, an able and ambitious politician, did not have features typical of a leader which Piłsudski had, but although he worked in Piłsudski's shadow he was not just an obedient follower of the latter. Piłsudski prevented Sikorski from coming too much to the fore, and after the *coup d'état* of 1926 (cf. XII, 3) dismissed him from active military service. Attacked by the Piłsudskites, Sikorski became one of the most prominent members of the opposition to the post-1926 régime. The first major conflict between Piłsudski and Sikorski took place as early as in 1915, and pertained to the evaluation of the military situation of the Central Powers and to the role of the pro-Austrian orientation, which Sikorski did not abandon until the beginning of 1918.

The year 1912 saw the formation of the Provisional Commission of Federated Political Parties, headed by Józef Piłsudski and Witold Narkiewicz. It united various groups, including the Polish Socialist Party active in the Prussian partition zone, but soon suffered a crisis. When that occurred, Wincenty Witos (1874—1945) broke up the Polish Peasant Party (cf. section 3 above) and organized the Piast Polish Peasant Party (whose name referred to the legendary founder of the Piast dynasty, himself allegedly a husbandman), and left the Commission. The Left Wing of the Polish Peasant Party came closer to the Wyzwolenie (Liberation) Polish Peasant Party, formed in Warsaw in 1915 by the fusion of several peasant organizations.

The National Democracy also prepared for taking over power in a future independent Polish state, but it banked on a victory by the Entente and at the same time expected certain concessions on the part of the tsarist régime. Only the left wing of the worker movement (the Social Democratic Party of the Kingdom of Poland and Lithuania and the Left Wing of the Polish Socialist Party), with which Lenin was in touch during his stay in Poland in 1912—14, was opposed to the war and waited for a political solution of the Polish issue by a revolution which it expected to take place soon.

The division of Europe, including the partitioning powers, into military blocs resulted in Polish territories becoming a theatre of war in the east; hence the attitude of the Polish population was important for both sides, which accordingly tried to win the support of the Poles by making promises but offering no official guarantees.

The first two years of the war which broke out in August 1914 did not contribute anything definite to the Polish issue. On the side of Austria, Piłsudski merged the various Polish para-military organizations into the Polish Legions, which were to take part in military operations against Russia. He expected that an uprising would break out in the Kingdom of Poland and with that end in view he left Cracow with his troops for Kielce on 6 August 1914, and announced that a National Government was already functioning in Warsaw. Having found no support in the Kingdom of Poland he had to agree to his Legions operating within the organizational framework of the Austrian army. The Supreme National Committee, which formed the political background of the Legions, was formed in Cracow on 16 August 1914. The Committee planned the annexation of the Russian partition zone to Austria. The Provisional Commission of Federated Political Parties and the conservative, National Democracy-oriented, Central National Committee (which had been formed earlier) were dissolved at the same time, but this merely led to new conflicts. Piłsudski accordingly started negotiations with the Germans to whom he offered co-operation on the part of the Polish National Organization, which he had just formed, and later of the Polish Military Organization.

The evolution of the political and military situation from late 1916, and in particular the prolonged war with the resulting immense losses on the part of the belligerents, induced the former partitioning powers to make declarations on the Polish issue. On 5 November 1916, the German Emperor and the Emperor of Austria-Hungary announced that they envisaged the possibility of organizing an autonomous — which did not mean independent — state that would, however, include only the territories of the former Russian zone. A Provisional Council of State, in which Piłsudski was in charge of military matters, was formed in December 1916. The point was to obtain Polish recruits and to set up a buffer state that would separate Germany from Russia; the Polish population was to be transferred from the Prussian zone to the territories of the planned state. The Tsar Nicholas II made some empty declarations about 'creating' Poland, too.

The attitude of the United States, and above all that of President Wilson, was of great, though primarily moral, importance for the Polish question. As early as January 1917 Wilson stated that the restoration of Poland was one of the conditions of peace, and one year later — to some extent influenced by the firm stand adopted on the Polish question by the leaders of the October Revolution in Russia — he included in his fourteen points, which defined the integral conditions of a future peace treaty, one point concerned with Poland: it stated that it was necessary to restore an independent Polish state which should have free access to the sea. The Polish question was more directly influenced by events in Russia and in Germany. The tsarist régime in Russia was abolished by the revolution of 16 March 1917, and the new Provisional Government proclaimed the restoration of Poland, but in the spirit of the declaration of 5 November 1916. The proclamation assumed in advance that the future Polish state would be linked to Russia by a 'free military alliance'.

International discussion on the Polish question and on Poland's future intensified. Polish units were being formed in Russia and in France, and the political activeness of Polish leaders was gaining in strength. A Polish National Committee, headed by Roman Dmowski and recognized by the Allies as the political representation of the Polish people, was set up in Switzerland in August 1917, soon to be transferred to Paris.

In the meantime Piłsudski, in view of the changing political and military situation, abandoned his orientation to the Central Powers, left the Provisional Council of State and adopted an attitude of opposition to the occupation authorities and especially to their representative, General Beseler, a German. Piłsudski's internment by the Germans and also his earlier work in the Polish Military Organization added considerably to his popularity in Poland. The so-called active attitudes, which counted upon co-operation with the belligerents, were losing influence. The Provisional Council of State dissolved itself.

The next move on the part of the emperors of Germany and Austria-Hungary consisted in establishing, on 12 September 1917, a new Council of State and the Regency Council in the persons of Aleksander Kakowski, the Archbishop of Warsaw, Prince Zdzisław Lubomirski, and Józef Ostrowski, a landowner. But the preparations of the circles connected with landowners for seizing power in a future state were foiled by a rise of democratic and revolutionary tendencies.

In the meantime revolutionary changes were taking place in Russia. The power was nominally wielded by the bourgeois Provisional Government, but Councils of the Delegates of Workers, Peasants and Soldiers, which represented the masses, were functioning simultaneously. The Petrograd Council of the Delegates took a stand on the Polish question by issuing, on 27 March 1917, a Proclamation to the Polish Nation, which stated that Poland 'had its right to full independence'. A similar stand was taken by the conference of the Social Democtratic Party of Russian Workers (the Bolsheviks), held in April in the same year. Lenin criticized the proclamation of the Provisional Government and claimed that it was a swindle referring to an allegedly free military alliance between Poland and Russia.

When the October Revolution abolished the Provisional Government documents were adopted which declared that Poland had its right to independence. On 7 November 1917, the second All-Russian Congress of Delegates in its proclamation To Workers, Soldiers and Peasants accorded all the nations that inhabited the Russian territories the right to self-determination. Further, the Decree on Peace was one of the first acts passed by the Council of People's Commissars. It called for the termination of the war and for a universal peace treaty without annexations and contributions. A special decree signed by Lenin on 29 August 1918, cancelled all the documents concerned with the partition of Poland, at one time signed by Russia, and recognized the Polish nation's right to independence.

Many Poles who stayed in Russia at that time took part in the revolution and the civil war, and many Polish revolutionaries played an important role in building up the Soviet State and held responsible party and government posts (Feliks Dzierżyński, Julian Leszczyński-Leński, Julian Marchlewski, Bronisław Wesołowski, Józef Unszlicht, and others).

The October Revolution was the second breach in the international situation, which paved the way for the resolution of the Polish question. As long as Russia remained a bourgeois state and a member of the Entente its allies had to reckon with its policy. The introduction in Russia of the socialist system and the declaration of the revolutionary authorities in favour of full independence for Poland changed the situation of the Allies and induced them to adpot solutions which were both supported by the Poles and prevented a possible revolution in Poland, and also set up a barrier between Russia and Western Europe in the form of independent Poland. It is in this light that we have to consider Wilson's points which presented the Western solution of the political systems in post-war Europe.

In March 1918 the Central Powers imposed harsh conditions upon Russia which was weakened by the revolution; on 3 March, a treaty was signed in Brest Litovsk, on the strength of which the German troops held Byelorussia, part of the Ukraine, Lithuania, Latvia, Finland and Poland under occupation. A German victory or the termination of the war in the form of a compromise would have limited the prospects for the restoration of an independent Poland — but the war ended in the defeat of the Central Powers. Austria-Hungary broke up into several states, and the revolution in Germany speeded up the capitulation of that country. The armistice agreement of 11 November 1918 forced Germany to renounce the treaty of Brest Litovsk, to leave the occupied territories, and to withdraw the troops within the frontiers of 1914. This created the conditions for the restoration of the Polish state.

Chapter XII

Between the World Wars: Successes and Failures (1918—39)

1. Reconstruction of the state. The first governments. The Constitution of 1921

The armistice signed near Compiègne (France) on 11 November 1918 imposed upon the Germans the obligation to leave all occupied territories in Europe except for those parts of Russia which the German troops held under the treaty of Brest Litovsk (cf. XI, 6), i.e. Byelorussia, Lithuania, and part of the Ukraine. The Allies supported the control of these areas by the German troops because of the advances of the revolution in Russia. Thus the Germans still held the former Prussian partition zone, and hence the territories in which the Polish state could be reconstructed were limited to the Kingdom of Poland and to part of the former Austrian partition zone (with Cracow), earlier recaptured by the Poles.

On 11 November 1918, organizational work in the Polish territories was quite advanced. Furthest-reaching measures had been taken in the former Austrian partition zone, because the Hapsburg Monarchy had almost completely collapsed by October 1918. Cracow became the seat of the Polish Liquidation Commission (formed on 28 October 1918), headed by Wincenty Witos, leader of the Piast Polish Peasant Party (cf. XI, 6). The Commission consisted of representatives of the various political groups, excluding the conservative landed gentry, discredited by their programme of preserving political links with Austria on the basis of autonomy or federation. Its active workers included Ignacy Daszyński, leader of the Polish Socialist Party in the former Austrian partition zone. The Polish Liquidation Commission seized power in Cracow and started winding up the former Austrian administrative system.

Cieszyn Silesia had at that time its National Council, while the Supreme People's Council, dominated by the national democrats, tried to seize power in Great Poland. (It had its predecessor in the Central Citizens' Committee, established in July 1918.)

The growing revolutionary attitudes found expression in the setting up, on 6 November 1918, of the short-lived Republic of Tarnobrzeg, not recognized by the Polish Liquidation Commission, which advocated that large estates be taken over by peasants.

In the meantime, the conservative Regency Council in Warsaw also strove to concentrate power in its hands, but realizing that, having been appointed by the former partitioning powers, it was not popular in the country tried to function as the medium which distributed power. It thus helped establish the National Democratic government headed by Józef Świeżyński, which also failed to win popular support.

This meant for the National Democrats the loss of a possible chance of seizing power, the more so as its leaders, gathered around the Polish National Committee, which had its headquarters in Paris, and the Polish army formed in France and led by General Józef Haller (cf. XI, 6), were far away. Its chances for seizing power were

Kapela dziecięca (A Children's Orchestra) by Tadeusz Makowski (1882–1932), one of the outstanding Polish 20th century painters (who had lived in France from 1908 on), whose production includes scenes from children's life, genre scenes, and grotesque landscapes

Zygmunt Wróblewski (1845–88) and Karol Olszewski (1846–1915), originators of the low temperature technique, the first to have liquefied oxygen and nitrogen in 1883

Maria Skłodowska-Curie (1867–1934), Polish physicist and chemist who worked in France, co-author of the science of radioactivity, twice awarded the Nobel Prize

Bolesław Prus (the pen name of Aleksander Głowacki, 1847–1912), author and jurnalist, co-founder of Polish critical realism

Henryk Sienkiewicz (1846–1916), mainly renowned for his historical novels, Nobel Prize winner

Stefan Żeromski (1864–1925), novelist, playwright and journalist

Stanisław Ignacy Witkiewicz (1885–1939), author, painter, art theorist, forerunner of the drama of the absurd (self-portrait)

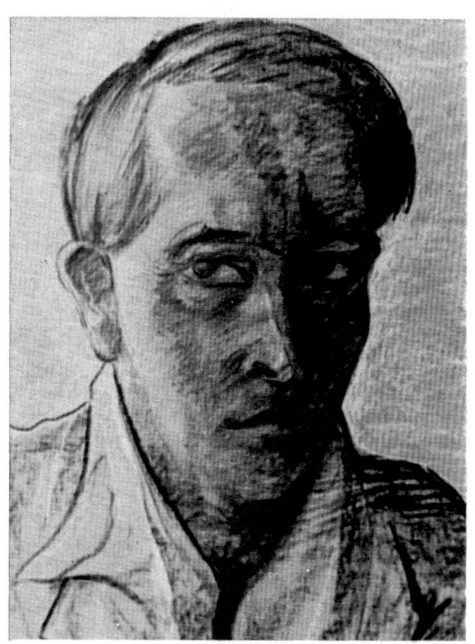

Czwórka (Four-in-Hands) by Józef Chełmoński (1849–1914), representative of realism in Polish art, painter of landscapes and genre scenes

Stanisław Wyspiański (1869–1907), poet, playwright, painter, theatre reformer, author of dramas concerned with Polish history (self-portrait)

Śpiący Mietek (A Sleeping Boy) by Stanisław Wyspiański

Władysław Stanisław Reymont (1867–1925), novelist, Nobel Prize winner, painted by Jacek Malczewski (1854–1929), a leading painter of the Young Poland period, representative of symbolism

Jan Matejko (1838–93), the most eminent Polish historical painter, whose large canvasses, painted in the partition period and recalling the finest moments in Poland's history, were of essential importance in preserving the national tradition and the belief in the regaining of political independence (self-portrait)

Ignacy Jan Paderewski (1860–1941), a pianist of international renown, composer, statesman, social worker, prime minister in 1919, Poland's representative in the League of Nations

Karol Szymanowski (1882–1937), composer, initiator of a very original style in music, based on elements drawn from the Polish folklore

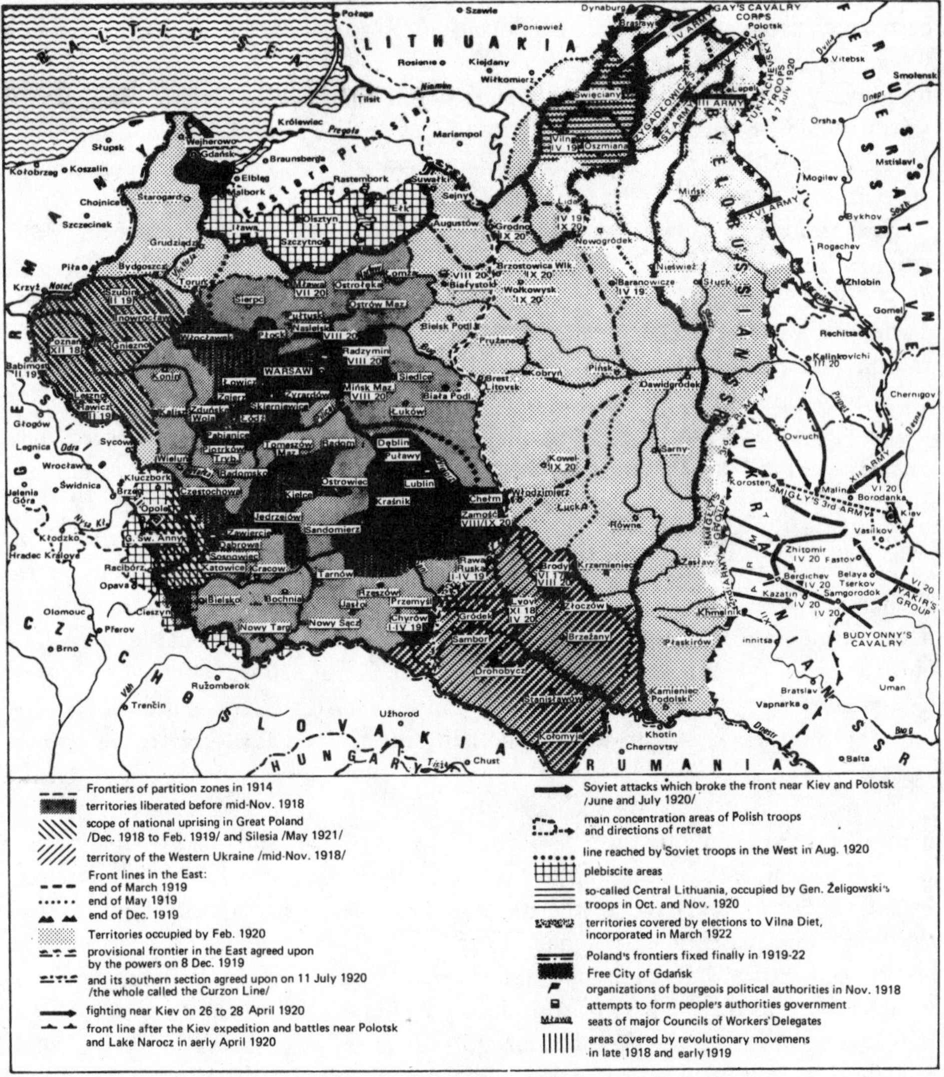

5. Reconstruction of the Polish State in 1918—22

also small because of the fact that the Allies did not support their undemocratic programme (cf. XI, 3) in view of the radical opinions which then prevailed in Europe. On the other hand, it was for the same reason that the model advocated by the October Revolution in Russia (seizure of power by councils of the delegates of workers, peasants, and soldiers) could not be put into effect in Poland. There were some such aspirations, but the existing conditions did not favour the outbreak of a revolution. The country was impoverished by the war; industrial installations had largely been taken from the Kingdom of Poland to Russia, and the working class was weakened numerically and scattered. Nor could any Polish government be blamed for poverty. The blame was on the former partitioning powers. Hence those groups which staked on parliamentary democracy, and not on a revolution, and proclaimed, be it even demagogically, the need for agrarian reforms and democratization of social and political life, had the greatest chances of gaining power.

Next to Cracow, Lublin turned out to be a centre of activity that had the restoration of an independent Polish state in view. On 5 November 1918, a Council of Workers' Delegates was formed there upon the initiative of the revolutionary parties, i.e. the Social Democratic Party of the Kingdom of Poland and Lithuania and the Left Wing of the Polish Socialist Party. Similar councils were then formed in Dąbrowa Górnicza (on the 8th), Częstochowa (on the 9th), Sosnowiec (on the 10th), Warsaw (on the 11th), Łódź (on the 13th), etc. In all some one hundred such councils were set up representing about 500,000 industrial workers and agricultural labourers. They failed, however, to establish a single leading centre; it was only in the Dąbrowa Basin that the councils combined to form a single organization. The lack of unity was due to the discrepancies between the Polish Socialist Party and the Communist Workers' Party of Poland, which developed from the merger of the Social Democratic Party of the Kingdom of Poland and Lithuania and the Left Wing of the Polish Socialist Party in December 1918 (cf. XI, 4) and was later to become the Communist Party of Poland. When the Polish Socialist Party withdrew its support the movement, suppressed by the authorities, gradually came to an end in 1919.

Even at the time when the Councils of Workers' Delegates were active a government supported mainly by the Polish Socialist Party, then called the Faction, and by the Wyzwolenie Polish Peasant Party (cf. XI, 6) was formed in Lublin on 7 November 1918 (while Warsaw had the Regency Council). It had Ignacy Daszyński as the prime minister, Stanisław Thugutt (1873—1941) as the minister of internal affairs, and Edward Rydz-Śmigły, the commander-in-chief of the Polish Military Organization, as the minister of war. This government, called the Provisional People's Government of the Republic of Poland, announced the establishment of a republican system of government, democratic elections, and social reforms, and proclaimed the dissolution of the Regency Council. The very fact that such a government was formed indicated that the radical views (though opposed to revolution) concerning the solution of the political and social problems of the country were quite strong. The situation was paradoxical because neither was the Lublin Government in a position to abolish the Regency Council nor could the latter come out against the former. A civil war would have meant an immediate outbreak of a revolution which all the parties wanted to avoid at any price. The solution came with the arrival in Warsaw, on 10 November 1918, of Józef Piłsudski, who had been freed by the

Germans (Wilhelm II abdicated on the previous day and a republic was proclaimed in Germany) and who enjoyed considerable popularity in Poland. The Regency Council passed its military authority over to him, and the Lublin Government dissolved itself upon his demand.

The Provisional People's Government of the Republic of Poland in Lublin had not, by the way, won the approval of the Piast Polish Peasant Party, i.e., of Witos, who preferred to co-operate with the national democrats; nor was it liked, as being too leftist, by Piłsudski who, according to his own statement, 'got out of the streetcar named socialism at the stopping place called independence.' It was also bluntly opposed by the revolutionary left-wing groups, which organized a general strike in Lublin. But, taking into account the powerful trends that were gaining the upper hand in both Western and Eastern Europe Piłsudski charged Ignacy Daszyński, the prime minister of the Lublin Government, with the task of forming a new government. Daszyński, under the pressure of the national democrats (in practice, politicians from Great Poland) ceded that task to Jędrzej Moraczewski who had formerly acted as a liaison between the Polish Social-Democratic Party and the national democrats, and was a socialist dedicated to Piłsudski. Piłsudski became a self-appointed Head of the State, with full political power.

The new government strove to obtain international recognition, primarily that of the Allies, but it was only Germany — which still controlled Great Poland, Pomerania, Silesia, and Warmia — that established diplomatic relations with it. France recognized only the Polish National Committee, headed by Roman Dmowski, which was ill-disposed toward the new government. No endeavours at all were made to establish relations with Russia.

Neither the right-wing (the national democrats) nor the left-wing parties (whose advice was consistently disregarded by the new government) wanted to accept Piłsudski. The left-wing parties closed their ranks — which applied to the trade union movement, too — and the national democrats prepared a *coup d'état* led by Colonel Marian Żegota-Januszajtis. The plot, handled very incompetently, collapsed, but Piłsudski, who already had at his disposal an army very well organized by himself, did not intend to engage in a conflict with the national democrats: he needed their support in his endeavours to fix the western frontiers of the nascent Polish state, and without them he could hardly weaken the left-wing parties and win approval of the landowners, rich peasants, and the bourgeoisie. That was why Moraczewski, to comply with Piłsudski's wish, after two months ceded the post of prime minister to Ignacy Paderewski (cf. XI, 5), extremely popular and connected with the national democrats. This took place several days before the elections to the Legislative Seym, held on the basis of a progressive and democratic electoral law which provided for a universal, direct, secret, proportional and equal vote; it was also for the first time that Polish women enjoyed full electoral rights. Yet even before the elections the Moraczewski cabinet issued several decrees intended to improve the situation of the masses and providing for an eight-hours working day and obligatory social insurance. It proved, however, more difficult to meet the demands of the peasants and agricultural labourers who clamoured for the fragmentation of large estates. In towns, demands were raised for the nationalization of banks and factories, and strikes and demonstrations were organized.

The elections, held on 26 January 1919, ended in a victory for the National Democratic Party and the peasant parties. The latter continued their parliamentary struggle for agrarian reform, which was intended to change, through fragmentation of large estates, the uneven distribution of land which was a result of the non-revolutionary agrarian reform in the 19th century (cf. X, 3). There were at that time nearly 2,000 large landed estates averaging three to four thousand hectares each and accounting for some 20 per cent of agricultural land, whereas some 100,000 small non-self-supporting farms of less than two hectares each accounted for not more than three per cent of land. Farm labourers, who together with their families accounted for some 12 per cent of the total population, were hardly protected by the law. For all these glaring inequalities and the threat of a revolution, the Agrarian Reform Act, which provided for a compulsory fragmentation of all landed estates of more than 180 hectares (the analogous figure for the former Prussian partition zone and for the eastern territories being 400 hectares) — i.e. the surplus being subject to fragmentation — and for the nationalization of the forests, was passed by a majority of only one vote. It marked the success of the progressive forces.

The developing parliamentary life resulted in the growth in the number of political parties and groups, although, on the other hand, there were mergers of the various groups following the gradual territorial integration of the state. The principal political battle was waged between the left, especially the revolutionary left, i.e. the communists, and the camp which represented the bourgeoisie and the landowners. The revolutionary wing of the left was represented by the Communist Party of Poland, allied on ideological grounds with the various groups within the socialist and the peasant movement, its right wing being formed from a considerable number of representatives of the Polish Socialist Party and the various peasant parties. The conflict between the national democrats and Piłsudski's adherents was in fact a family quarrel: it was a struggle for power, and not a controversy over the social foundations of the state, which in any case aimed to secure the supremacy of the propertied classes.

At first 296 deputies were elected to the Seym which had as its speaker Wojciech Trąmpczyński (1860—1953), member of the Supreme People's Council in Great Poland, who had parliamentary experience as a former deputy to the German parliament. As the German occupation of the Polish territories in the west was being eradicated and the political frontiers of the state were becoming stabilized the number of the deputies rose to 432 in November 1922, i.e. at the end of the extended term of office of the Seym.

As early as 20 February 1919, the Seym adopted what was commonly called the short Constitution, which transferred power to the Seym; this was also supported by the right-wing parties which strove to restrict Piłsudski's prerogatives, as at one time the aristocracy defended the gentry republicanism (cf. VIII, 2). This ultimately led to a division of prerogatives: the Seym was in charge of internal affairs, and Piłsudski, of the army and foreign policy. On 14 February 1919, a commission of 30 deputies started working on a draft constitution, which ultimately resulted in the adoption of what is known as the March Constitution (passed on 17 March 1921). It consolidated the principle of parliamentary bourgeois democracy, then typical of European countries, which took into account the political activeness of the population that wanted to have its share in the government. The March Constitution adopted a two-chamber parliament consisting of the Seym and the Senate, their term of office being five years, while that of the president was to be seven years. The prerogatives of the president were restricted by the principle of countersignature: any official act signed by the president had to be countersigned by the prime minister and the appropriate cabinet minister. The Cabinet was appointed by the president with the support of the majority of the Seym. The Constitution provided for the democratic rights and the protection of life, freedom, conscience and religion of every citizen regardless of his origin, nationality, and race, and also for the minorities' rights to preserve their national features; this was an important point because the minorities were very numerous at that time and consisted mostly of Byelorussians and Ukrainians. As decided in 1922, the Seym was to consist of 444 deputies, and the Senate, of 111 senators.

2. Gradual demarcation of the frontiers. The social, ethnic, and economic structure of Poland (up to 1922)

When the March Constitution was being passed the frontiers of Poland were not yet fixed. After World War I, decisions concerning the new order in Europe were to be made by a peace conference, but the Poles, without waiting for such decisions, were spontaneously disarming the troops of the former partitioning powers (in practice the German and Austrian troops) in order to restore to Poland the territories which belonged to it immediately before the partitions.

The uprising in Great Poland in 1918—19 was the first organized military action that enjoyed popular support. The uprising was speeded up by the formation by the Prussian government of special troops intended to defend 'the German East', namely the *Heimatschutz* (Guard of the Fatherland) and later the *Grenzschutz* (Frontier Guard). The uprising started in Poznań on 24 December 1918, and soon covered the whole of Great Poland. Spontaneous activities of groups of insurgents who liberated the various localities were combined with organized military operations. Three weeks later the Supreme People's Council appointed General Dowbór-Muśnicki to be the commander-in-chief of the insurgent detachments (that function was at first in the hands of Major Stanisław Taczak), who soon transformed them into a regular army of 70,000 men and drove the Germans out of the territories that corresponded to the former Grand Duchy of Poznań. During the negotiations in Trier concerning a consecutive prolongation of the armistice agreement of 11 November 1918 (concluded for a period of six weeks) Marshal Ferdinand Foch had its conditions extended so as to make them apply to the area conquered by the insurgents in Great Poland. Great Poland was thus free, but German military provocations continued to the middle of 1919. The uprising owed its success to many factors: the patriotism and vigour of the local population, the fact that it took the Germans by surprise, and the revolution in Germany which for some time gave power to councils of workers' delegates. Germans were leaving the former Prussian partition zone by hundreds of thousands, the figure being some 350,000 for Great Poland alone. The percentage of the German population in Great Poland accordingly fell from 38.4 to ca. 16.

The situation in the Cieszyn region of Silesia seemed less complicated. The demarcation line separating the regions disputed by both the Poles and the Czechs was agreed upon in November 1918 and based on the ethnic principle; following that agreement Poland received the Transolzan region (with Bogumin and Karwina), i.e. the region beyond the Olza River. But the agreement was broken by the incursion of the local Czech military commander. He was stopped in a battle near Skoczów, but Transolzania was to be kept by the Czechs until the issue would be resolved by the approaching peace conference.

At that conference, which opened in Versailles on 18 January 1919, and was attended by 27 states, the conditions were dictated above all by the United States, France, and Britain. As a result of that, Polish interests were affected by the controversy between Britain and France. The former feared that France would become excessively influential in continental Europe and accordingly supported Germany, whereas France wanted to strengthen those countries which could be its allies in a possible conflict with Germany, and accordingly supported the Polish demands, which had gifted advocates in the person of Ignacy Paderewski and Roman Dmowski, the Polish delegates to the conference.

Ultimately, primarily owing to the anti-Polish attitude of the British delegation, headed by Lloyd George, and the vigour of the Germans, the Polish proposals concerning the demarcation of the frontier were not accepted. The peace treaty sanctioned the success of the uprising in Great Poland and accorded Gdańsk Pomerania to Poland, but Gdańsk itself, together with a small surrounding region, was made a free city under international supervision to be exercised by the League of Nations. Eastern Prussia was retained by Germany, and the future of Upper Silesia, Masuria, Warmia, and the region on the Lower Vistula was to be decided by a plebiscite. Dissatisfaction of the population in Upper Silesia and its desire to be united with Poland was, however, so strong that three uprisings broke out there in

6. Upper Silesia during Uprisings and Plebiscites (1919—21)

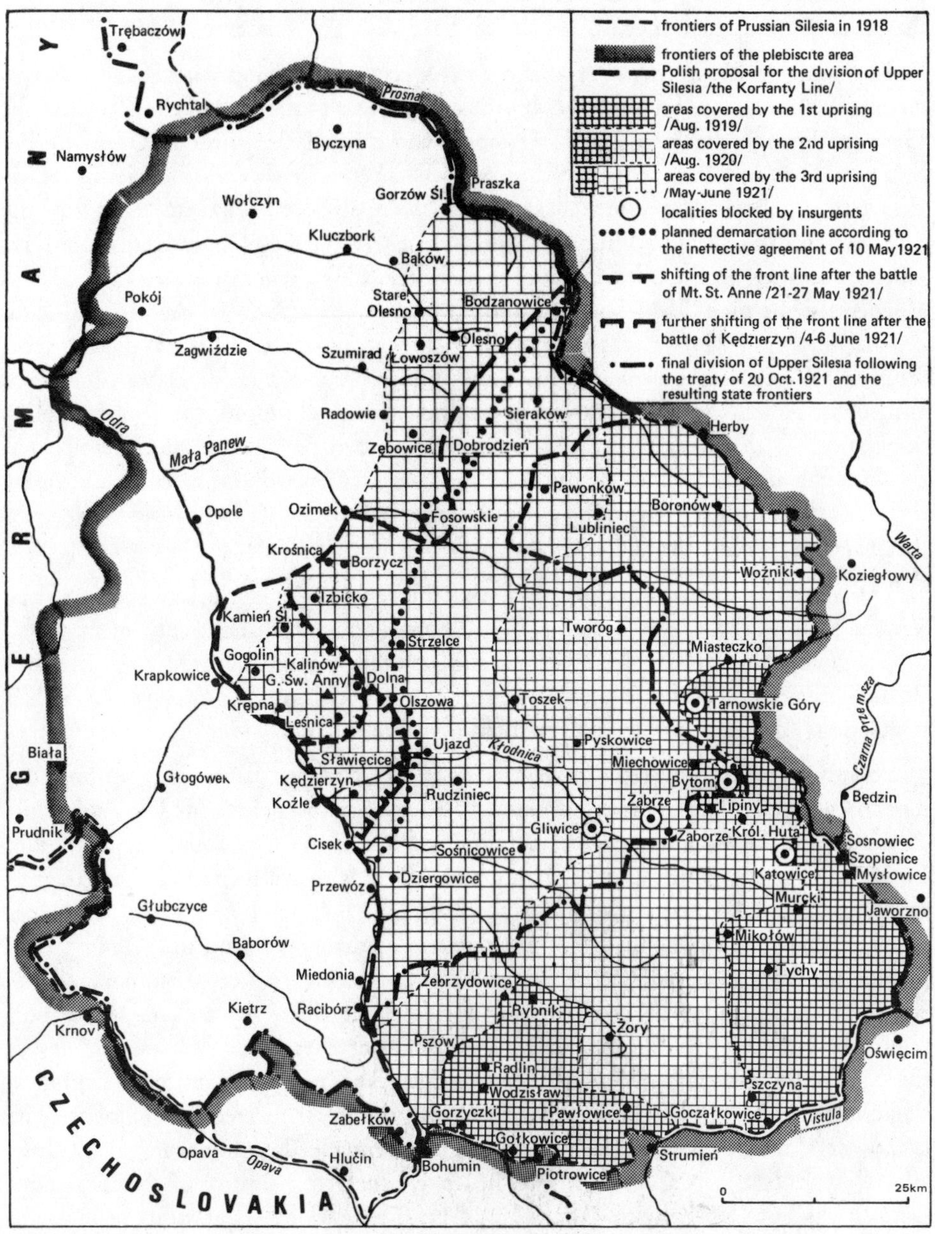

succession (1919, 1920, 1921); they were proletarian in character and connected with widely spread strikes and demonstrations. These uprising influenced the outcome of the plebiscite and the resulting division of the contended territories between Poland and Germany. Wojciech Korfanty (1873—1939), a former leader of the National League and one of the leaders of the uprising, was appointed the plebiscite commissioner on behalf of the Polish government.

In the plebiscite, 40 per cent of the votes were for the union with Poland. It was a considerable success for the Poles if we consider that at the time of the plebiscite the Germans brought back to Silesia all those who resided elsewhere in Germany but had been born in Silesia, and that the vote was taken after several centuries of a Germanization policy while some Silesian Poles were still somewhat mistrustful of the newly born Polish state. When after the plebiscite the Allied Commission could not reach unanimity on the Silesian issue, the workers took the matters into their hands: a general strike on 2 May 1921 was followed by the outbreak of the third uprising on the following day. It was very well organized and ably led by Wojciech Korfanty, who acted in agreement with the Polish government in Warsaw. Bloodshed ensued, in which the Germans did not refrain from massacring the Polish civilian population — this estranged them even from the British, who originally supported the German demands. The attitude of the Silesians was decisive for the ultimate decisions of the Allies concerning the political future of that region: Poland regained the principal part of the industrial areas in Upper Silesia.

The plebiscite in Warmia, Masuria, and the region near the lower course of the Vistula took place on 1 July 1920. The German terror and the involvement of the Polish government in the war with Russia resulted in a Polish defeat: in Masuria Poland obtained only three villages out of the 28 with the majority of the Polish population; in other regions Poland obtained five villages.

Poland's eastern frontier was at that time still an open issue. The national democrats wanted to incorporate Lithuania, Byelorussia, and part of the Ukraine, while Piłsudski and his adherents were in favour of a federation of those regions under Polish sovereignty. On the other hand, the Allies, who still expected that counterrevolution would emerge victorious in Russia and remembered their assurances made in 1917, recommended that the frontier be demarcated on the ethnic principle, i.e. on the so-called Curzon line along the former eastern boundary of the Kingdom of Poland. The problem was extremely intricate, because in the eastern region in question ethnic boundaries went not only across territories, but across the population as well: the peasants were Lithuanians, Byelorussians, or Ukrainians, while in towns (e.g. in Vilna, Lvov, Tarnopol) the Poles formed the majority. The landowners, that is those strata which were most advanced economically and culturally, were Polish, too. On the whole, however, the vast majority of the local population was not Polish, with growing and justified national aspirations of its own. The Ukraine, which covered Eastern Galicia, saw the emergence — in rapid succession — of three political entities: the revolutionary Ukrainian Soviet Republic, and the bourgeois People's Republic on the Dneper, and the West-Ukrainian People's Republic, which included the town of Przemyśl. The Lithuanian and Byelorussian

Soviet Republic came into being between December 1918 and February 1919. At the same time the territories evacuated by the German army were being occupied by Polish troops, which in April 1919 took Vilna and somewhat later the region of Suwałki; the Poles unsuccessfully tried to induce Lithuania to form a union with Poland.

In Eastern Galicia and Volhynia Polish troops fought the armies of the above-named two bourgeois republics and the Red Army. Eastern Galicia was soon taken by the Poles. An armistice was signed with the army of the Ukrainian People's Republic on the Dneper (led by Ataman Semen Petlura), the demarcation line being fixed along the Zbruch. In the conquered territories the Polish administrative agencies resorted to brutal methods, which estranged the local population. The Polish offensive in Eastern Galicia and in Volhynia met with a protest on the part of the Allies who expected that the Ukrainian troops could play an important role in fighting the Bolsheviks. After the Polish victories, followed by secret negotiations with Soviet Russia and refraining from supporting the offensive against Moscow, undertaken by the counter-revolutionary General Anton Denikin, the Supreme Allied Council in Versailles, alarmed by Piłsudski's stand, accorded autonomy to Eastern Galicia. This greatly weakened the authority of Paderewski, whose cabinet fell on 13 December 1919. The next, centrist, cabinet was formed by Leopold Skulski (b. 1878, d. between 1939 and 1945).

Piłsudski was still staking on his federative plans, the implementation of which was supposedly favoured by the weakness of Soviet Russia. Denikin had been defeated, but General Pyotr Wrangel was still fighting in the south. At that time the Soviet state suggested a peaceful settlement of the territorial problems, because peace was needed for reconstruction and stabilization. As Lenin claimed, Soviet Russia did not want 'a war over territories, because it wanted to do away with the cursed past when every Great Russian was considered an oppressor'. The masses in Poland organized demonstrations and strikes in favour of a peace, but Piłsudski thought that a war would help reduce the growing unemployment and sweep aside the danger of internal disturbances. After having made an agreement with Petlura he launched his offensive on 21 April 1920, which meant a Polish-Soviet war. After initial Polish successes the initiative was taken by the Red Army, which occupied Brest Litovsk on 1 August 1920, and moved westward. In view of a difficult situation it was Władysław Grabski (1874—1938) who was charged with the mission of forming a cabinet — this time even more rightist in character; upon Grabski's motion a Council for State Defence, endowed with vast prerogatives, was appointed. A lack of support on the part of the Allies, who formulated new conditions, and Grabski's considerable concessions in that respect brought about the fall of his cabinet and the formation of a government of national defence, headed by Wincenty Witos (24 July 1920). In the meantime, a revolutionary government, called the Provisional Revolutionary Committee of Poland, headed by Feliks

Dzierzyński and Julian Marchlewski, was formed in Białystok which had been taken by the Red Army. That army was then approaching Warsaw, Toruń, Płock, and Brodnica, and peasants and labourers were taking over the estates in the territories it had occupied. But soon the Polish counter-offensive, after the heavy fighting near Warsaw in August 1920 gave the victory to the Poles. The Red Army was driven out, and the Polish troops on the way took back Vilna, which was kept by General Lucjan Żeligowski despite Lithuanian resistance. The Polish-Soviet conflict was then settled by the treaty signed in Riga on 18 March 1921. Poland's eastern frontier was fixed on the Zbruch, that is, some 200 kilometres to the east of the Curzon line. The Polish losses in the operations in the East were considerable as they amounted to some 250,000 men in 1919—20.

When the Polish frontiers were ultimately fixed (Silesia was incorporated into Poland in June 1922), the area of the reborn Polish state was 388,390 sq. kilometres, with a population of 27.2 million (it had increased to 35.1 million by 1939), being the sixth state in that respect in Europe. Poland had access to the sea along a coast-line of 101 kilometres, and the estuary of the Vistula was within the territory of the Free City of Gdańsk. The country had to take over the inheritance of economic and social backwardness, caused by several centuries of the agrarian system based on demesnes resorting to corvée (cf. VI, 4), and by the partitions. The rural population amounted to 74 per cent of the whole, the figure being as high as 87 per cent in the case of the eastern regions. Agriculture was the basis of subsistence for over 17 million people (63.8 per cent of the population); only 26 per cent of all inhabitants lived in towns. The working class — agricultural labourers excluded — accounted for 16.5 per cent of the population (4.5 million), of which industrial workers formed a mere four per cent (1.1 million).

Poland was marked by a large percentage of the minorities, which caused conflicts, raised problems, and accounted for the weakness of the state. According to the census of 1921, there were 69 per cent of the Poles, the corresponding figures being 14.3 per cent for the Ukrainians, 3.9 per cent for the Byelorussians, 3.9 per cent for the Germans, and 7.8 per cent for the Jews, the rest consisting of other minorities. The Jews, who had been leaving Russia during and since tsarist times, lived mainly in the territories to the east of the Bug. In the case of the major towns the percentage of the Poles was 94 for Poznań, 84 for Cracow, 72.3 for Warsaw, 62.2 for Łódź, 61.8 for Lvov, 56.2 for Vilna. Nationality did not strictly coincide with religion: 29 per cent of the Protestants, 20 per cent of the Orthodox Catholics, and 25 per cent of professors of Judaism declared themselves to be Poles.

While the economic heterogeneity of reborn Poland was due to the partitions, the striking differences in the economic level of the various territories (the more advanced ones being often called 'Poland A' and the backward ones, 'Poland B') were largely a result of the inclusion of the backward territories in the East. There were no developed transport routes between the various regions: for instance, there was no direct railway line between Poznań and Warsaw. As compared with other countries, the indicators of the level of economic life were very low for Poland; the value of the annual production per capita was only one-third of that in France and Germany, and one half of that in Czechoslovakia. The same applied to foreign trade, consumption, savings, etc. Because of the necessity for organizing and maintaining the army more than one half of the budget in 1920—21 was spent by the Ministry of Military Affairs. Due to the lack of coal several hundred factories could not be opened. During the war (both World War I proper and the war between Poland and Russia) nearly two million buildings were destroyed and four million head of cattle were requisitioned. The credits obtained abroad were used for purchase of goods and for national defence. Much aid was provided by the Poles residing abroad, especially those in the United States.

In order to reconstruct the national economy the authorities tried to attract foreign capital to be invested in Poland, but at first there were no appropriate conditions for this. The income of the state was low, largely because of the fact that the taxes collected from the population impoverished by the war were very low. The growing budgetary deficit induced the authorities to print excessive quantities of paper money, which was not counterbalanced by the amount of the commodities on the market. This in turn led to a rise in prices and a drop in the value of money (at that time its unit being called the Polish mark). Growing inflation was temporarily a source of income for the state and caused a further impoverishment of the population, even though endeavours were made to raise salaries and wages as the prices were going up. The prices of food in Warsaw increased more than sixfold between January 1921 and October 1922. Inflation did not hamper the reconstruction of industry and offered a premium in the case of exports, but caused disaffection of the masses, which found expression in strikes.

The galloping inflation resulted in a crisis in 1923. In June of that year the food prices in Warsaw, as compared with those in October 1922, had increased more than tenfold. Implementation of the agrarian reform provided for by an act passed in 1919 encountered obstacles, and all that led to an extremely tense situation in the country. Revolutionary movements were on the rise, and the number of those who left the country in search of jobs was growing.

National conflicts in the eastern parts of the country were a serious problem, too. The Byelorussians, Lithuanians, and Ukrainians opposed the Polish administrative authorities which hampered their national advancement. The provisions of the March Constitution were not observed, nor was the Ukrainian Population Act of 26 September 1922. Until 1926 there were only 50 Ukrainian secondary schools; the number of Byelorussian elementary schools dropped from 186 in 1920 to 23 in 1924—25. The revolutionary left was quite influential with the Ukrainian population; it was represented by the Ukrainian Social-Democratic Party (later changed into the illegal Communist Party of Western Ukraine), the Communist Party of Western Byelorussia, and the Byelorussian Party of Peasants and Workers called Hromada (Community).

The majority of the Jewish population at that time consisted of the petite bourgeoisie, the proletariat accounting for some 20 per cent. The Jewish socialist workers party, called the Bund (Union), founded much earlier (cf. XI, 4) and co-operating with the Polish Socialist Party, was influential with the Jews, among whom, however, nationalist ideas, such as Zionism, were spreading, too. The Jews had a vigorous cultural life of their own, which included publication of books and periodicals in Yiddish and operation of theatres with performances in that language.

Well-to-do people predominated among the Germans, who accounted for some 10 per cent of owners of large landed estates (the figure being some 30 per cent in Pomerania and 56 per cent in Silesia). In the case of Upper Silesian industry the German capital amounted to about one half of all investments. The position of the German minority was much better than that of the other non-Polish nationalities. It ran its own schools, learned societies, organizations of various kinds, and cultural institutions, and had its own press and other publications. The German population in Poland was under the strong influence of the increasingly chauvinistic German authorities (under the Weimar Republic), which strove for a revision of the Treaty of Versailles. The Polish-French alliance — the key-stone of Polish foreign policy — was treated by German politicians as a threat to their country. The problem was much more complicated than it might seem, because the German left, too, although in the past traditionally friendly to Poland, largely supported the revisionist tendencies. In 1920, when Poland was involved in the war with Russia, Germany resorted to an economic blockade.

For all that the first four years of independent Poland were a period of astonishing achievements, especially if we consider the fact that Poland had to cope with difficult conditions in practically all fields. The radical attitude of the nation at large prevented a victory of the conservative forces and contributed to the spreading of democratic ideas. This was among other things due to the revolutionary left which by its attitude and success exerted extra-parliamentary pressure upon the political life and forced the authorities to seek progressive solutions, be it only for fear of a revolution.

The state became integrated to a large extent. Popular uprisings helped Poland regain the region of Great Poland and a large part of Upper Silesia. But, on the other hand, Poland had unfriendly relations with Soviet Russia.

As early as 9 February 1919, the decree on compulsory primary education was passed, which meant that for the first time in Polish history all children would be subject to obligatory schooling. There were new achievements in science, artistic life was extremely vigorous (see section 5 below). The construction of a modern harbour was started in Gdynia in 1920 in order to make the country independent of Gdańsk, where the Germans obstructed the functioning of the Polish authorities.

3. Internal political conflicts (1922—26). The coup d'état of May 1926

The next four years brought many important events in the political life of the country. The tide of revolutionary movements and actions was rising (not only in Poland), the aspirations of the national democrats grew stronger, and finally the *coup d'état* in 1926 gave the power into Piłsudski's hands.

When the new Constitution was adopted in March 1921 (cf. section 1 above) new elections were to be held in accordance with its provisions. In the meantime acute parliamentary conflicts were taking place between the national democrats, on the one hand, and Piłsudski and his adherents on the other (the so-called Belvedere Palace group, so named after the historical palace in Warsaw where Piłsudski had his residence as the head of the state). The intensifying strikes activated the forces of the revolutionary left. The Communist Party of Poland (until 1923 called the Communist Workers' Party of Poland) began to revise its too rigorous stand on co-operation with the socialists and the peasants, and started advocating a uniform workers' front and the worker-peasant alliance. The Communist Party spread its activity among the intelligentsia and the young people. March 1922 saw the convocation of the First Congress of the Union of Communist Youth. In the meantime a vigorous electoral campaign was going on. The communists took part in the elections as a semi-legal organization called the Union of the Urban and Rural Proletariat. The Polish Socialist Party increased its activity and broadened the scope of its democratic appeal. The communists saw the necessity for a revolution which would pass the power into the hands of the masses, and of a close co-operation with Soviet Russia. The right-wing groups merged to form the Christian Union of National Unity.

The election returns were as follows: the Christian Democrats won 28.8 per cent of the votes and 169 seats, the corresponding figures for other parties and groups being: the Piast Polish Peasant Party, 12.9 and 70; the Bloc of National Minorities (which to some extent co-operated with one another), 15.1 and 66; the Wyzwolenie Polish Peasant Party, 10.9 and 49; the Polish Socialist Party, 10.11 and 41; the National Workers' Party, 5.36 and 18; the communists, 1.43 and 2. In all, the influence of the parliamentary left increased by 6.6 per cent, and that of the right, by 3.2 per cent. The number of the deputies who represented national minorities increased from 17 to 89 (i.e. from 3.9 to 21 per cent) and included 35 Jews, 25 Ukrainians, 17 Germans, 11 Byelorussians, and one Russian. Maciej Rataj (1884—1940), representative of the Piast Polish Peasant Party, was elected the Speaker of the Seym. There were also separate elections to the Silesian Seym, where the Christian Democrats were extremely strong.

Under such conditions the emergence of a parliamentary majority that would be able to form a stable cabinet was a serious problem, especially in view of the acute conflicts among some of the political parties. The only solution could consist in a rapprochement between the centrists, on the one hand, and either the right or the left, on the other. It took place in the form of an alliance between the Christian Democrats and the Piast Polish Peasant Party. Next the Seym faced the problem of choosing the president. Piłsudski, who seemed a likely candidate, refused and suggested that someone who was less involved in politics be chosen. Count Maurycy Zamoyski, the candidate of the right, failed to obtain the majority of the votes in a number of rounds. Only the joint support by the Piast representatives and those of the national minorities of Gabriel Narutowicz, who was the candidate of the Wyzwolenie Polish Peasant Party, proved decisive and Narutowicz was elected president. This aroused a violent resistance on the part of the national democrats, who came out against the newly elected president by organizing demonstrations and stirring up young people. In an atmosphere of tension, Eligiusz Niewiadomski, a fanatical chauvinist, shot Narutowicz dead a few days affter his election. The news of the assassination excited the masses which were ready to attack the national democrats. Piłsudski's adherents tried to take advantage of the excitement of the masses in order finally to defeat the national democrats and to seize full power, but their plans were foiled by Rataj, the Speaker of the Seym, who entrusted General Władysław Sikorski, and not Piłsudski, with the task of forming a new cabinet. On 20 December 1922, Stanisław Wojciechowski (1869—1953), the candidate of the centrist parties, was elected president.

The new cabinet had to face enormous problems, mainly in the fields of the national economic and social relations, aggravated by the worsening conflict between the Piłsudskites and the national democrats. The conflict took the form of extraparliamentary activities as well, formation of various organizations, including clandestine ones, provocations by the police who were inspired by the Piłsudskites, etc., which revealed a grave crisis in Polish parliamentary life. Piłsudski sharply criticized the composition and the political programme of the cabinet and started opposing it ruthlessly. The agreement between the Christian Union of National Unity and the Witos-led Piast Polish Peasant Party signed in Warsaw in May 1923 brought about the fall of Sikorski's cabinet and passed the power into the hands of the centrist and right-wing parties.

The Witos cabinet survived for seven months (May to December 1923) and marked a shift to the right: social welfare legislation was limited, Polonization of the eastern territories intensified, and the position of the Roman Catholic Church was strengthened (which eventually led to the signing of the concordat in 1925: the financial status of the clergy, who became more active politically, was improved, and this disclosed its connections with the dominant classes and weakened its influence among the masses). The policy of the Witos cabinet also meant abandonment of the agrarian reform as envisaged by the recently adopted legislative acts (cf. section 1 above) in favour of solutions more favourable to the owners of large estates, and the revival of measures to be taken against the labour movement.

The events in Poland were, to some extent, part of the processes taking place on a European scale: the rise of the revolutionary tide and the opposition to it in the form of intensifying rightist trends. In Italy, Mussolini seized power (1922) following the fascist *coup d'état;* similar events took place in Spain in 1923; Germany witnessed the first attempt on Hitler's part to seize power (the Munich putsch); in Bulgaria, the Tsankov government seized power as a result of an armed coup, opposed by workers and peasants.

In Poland, swept by new waves of strikes, the communists intensified their activity: they appealed to the parliamentary left that it campaign for the formation of a workers' and peasants' government. Within the Communist Party of Poland the tendency to broaden its activity by organizing a uniform front of the working class (cf. section 2 above) was growing stronger. This was connected with the adoption of Lenin's conceptions on the national issue and on the attitude of the state toward the peasants. It is to be noted that the principle of the mobilization of the masses within a united front was then launched by the Fourth Congress of the Communist International.

In that respect the turning point in the Polish revolutionary movement was marked by the Second Congress of the Communist Workers' Party of Poland, held between 19 September and 2 October 1923. Those leaders who realized that it was necessary to abandon the dogmatic stand included Adolf Warski, Maria Koszutska ('Wera'), Henryk Lauer-Brand, and Henryk Walecki. The principal report to the Congress was submitted by Adolf Warski. On the agrarian issue the Congress declared that the communists were for the passing of the large landed estates into peasant hands without indemnification and came out against the government policy in social and national questions.

The strikes which swept the country in 1923 had their culminating point in the uprising in Cracow aimed at the Witos cabinet. In November workers clashed there with the police and with troops. Some troops, however, and some groups of the Piłsudskites joined the workers (Piłsudski, who sharply criticized the national democrats and the cabinet, still enjoyed considerable popularity with the masses). The rioting resulted in 18 dead and nearly 200 wounded. Similar riots took place in Borysław. The movement was spontaneous in nature; it was dominated by the socialists who ultimately helped master the situation. The days of the Witos cabinet were numbered, since some peasant groups were also against its policy. Inflation was galloping and moreover the cabinet could not boast of any successes on the international scene.

The new cabinet, which came into being on 19 December 1923, was headed by Władysław Grabski, who had earlier worked out a plan for the improvement of the economic situation of the country (the so-called stabilization plan). His measures coincided with the then already noticeable upward trend in the international economy. Since Britain and the United States — which tried to prevent France from becoming too strong, and also to create a counterbalance to the Soviet Union which was growing in strength — pursued the policy which tended to reconstruct Germany militarily and economically, Poland was forced to improve its internal situation even more. The focal point of the reform was increased taxation which would draw money from both the propertied classes (direct taxes) and the masses (indirect taxes), an improvement in public administration, and intervention on the stock exchange to prevent the Polish mark from falling still more. The mark was replaced by the złoty, the conversion rate being 1,800,000 marks to one złoty, which illustrates the level of inflation. The Bank of Poland was founded. All this yielded good results, which is remarkable in view of the fact that all these measures were taken without foreign aid. But the inflow of foreign capital began, too, loans were contracted abroad, and the native capitalists started — by lowering the wages (which was made easier by the fact that unemployment was on the rise) and lengthening the working day — to shift the costs of the reforms onto the masses. The government had to counteract this at least to some extent; the same applied to the overdue issue of the agrarian reform, which was regulated by a new act, passed by the Seym in December 1925. From 1919 to that date some 1.25 million hectares of land had been passed to peasants. In most cases it was a voluntary breaking up of large estates, and against indemnity, so that the land was purchased mostly by well-off peasants. Despite a certain improvement in the economic situation the country came to face new problems in 1925, the more so as the crops in 1924 were very poor, and on the other hand the price of sugar, one of the principal commodities at that time exported by Poland, dropped by some 40 per cent. In June 1925 Germany stopped importing coal from Poland, and the Polish government had to restrict imports from Germany. This led to the so-called tariff war between Germany and Poland, which — as the leading politicians of the Reich expected — was to bring about economic collapse in Poland. The Polish balance of trade deteriorated, and foreign currencies started flowing out of the Bank of Poland.

At the same time the political system in Europe was undergoing an essential modification: the Locarno conference in October 1925, which reflected the agreement beween Britain and an already stronger Germany, meant a departure from the system based on the Treaty of Versailles, and hence a worsening of the political situation of Poland, Czechoslovakia, and the Soviet Union. This in turn led to a temporary improvement of Poland's relations with these two countries. The Locarno treaties guaranteed the western frontiers of Germany which in turn assumed the obligation not to change its eastern frontiers by resorting to force, but the possibility of a change as such was not excluded.

The implementation of Grabski's programme, which largely depended on the international situation, collapsed, and his cabinet fell. This resulted in increased activity among Piłsudski's adherents, especially in the army. The ex-servicemen closed their ranks and circulated the myth of their contribution to the reconstruction of the Polish state and promoted the worship of Piłsudski, also strengthened by the Polish Socialist Party with Daszyński as its leader. A coalition cabinet was formed, representing the National Democrats, the Christian Democrats, the Piast Polish Peasant

Polish gunners during the uprising in Great Poland (1918–19), organized to win the incorporation of the former Prussian partition zone into Poland

Józef Piłsudski (1867–1935), statesman, founder of the Polish Legions in 1914, Head of the State in 1918–22, from 1920 the Marshal of Poland and the Supreme Commander of the Polish Army

Wincenty Witos (1874–1945), peasant leader, politician, journalist, prime minister in 1920–21, 1923 and 1926

The Chamber of Deputies during the first meeting of the Diet on 10 February 1919

The harbour in Gdynia, the largest Polish investment project between the World Wars

The National Museum in Warsaw, built in 1926–39

Warsaw in the 1930's

Polish aircraft designers (from the left) Stanisław Gliński, Janusz Lange, Jerzy Rudnicki, Witold Grabowski, Marian Bartolewski and Jerzy Teisseyre, shown with the passenger airplane Lublin R IX, with an R X in the background (in the period between the World Wars Poland was noted for gifted aircraft designers)

Ludwik Hirszfeld (1884–1954), physician, serologist and immunologist, co-founder of the science of blood groups

Kazimierz Funk (1884–1967), biochemist active in Germany, Britain, Poland, and the United States, co-founder of the science of vitamins

Stefan Banach (1892–1945), eminent mathematician, co-founder of the theory of functional analysis

Tadeusz Kotarbiński (1886–1981), philosopher, logician, principal originator of praxiology

Zofia Nałkowska (1884–1954), writer, representative of realistic prose concerned with psychological and moral issues

Maria Dąbrowska (1889–1965), writer, representative of realistic prose concerned with psychological and social issues and manners

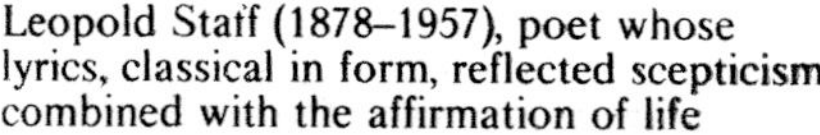

Leopold Staff (1878–1957), poet whose lyrics, classical in form, reflected scepticism combined with the affirmation of life

Leon Schiller (1887–1954), stage director, theatre historian, teacher of theatre art, author of monumental stagings of poetic plays

Władysław Broniewski (1897–1962), the leading Polish revolutionary poet who referred to the Polish romantic traditions

Jarosław Iwaszkiewicz (1894–1980), prose writer, poet, playwright, co-founder of the Skamander group

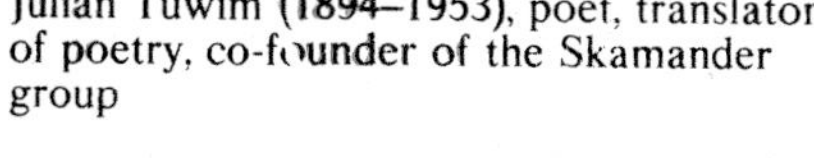

Julian Tuwim (1894–1953), poet, translator of poetry, co-founder of the Skamander group

Czesław Miłosz (b. 1911), poet, member of the Żagary group, since 1951 living abroad, Nobel Prize winner in 1980

General Karol Świerczewski (1897–1947), participant in the October Revolution, commander of the 14th International Brigade during the Civil War in Spain, one of the organizers of the Polish troops in the Soviet Union and commander of the 2nd Polish Army during World War II (shown – first from the left – in the company of Dolores Ibárruri when watching the parade of the international brigades in Spain in 1937)

Party, the Polish Socialist Party, and the National Workers' Party. Piłsudski opposed endeavours to subject the army to parliamentary supervision, attacked Sikorski, and activated his own supporters in the army. A group of intellectuals and professionals, headed by Kazimierz Bartel (1882—1941), professor at the Lvov Technical University, organized a Labour Club (Labour Party) that supported Piłsudski. The improving economic situation also worked to Piłsudski's advantage. His breaking the negotiations with the cabinet concerning his assuming a post in the army and his attacks aimed at many important personages in the army exacerbated the situation. Piłsudski's adherents, whom Sikorski had transferred to the provinces, started returning to Warsaw. The cabinet resigned, and a new one was to be formed by Witos. He did form a cabinet on 10 May 1926, but two days later Piłsudski with those troops which were loyal to him, left his residence in Sulejówek near Warsaw and marched his troops on the capital. After a brief period of fighting (the casualties being 300 dead an 1,000 wounded) the cabinet resigned on the night of 14 May 1926, and President Wojciechowski did the same. Upon Piłsudski's proposal Rataj, the Speaker of the Seym, entrusted Kazimierz Bartel with the task of forming a new cabinet. Professor Ignacy Mościcki (1867—1946), supported by Piłsudski, was elected president (re-elected in 1933 he held that post until Poland's defeat by Germany in 1939). This opened the period of political control of the country by the Piłsudskites, who promised to sanify the political life of the country — and hence their rule was labelled the *sanacja* or 'sanification' period. After the *coup d'état* of May 1926 the power élite was reduced to a small number of persons, and the power apparatus, consisting of several dozen thousand persons, became dominated by the 'sanification' group. This gradually led to the consolidation of the dictatorship of the 'sanification' group, exercised by civil servants and the military. For the next nine years the power was to be wielded by Piłsudski, and later by his political successors, who, however, started revealing differences within their group. The military were playing an increasing role within the ruling group.

4. Poland under the 'sanification' cabinets (1926—39). Growth of radical attitudes. The danger of war

The leftist groups, which had believed that Piłsudski fought for democratic principles and opposed the rightist orientation in politics, were soon disenchanted and had critically to assess their attitude. It was the *coup d'état* of 1926 which, by destroying parliamentary democracy and restricting the size of the governing élite, laid the foundations for making the political rule in Poland rightist in nature. It was true that it limited the influence of the national democrats, but at the same time it was a blow to the parliamentary left and a serious danger to the revolutionary left that was clandestinely active. The capitalists supported the new situation as they saw in it a better guarantee of restricting the demands raised by the workers; moreover, the strong rule made foreign capitalists more confident of the situation in Poland. Foreign capital and loans started flowing in quite freely. Considerable influence was acquired in Poland by American, British, and French capital. All this improved the business trends and stimulated investments, but at the same time Poland's indebtedness was growing, which was not without influence upon the country's political dependence on others. In order to obtain credits more easily enterprises made cartel agreements, which in turn increased Poland's dependence upon other countries in the sphere of capital supply. But on the whole production was increasing and so was employment; the material status of the workers continued to improve. Industry was modernized and housing construction expanded. In 1926—29, industrial production increased by some 40 per cent. The construction of the harbour in Gdynia was making rapid progress, and Gdynia soon became one of the largest harbours in the Baltic (in terms of turnover of goods), second only to Copenhagen. The construction and extension of the Gdynia harbour was primarily due to Eugeniusz Kwiatkowski (1888—1974), at that time the Minister of Industry and Commerce. Railway lines connecting Gdynia with Silesia were also built.

The situation of agriculture improved considerably. In 1926—29, the incomes from peasant farms, calculated per one hectare, rose by 60 to 70 per cent. This expanded the home market for industrial goods, and at the same time, in view of the increased prices of land, induced the owners of large estates to sell some of their land. The policy pursued by the 'sanification' cabinets promoted the development of capitalist relations in the country and saw in well-to-do peasants the principal figures in the rural areas. But this policy was hampered by enormous over-population of the rural areas; the surplus manpower was not absorbed by industry in spite of an increasing output of industrial goods. This was why the number of emigrants, mainly landless peasants and owners of dwarf and small holdings, reached 500,000 between 1926 and 1929. Moreover, the prospects for the future were not good: the great depression, which came soon, dragged on in Poland for an exceptionally long time, namely from 1929 until 1935.

For the time being, however, the improvement in the economic situation obviously played into the hands of the 'sanification' group and facilitated the implementation of its policies. The first step consisted in strengthening the position of the army within the political system. The office of the General Inspector of the Army was formed, its holder being responsible to the President only. Provisions of the Constitution were being violated; political storm troopers assaulted writers and politicians who criticized the 'sanification' governments or Piłsudski personally. The position of the cabinet ministers changed markedly: while before they had represented definite political ideas according to their party allegiance, they were now selected as experts in their respective fields for whom political decisions were made by the power élite consisting of former members of the Polish Legions and obedient to Piłsudski. Even the President had liaison officers who were assigned to him either by General Felicjan Sławoj-Składkowski (1885—1962) — appointed prime minister in 1936— or by Piłsudski himself. Endeavours were also made to win over the Ukrainian and Byelorussian population, but concessions were made dependent on support to be given by those ethnic groups to the 'sanification' group, which, however, did not have any definite conception in that respect. All this required further restrictions of the prerogatives of the Seym and the establishment of a *sui generis* presidential system, which was, however, based not on the authority of President Mościcki, but on Piłsudski's political position. At the end of 1926 Piłsudski was simultaneously the Prime Minister, the Minister of Military Affairs, and the General Inspector of the Army. Yet all the time the point was to keep the appearances of a form of government based on parliamentary democracy.

The situation brought about by the *coup d'état* of May 1926 had considerable repercussions, and led to divergences in the existing political parties and groups on the issue of their attitude toward the 'sanification' group, and also — in the case of the Communist Party of Poland — on the issue of its co-operation with the parliamentary left. The Communist Party was approached by the Independent Peasant Party, the Hromada Byelorussian Party of Peasants and Workers, and the Left Wing of the Polish Socialist Party, which broke off with the Polish Socialist Party that still supported the government. This meant a danger for the 'sanification' group, which reacted with arrests and the delegalization of the Independent Peasant Party and the Hromada Byelorussian Party.

The Communist Party of Poland, which in 1923—33 had some 16,000 members, was the most consistent of all in opposing the 'sanification' group. The legal, i.e. parliamentary, opposition consisted mainly of the National Party (ca. 200,000 members in the late 1930's), the Peasant Party (which came into being through the merger, in 1931, of the Piast Polish Peasant Party, the Wyzwolenie Polish Peasant Party, and another peasant party), with some 150,000 members in 1939, and the Polish Socialist Party, which had only some 30,000 members but whose influence with the masses was incomparably greater.

The striving of the 'sanification' group to win more influence and the opposition's attacks upon the policies of that group continued. In order to gather as many people around the government as possible the Piłsudskites formed, before the elections of 1928, the so-called Non-Party Bloc for Co-operation with the Government, which was intended to unite the various groups, social classes, and political trends. But the Bloc failed to win the majority in the election, and thus lost the chance of having the Constitution changed. There were 34 electoral lists at that time; the communists received nearly one million votes and, together with groups whose programmes were similar to theirs, won 15 seats in the Seym.

The Bloc's striving to limit the role of the Seym and the formation, in 1929, of the cabinet headed by Kazimierz Świtalski, with Piłsudski's trusted men, resulted in a closer co-operation of the centrist and leftist parliamentary clubs. The Piłsudskites left the Polish Socialist Party, which was accordingly strengthened ideologically and won more support from other opposition groups. Six parliamentary clubs merged to form an opposition bloc called Centrolew (probably the closest corresponding term being the Italian *Centro-sinistra*) and abolished the Świtalski cabinet with a considerable majority of votes. A new cabinet was formed by Bartel, who, having passed the state budget in the Seym, which was his principal task, resigned soon after. The next cabinet was headed by Walery Sławek (1879—1939), but the composition of the successive cabinets varied little. The Congress for the Rights and Freedoms of the People, organized by the Centrolew, announced a campaign against Piłsudski's dictatorship and won growing support in society. This spread the political conflict outside the parliamentary arena. The process coincided with the deteriorating economic situation. It was the beginning of the great depression, which covered all capitalist states. In Poland, as has been said, it was particularly acute and lasted longer than elsewhere. As compared with 1929, industrial production fell by 18 per cent in 1930, by 31 per cent in 1931, and by 46 per cent in 1932, which was followed by a certain improvement: if the 1929 level is taken as 100, then the indicator of industrial production was 56 in 1933, 63 in 1934 and 66 in 1935. The fall was larger than that of world production as a whole, and was due to a considerable shrinking of the home market (as a result of the fall of incomes) and also to the activity of the cartels, which strove to raise prices rather than to increase production. Unemployment was growing and the overpopulation of the rural areas was even more acutely felt. In the textile industry unemployment affected as many as one half of the workers. In 1931, unemployment covered — according to the branch of industry — from 25 to 80 per cent of all gainfully employed. Craftsmen and small shopkeepers suffered from the depression, too, their volume of business having dropped, between 1928 and 1932, by some 60 per cent on the average. In agriculture, the depression took mainly the form of a fall of incomes due to the drop in the prices of agricultural produce by nearly 70 per cent, and not to the shrinking of production. The peasants accordingly found it difficult to make investments and to pay back the debts contracted earlier, when their financial position was better. Small holders could not cover their expenses by the same surplus of agricultural produce as before. Poverty and backwardness in the rural areas intensified. In the eastern provinces of the country peasants almost ceased to purchase industrial and consumer goods. The smaller the farm the more acute were the consequences of the depression. The financial situation of the country deteriorated, and the same applied to its foreign currency reserves. Poland was becoming more and more dependent upon foreign capital.

The elections held in November 1930 were marked by a political offensive by the 'sanification' group. The Centrolew formed an electoral bloc called the Union for the Rights and Freedoms of the People, but its activity was hamstrung by arrests of such prominent politicians as Stanisław Dubois and Norbert Barlicki of the Polish Socialist Party, Józef Putek of the Wyzwolenie Polish Peasant Party, Wincenty Witos of the Piast Polish Peasant Party, and Wojciech Korfanty of the Christian Democratic Party. They were placed in a military prison in Brest Litovsk, where they were terrorized. In all, arrests affected some 5,000 persons, primarily adherents of the Centrolew.

In the elections the 'sanification' group (i.e. the Non-Party Bloc for Co-operation with the Government) received 46.2 per cent of the votes, the analogous figures being 17 per cent for the Centrolew and 2.3 per cent for the communists. In the new cabinet the majority of the ministers again consisted of ex-servicemen. In the meantime the news about the terror applied in the Brest prison was spreading throughout the country, and public opinion demanded explanations. Piłsudski's popularity dropped sharply.

The new cabinet, and those which followed but remained within the same political orbit, faced as its main problem the countermeasures to be taken to reduce the worsening economic depression and the resulting restlessness of the masses. The cabinets were, however, more consistent in fighting the opposition than in counteracting the depression. The measures taken against the communists were intensified, especially in the Ukraine. There was a number of political trials, including that of the leaders of the Centrolew, imprisoned in Brest. Wincenty Witos left the country to protest against the sentence, but he announced that he would continue his campaign against the 'sanification' group from abroad. Workers' parties were crushed or delegalized (this applied to the Byelorussian Hromada, the Independent Peasant Party, and the Left Wing of the Polish Socialist Party). There were many strikes and demonstrations, also of the peasants, particularly marked in Little Poland in 1933. The school system was changed and the fees were raised in the schools of university standing, which limited the access to secondary and higher education of young people from the poorer strata of the population, primarily young peasants. The courts, the bar, and the Supreme Administrative Court were made dependent upon the cabinet. Social insurance was restricted. Finally, in April 1935, a new Constitution was passed without the due process of law, which replaced the March Constitution of 1921 (cf. section 1 above). In the new Constitution, it was not the nation but the state (governed by its élite) which was moved to the fore. In this connection the prerogatives of the Seym and the Senate were limited considerably, while those of the president were enhanced greatly; he was thenceforth to be responsible only 'to God and History'. Under these circumstances some adherents of the national democracy (the Union of Young National Democrats), who always had such a model of the state in view, began to come closer to the 'sanification' group; on the other hand, the left-wing groups were growing more and more radical. The Left Wing of the Polish Socialist Party, already mentioned, was formed in 1934; in the Peasant Party an internal controversy was taking place over that party's attitude toward the 'sanification' group. Actions undertaken jointly by the communists and the socialists, which were a prelude to the emerging popular front recommended by the Seventh Congress of the Communist International in 1935, were increasing in number. The new elections, which took place under new conditions, namely after Piłsudski's death on 12 May 1935, ended in an utter defeat of the 'sanification' group as they were boycotted by the population: the attendance at the polls was merely 46.5 per cent, and as many as one-fourth of all votes were invalid. The Non-Party Bloc for Co-operation with the Government was dissolved, and two subgroups began to take shape within the 'sanification' group: one, consisting only of military men and ex-servicemen, was gathered around Edward Rydz-Śmigły, the then General Inspector of the Army, and was nicknamed the Belvedere Palace group (after the official residence of Rydz-Śmigły), and the other, more civilian in its composition, was gathered around Ignacy Mościcki and was nicknamed the Royal Castle group (after the official residence of the president).

Józef Beck (1894—1944), who was the Polish Minister for Foreign Affairs from 1932, succeeded in securing an independent position between the Belvedere Palace group and the Royal Castle group. The guiding idea of his policy, based on the principles adopted by Piłsudski, was to strive for an understanding with Germany while traditionally seeking the support of France, and also, on an increasing scale, of Britain. While a pact of non-aggression was signed with the Soviet Union in 1932, it did not have any major influence upon the political conceptions of Piłsudski and Beck, which recommended balancing between France and Britain, on the one hand, and Germany on the other. That policy was to be changed only when the German danger became an undisputable fact. For the time being a declaration of non-aggression was signed with Germany in 1934. While Poland adopted it as the focal point of its foreign policy, which was manifested by the rejection by Poland of the idea of the so-called Eastern Pact that would unite France, the Soviet Union, Poland, Czechoslovakia, and Germany, for the Germans it was merely an element of political tactics in the drive intended to put into effect the expansionist plans outlined by Adolf Hitler in his *Mein Kampf*.

In 1935 and 1936 Poland witnessed vigorous demonstrations and numerous strikes aimed against the policy of the 'sanification' group. The major events in that respect included the sit-in strike in the Semperit Plant in Cracow in May 1936, which provoked an avalanche of demonstrations of solidarity such as the great demonstration of the peasants in the village of Nowosielce in June 1936, the Congress of Culture in Lvov ('Cultural Workers for Peace') and the demonstrations undertaken by the Union of Polish Teachers. At that time some 5,000 Poles, mainly communists by conviction, fought in the International Brigades in the defence of the popular government during the civil war in Spain (1936—39); they included Karol Świerczewski (1897—1947), who proved a very capable commander.

In the meantime two factors made themselves felt and considerably influenced the political life of the country in 1936—39: a revival of the national economy and the intensifying threat of a conflict with Germany. The economic revival was largely due to the interference of the state (in the form of state interventionism) and an upward business trend in agriculture. The government announced its economic programme called the Four-Year Investment Plan for the period from 1 July 1936 to 30 June 1940. Economic matters were at that time in the hands of the left wing of the 'sanification' group, headed by Eugeniusz Kwiatkowski, the principal advocate in Poland of the policy of driving up the business trend. Planned investments were initiated, the pride of place going to the Central Industrial District in Little Poland. Many commercial agreements were concluded and exports were growing. The volume of Polish foreign trade in 1938 was about 40 per cent greater than that in 1935. The Investment Plan was carried out by March 1939, and a new one, covering a period of three years, was made, but its implementation took place in a very tense political climate and coincided with preparations for war the threat of which was looming larger. Some of the investments were in the armaments industry, and endeavours were made to modernize and to expand the air force and the navy.

All these undertakings, combined with an upward business trend and increased incomes of the population — mainly those engaged in agriculture, in view of the rising prices of agricultural products — caused industrial production to go up. The situation in agriculture was also improved by the measures, taken from 1933 on, to reduce the burden of debts.

The danger of war intensified following the successive steps taken by Nazi Germany after Hitler's rise to power in 1933, and also in the atmosphere of a general political offensive of the fascist forces. In 1935, the Third Reich, having left the League of Nations in 1933, denounced those provisions of the Treaty of Versailles which applied to the limitation of armaments, and on 7 March 1936 sent troops to the Rhineland, which formerly was to be a demilitarized zone. The year 1936 saw the civil war in Spain following the rebellion by General Franco. In July 1937, Japan, where pro-fascist forces gained the upper hand, started a war with China. In 1938, Germany annexed Austria by resorting to force and made the governments of Britain, France, and Italy, which wanted to preserve peace at any price, agree — at the Munich Conference in September 1938 — to the annexation of the Sudetenland by the Germans. The Polish government stuck to its policy of maintaining good relations with Germany; the opinion — not shared by the military and sober-thinking politicians — was upheld that further German expansion would be in the Danubian Basin. Taking the Czech action in 1919 (cf. section 2 above) as a pretext at the beginning of October Poland annexed the Transolzan region, which was politically convenient to the Germans.

As soon as 24 October Germany laid bare its intentions with regard to Poland. Joachim von Ribbentrop, the German minister for foreign affairs, at a meeting with Józef Lipski, the Polish ambassador in Berlin, presented the German demands, to be renewed until April 1939, which included the incorporation of the Free City of Gdańsk into Germany and the construction of an extraterritorial highway that would connect Germany proper with East Prussia.

Ribbentrop's proposals were in fact a way of finding out whether Poland could be subordinated to the Third Reich and thus deprived of its sovereignty. The acceptance of those proposals, which were constantly escalated, would not have preserved the peace and would have made the Allied victory over Germany much more difficult. Hitler's plans did not end at Gdańsk and the highway: as the future was to show, his goals were much more comprehensive.

The rejection of the German proposals was the first 'no' to the Nazi expansion. It meant an essential change in Polish foreign policy, a change made easier by the attitude of Britain which was now determined to stop — also in its own interest — the further expansion of Germany which in the meantime (14 March 1939), occupied Bohemia and Moravia. All this led to the conclusion, on 6 April 1939, of a Polish-British treaty of guarantees. In the same month Germany denounced the Polish-German declaration of non-aggression of 1934. Despite all this the change in the Polish foreign policy was not quite consistent, because Beck did not support the Soviet endeavours which had a treaty of collective security in view (the Polish government did not agree to possible movements of Soviet troops through the Polish territory). Previously (1935) the Polish government also refused to support the Soviet and French endeavours to conclude the so-called Eastern Pact.

Under the circumstances the Soviet Union signed, on 23 August 1939, a pact of non-aggression with Germany, sometimes referred to as the Ribbentrop-Molotov pact.

The escalation of Hitler's demands continued in the meantime. He was convinced that the Western Powers would not support Poland and there would be accordingly no second front. The preparations for the offensive against Poland were proceeding at a rapid pace. The broad propaganda campaign was reinforced by many anti-Polish provocations, including the fictive Polish action against the broadcasting station in Gliwice. On 22 August 1939, Hitler declared that the destruction of Poland was his first goal, and that for propaganda purposes he would give any cause for the outbreak of the war, whether believable or not. The demands addressed to Poland were increased incessantly although the date of the offensive was already fixed; in the last moment it was shifted from 26 August to 1 September 1939.

5. Culture and society. The historical values of the period

The brief period of two decades (1918—39) has an important place in the history of Poland. It was a school of political thinking and political practice, which brought in full relief the creative forces of the Polish nation and also the immense tasks that faced the Poles who were organizing anew their lives as citizens of a sovereign state.

The period in question marked a further stage in the development of the Polish nation. First of all, the Polish territories with their population, separated from one another as a result of the partitions, were reintegrated. In fact those integrative processes which took place in this period were the most important contribution of the epoch to the history of the Polish people.

An immense part was played by education, science, and other spheres of culture. While Poland was till largely a country of peasants and its social structure did not change much, nevertheless the share of the intelligentsia increased by 12 per cent, the analogous figures for the working class and the petite bourgeoisie being nine per cent and seven per cent, respectively. This had a considerable impact upon the content of cultural life and the number and the differentiation of those who participated in it.

First of all, advances in education were of considerable significance. The various regions had been greatly differentiated in that respect (cf. XI, 5): while in Great Poland and in Pomerania there were practically no illiterates, in Central Poland the indicator of illiteracy was 30 to 40 per cent; in the western part of Little Poland, 20 to 30 per cent; and in the eastern territories, 40 to 70 per cent; the average for the whole country being about 33 per cent. Compulsory primary education became a fact in the 1930's, but there was still the danger of the so-called recurrent illiteracy (people forgetting how to read and write years after they had left the school), especially in the rural areas. The percentage of children of workers and peasants in the secondary and university schools was falling. In 1922—23, out of the total of 227,000 pupils in secondary schools less than four per cent were of working class origin, and 13 per cent, of peasant origin. Out-of-school education continued to spread, being promoted by farmers' circles, the Wici (Call to Arms) Union of Peasant Youth, and the Society for Promotion of Popular Universities, which co-operated with the Polish Socialist Party and was active among workers. A Peasant University was active until 1929, when it was closed down by the authorities. The network of public libraries and museums became quite dense. The National Museum was founded in Warsaw, the Museum of Modern Art was organized in Łódź. There were in all 27 schools of university standing, concentrated in Warsaw, Cracow, Lvov, Poznań, and Vilna, including five universities (Poznań University was only opened in 1919; earlier endeavours to have it founded there (cf. X, 2) failed in view of the refusal of the German authorities). The sixth university, namely the Roman Catholic University, was soon opened in Lublin. The so-called Warsaw Free University, with a branch in Łódź, founded in 1928, also proved important in the advancement of culture. The technical universities (colleges of science and technology) in Warsaw and Lvov (cf. XI, 5) and the Warsaw Academy of Fine Arts continued their work. The Cracow School of Mining was founded in 1919 and, the Warsaw School of Political Science in 1922. In all, in the 1930's there were some 50,000 students in all those schools. The number of dailies and periodicals was 2,692 in 1937, of which 130 were Jewish, 125 were Ukrainian, 105 were German, nine were Russian, eight were Byelorussian, etc. The network of state archives was organized, and over a dozen research institutes were established, which reflected the vigorous development of research (in 1938 the number of research workers reached the level of some 4,000 persons).

International renown was won by Polish mathematicians, grouped in two principal schools, that in Warsaw with Wacław Sierpiński (1882—1969) and Kazimierz Kuratowski (1896—1980), and that in Lvov with Stanisław Mazur (b. 1905—83) and Stefan Banach (1892—1945), one of the founders of functional analysis (cf. the Banach spaces, one of the fundamental concepts in that branch of mathematical analysis). Outstanding achievements were also recorded in logic: Jan Łukasiewicz (1879—1956), Stanisław Leśniewski (1886—1939), Alfred Tarski (b. 1901); in physics: Stefan Pieńkowski (1883—1953), Leopold Infeld (1898—1968), a close collaborator of Albert Einstein, and Czesław Białobrzeski (1878—1953); in chemistry: Wojciech Świętosławski (1881—1968); in technology: Stefan Bryła (1886—1948), the constructor of the first fully welded bridge in the world; in geography: Eugeniusz Romer (1871—1954); in antropology: Jan Czekanowski (1882—1965); in botany: Władysław Szafer (1886—1970); in medicine: Ludwik Hirszfeld (1884—1954). The Lvov-Warsaw school of philosophy won world recognition for its studies in logic and semantics. Its chief representatives included Kazimierz Twardowski (1866—1938), Tadeusz Kotarbiński (1886—1981), and Kazimierz Ajdukiewicz (1890—1963). The phenomenological trend in philosophy had its prominent representative in Roman Ingarden (1893—1970), largely concerned with the theory of aesthetics, and the history of philosophy and aesthetics was the field of interest of Władysław Tatarkiewicz (1886—1980).

A notably high level was reached in economics and statistics by Adam Krzyżanowski (1873—1963), Edward Taylor (1884—1964), and Edward Lipiński (b. 1888). In sociology and ethnography the pride of place goes to such names as Ludwik Krzywicki (1859—1941), Stefan Czarnowski (1879—1937), Florian Znaniecki (1882—1958), Kazimierz Moszyński (1887—1959), Jan Stanisław Bystroń (1892—1964), and Bronisław Malinowski (1884—1942), who conducted field work and taught abroad. Psychology had its main representatives in Władysław Witwicki (1878—1948), Stefan Baley (1885—1952), and Stefan Szuman (b. 1889). In jurisprudence special mention is due to the theorists of law Leon Petrażycki (1867—1931) and Czesław Znamierowski (1886—1967), to the historians of law Stanisław Kutrzeba (1876—1946), Przemysław Dąbkowski (1877—1950), and Rafał Taubenszlag (1881—1958), and to Ludwik Ehrlich (1889—1968), an expert in international law.

The historical disciplines accompanied, or even went ahead of, the general advances in that field, studies in the history of prices being a particularly creditable achievement.

The period now under consideration also witnessed the laying of the foundations of linguistics, which was the work of Kazimierz Nitsch (1873—1968), Tadeusz Lehr-Spławiński (1891—1965), Ananiasz Zajączkowski (1903—70), and many others. Kazimierz Nitsch was the first in the Slavonic countries to publish a linguistic atlas. Remarkable advances were noted in the study of literary history: Aleksander Brückner (1856—1939), Stanisław Pigoń (1885—1968), Juliusz Kleiner (1886—1957), and Julian Krzyżanowski (1892—1976); and musicology: Adolf Chybiński (1880—1952) and Zdzisław Jachimecki (1882—1953).

Interest in literary history was probably due to an unprecedented outburst of Polish literature, and especially poetry. In poetry, among the many groups the greatest and lasting influence was won by those connected with the monthly *Pro Arte et Studio,* founded in 1920, and next with the *Skamander.* The members of the latter group were rather traditional in the forms of their poetry, but novel in its content: to the moodiness and symbolism typical of the Young Poland period they opposed the poetry of everyday life. The remarkable representatives of that group included Julian Tuwim (1894—1953), Kazimierz Wierzyński (1894—1969), Jarosław Iwaszkiewicz (1894—1980), Antoni Słonimski (1895—1976), Jan Lechoń (1899—1956), and two poetesses, Kazimiera Iłłakowiczówna (1892—1983) and Maria Jasnorzewska-Pawlikowska (1893—1945). Much influence was also won by the group named the Cracow Avantgarde with Tadeusz Peiper (1891—1969), Julian Przyboś (1901—70) and Jalu Kurek (1904—83). The socially revolutionary trend in poetry was represented by Władysław Broniewski (1897—1962), Bruno Jasieński (1901—39), and others. Leopold Staff continued his work as a poet, and the same applied, in the early years of the period, to Jan Kasprowicz (d. 1926).

Social and political issues were forcefully reflected in prose works, especially in novels. The period witnessed the appearance of such outstanding works as *Przedwiośnie* (Early Spring) by Stefan Żeromski (1925), *Romans Teresy Hennert* (The Love Affair of Teresa Hennert) by Zofia Nałkowska (1924), *Pokolenie Marka Świdy* (Marek Świda's Generation) by Andrzej Strug (1925), *Czarne skrzydła* (The Black Wings) by Juliusz Kaden-Bandrowski (1928—29), *Noce i dnie* (Nights and Days) by Maria Dąbrowska (1932—34), *Krzyżowcy* (The Crusaders) by Zofia Kossak-Szczucka (1935), *Kordian i cham* (Kordian and the Churl) by Leon Kruczkowski (1932), *Czerwone tarcze* (Red Shields) by Jarosław Iwaszkiewicz (1934), *Cudzoziemka* (The Stranger) by Maria Kuncewiczowa (1936), *Ferdydurke* (a non-translatable nonce-word) by Witold Gombrowicz (1937), and *Sklepy cynamonowe* (Cinnamon Shops) by Bruno Schulz (1937).

In the drama the manner of writing typical of the Young Poland and the expressionist period prevailed still, represented, e.g., by Karol Hubert Rostworowski (1877—1938). Many comedies were written in that period, which also saw the appearance of avantgrade works, whose revival we are witnessing today: this applies above all to the dramatic production of Stanisław Ignacy Witkiewicz (also known under his pen name of Witkacy), a forerunner of the absurd in the drama (1885—1939). Jerzy Szaniawski (1886—1970) also ranked as one of the greatest Polish playwrights of that period. Special mention is due to literary criticism, represented above all by Tadeusz Boy-Żeleński (cf. XI, 5) and Karol Irzykowski (1873—1944).

Theatrical life was very brisk, and the number of permanent theatres reached 26 in 1936. The most active and at the same the most ambitious ones included the Polski (Polish) Theatre, the Narodowy (National) Theatre, the Atheneum Theatre (all in Warsaw) and the Municipal Theatres in Lvov. The best productions included those of Żeromski's *Uciekła mi przepióreczka* (My Little Quail Ran into the Millet — the title drawn from a folk song) by Juliusz Osterwa in 1925, Krasiński's *Nie-Boska Komedia* (The Undivine Comedy, 1926), Mickiewicz's *The Forefathers' Eve* (1930) and Słowacki's *Kordian* (1932), all by Leon Schiller. The most prominent stage directors and stage producers included, next to Osterwa and Schiller, Stefan Jaracz (1883—1945), Stanisława Perzanowska (1898—1981), Wilam Horzyca (1889—1959), and Ludwik Solski (1855—1954).

The development of the film art in Poland was largely due to novel technological ideas, in which connection mention is due to Jan Szczepanik (1872—1926), nicknamed the Polish Edison, who had to his credit several dozen patents in weaving, television, colour photography, and colour film.

The period under consideration also witnessed the growing popularity of the radio; in 1931 a broadcasting station was built at Raszyn near Warsaw, which was at that time most powerful in the world and whose programmes could be received almost all over the country.

The search for novelty was also characteristic of the visual arts and music. In architecture, reference was made to the old styles and forms, but new ones were adopted, too. After the domination of *Art Nouveau,* characteristic of the Young Poland period, followed by a tendency to erect monumental buildings, Polish architects adopted the modern trends of functionalism and constructivism with their fondness for geometrical forms. This applied to both public buildings, erected in large numbers for new institutions, and housing. Due to close contacts with French art, post-impressionism played a considerable role in Polish painting (Jan Cybis, 1897—1972; Artur Nacht-Samborski, 1898—1974). Avantgarde trends such as formism developed (Tytus Czyżewski, 1880—1945; Stanisław Ignacy Witkiewicz, 1885—1939), and the Polish version of abstract art known as unism (Władysław Strzemiński, 1893—1952). Links between visual arts and architecture were sought (art groups Blok and Praesens), and Cracow became an important centre of artistic and literary avantgarde (Group Cracow). Tadeusz Makowski (1882—1932), active in France, developed his own original style of painting. Graphic art was influenced by folk art and woodcutting traditions (Władysław Skoczylas, 1883—1934) and expressionism (Tadeusz Kulisiewicz, b. 1899; Stanisław Ostoja-Chrostowski, 1897—1947; and Konstanty Brandel, 1880—1970).

Music was additionally stimulated by the development of schools (seven conservatoires) and the amateur choirs which had old traditions. It was dominated by the artistic personality of Karol Szymanowski (cf. XI, 5). Also important for the development of Polish music in that period were Feliks Nowowiejski (1877—1946), Tadeusz Szeligowski (1896—1963), Bolesław Szabelski (1896—1979), Bolesław Woytowicz (b. 1899), Grażyna Bacewicz (1913—69), Witold Lutosławski (b. 1913), and Michał Spisak (1914—65). An Association of Young Polish Musicians was organized in Paris, where many talented Poles continued their studies and at the same time propagated Polish music. In 1922—29, over 70 concerts were given in Paris with programmes largely consisting of compositions of young Poles. Since 1927 on the International Chopin Piano Competitions have been held in Warsaw every five years. The Seventeenth Festival of the International Society of Modern Music was held in Warsaw in April 1939, having been prepared by the Society's Polish Section headed by Zbigniew Drzewiecki (1890—1971) and Roman Palester (b. 1907). Most eminent musicians from various countries were being invited to perform in Poland. The radio had its growing share in the popularization of music.

For all the problems faced in the various fields the very existence of the reborn state proved a very strong catalyst of cultural and artistic life. One cannot fail to see the role of these achievements in the Polish nation's survival of the Nazi occupation of the country. On the other hand, however, the barriers which prevented the masses from participating in culture on a large scale should also be noticed.

The interwar period was marked by the spreading of the radio and the film, and also of the press, increased publication of books, and the advent of new means of transportation (the automobile, the airplane), but all that did not change much the way of life of the overwhelming majority of the inhabitants of the rural areas. While urban culture evolved and developed considerably, its patterns did not penetrate the rural areas. Nevertheless there was a considerable standardization of material civilization due to the mass production of consumer goods. In nearly every field the processes which started quite clearly in the second half of the 19th century were continued and intensified.

Chapter XIII

Poland and the Poles During World War II. The Origins of People's Poland (1939—45)

1. The defence war in 1939

The last elections before the outbreak of the war, held in November 1938, were a manifestation of civic discipline in face of the growing danger of a war. Attendance at the polls was almost 70 per cent despite the fact that the elections were boycotted by such influential political parties as the Polish Socialist Party, the Peasant Party, and the National Party. The 'sanification' group did not draw any conclusions therefrom, and even when the cabinet was being reorganized after the outbreak of the war (on 3 September 1939) it barred the opposition from the cabinet and thus failed to form a government of national defence.

The Polish people were watching with apprehension the German preparations for the war and the Nazi escalation of demands. A large part of the German population in Poland intensified its anti-Polish activities, systematically instigated by Nazi propaganda. In the case of those Germans residing in Poland who favoured Nazism the Germans engaged in political propaganda, but they did not stop at that: they trained them as spies and soldiers, amassed arms, and organized subversive groups. The activities of the fifth column came to be acutely felt during the military campaign of September 1939, when subversive activities of those German groups intensified greatly.

The arrival in Gdańsk, on 25 August 1939, of the *Schleswig Holstein,* the German cruiser, for a 'courtesy visit' was an announcement of war: it was that battleship which on 1 September started bombing the Polish garrison in Westerplatte, a small peninsula in Gdańsk, which was heroically defended by 182 Polish officers and soldiers led by Major Henryk Sucharski (1898—1946). At the same time the German air force started bombing Poland and German troops crossed the Polish frontiers. The Nazi plan of the invasion of Poland (the so-called *Fall Weiss*) was being put into effect.

Poland was attacked by some 1.8 million German soldiers who had at their disposal modern equipment and were supported by some 2,000 aircraft. The German army was almost fully motorized.

To this Poland could oppose an army of only about one million soldiers, much worse equipped and having only 400 aicraft — not very advanced technologically — at its disposal. Besides, the previous occupation by the Germans of Czechoslovakia enable them to encircle Poland from the West, North, and South, which greatly facilitated their offensive.

The Polish plan for the war, called Plan West, provided for concentrating resistance in the western part of the country and waiting for further developments after the expected French and British offensive in the West, but events took a different course. While Britain and France declared war on Germany on 3 September 1939, in accordance with the agreements earlier concluded with Poland, Poland remained isolated in its armed resistance because its allies abstained from engaging immediately in military operations against Germany. Under such circumstances the

German troops shown crossing the Polish frontier on 1 September 1939

The Polish horse artillery in the Battle of Bzura, the biggest battle during the Nazi invasion in 1939

The Hubalians, a special Polish Army force organized after the termination of regular military operations in 1939 by Major Henryk Dobrzański, who adopted the name of Hubal

Auschwitz-Birkenau, in 1940-45 the largest Nazi concentration and extermination camp, where some four million prisoners found their death

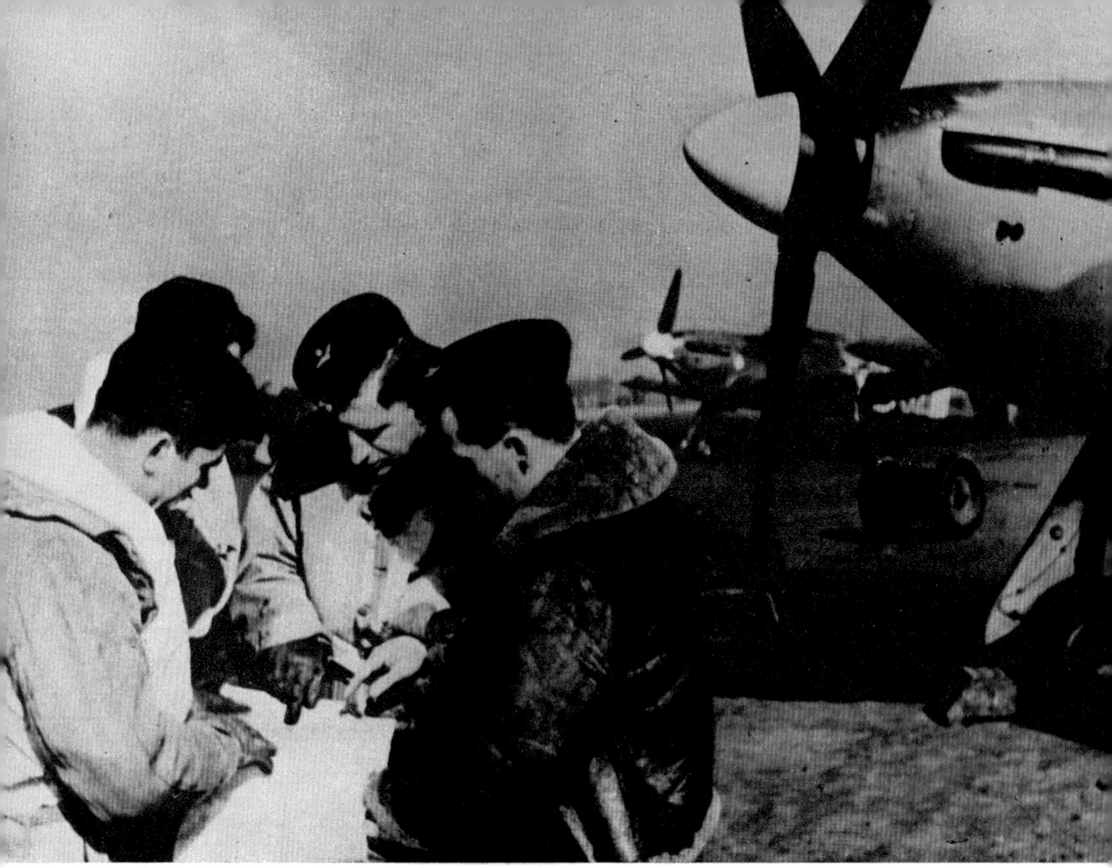

The Polish air squadron No. 303, which took part in the Battle of Britain

Soldiers of the Polish Second Corps after the storming of Monte Cassino on 12 May 1944

General Władysław Sikorski (1881–1943), politician, prime minister of the émigré government and commander-in-chief in 1939–43

The oath taken by the 1st Infantry Division (named after Tadeusz Kościuszko), the oldest unit of the Polish People's Army, formed in the Soviet Union at Seltsy-on-the-Oka in 1943

The first battle fought by the 1st Infantry Division against the Nazi troops at Lenino on 12–13 October 1943

A German military transport train derailed by members of the Polish resistance movement

The uprising in Warsaw, which broke out on 1 August 1944

The parade of the Polish First Army units in liberated Warsaw on 17 January 1945

The Polish First Army units at the Brandenburger Tor in Berlin on 2 May 1945

Distribution of land following the promulgation by the Polish Committee of National Liberation of one of its first decrees, namely that on the agrarian reform of 6 September 1944

Bolesław Bierut (1892–1956), worker leader, in 1943–44 member of the Polish Workers' Party Central Committee and chairman of the National Council, after the liberation president of the Polish People's Republic and First Secretary of the Polish United Workers' Party (here shown when working on the reconstruction of Warsaw)

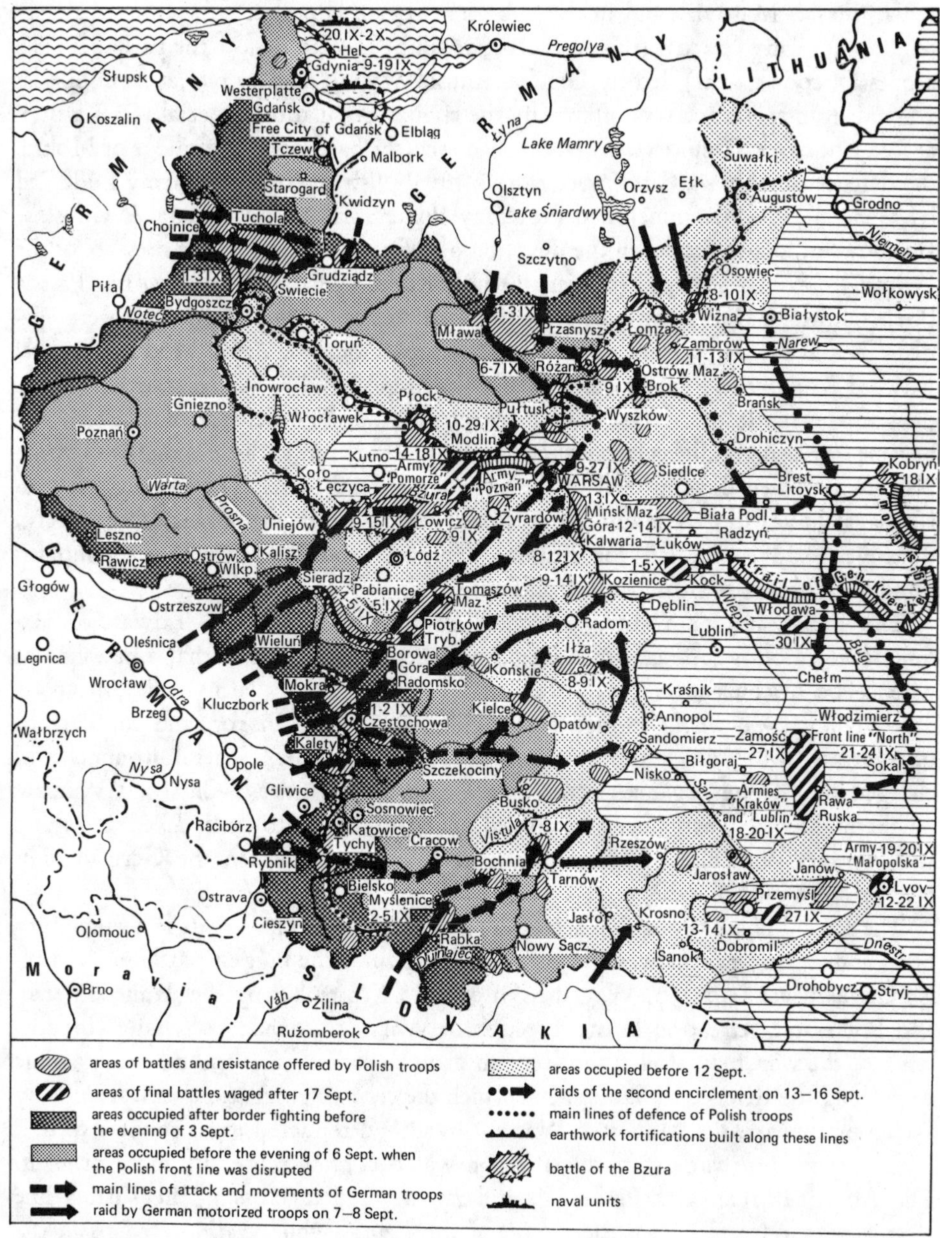

fact that Poland succeeded in resisting the Germans for over one month must be viewed as a military success and a manifestation of Polish patriotism. Poland failed to ward off the German attack, but its resistance helped its allies to gain strength.

Poland, encircled by the German troops, was attacked simultaneously in Pomerania, Silesia, Masovia, and in the Subtatran region (Podhale). As soon as 2 September the Army Cracow (this formulation will be used to denote the various Polish armies by code names), led by General Antoni Szyling, had to retreat from Silesia, where heroic resistance was offered by the civilian population, especially in Katowice and Chorzów. Despite considerable successes (the battle near the village of Mokra, the defence of Borowa Góra, operations of the Polish air force) the Army Łódź, led by General Juliusz Rómmel, and the Army Pomerania, led by General Władysław Bortnowski, had to retreat in the direction of Warsaw in view of the pressure of the German troops. The Army Carpathians (General Kazimierz Fabrycy) and the Army Prussia (General Stefan Dąb-Biernacki) were defeated, and the Army Poznań (General Tadeusz Kutrzeba) also started reteating. On 4 September, the Army Modlin (General Edward Krukowicz-Przedrzymirski), after having offered heroic resistance for three days in the battle of Mława, began to retreat, too. The defence of Westerplatte became increasingly difficult, but the garrison succeeded in withstanding the German assaults for seven days instead of the expected several hours. The two largest Polish naval units, the *Gryf* and the *Wicher,* were sunk in the Baltic (three Polish destroyers had earlier left for Britain). German subversive groups were intensifying their activities behind the frontlines.

The Polish army's resistance having been broken, Marshal Edward Rydz-Śmigły, the Polish commander-in-chief, on 6 September ordered that a new line of defence be organized on the Vistula and the San. A new army, with the code name Lublin, was being formed under General Tadeusz Piskor, and the defence of Warsaw, with which the new Army Warszawa under General Rómmel was charged, was being organized, too. The Polish Commander-in-Chief left Warsaw on the night of 6 September and moved his headquarters to Brest Litovsk. It was still expected that allied operations in the West would lessen the German military pressure on Poland.

The second phase of the defence of the country began. The largest Polish military operation in that period was the battle of the Bzura, the biggest battle in the Polish-German war in 1939. Waged from 9 to 17 September by the Armies Poznań and Pomerania retreating in the direction of Warsaw, it could not change the fortunes of the war, but it foiled the German plans to some extent and made it possible to prolong the defence of Warsaw, in which the civilian population, enheartened by Stefan Starzyński, the Mayor of Warsaw, who had rendered great services to that city, took part *en masse.* But the situation was becoming more and more difficult. The Armies Poznań and Pomerania did not succeed in crossing the Vistula line after having retreated from the region of the Bzura, while German troops in the meantime reached the Vistula, the Bug, and the towns of Zamość and Lvov, which meant the encirclement of the Polish detachments, scattered and operating in isolation from one another. There were still centres of resistance in Gdynia (by volunteer formation consisting of industrial workers), in Kłecko, Mogilno and Lvov (by civilian population), the garrison of the Hel Peninsula had not surrendered yet, and scattered detachments of the Armies Cracow and Lublin were still engaged in defensive operations. The headquarters of the Commander-in-Chief and the government with President Ignacy Mościcki reached the Rumanian frontier on 14 September and decided to cross it to be interned in Rumania on 17 September.

On the same day the Polish ambassador in Moscow was handed a note stating that in view of the Polish defeat the Soviet government ordered the Red Army to cross the Soviet-Polish frontier and that the Soviet troops entered the territory of Western Byelorussia and the Western Ukraine. In early November 1939 these regions were formally incorporated into the adjacent Soviet republics.

The evacuation of the Polish authorities to Rumania opened the third phase of operations in the autumn of 1939 (traditionally called the September campaign). The Germans prepared to storm Lvov, defended by the Polish troops led by General Władysław Langner, who on 19 September gave the city into the hands of the Soviet troops. On 18 to 20 September the remnants of the Armies Cracow and Lublin offered resistance near Tomaszów Lubelski, but failed to break through. Warsaw, surrounded by the German troops and bombed from the air, surrendered on 27 September, and the German troops entered the city two days later, when the defence of Modlin also came to an end.

The garrison on the Hel Peninsula defended its post until 2 October; it was on that day, too, that the last battle of the September campaign took place near Kock (in Polesie) between the German troops and the Operational Group organized by General Franciszek Kleeberg; the Group capitulated on 5 October. Major Henryk Dobrzański ('Hubal') refused to capitulate and on 23 September organized from scattered units a detachment which fought for a couple of months thus giving rise to the guerilla warfare against the Nazis.

2. The Nazi occupation of the Polish territories. The Nazi terror

The Nazi occupation was the most dramatic period in the whole of Polish history, because not only the existence of the Polish nation *qua* nation but its very biological existence was threatened. The German drive against Poland from the very beginning was not only intended to conquer the country but had in view the extermination of the Polish people in order to win 'a living space' (*Lebensraum*) for the Germans, which was the policy envisaged by Hitler in his *Mein Kampf.* Those who would survive would be used as slave manpower. Hitler's instructions to the commanders of the German army stated that the goal was not just to reach a definite line, but to annihilate the enemy. Now it depended upon the German officers and men what methods they would use. Thus, while Major Henryk Sucharski, who commanded the Polish garrison in Westerplatte, after capitulation with honour on 7 September was given back his sabre in recognition of his valour, in other territories the Wehrmacht murdered the civilian population. Between 1 September and 25 October 1939, when the Polish territories were controlled by the Wehrmacht, i.e. by the commander in charge of its operations in Poland (General Walter Brauchitsch), and later by the military administration under General Gerd Rundstedt, the Nazis held 714 mass executions in which over 16,000 Poles lost their lives. Some 60 per cent of these crimes were committed directly by the Wehrmacht, and the remaining 40 per cent of them, by the various police forces and special organizations which were ordered to exterminate the Polish intelligentsia. Even after the cessation of hostilities the German troops burnt 55 towns and 476 villages.

After 25 October 1939, the Polish territories seized by the Germans were divided into those incorporated into the Reich (*eingegliederte Ostgebiete*) and the so-called *Generalgouvernement* with Hans Frank as the Governor General, who had his residence in Cracow. The territories incorporated into the Reich included Pomerania, the region of Poznań, the larger part of the province of Łódź, the western part of the province of Cracow, the northern part of the province of Warsaw, and the districts of Augustów and Suwałki. These territories were annexed to four administrative districts: Eastern Pomerania (with *Oberpräsident* Erich Koch), the newly formed district of Gdańsk and Western Pomerania (with *Oberpräsident* Albert Forster), Silesia — in early 1940 split into Lower and Upper Silesia (with *Oberpräsident* Fritz Bracht), and the Region of the Warta (Wartheland), transformed from the district of Poznań on 29 January 1940. The Region of the Warta included the former Polish province of Poznań and parts of the provinces of Pomerania, Łódź, and Warsaw, and was subdivided into administrative units with their local capitals in Poznań, Inowrocław and Kalisz (transferred to Łódź in 1940).

The whole system of the occupation of the Polish territories was intended to serve the economic and military goals of the Third Reich, one of the principal elements of German policy being the gradual extermination of the Polish population, primarily the Polish intelligentsia as the culture-making group which guided the spiritual life of the nation. This was combined with a systematic destruction of cultural goods, oppression of the Roman Catholic Church, and closing down of Polish schools. Those most exposed to the danger of extermination included the Polish population in the areas incorporated into the Reich and the entire Jewish population, which — crowded into the ghettos — was being ruthlessly murdered. The *Generalgouvernement*, under the sovereignty of the Reich, was called 'the State of Terror'. The Polish population there — all the time facing the danger of persecution, deportation and death camps — was to be almost completely exterminated (the Nazi plans provided for the possible deportation of some Poles to the areas which were to be seized in Russia).

In the areas incorporated into the Reich the consistent extermination of the Poles — through the allocation of food rations at starvation level, restrictions imposed on marriages, deportation to forced labour camps, etc. — was accompanied by the

Germanization and the settling of Germans (some of them brought in from the Baltic States). The Poles were prohibited from owning farms and industrial and commercial enterprises. Poles of German origin were put on the so-called German nationality list (*Volksliste*), divided into four categories, which did not, however, mean the automatic granting of the citizenship of the Reich. Poles from Silesia, Pomerania and Masuria were put in the lower categories of that list, their gradual Germanization being planned. Some 15 per cent of the population of the Wartheland, i.e. some 700,000 persons, were deported to the *Generalgouvernement* or sent to forced labour in the Reich. In most cases they were deprived of their flats or houses (together with household goods) and farms, which were given to the German settlers and the Germans employed in the occupation authorities. In total, some 750,000 Germans were brought to the occupied Polish territories either from the Reich or from other areas. Great numbers of people were deported from the Polish territories to the Reich: the estimates are ca. 2.8 million, which includes the 700,000 mentioned above plus some 1.2 million people from the *Generalgouvernement* and some 500,000 from the eastern Polish territories, occupied by the Germans after 22 June 1941, i.e. after their invasion of the Soviet Union, where ruthless terror was the rule, too.

In the areas incorporated into the Reich the Poles lived in conditions which resembled those of an immense penal camp. In the Wartheland in 1941 there were 4.4 newly concluded marriages of the Poles and 8.1 such marriages of the Germans per 1000 inhabitants, the analogous figures for 1942 being 1.2 and 7.2, respectively. The natural increase of the population for the Poles there was 4.3 per mil. in 1942 and 3.0 per mil. in 1943, the analogous figures for the Germans being 17.1 per mil. and 15.2 per mil., respectively. These data tellingly bring out the difference in the situation of the two groups and the effects of the policy of extermination of the Poles. The Poles were treated as subhuman beings (*Untermenschen*), they were deported to other places, deprived of better dwellings, and their opportunities for vocational training were drastically limited. The system was set on terrorizing the Poles and destroying their physical and mental resistance. Here are some of the rules issued in the Wartheland: the Poles had to bow to the Germans; letters addressed to the Poles could not have the word *Herr* (Mr.) used in the address; the Poles were forbidden to have motorcars and motorcycles (in exceptional cases they could have bicycles with special marks on the licence plates); they were forbidden to have radios, telephones, and gramophones; the possibility of using the postal services were limited; they could travel in the area only with special passes; they were forbidden to enter public parks and use stadiums and other sports facilities; they could not go to the cinemas; the schools were closed down, and only a limited number of Polish children were allowed to learn how to read and count. There were, of course, no Polish theatres, no public concerts for Poles, etc., although the Poles tried to make up for this by organizing clandestine cultural activities.

In the *Generalgouvernement* the Poles were somewhat freer to act, but the region was terrorized by the numerous police. They were divided in the public order police (*Ordnungspolizei*) and the security police (*Sicherheitspolizei*), the latter including its most feared group, namely the secret state police, commonly known as the Gestapo (from *Geheime Staatspolizei*). The two police forces had their activities coordinated by an SS and police commander, subordinated to Heinrich Himmler, who was in charge of the entire Nazi police.

The extermination drive was directed by the Governor General and his functionaries. The first major actions were aimed at the intelligentsia. International public opinion was shocked by the news of the arrest and imprisonment in a concentration camp of professors and research workers of the Jagiellonian University in Cracow. When Lvov was occupied after the German attack on the Soviet Union, the Nazis murdered there, in July 1941, a group of 25 Polish intellectuals, including Tadeusz Boy-Żeleński (cf. XI, 5). During World War II Poland lost some 40 per cent of university professors, some 34.5 per cent of physicians, some 18 per cent of the clergy. Statistically, nearly 2,900 Poles were losing their lives every day. In all Poland lost six million people (i.e., 220 per thousand of the population), of whom only 11 per cent lost their lives as a result of military operations. These were the greatest losses of all the countries occupied by the Nazis, when calculated on a percentage basis. The material losses are estimated to have amounted to some 38 per cent of the national property. In the Polish territories the Nazis organized more than 2,000 extermination camps (including their various branches). In the Auschwitz (Oświęcim) camp alone between 2.8 million (as estimated by the Supreme National Tribunal in Poland) and four million (as estimated by the Soviet Extraordinary State Commission for investigating Nazi crimes) people perished in gass chambers, from hunger, slave labour, illnesses and in executions.

Mass executions, either intended to intimidate the Polish population or undertaken as reprisals for the activities of the resistance movement, were almost a standard feature of life in the *Generalgouvernement.* In Warsaw alone, between October 1939 and July 1944, the Nazis held some 250 executions, murdering from several to several hundred people in each case. For instance, at least 359 persons, including the political leaders Maciej Rataj and Mieczysław Niedziałkowski, and Janusz Kusociński, winner of the ten kilometre race at the Olympic Games in Los Angeles in 1932, were killed at Palmiry near Warsaw on 20 and 21 June 1940. In the rural areas, the major intimidation and repressive actions cost some 15,000 Polish lives up to 1943. Many inhabitants of the rural areas lost their lives when trying to save thousands of Jews. On the whole, some 100,000 Jews have survived thanks to this assistance.

The Jews who had lived in Poland were on the largest scale affected by what the concept of genocide implies. The first ghettos were formed at the turn of 1939, the largest ones being that in Warsaw (nearly half a million people) and in Łódź (160,000 people). People there were dying daily by thousands of both starvation and disease. In the Warsaw ghetto there were eight to ten persons per one room. A systematic extermination of the Jews began in 1941. In the Ukraine and Byelorussia the Nazis murdered about half a million Jews immediately after having occupied those territories. In the other areas Jews were murdered in extermination camps (Chełmno-on-the-Ner, Bełżec, Sobibór, Treblinka, Majdanek).

Polish children were kidnapped for Germanization purposes, selection being based on pseudo-scientific racialist criteria. Children were dying together with adults in camps, in prisons, in the streets. Out of the 30,000 children deported from the region of Zamość only 4,500 survived. Children accounted for more than one-third of the six million Polish citizens murdered by the Nazis. The conduct of Janusz Korczak, physician and author, who specialized in child education and who during the liquidation of the Warsaw ghetto decided to die together with the children from the orphanage he headed, even though owing to the assistance offered to him from the outside he could have left the ghetto and go into hiding, had very broad repercussions.

3. The Polish nation's struggle for survival and freedom

The Nazi system which had the extermination of the Polish people in view was opposed by the Poles from the very beginning. Regardless of the fact that they had to risk their lives all the time and regardless of the most ingenious forms of terror, they developed various forms of struggle, both organized and spontaneous. Such a struggle, with intensity varying from country to country, was waged by all the opponents of Nazism. There emerged the concept of underground Europe which was becoming more and more active as the war dragged on; this applies to both the initial period of Nazi victories, and to the later one, after the German defeat in the Battle of Stalingrad (17 July 1942 to 2 February 1943), when the Nazi 'empire' began to disintegrate. Underground Europe included the Polish government in exile, which continued the Polish struggle against the Third Reich. That government consisted at that time of representatives of the former opposition to the 'sanification' group, and was headed by Władysław Sikorski, who also acted as the Commander-in-Chief and was supported by France, where his government had its residence. By representing the continuity of the Polish state the Polish government in exile made it possible for Poland to be recognized as a country which was not completely conquered.

The politicians from the 'sanification' group tried to keep the power in their hands (Władysław Raczkiewicz, who became the new president after the resignation of Ignacy Mościcki, tried to form a 'sanification' government to be headed by August Zaleski), but such a solution was opposed both abroad and at home, where the government which was responsible for the disaster and fled the country was sharply criticized. All this also meant the end of the myth of the Legions and the Piłsudskites. The class antagonisms, pushed into the background by the Polish defeat in September 1939 and the danger that became common to all, started surfacing again. A new type of national solidarity began to shape. Sikorski's government was universally approved and it was believed that the war would end soon.

Britain, France, and the United States formally recognized the new Polish authorities. But in the course of time it turned out that the politicians connected with the pre-1939 political system in Poland, whether adherents or opponents of the 'sanification' group, failed in their majority to perceive the emerging new complex of international forces which was of decisive importance for the Polish issue. It can clearly be seen in the historical perspective that the continuation of the old conflict between the 'sanification' group and the legal parliamentary opposition, whether carried on in exile or in the underground movement at home, did not have any major significance for the future of Poland. The essential confrontation was at a different level: continuation of the old political structure versus changes in the direction advocated by the revolutionary left.

The growing political role of the Soviet Union within the anti-Nazi coalition gave a chance to the left in the struggle for power, which nevertheless proved to be difficult. The Polish government in exile soon came to face a crisis in connection with the issue of the attitude to be adopted toward the Soviet Union. The occupation by the Germans of Western Europe gave rise to a new situation. Many far-sighted politicians realized that Hitler would break the non-aggression agreement concluded with the Soviet Union in 1939 and would attack that country. This was perfectly well understood by the political leaders of Britain and the Soviet Union, who as early as in June 1940 started negotiations concerning a closer co-operation between the two countries.

This was also understood by Sikorski, who submitted to the British government a special memorandum that envisaged the formation of an army of 300,000 men from among the Poles who stayed in the Soviet Union, including former participants of the September campaign. The memorandum was prepared without the approval of his cabinet and President Raczkiewicz, who in the meantime, acting together with August Zaleski, the minister for foreign affairs in Sikorski's cabinet, and with General Kazimierz Sosnkowski, declared that Poland was in a state of war with both Germany and the Soviet Union, and treated any endeavour to come to terms with the latter country as a betrayal of the national cause. The acceptance by the 'sanification' politicians of the principle that Poland was in a state of war with the Soviet Union and their demands that the frontiers fixed by the Treaty of Riga in 1921 be accepted, was a view which astounded even those politicians in the West to whom any leftist orientation was completely alien. When Sikorski signed with Maisky, the Soviet ambassador to the Court of St. James, a Polish-Soviet agreement on 30 July 1941, the 'sanification' politicians maintained their standpoint and some members of the cabinet resigned in protest. The new ones, appointed to replace them, included Stanisław Mikołajczyk (1901—66), of the Peasant Party, who became the deputy prime minister. Some members of the Polish Socialist Party (those of the Freedom, Equality and Independence Group of that party) also refused to accept the agreement with the Soviet Union.

The Polish army, formed in the Soviet Union and commanded by General Władysław Anders, did not take part in the operations together with the Red Army, because — with the assistance of western powers and Britain in particular — it was led out of the Soviet Union to the Middle East in the period between 23 March and 20 September 1942: the operation covered some 67,000 officers and men and 47,000 civilians. Sikorski was not in a position to prevent this. Tension in Polish-Soviet relations increased perceptibly, which was accompanied by attack on Sikorski, who was also not able to change his policy. The Maisky-Sikorski agreement proved shaky in view of the extremely complicated Polish-Soviet relations. The vehement discussion concerning the Polish frontier line, combined with the 'Katyń issue' and the resulting activities of the Nazi propaganda led to the denouncement of that agreement on 25 April 1943. Despite the endeavours of Britain and the United States which strove to have the Polish-Soviet relations improved, the diplomatic relations between the Polish emigré government and the Soviet government were broken or, as Stalin put it, suspended. This started the isolation of the Polish emigré government in the international arena. General Sikorski's death in an air accident on 4 July 1943, in circumstances which have not been fully clarified to this day, meant another blow. General Sosnkowski was appointed commander-in-chief, while Stanisław Mikołajczyk, a Peasant Party politician of the Witos school, was made prime minister under the pressure of the British government which wanted to avoid having a too strongly anti-Soviet person in that role. Mikołajczyk, howver, also failed to come up to the British expectations in that respect.

In the meantime, spontaneous anti-Nazi resistance was intensifying at home, accompanied by an organized movement intended to oppose the Nazi terror. There was an underground Polish cultural life, a clandestine school system was organized and the same applied to some extent to research and studies at the university level. 'Sanification' politicians, headed by Rydz-Śmigły, strove to secure influence in that underground movement by initiating organizational solutions that would ensure the ideological and political continuity of the prewar system. While their plans had to undergo essential revision as a result of the fact that the opposition groups voiced their opinion in exile, people connected with the 'sanification' group were still the most influential ones not only in the Service for Poland's Victory organization, formed as early as on 27 September 1939, but also in the Union for Armed Struggle, formed upon the initiative of the Polish government in exile and headed by General Stefan Rowecki. But at home the masses just wanted to fight for survival and freedom. As General Michał Tokarzewski, commander of the Service for Poland's Victory, wrote to General Kazimierz Sosnkowski, Polish people 'experienced an unquestionable revaluation of concepts and authorities in general whether they be party-based or organizational'. Numerous independent groups and conspiratorial organizations, both military and non-military in character and of various political shades, were formed, and the differences of programmes had little effect upon their rank-and-file members, largely young people, who just wanted to prove they were patriots.

Such organizations emerged in all parts of the country, including those incorporated into the Reich, where the struggle against the Germans was particularly difficult. Great Poland was very active is that respect: in December 1939 several organizations there merged to form the Volunteer Army of the Western Territories. The organization called Motherland, ideologically linked to the national democrats, was formed in October 1939. The Peasant Party, which adopted the cryptonym Roch, set up its own military organization named Peasant Battalions, which was faithful to Sikorski's government but established no political connections with the Union for Armed Struggle because of the pro-'sanification' attitude of the latter organization. Even when the Union for Armed Struggle was transformed, in February 1942, into the Home Army, the Peasant Battalions, although subordinated to the latter, retained a considerable autonomy.

Jewish organizations were formed, too, and included the Jewish Military Union (November 1939) and the Jewish Combat Organization (October 1942). The Jewish Bund was very strong, and communist groups were being formed in ghettos.

The former scouting organization continued its activities in the organization called the Grey Ranks (from the grey uniforms the Polish scouts wore before the war). The conspiratorial movement was consolidating despite incessant persecution and reprisals.

At the same time the communists became very active, especially after the outbreak of the German-Soviet war. Also active were the various groups of left-wing socialists, at first led by Stanisław Dubois; they circulated the clandestine periodical called *Barykada Wolności* (The Barricade of Freedom).

In April 1943 there was a split in the Polish Socialist Party: its left wing formed the Workers' Party of Polish Socialists and broke with the Freedom, Equality, Independence Group of the Polish Socialist Party, but since it adopted a centralist attitude, an opposition group led by Edward Osóbka-Morawski and Stanisław Szwalbe emerged in turn.

In Paris endeavours had been made since early 1939 to reconstruct the Communist Party of Poland, dissolved by the Communist International in mid-1938. From mid-1941 on that work was continued in the Soviet Union, whereas at home numerous leftist and communist organizations were being formed from late 1939. In Warsaw, the editors of the clandestine *Radio Bulletin,* and later the Union for Liberation Struggle, played a particularly important role in preparing for the reconstruction of the Communist Party of Poland and its ideological programme, which was subsequently to lead to the formation of a broad front of anti-Nazi struggle. On the night of 28 December 1941, a group of communist leaders, including Marceli Nowotko and Paweł Finder, was parachuted from the Soviet Union into the vicinity of Warsaw.

When contacts with leaders of some groups active in Warsaw were established, the Polish Workers' Party, with Marceli Nowotko as its secretary, was formed on 5 January 1942. It had the *Trybuna Wolności* (The Tribune of Freedom) as its clandestine press organ, of which Bolesław Bierut was one of the first editors, while Paweł Finder and Władysław Gomułka were responsible for the periodical on behalf of the party authorities. The Polish Workers Party set forth the programme of having the whole nation concentrated on the anti-Nazi struggle. While it considered the existence of the Polish emigré government in London to be a favourable circumstance it indicated that the attitude of the left toward that government would depend on the steps to be undertaken by that agency.

The acceptance of the ideas advanced by the Polish Workers' Party on the part of the Polish nation at large was made difficult by the fact that the majority of the Poles favoured the Sikorski government and by the active propaganda aimed at the Polish Workers' Party by other underground groups. But gradually, as the party was carrying out its programme of armed struggle against the Nazis and as the party press increased its clandestine circulation, the authority of the Polish Workers' Party in Polish society grew and the endeavours to bring about its political isolation ended in failure.

The Polish Workers' Party set up in early 1942 its military organization, named the People's Guard, and in 1943, the Union of Fighting Youth (headed by Hanka Szapiro-Sawicka, and after her death in June 1943 by Janek Krasicki, who lost his life in September of the same year). A Polish Workers' Party organization was also formed in the Warsaw ghetto. In January 1944, the People's Guard developed into the People's Army, led by General Michał Żymierski. In 1944 alone the People's Army engaged in some 1,100 military operations including eight major guerilla battles. There were also other military organizations, such as 'Poland Is Not Yet Lost', headed by Robert Satanowski and active in the eastern territories in co-operation with the Soviet command.

The effort involved in all these underground activities was enormous, and shared by all social classes — among them by the peasants, and that on a very large scale — which strengthened the national bonds. It was one huge battle waged by the entire nation, which met with ruthless reprisals but made it impossible for the Nazis to exterminate the Polish people with impunity and, by tying up considerable Nazi forces, helped the Allies to fight the Germans. In all some 10,000 military operations were carried out, of which several hundred major battles in forest-covered regions in 1943—44 (including the Battle in Janów and Lipsk Forests and that in the Solska Forest).

In the peak period the guerilla movement involved about half a million people, the Home Army and the Peasant Battalions being the most numerous organizations. The forms of struggle varied. Next to defensive operations against the Nazi troops whose task was to fight the guerillas and the operations intended to prevent 'pacification' the most common measures consisted in destroying railway and other lines of communication, in shooting persons of a high rank in the Nazi machinery of terror and espionage, and sabotage of all kinds. There were also some very special operations, like the one which resulted in transmitting to the Allies the data about the production of the V missiles at Peenemünde. In 1941—44 the Union for Armed Struggle and Home Army units derailed and blew up nearly 1,200 trains with 20,000 trucks, and burnt 272 German army stores.

Special mention is due to the uprisings: that in the Warsaw ghetto in April 1943, and the Warsaw Uprising (see section 4 below). The uprising in the ghetto, preceded by an armed struggle in January 1943, went on for several weeks although the Germans had thought that they would not face major problems in sending the Jewish population of the ghetto to gas chambers. But the Jews, doomed to extermination, offered stubborn armed resistance. They were assisted by the Home Army and the People's Guard, but they had no chance of survival in face of the overwhelming superiority of the German troops engaged in combat. There were more than 20 Polish solidarity operations: supplies of arms, assistance in escapes from the ghetto, participation in the fighting within the ghetto, strafing of German posts, etc. There was also a special Council for Assistance to the Jews, known under the code name of Żegota.

Resistance was also taking place in the sphere of cultural life. It was particularly needed because the Germans ruthlessly destroyed monuments of Polish culture, closed down the schools at the university and secondary level, and permitted elementary education on a reduced scale only. In the *Generalgouvernement*, clandestine secondary schooling covered as much as 70 per cent of young people, and elementary schooling, about 1.5 million children and young people.

The Clandestine University of the Western Territories functioned as the continuation of Poznań University, closed down by the Nazis; throughout the war period it had more than 2,000 students. Warsaw University, with some 4,000 students, and Vilna University also worked clandestinely. Lvov University functioned as the Ukrainian Ivan Franko University in 1939—41. When Lvov was taken by the German troops the Nazis executed 24 professors of that university, but clandestine schooling went on. In the *Generalgouvernement*, some vocational schools approved by the German authorities in fact continued schooling at the post-secondary level. The Warsaw Technical University issued clandestinely almost 200 diplomas. In all some 70,000 persons studied clandestinely, which illustrates the amount of organizational effort and urge for knowledge, on the part of both the teachers and the students. Polish schools, including some at the university level, also functioned in exile: for instance, a Polish School of Medicine was organized in Scotland.

At home, scholars and scientists continued their research work as far as that was possible under the circumstances and wrote books to be published after the war. Those monuments of culture which had not been destroyed were being preserved. The Polish Academy of Learning held its meetings in secret, poets read their poems at private gatherings, authors wrote books. Clandestine literary periodicals grouped writers around them. Clandestine publications, both printed and mimeographed, were circulated: as early as 1939 there were about 30 such periodicals, the number being over 200 in 1940, 300 in 1941, 380 in 1942, 500 in 1943, and 600 in 1944, of which 15 succeeded in appearing continuously during the five years of the Nazi occupation. Considering the circumstances, the clandestine publication of books was quite considerable: the incomplete data available today list over one thousand titles. The ruling of the Nazi authorities which forbade the sale and lending of books by some 1,500 authors was not observed.

Theatrical and musical life had to go underground. Plays were staged in private homes. Warsaw had four experimental troupes and 20 theatres (including two professional ones) which specialized in poetry reading; outside Warsaw there were at least ten amateur theatres with young people working as actors, and eight theatres of other kinds (mainly in Cracow), which included the troupe that after the war developed into the renowned Rhapsodic Theatre. Actors were being trained, too. In Warsaw, in 1942 alone, several hundred concerts were organized in private homes, attended each time by from 40 to 150 persons. Grażyna Bacewicz, Witold Lutosławski, Jan Krenz, and Kazimierz Wiłkomirski were among the musicians who were most active in the underground propagation of music. Cartoonists, poster artists and book illustrators — their works being circulated clandestinely — were also directly engaged in the resistance movement.

4. Liberation of the Polish territories. Formation of the new political model of the state. The end of World War II

The Polish contribution to the defeat of Nazi Germany consisted not only in underground and guerilla activities which tied up a large number of Nazi troops, but also in the direct participation of the Polish Armed Forces (totalling some 500,000 soldiers) in Allied operations outside Poland. Poles took part in the resistance movement in the Soviet Union, France, Yugoslavia, and other countries, and also in Germany itself, where German anti-fascists were active.

The Polish Armed Forces, termed so by the emigré government which strove to organize them, were formed both in France and Britain and in the Soviet Union. In France, in the spring of 1940, the Polish units had some 84,000 men, of whom nearly 40,000 managed to reach France by clandestinely leaving occupied Poland.

A Polish infantry brigade took part in the Battle of Narvik (in Norway) at the turn of May 1940. After the surrender of France Sikorski's government succeeded in evacuating some 25,000 soldiers to Britain, where they formed the I Polish Corps, stationed in Scotland and incorporated in the anti-invasion services.

Polish pilots and Polish warships took a direct part in the operations against the German air force and the German navy. In the Battle of Britain (July to 31 October 1940) the Polish squadrons 302 and 303 won special renown: out of the 1,733 German aircraft shot down at that time the bringing down of 250 went to the credit of the Polish pilots. Per every lost Polish airplane there were nine German aircraft shot down (in the case of RAF the ratio was one to three). The Polish Armed Forces also included a paratroop brigade.

The Polish navy, to which some warships were added in Britain, escorted 787 convoys and tooks part in 1,162 naval operations. It certainly sank nine enemy warships (probably plus five) and 39 merchant and transport vessels; it also damaged 29 enemy ships and shot down some 30 enemy aircraft.

The Polish units evacuated from the Soviet Union (cf. section 3 above) were organized as the II Polish Corps, which late in 1943 was moved from Palestine to Italy. The Polish Armed Forces in the West fought arm in arm with their allies and distinguished themselves by valour and many important military successes. The so-called Carpathian Riflemen Brigade, formed in Syria, fought on the North African front, while the II Corps during the operations in Italy stormed Monte Cassino, occupied Ancona and helped occupy Bologna. The division led by General Maczek played an important role in the battles of Falaise and in Belgium and the Netherlands, and the Paratroop Brigade took part in the biggest air-borne operation during World War II, i.e. in the Battle of Arnhem (1944). Separate mention is due to the breaking by Polish mathematicians trained as cryptographers of the code of the German Enigma coding device, which was of immense importance for the operations conducted by the Allies.

At the same time the leftist trend in the striving for independence, staking on the alliance with the Soviet Union, was becoming more active. It was represented at home by the Polish Workers' Party and in the Soviet Union by the Union of Polish Patriots, organized there. As the Polish government in London was becoming more and more isolated because of its unchanging anti-Soviet attitude and the rigid stand on the issue of Poland's eastern frontiers, the position of the representatives of the leftist trend was growing stronger in the Allied camp, even though at home the Polish emigré government in London and its Delegate for Home enjoyed the support of the majority. It was only the growing activation of the masses and their increasing share in devising the new, socialist, model of the state which brought about an evolution in the political consciousness of the Polish nation. It was, however, a process which, originating at that time, was later to become the core of political changes in Polish postwar history (cf. XIV).

In order to have political authority of their own the leaders of the revolutionary left set up, on the night of 31 December 1943, an underground parliament called the Home National Council, headed by Bolesław Bierut. The Home National Council ordered the transformation of the People's Guard into the People's Army (cf. section 3 above) and announced that it would strive for fundamental social and economic reforms.

The Union of Polish Patriots was active in the Soviet Union, where Wanda Wasilewska played an important role in its work. It was upon the Union's initiative that the Polish First Infantry Division, named after Tadeusz Kościuszko, was organized; in October 1943 it was for the first time engaged in action in the Battle of Lenino (Byelorussia). It was later expanded into the I Corps of the Polish Armed Forces in the Soviet Union, in turn reorganized into the Polish First Army, led by General Zygmunt Berling (who remained in the Soviet Union after the evacuation of the Anders corps to Iran). Berling had Generals Karol Świerczewski and Aleksander Zawadzki as his deputies. In 1944, more than 200,000 Poles wore Polish uniforms both in the East and in the West, and their number was still growing. When the war ended Poland ranked fourth among the Allies as to the number of its ground forces (after Britain but before France).

As the Soviet troops were approaching the Polish-Soviet frontier of 1939 (they crossed that line on the night of 3 January 1944) the Polish government in London, headed by Stanisław Mikołajczyk, and in particular the General Command of the Home Army, voiced their protest against the establishment of the future Polish eastern frontier on the Curzon line, that is, along the Bug. Nonetheless, these recommendations were put forward at the first conference of Roosevelt, Churchill, and Stalin as the leaders of the anti-Nazi coalition, held in Teheran at the turn of November 1943. Reference was then also made to the moving of Poland's future western frontier to the Odra. Mikołajczyk's protests were, accordingly, at variance with the main lines of the Great Powers' policies. Mikołajczyk failed to win British support on the issue and Churchill stated that this plan would be the solution of the Polish issue on a large scale. Nor was Mikołajczyk successful in his talks with Stalin. The Polish emigré authorities then tried to put into effect their plan known under the code name *Burza* (Storm). According to this plan, the Home Army and delegates of the Polish government-in-exile were to take over civilian and military power in the territories between the Polish-Soviet frontier of 1939 and the Curzon line before the Soviet troops could enter them. This, too, failed to win the support of the western powers.

Sosnkowski then proposed to use the Home Army for a new operation, this time directed against the Soviet troops, but his idea was not supported by the emigré government which had been reorganized in the meantime. While all this was going on, the People's Army, the Peasant Battalions, and other minor organizations were active behind the front-line, accompanied by some detachments of the Home Army.

The aim of the emigré government was to have at least the territories to the west of the Curzon line liberated with the participation of its troops, and hence the Polish government adopted a double course. It organized an uprising in Warsaw to liberate the city before this could be done by the Soviet troops (which had, in the meantime, reached the Vistula). But these troops, having advanced on the so-called Byelorussian front for 500 kilometres instead of the 250 originally planned, needed much time to prepare for a new offensive, the more so as they had encountered stubborn German resistance which General Komorowski, the commander of the Home Army, did not consider since he counted on the Soviet Army crossing the Vistula. At this time, Mikołajczyk paid his next visit to Moscow as he wanted to conclude an agreement on the take-over by the emigré government of the territories liberated by the Soviet Army. The taking of Warsaw, which was planned by the London government as a relatively short campaign, was to be his trump card.

The Warsaw Uprising, which — contrary to the opinion of some leading representatives of Polish emigré circles in Britain — broke out on 1 August 1944, was brutally suppressed. It was, nevertheless, a great demonstration of patriotism on the part of both the Home Army and other groups (including the Warsaw group of the People's Army whose commander, Bolesław Kowalski, lost his life in Warsaw) and the civilian population. Everybody expected the liberation and wanted to expedite it; it was also believed that the Uprising had been well prepared both militarily and politically. But in fact it had no chance of success — even though the Soviet and Polish troops after heavy fighting occupied Praga (the part of Warsaw on the east bank of the Vistula). The Uprising lasted 63 days and cost the lives of some 200,000 Poles of whom some 22,000 were soldiers. The German losses amounted to about 26,000 while the losses of the Soviet air force in the region of Warsaw were about 250 men, of whom about 100 were Poles. Following a direct order from Hitler, about 80 per cent of the city of Warsaw, including many treasures of Polish culture, was destroyed.

The plans of the Polish emigré government were collapsing even regardless of the disaster in Warsaw. There was already in Poland an organized centre of power which had to be reckoned with because it enjoyed the support of the Soviet Union. In March 1944 the Home National Council approached the Soviet government and the Union of Polish Patriots through its representatives in Moscow and obtained Stalin's approval to set up the Office of the Home National Council's Delegates for the Liberated Areas. This was made easier by Mikołajczyk himself, who — counting in vain on the support this time of the United States — refused all compromise with the Home National Council.

When the Soviet troops liberated Chełm, the first major town to the west of the Curzon line, the Office of the Home National Council's Delegates for the Liberated Areas converted itself into the Polish Committee of National Liberation (21 July 1944), and the next day, issued its Manifesto. The Polish Commitee of National Liberation, in which the Polish Workers' Party played the principal role, had in its programme the restoration of the March Constitution (cf. XII, 1), co-operation with the Soviet Union and acceptance of the recommendations concerning Poland's frontiers put forward at the Teheran conference. It also proceeded immediately to offer full assistance to the Red Army and had all the liberated areas working for the army. The Polish First Army and the People's Army were merged into the uniform Polish Army. At the same time the Polish Second Army and other units were being formed in the liberated areas. The Polish Committee of National Liberation, functioning as a provisional government, took Lublin as its headquarters. During his talks in Moscow in August 1944, Mikołajczyk rejected Bierut's proposals (to be himself prime minister and to allocate three posts in a joint cabinet) as he still counted upon the success of the Warsaw Uprising which had broken out only ten days earlier.

Between July 1944 and January 1945, when the new Soviet offensive began, the Polish Committee of National Liberation was engaged in direct activity in the liberated territories (those to the east of the Vistula). The Peasant Party and the Polish Socialist Party were reconstructed (the latter on the basis of its former left wing), and the same applied to the trade unions and youth organizations. The Polish Workers' Party and the Polish Socialist Party became mass organizations. Local self-government (people's councils) was set up, and the police and security forces were established. A decree on agrarian reform was issued and its enforcement began immediately; the reform covered land which had previously been owned by the state, by Germans, and by people who held estates of 50 hectares or more (in the Western territories the lower limit was 100 hectares). This meant the elimination from the social structure of the class of owners of large estates. At the same time, guerilla warfare intensified in the areas still occupied by the Germans; these regions were also penetrated by Soviet reconnaissance groups, which availed themselves of the assistance of the local population.

In the meantime, negotiations concerning the future Polish government were continuing, but no agreement was reached in the talks held on 13—14 October 1944; the emigré government in London refused to make concessions on the issue of Poland's eastern frontiers, despite the lack of support by Churchill and Roosevelt; Mikołajczyk, considered to have been too conciliatory, had to resign and the new cabinet, headed by Tomasz Arciszewski, proved even less flexible. Wincenty Witos, already gravely ill, if he could be brought to London, was then another candidate for prime minister of the emigré cabinet. There was also a campaign for the international recognition of the Polish Committee of National Liberation. Polish organizations which supported that political body were formed in France and Belgium.

On 31 December 1944, the Home National Council appointed the Provisional Government of the Republic of Poland, recognized by the Soviet Union, with which that government signed, on 21 April 1945, the Treaty of Friendship, Mutual Aid and Postwar Co-operation (to be in force for 20 years and subject to prolongation).

This signing took place after the next Big Three Conference, held at Yalta on 4—11 February 1945, which confirmed Poland's eastern frontier on the Curzon line, spoke about the necessity of adding to Poland territories of a considerable area in the West and in the North, and demanded the establishment of a government of national unity that would enjoy the support of the Western Powers. Agreement was finally reached at a new conference in Moscow: a Provisional Government of National Unity was formed, with Edward Osóbka-Morawski as prime minister and Władysław Gomułka and Stanisław Mikołajczyk as his deputies. The Polish Workers' Party and the Polish Socialist Party received nearly two-thirds of the portfolios, the rest going to the Peasant Party and the Democratic Party. The state of specific diarchy came to an end, and an amnesty was proclaimed for those who had participated in the conspiracy that supported the emigré government in London.

The liberation of the whole country followed the above-mentioned Soviet offensive (started in January 1945). The Polish First Army took part in breaking through the so-called Pomeranian Wall, in reconquering Kołobrzeg, Gdynia, and Gdańsk, and in the Battle of Berlin. The Second Army, led by General Świerczewski, at first moved toward Pomerania and later turned in the direction of Dresden and was engaged in the Battle of Bautzen, important for the taking of Berlin; it also took part in the Prague campaign and liberated a number of places in Czechoslovakia. In spite of imminent defeat, the Germans to the last moment continued to exterminate Poles.

New organization of normal life, protection of national property, putting factories in operation, opening schools and launching cultural undertakings accompanied the liberation of towns and rural areas. Nuclei of local power were set up before contacts with the central authorities could be established, which, however, happened quickly. The hard work on the reconstruction of the country began.

Poland's western frontiers were fixed at the Big Three Conference in Potsdam (17 July to 2 August 1945), attended by the Polish delegation with Bolesław Bierut. It was decided that the remaining German population (most Germans had fled to the West before the arrival of the Soviet army) would be transferred from Poland and other countries to Germany.

Chapter XIV

Development of People's Poland. Formation of Modern Society and a Socialist Nation. Democratization of Cultural Life (1945—80)

1. Historic tasks of the period. Reconstruction. The first reforms. Stabilization of people's rule

Poland suffered enormous losses during World War II (cf. XIII, 2). While in 1939 Poland had 35.1 million inhabitants, the census of 14 February 1946 showed only 23.9 million inhabitants instead of the expected ca. 40 million. The losses in national resources amounted to about 38 per cent. The Polish nation was faced with the extremely difficult task of reconstruction, which did not mean simply the return to previous conditions because these reflected backwardness inherited from the past and not fully eliminated in the period between the two World Wars: Poland, then, was still a backward agricultural country with an obsolete social structure, marked by only small participation in culture by a large proportion of the population, especially in the rural areas. The wounds inflicted by the war brought all those problems into sharp focus.

The nation and the state authorities were faced with a task of historic significance: reconstruction had to be combined with restructuring the national economy and society, and also with shaping a new mode of cultural life. In the first postwar years the principal task was to reconstruct the areas which had earlier formed parts of Germany, namely Silesia, Western Pomerania, the region of the middle Odra, Warmia, and Masuria, and also to stabilize the power taken over by the left. The ethnic unity of the population, resulting from the shifting of the frontiers, proved conducive to this process. Conditions were also secured for a new settlement of the relations between State and Church.

Poland now had an area of 312,700 sq. kilometres, one-third of which consisted of the aforementioned regions in the West and North and the area of the former Free City of Gdańsk. Even though the area of the state was reduced by 77,000 sq. kilometres the conditions for industrialization were now much better: the territories in the West and in the North, now incorporated into Poland, had in 1937 an industrial production that amounted to from 60 to 70 per cent of the entire industrial output of prewar Poland, while the analogous figure for the territories to the East of the Bug was merely 12 to 13 per cent. The disposition of the national resources in the newly incorporated regions helped the process of economic reconstruction.

The implementation of the immense tasks which the reconstruction of the country involved was, for the period of over one year immediately after the termination of the war, intertwined with the new government's struggle for the stabilization of its power. This was made even more difficult by the fact that a considerable part of society, despite marked general radicalization during the war, was still mistrustful of the new government, and this attitude was to change only in the process of reconstruction and — at the same time — the shaping of a new life. The refusal by Britain and the United States to recognize the emigré government in London certainly did help in that process, but, on the other hand, the fact that Mikołajczyk (cf. XIII,

4) became a member of the cabinet at home meant that the struggle for power was to continue. Mikołajczyk, in his striving to secure a social basis for his political activity, tried to become the leader of the entire peasant movement. When he failed to dominate the left-wing Peasant Party, founded on 25—26 March 1945, he formed his own party, called the Polish Peasant Party (22 August 1945). Paradoxically, this became an opposition party within the government and at the same time the centre of those forces which were openly hostile to the new political and social system. Many members of the Polish Peasant Party had nothing in common with the peasants or even with the rural areas in general. The National Democratic Party also tried to renew its activity.

The liberation of Poland by the Red Army was decisive for the left keeping the power in its hand, and the presence of Soviet troops in the country prevented a civil war from breaking out (even though there was some fighting in certain regions). The first postwar period witnessed the great battle of classes which was decisive in the struggle for power. The people's power was opposed by both the political underground, consisting partly of members of Polish organizations active during the war (for example, those members of the Home Army who did not recognize the dissolution of that organization in August 1945), and by the legal opposition consisting of various social groups; it is to be noted that in some cases the demarcation line between the legal and the illegal opposition was rather difficult to draw.

Suppression of the armed underground movement was not an easy task. Between 22 July 1944 and 1 January 1946, members of the armed underground killed more than 7,000 people, primarily local activists of the Polish Workers' Party, militiamen, officers and soldiers of the Polish Army, and members of the security forces. There were more victims later because the armed underground movement was finally suppressed only in 1947. At the same time the struggle against the Ukrainian nationalists and pro-Nazi organizations which called themselves the Ukrainian Insurgent Army went on for three years, mainly in the southeastern part of the country.

The Polish Peasant Party (PSL) advocated the solution that was termed agrarianism, that is a capitalist political system based on a peasant party and having the features of parliamentary democracy. Hence the main catchword of the Polish Peasant Party was 'the defence of democracy', which repudiated the values of the emergent socialist model of the state, in which power was to be wielded by the working class in an alliance with the peasants, the petite bourgeoisie and the intelligentsia. The PSL did not in principle come out against the reforms (the nationalization of industry and agrarian reform), because that would not have been supported by the majority of the population. But the PSL nevertheless overestimated its own strength. In the referendum held on 30 June 1946, before the elections to the Seym, victory went to the bloc of the democratic parties, consisting of the Polish Workers' Party, the Polish Socialist Party, the Peasant Party, and the Democratic Party. Attendance at the polls was 85.8 per cent. In reply to the first question: 'Are you for the abolition of the Senate?' the 'ayes' accounted for 68.2 per cent of the replies. Their number was 77.3 per cent in the case of the second question, namely that concerning the approval of the nationalization of industry and of the agrarian reform, and 91.4 per cent in the case of the third question, namely that about the fixing of the Polish western frontier along the Baltic coast, the Odra, and the Lusatian Nysa. The Polish Peasant Party, which recommended a 'no' answer to the first question, thus won only 31.8 per cent of the votes.

The defeat of the PSL was even greater in the elections to the Seym, held on 19 January 1947: it received only 10.3 per cent of the votes, which secured it merely 28 seats. Mikołajczyk's opposition was thus eliminated as a major political force, and he himself fled the country in October 1947 to join the emigré government in London. Bolesław Bierut was elected the president of the Republic of Poland, while the cabinet had Józef Cyrankiewicz (Polish Socialist Party) as prime minister, Władysław Gomułka (Polish Workers' Party) as the first deputy prime minister and Antoni Korzycki (Peasant Party) as the second deputy prime minister. The Seym passed what was currently called the Short Constitution, replaced by the full Constitution on 22 July 1952; according to the latter 'Poland is a people's democracy' and power belongs to the working people of town and country, through their representatives elected to the Seym and people's councils in universal, equal, direct and secret suffrage'.

An essential step in the consolidation of the people's rule consisted in the unification of the workers' movement, which took place in 1948. The Polish Workers' Party, which in December 1948 had over one million members (as compared with 820,000 in 1947 and 235,000 in 1945), merged with the Polish Socialist Party, which had over 500,000 members and revealed a strong tendency to grow, to form the Polish United Workers' Party (PZPR). The youth organizations also merged into the Union of Polish Youth (ZMP). This did not take place without discussions concerning the political programme of the new party: it envisaged the construction of a socialist system on the basis of a broad front of national unity. The Jewish Socialist Party (the Bund) also acceded to the PZPR and the peasant movement was reorganized in 1949, into the United Peasant Party (ZSL). The Labour Party was dissolved after a short period of existence, and the bloc of the democratic parties included the Polish United Workers' Party, the United Peasant Party, and the Democratic Party, the latter two recognizing the leading role of the former and acting as its allies.

It is to be noted that essential political divergences developed within the Polish Workers' Party a few months before the fusion of the two workers' parties. The controversy was over the attitude to be adopted toward the decisions — passed by the Information Bureau of the Communist and Workers' Parties that had replaced the Communist International — concerning the collectivization of agriculture in people's democracies, the situation within the Communist Party of Yugoslavia (which opposed the Stalin cult), and also the assessment of the traditions of the Polish workers' movement. In the atmosphere which then prevailed in the workers' movement, dominated by the dogmatic personality cult, those who opposed uniformity in the methods of building socialism and saw the necessity of taking the distinctive national features into account were easily labelled 'rightist' and 'nationalist deviationists'. They included a group of prominent party leaders with Władysław Gomułka, who was expelled from the party authorities in 1949. The resolution concerned with the rightist and nationalist deviation was revoked in October 1956, and formally rescinded at the Third Congress of the Polish United Workers' Party in 1959.

At the time of the struggle for the stabilization of the people's rule, basic social and economic reforms were being carried out. There were also large-scale migrations, due not only to the shifting of the Polish frontiers but also to the population movements that had taken place during World War II. All this was accompanied by the reconstruction of the war-devastated country.

The agrarian reform was continued in the territories to the West of the Vistula as soon as these were liberated. Those peasants who did not receive plots because of a shortage of land in the area were advised to move to the western and the northern territories. The decree on the agrarian reform of 6 September 1944 encompassed 9,300 estates. It covered over six million hectares which were divided among over one million peasant families. 814,000 new farms were formed and over 254,000 existing ones were expanded.

There were, it is true, considerable differences in the way the agrarian reform was carried out in the various regions; additional plots were given in the most overpopulated areas (Little Poland), which did not, however, alter the social status of that population. In Great Poland and in Pomerania, where there was more land, obtaining it as a result of the agrarian reform often meant social promotion. On the whole, the size of the new farms was primarily determined by the size of a given family. In Great Poland and in Pomerania small holders tended to form co-operative farms but the authorities did not support such undertakings, in order to avoid the impression that agriculture was going to be collectivized after the Soviet pattern.

The agrarian reform was connected with migrations, especially to the territories regained in the West and the North, where by the end of 1947 over two million people had settled, nearly one half of them being Poles resettled from the territories to the East of the Bug. The agrarian reform led to the emergence of many independent farms: nearly 22 farms out of every 100 private farms originated totally or in part from the agrarian reform and the shifting of the population. There was also a novel element in the structure of agriculture in the form of the State Farms, which by 1950 had covered about nine per cent of all land (ca. 2,200,000 hectares). Some 3.5 million hectares of forests were nationalized, which made it possible to cultivate the forests more rationally than previously.

The situation of the rural population after the war was far from good: 470,000 farmsteads were destroyed, there were shortages of farm animals (including draught animals), fertilizers, and implements. In 1946 the level of agricultural production was only about two-thirds of that in 1937. To ensure food supplies to the towns, compulsory deliveries of agricultural produce by the farmers were introduced for a certain period. The ratio of prices also was bad for the farmers, because the prices of industrial goods were very high, following the destruction of numerous factories. Loans for the reconstruction of farms were provided by the state. The rural population was greatly differentiated and not free from internal conflicts. At first strong differences were felt between the old residents in a given area, on the one hand, and those who had settled there as repatriates or migrants, on the other, but the adaptation of the latter groups to the new conditions was quick, which led to the integration of the rural population in the various regions. Until about 1948 there was little marriage between those groups, but gradually this changed. On the whole, the social position of the peasants improved and this gradually began to influence their political attitudes: the political self-consciousness of the peasant was determined by such new criteria as the origin of his farm (inherited, acquired as a result of the agrarian reform, etc.) and the political traditions of his family, rather than by the mere size of his farm. An important role was played in this respect by the abolition in 1946 of the compulsory deliveries of agricultural produce, better supplies of industrial goods, the decline of the importance of the PSL, and the collapse of the militant underground movement. It is to be noted, however, that compulsory deliveries were reintroduced at the time of the great industrialization drive in 1951 (cereals) and in 1952 (pigs and milk).

The development of industry, which after its nationalization passed into the hands of the state except for small workshops, was also far from easy. The devastations had been immense: by 1945 148,000 (305 million cu. metres) of all buildings had been destroyed in towns in the western and northern regions. Warsaw lay almost completely in ruins. (It is worth noting that Hans Frank during his first stay in Warsaw on 10 October 1939 personally helped destroy what had been left of the Throne Hall in the Royal Castle and that in November 1939 German officials were formally permitted to plunder the ruins of the castle). Harbours, major bridges and high-tension lines, and many factories had been destroyed. In the mining, mineral, metallurgical, precision, electrical engineering, chemical, textile, and building industries, the devastations accounted for 50 to 90 per cent.

Until the middle of 1945 the Polish national economy practically had all the features characteristic of wartime. The period from mid-1945 to the end of 1949 can be defined as that of economic stabilization and reconstruction based on short-term and long-term planning. The principal role was played in that respect by the economic reconstruction plan for 1947—49; particularly good results were obtained in the reconstruction of industry and land transport and in the maintenance of a balanced budget. The national income rose in that period by 45 per cent, which meant that the prewar level was exceeded by 25 per cent and by some 36 per cent when calculated per capita. There were also visible changes in the structure of the process whereby that income was created: in 1949 the ratio of industrial to agricultural output was approximately 2 : 1, while in 1937 it was 1 : 1. Industrial production increased, as compared with 1937, by 76 per cent, that of hard coal twice, and that of electric power, 2.3 times.

Accelerated economic growth through industrialization was then achieved mainly by the maximum use made of manpower, that is, practically by the elimination of the latent unemployment in the rural areas, typical of the prewar period, and less by increased labour productivity. Considerable exodus of people from country to town could be observed.

This townward flow of the population must be counted, next to repatriation from the eastern areas and migrations to the western and northern regions, among the greatest manifestations of vertical and horizontal social mobility in People's Poland. They were two processes of great significance for the country, which made it possible to incorporate the western and northern territories into the national economic system and to transform the country from a predominantly agricultural into a predominantly industrial one.

The number of people repatriated from the Soviet Union in 1944—48 amounted to over 1.5 million, while that of repatriates and re-emigrants from Germany and other countries was nearly 1.5 million between 1945 and 1948. All those Poles who found themselves in the Reich and in Austria (mainly as forced labour deportees) were repatriated during 1945. The converse process, that is the return of aliens to their respective countries, was on a much smaller scale, mainly because the Germans had largely fled from the territories that belonged to Poland prior to 1939 before the arrival of the Soviet and the Polish army.

Population transfer resulting from the shifting of the Polish-Soviet and the Polish-German frontiers, decided at the Potsdam Conference, was a separate problem. Poles were moving from the Soviet Union to Poland, while Ukrainians, Byelorussians, and Lithuanians were leaving Poland for the Soviet Union. In 1944—46 1.5 million people arrived in Poland from the Soviet Union, while 518,000 Ukrainians, Lithuanians and Byelorussians were repatriated from Poland to the Soviet Union. The postwar transfer of population also included those Germans who stayed in the area between the former Polish-German frontier and the Odra and Lusatian Nysa line; at the end of the war they numbered about 8.5 million; the majority had either been evacuated to the West or had fled from that region, suffering considerable losses in this dramatic period. By the end of July 1945 many Germans had moved on their own initiative to the other bank of the Odra and the Lusatian Nysa, into the Soviet occupation zone, while the planned resettling of Germans to the British and the American zone affected about three million people. They have quickly settled in the local community and have come to play a considerable part in the economic development of West Germany.

As a result of all these migrations and the natural increase of the population, Poland had 25 million inhabitants in 1950.

2. Changes in the political and economic system. The foreign policy of People's Poland

The 1952 Constitution (cf. section 1 above) stated that the Polish People's Republic was a State of people's democracy and that the power belonged to the working people of town and country. That power was to be exercised directly by representatives elected to the Seym and to the people's councils. The social ownership of the basic branches of the national economy and the state monopoly of foreign trade were confirmed. The fundamental tasks of the Seym were to consist in passing laws, supervising public administration, adopting long-term economic plans and approving the state budget. The legislative initiative was vested in the Council of State elected by the Seym, the cabinet and the deputies to the Seym. The cabinet (literally called the Council of Ministers) with its prime minister was to be the highest executive and administrative agency of the state. The Constitution guaranteed to the citizens of People's Poland the right to work, to rest, to the protection of health, to education, and to access to cultural achievements. It also stated that women and men had equal rights, that the state would protect the family as a social institution, that all citizens would enjoy the same rights regardless of nationality, race, and religion, and freedom of conscience. The Church was separated from the State.

Among the socio-economic changes which took place between the merger of the workers' parties and the passing of the 1952 Constitution the most radical was the drive (undertaken despite a shortage of agricultural implements and machines, mainly tractors) to form collective farms. This was intended to unify the agrarian organization of the countries engaged in the building of socialism and rapidly to transform peasant farms concentrating on marketable production on a small scale into socialist ones. The 1952 Constitution included both a provision which promised support to the formation of co-operative farms, and one which ensured protection to individual (private) peasant farms.

The tentative collectivization of agriculture, undertaken in 1949—56, failed to achieve the expected results. At the time when the rapid industrialization of the country (cf. section 3 below) was followed by a shortage of consumer goods among other things, when food rationing was abandoned in January 1953, it was believed that an accelerated socialist reconstruction of agriculture would improve the market situation. This would remove one cause of the dissatisfaction of the workers, which was occasionally making itself felt in social and political life. But the combination of shortage of means of production with sometimes too vigorous promotion of the idea of collective farming, resulted in the failure of those farms to achieve the desired developments. Despite the support of the state authorities, many peasants were alienated from this organizational form of agriculture — to such an extent that 85 per cent of all co-operative farms were dissolved in 1956.

The process was being noted by members of the PZPR with a growing clarity. A new agrarian policy began taking shape at the PZPR's 2nd Congress in March

1954 (preceded by the 9th Plenary Meeting of the Party's Central Committee). The new policy was to consist in the search for diversified methods of socializing agricultural production, with the proviso that such measures should promote the growth of production. It was also decided to increase allocations to agriculture, combined with increased allocations to consumption in general, and a reduction of expenditure on investments. At the same time the Congress tried to assess critically the influence of the personality cult that was still persisting in the international workers' movement, and to see to it that the provisions of the Constitution concerning socialist democracy were enforced. That implied large-scale participation in the process of government, *inter alia* by work in the PZPR and the allied parties. The point was to ensure the efficient action necessary for the implementation of the very ambitious plan to industrialize the country and thus to lift it out of the backwardness inherited from the past. These ideas could not easily be carried out because many activists of the PZPR upheld the belief that the class struggle was increasing as socialism was being built, and because of the strong dogmatic tendencies within the party. This led to the preservation of the concept of the rightist and nationalist deviation.

The year 1956 saw a new stage in the evolution of political life in Poland. In February of that year the Communist Party of the Soviet Union held its 20th Congress, which proved of vital importance for the international workers' movement as it revealed the consequences of the personality cult and thus stimulated a more penetrating revaluation of the methods of introducing socialist conditions both in Poland and in other people's democracies. Society at large pressed for the same since it was increasingly disenchanted by the growing problems, falling real wages, insufficient measures intended to raise living standards, bureaucratization of the state agencies, and infringements of the rule of law (for instance, with respect to the former members of the Home Army and to the Church). The measures, undertaken by the PZPR after 1954, intended to democratize political life and to raise living standards, proved insufficient, the more so as industrialization and advances in education and culture (cf. sections 3 and 4 below) had resulted in a numerical increase of the working class and a general rise in the political awareness of the nation, which wanted to take a more active part in the process of government and in the programming of social change. This meant that the entire system of the feedback between the national economy, on the one hand, and the social structure and the processes taking place in social consciousness, on the other, became extremely intricate. The strike in the Cegielski Works (then called the Stalin Works) in Poznań, which broke out as a result of bureaucratic incompetence and tardiness, was a drastic indicator of the growing contradictions and problems. The strike was not only economic but also political in character and led to mass demonstrations by the inhabitants of Poznań. An attempt to suppress the unrest by force resulted in attacks on public buildings and clashes with security forces, and consequently in casualties.

Under those circumstances further steps were taken to restore the socialist rule of law, in which an essential role was played by the 8th Plenary Meeting of the PZPR Central Committee, held in a very tense atmosphere in Warsaw on 19—21 October 1956. While emphasizing the unchanging observance of the principles of Marxism-Leninism the meeting stressed the necessity of democratizing political life and improving living standards. The concept of the rightist and nationalist deviation was totally abandoned. Władysław Gomułka was elected First Secretary of the Central Committee.

The events in October 1956 created a new political climate in the country and revealed — as had been the case immediately after the end of the war — the spirit of the masses.

Co-operation among the political parties was now reorganized on a partnership basis, the United Peasant Party and the Democratic Party recognizing, however, the leading role of the Polish United Workers' Party.

The Union of Polish Youth, which had experienced a crisis and had been dissolved in January 1957, was replaced by the Union of Socialist Youth and the Union of Peasant Youth, which continued the traditions of the radical youth movement.

A broadly-based socio-political organization, the National Front, formed the Front of National Unity (FJN) in December 1956 with the intention of uniting all strata of the nation. Elections to the Seym were held in January 1957; attendance at the polls was 94.19 per cent, and 94.4 per cent of the votes were cast for the candidates of the Front of National Unity. Poland's position in the international arena was strengthened, and changes in the economic policy at home brought about a rise in living standards. Real wages in 1959 were about one-third higher than those in 1955. Cultural life (see section 4 below) became much more dynamic. The political consciousness of the nation increased markedly, and people became determined to eliminate the sectarian tendencies which restricted social activity in general. The programme of a political and economic restructuring of the country won the support of growing numbers of the population. The successive five-year plans (1956—60, 1961—65, 1966—70) meant further advances in the national economy, and the gap between Poland and the highly developed countries was being gradually reduced.

But then it again transpired that it was no easy matter to avoid the contradictions between carrying out production plans and satisfying current needs, i.e. the contradiction between future needs and present needs; this rendered keeping the proper ratio of the accumulation fund to the consumption fund difficult. The development of agriculture proved inadequate in view of the insufficiently flexible agrarian policy. Concentration of efforts on carrying out difficult tasks favoured the growth of centralist tendencies and put a brake on the democratization of public life. The growing population experienced pressing needs in the sphere of housing, yet the authorities tried to resolve the emerging problems by keeping incomes on an unchanged level. The most important decisions were in the hands of a small group of party leaders closely associated with Władysław Gomułka, which caused growing dissatisfaction in party ranks as well. The announcement, shortly before Christmas 1970, of large increases in prices (mainly of meat) resulted in workers' demonstrations and strikes, chiefly in Gdańsk and Gdynia, which led to essential corrections in the economic and social policies to take the growing aspirations of the population into account. Dissatisfaction had, by the way, been voiced much earlier, especially during student revolts in March 1968, but the vicious circle was broken only by the 7th Plenary Meeting of the PZPR Central Committee, held in December 1970, which removed from power those who had been responsible for the errors in the economic and social policies and those who, by taking the decision to suppress the unrest by force, caused casualties among the population. Edward Gierek was elected First Secretary; Piotr Jaroszewicz was appointed prime minister, the functions of the chairman of the Council of State being exercised at first by Józef Cyrankiewicz and later by Professor Henryk Jabłoński.

Thus began a new stage of economic development, rapid at the beginning and gradually, in view of excessive centralization and errors in investment policies, slumping in the later period. The living standards rose markedly as a result of increased salaries and wages and a new market policy (for instance, the prices of staple articles of food were frozen for a period of several years). Housing construction was greatly intensified, the agrarian policy advanced the idea of a gradual restructuring of agriculture by supporting those forms of individual farming which brought it closer to the socialist economy. The 6th Congress of the PZPR, held in December 1971, stated that increased participation of the working people and their various organizations in the process of government should be one of the main principles of the further development of socialist democracy; it was to serve the common interests of building socialism and to counteract the contradictions which emerge in that process. These directives were confirmed in greater detail at the 7th Party Congress (December 1975), which stressed the importance of better quality of work and a further improvement of living conditions. In 1976, a resolution for amending the Constitution was passed.

The local-government administration was reorganized with great costs involved. Poland had been previously divided into 17 voivodships (provinces), with the five largest cities each having, additionally, the status of a voivodship; the voivodships were subdivided into 392 counties and these in turn into 2,365 (rural) communes. Now the number of the voivodships was raised to 49 and the administrative division at the county level was abolished, which added to the status of the rural communes.

All these transformations were accompanied by changes in the international situation, marked by the break-up of the colonial system, increased importance of the socialist states, and — after a period of cold war — by the growing tendency to work out the principles of peaceful co-existence among countries with different political systems.

Polish foreign policy has been based on the alliance with the Soviet Union and other socialist states. The Treaty of Friendship, Mutual Aid and Postwar Co-operation of 1945 (cf. XIII, 4) was renewed in 1965 to cover the next 20 years. The Soviet Union also became Poland's most important partner in all economic matters. Treaties of friendship and co-operation were also concluded with other socialist states.

Quite understandably, relations between Poland and the two German states held a special place in Polish foreign policy. The birth, in 1949, of the German Democratic Republic meant that one part of Germany recognized the consequences of the war started by the Nazi régime, including the acceptance of the Odra and Nysa line as Poland's western frontier. In the so-called Zgorzelec Agreement of 6 July 1950 the German Democratic Republic recognized the existing Polish-German frontier on the Odra and the Lusatian Nysa. At first there were practically no political contacts between Poland and the other German state, i.e. the Federal Republic of Germany, which refused to recognize that frontier. Territorial revisionism and the claim by the Bundesrepublik to be the sole representative of Germany, combined with a policy of negotiation from a position of strength, pursued by Adenauer and his party, could mean only one thing in the eyes of Polish public opinion: German striving for enforcing a change in Poland's western frontier, despite the fact that the frontier had been recognized by the Allies at the Potsdam Conference.

The problems bred by the cold war determined Poland's attitude towards them, and hence also delineated Poland's foreign policy, which consisted in repeated initiatives intended to consolidate international peace and security, to bring about a détente, to limit the arms race, and to promote everything conducive to mutual understanding. Intensified activity in favour of détente in Europe was manifested in Poland's decision to terminate the state of war with Germany (February 1955), the repeated endeavours (1955—57) to establish diplomatic relations with the Federal Republic of Germany, and also suggestions that an atom-free zone be created in Central Europe and nuclear armaments frozen. All this culminated in the Polish proposal that a European conference on security and co-operation be convened, submitted on 14 December 1964 at the 19th session of the UN General Assembly. Cultural and economic contacts between Poland and the Federal Republic of Germany were developing throughout that period, but they intensified only on the strength of an agreement between the two countries, signed in Warsaw on 7 December 1970, concerned with the bases of normalization of relations between Poland and the Federal Republic of Germany: both parties to the agreement confirmed that the existing frontier defined at the Potsdam Conference was the western frontier of Poland. The agreement confirmed the inviolability of existing frontiers in the present and in the future (Art. 1) and declared that the two states had no territorial claims against one another and that they would not advance any such claims in the future. The agreement was an important international event in the post-1945 history of Europe and contributed to a détente on that continent.

Diplomatic relations between Poland and the Federal Republic of Germany were established in September 1972, following the ratification of the 1970 agreement by the Polish Council of State and the Bundestag. The agreement laid the foundations for normalization of relations between the two countries and made it possible to solve bilateral problems.

The First Secretary of the Central Committee of the PZPR and the Chancellor of the Federal Republic of Germany, who met in Helsinki after the signature of the Final Act of the Conference on Security and Co-operation in Europe, decided that a number of agreements would be concluded concerning important issues still pending. These agreements were subsequently signed in Warsaw by the foreign ministers of both countries which confirmed their intention to continue constructively the process of normalization of relations in the spirit of the 1970 agreement. When Edward Gierek visited the Federal Republic of Germany in June 1976 a joint declaration was signed on the development of the relations between the two countries, while a common declaration stating that both sides were ready to continue the process of normalization of relations between them and to conclude new agreements was signed when Helmut Schmidt visited Poland in October 1977. This terminated the first period of the relations between Poland and the Bundesrepublik.

In the history of both countries the 1970's were a period of vigorous development of contacts, in the form of visits of political leaders and parliamentarians and regular consultations between the foreign ministries of the two countries, concerned with bilateral and international issues. There were also meetings of economists, scientists, and journalists, contacts between youth organizations were established, and four Polish and West German cities began to co-operate on a special basis. The problem of bringing separated families together was also successfully solved, following which some 125,000 people left Poland for the Bundesrepublik in 1976—79.

Exchange of tourists increased: in 1979, 303,000 West Germans visited Poland, while over 130,000 Poles saw the Bundesrepublik, which shows that the process was balanced as the West German population is nearly double that of Poland.

While working within the national UNESCO Commissions on school textbooks Polish and West German experts reached agreement on the recommendations to be made concerning the verification of the textbooks for history and geography, used in both countries, so that these textbooks should further the education of the peoples of both countries in the spirit of peace, mutual respect, and trust. In the cultural agreement signed on 11 June 1976, both parties undertook to put these recommendations into effect by correcting the textbooks, but the process has encountered difficulties in the Federal Republic.

The principal obstacle to the normalization of relations between the two countries lies in the fact that the legal consequences of the 1970 agreement (which in the Federal Republic is presented as a *modus vivendi,* or a temporary solution), and hence the recognition of the Odra and Nysa line as an inviolable frontier, are not observed in the legislation and judicial decisions in the Federal Republic of Germany. This is manifested in legal acts which suggest that the German Reich formally continues to exist within the frontiers of 1937. Nor does it contribute to the creation of a proper atmosphere between the two countries if all the persons leaving Poland permanently for the Bundesrepublik are formally assigned there the status of 'expelled' persons (*Vetriebene*). The same can be said about the revisionist activity of the organizations of people from the territories now belonging to Poland (*Landsmannschaften*), financed also by the German federal authorities; such organizations reject the 1970 agreement as the basis of normalization of the relations between Poland and the Bundesrepublik.

3. Industrialization and social changes. Intensification of national bonds

The drive for industrialization, launched immediately after the war and particularly intense in the period covered by the Six-Year Plan (1950—56), led to the construction of many new industrial plants (the Lenin Iron and Steel Works in Cracow, the Motorcar Factory in Warsaw, the Lorry Factory in Lublin, and the Chemical Works in Oświęcim), including a number of new industrial town districts, such as Nowa Huta in Cracow, Nowe Tychy and the new districts of Konin in Great Poland. The petrochemical industry was located at Płock, the chemical works in Puławy, Włocławek, Police, and other towns. New coal-mining districts have emerged, such as the Rybnik Coal Basin, the collieries in the Lublin region, still largely under construction, and the brown coal strip mines in the Turoszów region. Sulphur is being extracted in Tarnobrzeg, while copper is mined in Lubin and Polkowice. The shipbuilding industry has developed remarkably, and a new Port North has been built in Gdańsk. Endeavours were made to industrialize regions with a backward economic structure, but industry in the western and northern territories was expanded, too. The Aluminium Works in Skawina, the Nitrogen Works in Kędzierzyn, the Czechowice Power Plant near Wrocław, and many others were built. In recent years a renewed drive has led to the construction of dozens of new industrial plants, such as the crude oil refinery in Gdańsk, the Katowice Iron and Steel Works, the huge power station at Kozienice and the Piast coal mine in Tychy.

In 1973, the level of industrial production in Poland was 20 times higher than it had been in 1938. The structure of industry changed, too: the role of the electrical engineering, chemical, motorcar and shipbuilding industries grew. In terms of per capita production Polish industry reached some four-fifths of the level typical of the industrialized countries in Western Europe, and Poland came to rank among the ten most industrialized countries in the world.

In 1950—79, industrial production grew by an average of 10 per cent annually. Agricultural production increased more slowly, the more so as agriculture provided the principal means that made accumulation, and hence investments, possible.

The central part of reconstructed Warsaw and the Lenin Iron and Steel Works in Cracow, the first large-scale industrial investment project in People's Poland. The reconstruction of the destroyed capital and industrialization of the country were possible thanks to the efforts of the whole society

The building which houses the Seym and the Council of State

The Belvedere Palace, residence of the Chairman of the Council of State

The building which houses the Prime Minister's Office

Prime Minister Edward Osóbka-Morawski in the presence of Joseph Stalin and Bolesław Bierut (standing first from the right) signing the Polish-Soviet Treaty of Friendship, Cooperation and Mutual Aid (April 1945)

Józef Cyrankiewicz and Otto Grotewohl, prime ministers of the two countries, signing the Treaty on the Demarcation of the Fixed and Existing Frontier between the Polish People's Republic and the German Democratic Republic (Zgorzelec, July 1950)

Prime Minister Józef Cyrankiewicz and Federal Chancellor Willy Brandt signing the Treaty on the Normalization of Relations between the Polish People's Republic and the Federal Republic of Germany (December 1970)

The staging of *Apocalypsis cum figuris*, shown in many countries by Jerzy Grotowski, founder of the experimental Laboratory Theatre

The Wedding Party, a film by Andrzej Wajda, the best known Polish film director, an adaptation of a play by Stanisław Wyspiański

Krzysztof Penderecki, the eminent Polish composer, representative of the avant-garde in music, conducting at the 19th International Autumn Festival of Modern Music in Warsaw

Tadeusz Trepkowski (1914–54), one of the best Polish poster painters, whose work includes the poster produced to mark the Fifth International Chopin Competition in Warsaw

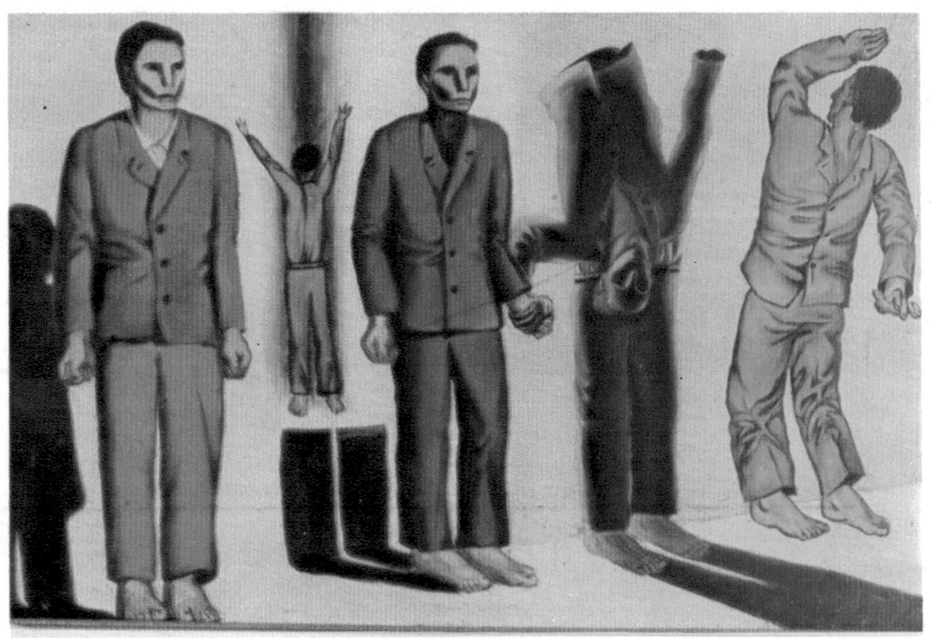

The Execution, painted in 1949 by Andrzej Wróblewski (1927–57), creator of expressionistic oil paintings

Pregnant Women by Xawery Dunikowski (1875–1964), one of the most eminent Polish sculptors

The central part of the city of Katowice, the principal town in the Upper Silesian Industrial Region, with the monument dedicated to the participants in the Silesian uprisings

The International Fair in Poznań (first held in 1925)

Port North in Gdańsk, the largest investment project of this kind in People's Poland and the largest harbour on the Baltic

In 1978 Cardinal Karol Wojtyła, Archbishop of Cracow, was elected Pope assuming the name of John Paul II. Ceremonial inauguration of John Paul II's pontificate

8. Economic Development in the Polish People's Republic

Nevertheless, in the period 1951—75 total agricultural production increased by nearly 90 per cent, the figures being some 75 per cent for plant production and almost 111 per cent for animal production. In 1971—75 alone agricultural production increased by 20 per cent. In the same period, the national income increased by some 60 per cent, the growth of real wages being 41.4 per cent. The average annual rate of growth of agricultural production, taking into account the years marked by poor crops, which recorded a fall of agricultural production in absolute terms, was 3.7 per cent in 1971—75, the analogous figure for 1966—70 being 1.8 per cent. The new agrarian policy, which provided for better supplies of the rural areas with industrial goods, started yielding results. In 1971—75, the socialized sector brought over 750,000 hectares of land under cultivation, so that the socialized economy in 1975 came to account for 29.5 per cent and in 1979 for 31.8 per cent of agricultural land. A large part of that increment came from the land transferred by farmers (especially those too old to work) to the state.

Industrialization and the growth of agriculture were closely linked to changes in the social structure. In that respect People's Poland has witnessed a far reaching revolution. Before World War II the rural population accounted for 73 per cent of the total, whereas in 1979 some 77.5 per cent of the population lived on earnings from non-agricultural sources, the figure being 50 per cent for the rural areas, which means a high degree of urbanization of those areas, accompanied by corresponding changes in cultural patterns. If we take the years 1950, 1960, and 1979, the percentage of the population which lived primarily on agriculture fell from 47.1 to 38.4 and 22.5 per cent, respectively. Correspondingly, the percentage of the urban population was growing rapidly, from 39 in 1950 to 48.3 in 1960 to 58.2 in 1979. While the population of the country increased by 11.7 million people, the corresponding figure for the urban population was 12.5 million, which shows that the towns absorbed not only the whole natural increase of the population, but also some people from the rural areas. The urban population swelled by nearly 3.5 million people between 1971 and 1979 and Poland's urbanization rate equalled those of Austria, Finland, Switzerland and Hungary. We witness the development of conurbations, the most important one being the Gdańsk-Gdynia-Sopot conurbation on the Baltic (with more than 700,000 inhabitants).

In all, the population of Poland rose from 25 million in 1950 to 35.6 million in 1980, which equalled the prewar level.

Next to the increase of the percentage of the population gainfully employed outside agriculture, the numerical increase of the working class, together with the changes in its structure, must be regarded as another significant process. While in 1931 there were 4.2 million workers in all branches of the national economy, of whom less than 30 per cent were employed in industry and the building trade, the figure for 1970 was 6.8 million, of whom 64.5 per cent worked in industry and the building trade. The number of workers employed in modern industries, including the automated ones, has grown to about 40 per cent, many of them educated on the secondary vocational level.

The growth of the intelligentsia is to be noted as the third important change in the social structure. The intelligentsia, decimated by the Nazis, accounted before the war for some 14 per cent of all those gainfully employed outside agriculture; that number rose to some 25 per cent in 1950, and to over 35 per cent in

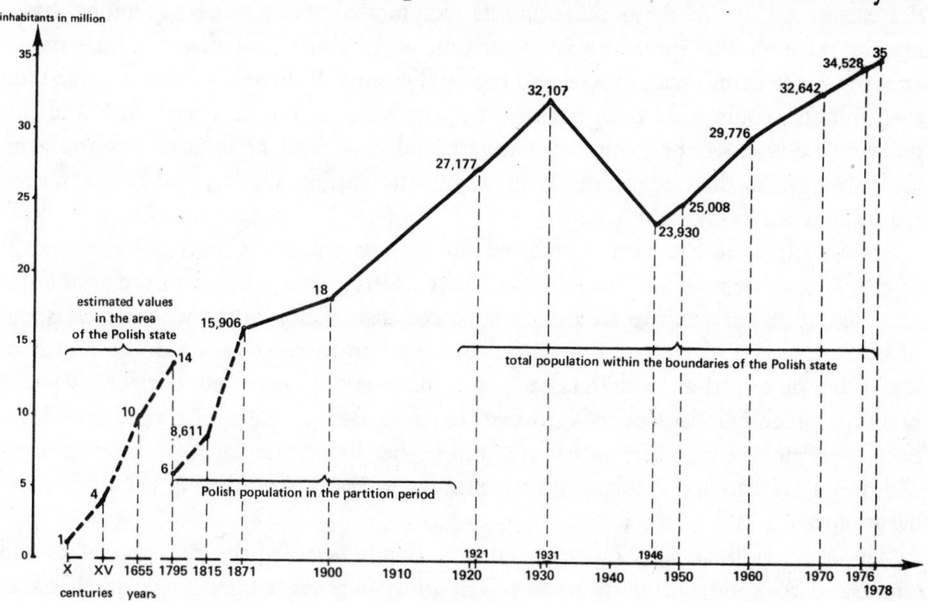

1973. It now originates mainly from workers (ca. 35 per cent) and peasants (ca. 20 per cent), from the former intelligentsia (ca. 40 per cent), and from among the petite bourgeoisie and the former upper strata of society (ca. 5 per cent). The process is closely associated with the increase in education: while between the two World Wars some 85,000 persons acquired higher education, the analogous figure for 1945—65 was 368,900 with an additional 797,800 in the following years.

The emergence of a modern urban and industrial society was not the only revolutionary change in the realm of social structure. The process has not only put an end to most age-old deformities in the social structure and placed the Polish population in that respect on a par with societies in highly developed countries, but has also penetrated to what might be termed the foundations of the social structure. We mean by this the multidimensional integration of the Polish people. The social changes that occur when socialism is being developed eliminate completely neither the various elements of social differentiation, nor contradictions of various kinds. However, this does not invalidate the fundamental significance of the process of integration which forms an intricate network of relationships and mechanisms (not free from conflicts) in the various areas of the life of the nation and the state. Some of these will be mentioned below.

The revolution has brought to an end antagonisms between social classes and this has totally changed the nature of the relationships between the state and the people. Further, the westward shifting of the frontiers, both in the East and in the West, has brought about the important macroprocess of cultural adaptation and integration of the various groups of the population (cf. section 1 above) on a cross-regional basis, mainly through the spreading of education and culture and through inter-marriages of people from various social and regional groups. In People's Poland, more than five million people have been born in the western and northern territories and this growing number of the genuinely native population must be regarded as the principal strength in the integration, both within the various regions and between each region and the rest of the country.

Industrialization has greatly reduced the differences in the level of development of the various regions and in the pace of the changes taking place in them, and has accordingly led to a territorially more balanced distribution of the working class and of other classes and strata as well, and hence to an increase in the development of social bonds. Further, industrialization, urbanization, increased horizontal social mobility, much quicker flow of information (the radio, TV), the effects of the educational system and advances in culture, and higher living standards of the rural population — all this has resulted, and continues to result, in reducing the differences between town and country.

The changes in social structure bred new bonds between the various classes and strata and consolidated existing ones. The most important phenomena in this area include the numerical growth within the intelligentsia of the group of technologists, which has yielded closer links between the working class and the intelligentsia. Other facts which, at least in some of their aspects, are manifestations of integration processes, are associated with what is technically termed breaking down of the characteristics of social status. This means that the three characteristics of social status, namely the nature of work, the level of income, and social prestige, which previously usually accompanied one another, no longer do so; hence a high place in the hierarchy of the prestige of professions and vocations need not correspond to a high income level, and vice versa. This brought about an increasingly uniform social structure. On the other hand new social differences emerged due to the redistribution of the national income, profits from additional sources of income, or nepotistic practices resulting in easier access to various goods. Despite various disintegrating processes social consciousness was gaining an increasing number of elements which were common to all and superior to existing differentiations.

4. Education, science, culture and artistic life

Broadly speaking, cultural life has played a major role in defining the processes of integration described above. In most general terms, life has become in a sense urbanized, which can best be seen in the rural areas. The process has had two features: the adaptation of the people from the rural areas who have moved to towns to the patterns of urban life, and the penetration by those patterns into rural life.

Traditional folk culture has begun to vanish and has changed into folklore in the sense of something ornamental, deliberately revitalized in order to exploit local colour. The most visible changes are observable in rural housing construction which frequently imitates second-rate urban models, while folk patterns have become popular with well-to-do town dwellers. The same applies to furniture. Here, modernization in the rural areas reached stoves and ovens first, spreading gradually to furniture and various household appliances (no more benches and chests, changes in interior decoration). There has been a general trend to increase floor space, also in towns, where — after the first period of reconstruction — housing conditions have been improving, though at too slow a pace.

Efforts have been made to improve the functioning of public utilities in towns and to embellish urban centres, also to adapt them to the growing number of motorcars. The car known as the Polski Fiat 126 p has begun to contribute to the development of tourism, with all the accompanying changes in the way of life. Farms have ceased to be self-supporting units in matters of food production. Even more striking changes have taken place in the sphere of dress: in this respect the differences between town and country have vanished for all practical purposes, except that in some regions folk costumes are still being worn on festive occasions; this has consequently led to the adoption by the inhabitants of the rural areas of fashion trends prevailing in the western world. Obliteration of the differences between town and country in the aspects discussed above took place between 1950 and 1960, especially in household equipment and the ways young people dress. Sports and tourism have become popular in the rural areas.

In the postwar period facilities for intellectual pursuits became increasing available, for example, the number of libraries and museums has grown.

The Manifesto of the Polish Committee of National Liberation (cf. XIII, 4) announced that the school system would be expanded and the intelligentsia given special protection, which was to be accompanied by the democratization of culture. This programme envisaged a *sui generis* revolution in the sphere of national culture. The enormous work in this field began with the removal of secondary illiteracy (caused by the conditions prevailing under the Nazi occupation). As Bolesław Bierut put it when speaking at the opening of the radio broadcasting station in Wrocław on 16 November 1947, the popularization and socialization of cultural production in all its fields and manifestations was the task set the present generation of the creative artists and the entire nation by the new period of our history, that of people's democracy.

When speaking about the development of cultural life in the broad sense of the word, it is important to remember the role played in the early period of People's Poland by the town of Lublin where many daily papers and periodicals were published. Lublin at that time was also the centre of a vigorous theatrical life (with such outstanding actors as Jan Kreczmar, Jacek Woszczerowicz, Władysław Krasnowiecki, Jan Świderski, and Aleksander Zelwerowicz), a strong literary milieu (with

Mieczysław Jastrun, Julian Przyboś, Jerzy Putrament, and Adam Ważyk), and an important centre of academic activity (with the first universities to be opened after the Nazi occupation, namely the newly founded Maria Curie-Skłodowska University and the Roman Catholic University).

Next the role of the Polish cultural centre was taken over by Łódź, with the periodicals *Kuźnica* and *Myśl Współczesna* and a strong academic centre with such eminent scholars as Tadeusz Kotarbiński, Stanisław Ossowski, Maria Ossowska, Józef Chałasiński, and Natalia Gąsiorowska. Theatrical life was very active here, with stage directors Leon Schiller and Juliusz Osterwa, and also those who had moved there from Lublin.

All this did not last long, because following the reconstruction of Warsaw, enthusiastically supported by all (as was later, in 1970, the idea of rebuilding the Royal Castle in Warsaw), the centre of cultural and academic life moved to the capital, which soon regained its leading position.

Wrocław also became a strong cultural and academic centre, which in some fields (mathematics with Hugo Steinhaus and Edward Marczewski and haematology with Ludwik Hirszfeld) soon won international renown. Literary life flourished, too. That the World Congress 'Intellectuals for Peace' was held in Wrocław in 1948 testified to Wrocław's rank in intellectual life.

Cracow was very active, too, with a number of university schools and was an important publishing centre. The local theatres (at the time with the stage director Arnold Szyfman and actors Ludwik Solski and Karol Adwentowicz) were of traditionally high standards.

Szczecin was slower to emerge as an intellectual centre: the process required the development of a kind of regional identity by the people who settled there from other parts of the country.

Zielona Góra and such towns as Toruń, Opole, Olsztyn, Białystok, Rzeszów, Bydgoszcz, Koszalin and Słupsk also appeared on the cultural map of Poland, with their own intellectual centres. Several prominent writers, scholars and artists began their career in Poznań, which had a considerable share in the animation of postwar cultural life.

Cultural co-operation developed at first primarily with the Soviet Union and other socialist countries that were in search of a new model of cultural life. Contacts with other countries were also being gradually established.

Education was the basis on which culture could develop and spread. Visions of the postwar system of education were mapped out as early as the Nazi occupation, e.g. by the Clandestine Organization of Teachers. It was to them that the Congress on Education, held in Łódź in June 1945, referred when the model of education in Poland was discussed. But discussions and modifications were numerous. The postwar period witnessed a growth in the number of schools and pupils: in 1945/46 there were 18,397 schools with three million pupils, and in 1949/50, 22,738 schools with 3.4 million pupils. The number of schools of higher education (both vocational and those of the university standing) rose from 46 (with 56,000 students) in 1945/46 to 67 (with 115,000 students) in 1949/50.

The circulation of newspapers increased from 1,118,000 copies daily in 1945 to 4,199,000 copies in 1949. The centralization of cultural life, observable after 1948, led to a reduction of the number of periodicals, but with an increase in the total number of copies. The press came to be avidly read in the rural areas, and many periodicals for the national minorities appeared. The production of books rose from 1,083 titles with a total impression of 10 million copies in 1945 to 4,611 titles with a total impression of 118 million copies in 1950.

The radio broadcasting system, completely destroyed by the Nazis, developed rapidly: in 1948 the number of receivers almost equalled the prewar level; electrification of the rural areas, which gradually covered the whole country, led to an increase in the number of radio receivers there. This last applies to TV sets as well, when TV broadcasts were started in the 1950's.

The state enterprise Film Polski, established in 1945, helped the cinematic art develop rapidly. Audiences were growing, and Polish films began to win recognition abroad. The first Polish postwar film, *Forbidden Songs,* concerned with the Nazi occupation, was first shown in Warsaw on 8 January 1947. People in the rural areas also started clamouring for cinemas and films.

The centralist tendencies in cultural life were overcome to a considerable extent in 1954—56, which stimulated cultural activity again. The number of pupils in secondary schools increased from over 0.5 million in 1950/51 to 2.4 million in 1979/80; the number of students in schools of university status rose from 125,000 in 1950/51 to nearly 500,000 in the 1970's. This illustrates the scale of the spreading of post-elementary education, and hence the better intellectual 'equipment' of the population. In 1979/80 Poland had 10 universities, 18 colleges of technology, 10 medical academies, nine agricultural academies, and 46 schools of other types (concerned with teacher training, physical education and sports, art, and theology).

The Polish Academy of Sciences, which now has branches in Cracow, Poznań, Wrocław, Katowice, and Łódź, and also research centres in France and Italy, was founded at the First Congress of Polish Science, held in Warsaw in 1951. Over 100 research institutes attached to the various ministries have been set up. The number of research workers increased signally: while the average rise in employment in the socialized economy was 7.6 per cent between 1970 and 1972, the analogous figure for the number of researchers and the academic staff was 55.7 per cent.

In many fields Polish science has won international renown; Polish scientists have striven to solve problems related to the rapid development of the country. Mathematics is among those disciplines which have won the greatest renown on an international scale; research in new branches has been added to that in the branches for which this country had been famous already before World War II (mathematical logic, set theory, topology). Notable achievements have been recorded in theoretical and nuclear physics and in optics. People's Poland has seen considerable advances in the technical sciences, geography, geology, the biological sciences, and sociology. In medicine, which has remarkable achievements to its credit, the pride of place goes to immunology, haematology, human genetics, orthopaedics, ophthalmic surgery, and pharmacology. The restructuring of agriculture has stimulated advances in the agricultural sciences.

In the social sciences, the methodological and theoretical inspirations of Marxism combined with the traditionally high standard of rigour in research have resulted in unprecedented attainments. Great progress has been noted in the methodology of sciences, drawing on the work of such past masters in that field as Tadeusz Kotarbiński and Kazimierz Ajdukiewicz. Sociologists have been given a laboratory on an immense scale in the form of study of the changes taking place in this country. Economics can boast of such scientists of international renown as Oskar Lange and Michał Kalecki. Important advances have been made in jurisprudence, also inspired by the problems emerging from a new political and economic system, special mention being due to international law, civil law, constitutional and legal theory, and legal history. Classical philology and Oriental studies have also reached international standards. Historical studies, which have had a long tradition in this country, marked a new stage in their development and gave rise to 'the Polish school in historiography'; they are probably the most expanded branch of the humanities in Poland. Art history received a considerable stimulus in connection with the need to restore works of art destroyed or damaged during the hostilities and the Nazi occupation. Polish archaeology and the history of material civilization are widely known abroad. Literary studies, and aesthetics also developed at a fair pace. There are regular and lively contacts between Polish and foreign scholars, in both socialist and capitalist countries.

Literary works have had a traditionally strong impact upon the formation of human attitudes. Next to 19th century classics the most widely read authors include Maria Dąbrowska, Jarosław Iwaszkiewicz, Jan Parandowski, Władysław Broniewski, Stanisław Lem, Konstanty Ildefons Gałczyński, and Tadeusz Różewicz. These are accompanied by such equally prestigious authors as Jerzy Andrzejewski, Kazimierz Brandys, Tadeusz Breza, Stanisław Dygat, Bohdan Czeszko, Stanisław Grochowiak, Andrzej Kuśniewicz, Sławomir Mrożek, Teodor Parnicki and Julian Tuwim. Some of the most renowned Polish authors have been living and writing abroad; they include the late Witold Gombrowicz and Kazimierz Wierzyński, and Czesław Miłosz, who was awarded the Nobel Prize in 1980. Polish literature has been greatly influenced by the experiences acquired during World War II and the Nazi occupation of the country, and also by the impact of the changes that have taken place here after 1945. This is why the novel, with the opportunities for description it offers, has been the most important literary genre.

In Polish films, too, the same experiences, the history of the nation, and recent transformations, have been decisive for the subject matter of the works produced by

Andrzej Wajda, Andrzej Munk, Jerzy Kawalerowicz, Krzysztof Zanussi, and many others.

Many Polish architects have gained international fame by winning first prizes in many competitions. The most important personalities in sculpture include Xawery Dunikowski, Stanisław Horno-Popławski, Marian Wnuk, Antoni Kenar, Alina Szapocznikow, and Władysław Hasior; in painting, the same may be said about Jan Cybis, Eugeniusz Eibisch, and Stefan Gierowski. The graphic arts and poster design have also contributed important achievements.

A special mention is due to the Polish theatre which has made itself known throughout the world. Perhaps the pride of place in that respect goes to Wrocław with its Laboratory Theatre run by Jerzy Grotowski and the Pantomime Theatre under Henryk Tomaszewski. Warsaw with its 35 professional theatres is the largest centre in the country's theatrical life, followed by Cracow, which, however, is given by critics the first place in originality in the approaches to stage direction. The most important stage directors include Kazimierz Dejmek, Adam Hanuszkiewicz, Andrzej Wajda, Józef Szajna, and the late Konrad Swinarski.

Music has been developing vigorously; already by 1948 there were six philharmonic halls, eight symphony orchestra houses, and four opera houses; by 1956 the numbers of the symphony orchestra houses had risen to 27, and that of the opera houses to nine, to which eight musical and operetta theatres were added. In the first postwar decade many important compositions were largely inspired by Polish folk culture (those by Stanisław Wiechowicz, Jan Maklakiewicz, Witold Lutosławski, Kazimierz Serocki, and others). A different type of music was represented by Bolesław Szabelski, Zbigniew Turski, Grażyna Bacewicz, Tadeusz Baird, and Bolesław Woytowicz. Contacts with the trends prevailing abroad became closer after 1956, and the Autumn Festivals of Modern Music, held annually in Warsaw, have become the most comprehensive presentations of modern music in the world, which also ushered in Krzysztof Penderecki, Henryk Górecki, Zygmunt Krauze, and others. The Chopin competition and the Wieniawski competition are being held regularly in Warsaw and Poznań, respectively. Works by Krzysztof Penderecki, Witold Lutosławski and Tadeusz Baird rank among major achievements in world music. Mention must also be made of outstanding conductors, such as Grzegorz Fitelberg, Walerian Bierdiajew, Henryk Czyż, Kazimierz Kord, Jan Krenz, Andrzej Markowski, Witold Rowicki, Robert Satanowski, Stanisław Skrowaczewski, Bohdan Wodiczko, and Stanisław Wisłocki, and of singers, including Andrzej Hiolski, Teresa Kubiak, Bernard Ładysz, Wiesław Ochman, Stefania Woytowicz and Teresa Żylis-Gara, pianists, such as Halina Czerny-Stefańska, Barbara Hesse-Bukowska, Adam Harasiewicz, Lidia Grychtołówna, Władysław Kędra and Krystian Zimerman, and violinists, including Wanda Wiłkomirska, Konstanty Andrzej Kulka, and Kaja Danczowska.

Cultural life in Poland is varied and marked by a creative search for novel elements. Active participation in culture is facilitated by the various institutions whose special task is to offer opportunities to the public, especially the young people, for direct contacts with artistic production. In 1979, there were 20,000 such centres, including 2,176 community centres and 18,000 clubs of various kinds, with more than 40,000 amateur groups (with a total membership of over 700,000 people).

Cultural and educational activity is promoted by the Popular Knowledge Society, which organizes various lectures and courses, attended in 1974 by some six million people.

Following the great acceleration in the sphere of cultural development observable in the postwar years and the above-mentioned blossoming of cultural initiatives after 1950, there came recurrently more difficult periods for culture. Processes of industrialization rather over-occupied the attention of those who handed out the funds for culture for them to devote the latter the attention that the assumptions of the democratization of the cultural process required. Due to this, particularly in the 1970's, the pulse of cultural life weakened, editions of books decreased in number, the amount of textbooks printed and records produced was insufficient, the circulation of newspapers, weeklies and other magazines dwindled. A contradiction outlined itself between the assumptions of the continuing democratization of culture and the real conditions of its development, which limited the possibilities of participation in culture for the ordinary citizen. This was not visible in an obvious way on the outside. The international prestige of Polish science and culture held fast.

*

Throughout the postwar period, Poland's cultural significance and her role in world science has been increasing. A large and constantly growing number of Polish citizens has won renown in the arts and various fields of intellectual activity.

The growth of Poland's prestige was a continuous process — and one evidence of this was the election of Cardinal Karol Wojtyła as pope — John Paul II — in 1978.

However, the foundation of the state's prestige is above all its economic power and its permanent growth. The implementation of the ambitious programme for further economic and cultural changes proved more difficult than expected and in the mid-1970's growing difficulties began emerging in the country's internal situation. It became necessary to adapt the state's structures of management and government to an increasingly modern society which aimed at a larger participation in government.

The failure to carry out such indispensable reforms which could help overcome these contradictions brought about in August and September 1980 mass protest by the workers who demanded changes. This opened up a new stage in the development of Poland.

Genealogical Tables

Table I

The Piast Dynasty
(compiled by Antoni Gąsiorowski)

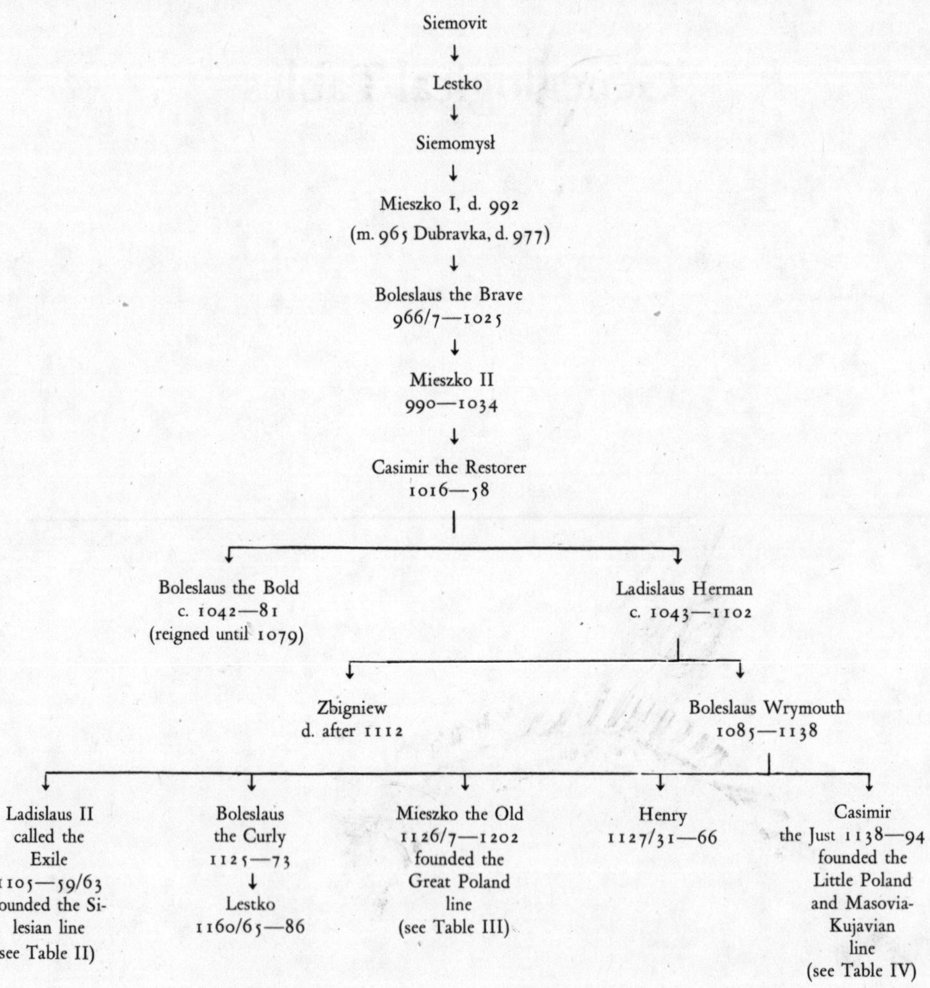
Siemovit
Lestko
Siemomysł
Mieszko I, d. 992
(m. 965 Dubravka, d. 977)
Boleslaus the Brave
966/7—1025
Mieszko II
990—1034
Casimir the Restorer
1016—58
Boleslaus the Bold
c. 1042—81
(reigned until 1079)
Ladislaus Herman
c. 1043—1102
Zbigniew
d. after 1112
Boleslaus Wrymouth
1085—1138
Ladislaus II
called the
Exile
1105—59/63
founded the Si-
lesian line
(see Table II)
Boleslaus
the Curly
1125—73
Lestko
1160/65—86
Mieszko the Old
1126/7—1202
founded the
Great Poland
line
(see Table III)
Henry
1127/31—66
Casimir
the Just 1138—94
founded the
Little Poland
and Masovia-
Kujavian
line
(see Table IV)

Table II

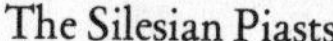

The Silesian Piasts

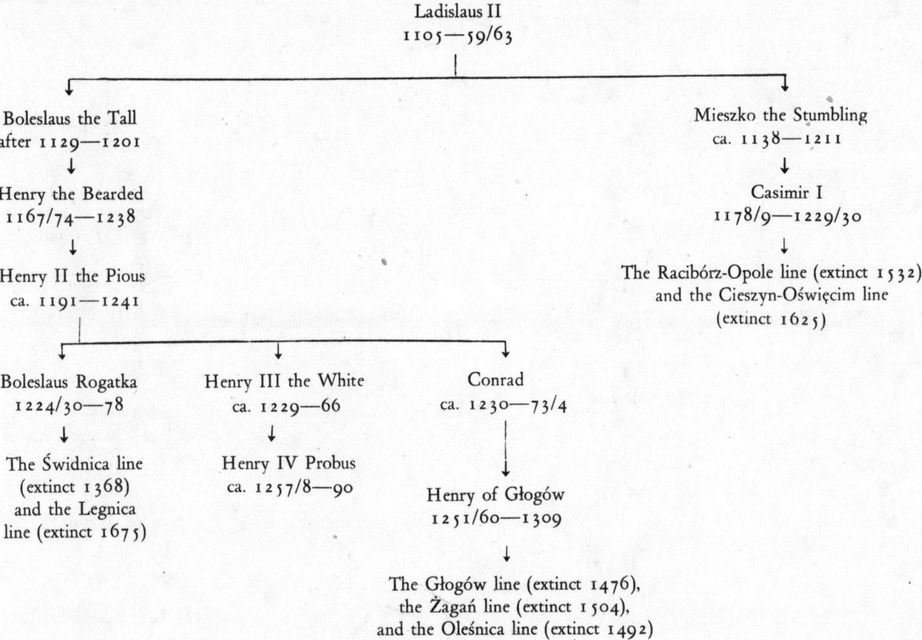
Ladislaus II
1105—59/63
Boleslaus the Tall
after 1129—1201
Henry the Bearded
1167/74—1238
Henry II the Pious
ca. 1191—1241
Mieszko the Stumbling
ca. 1138—1211
Casimir I
1178/9—1229/30
The Racibórz-Opole line (extinct 1532)
and the Cieszyn-Oświęcim line
(extinct 1625)
Boleslaus Rogatka
1224/30—78
The Świdnica line
(extinct 1368)
and the Legnica
line (extinct 1675)
Henry III the White
ca. 1229—66
Henry IV Probus
ca. 1257/8—90
Conrad
ca. 1230—73/4
Henry of Głogów
1251/60—1309
The Głogów line (extinct 1476),
the Żagań line (extinct 1504),
and the Oleśnica line (extinct 1492)

The Great Poland Piasts

Table III

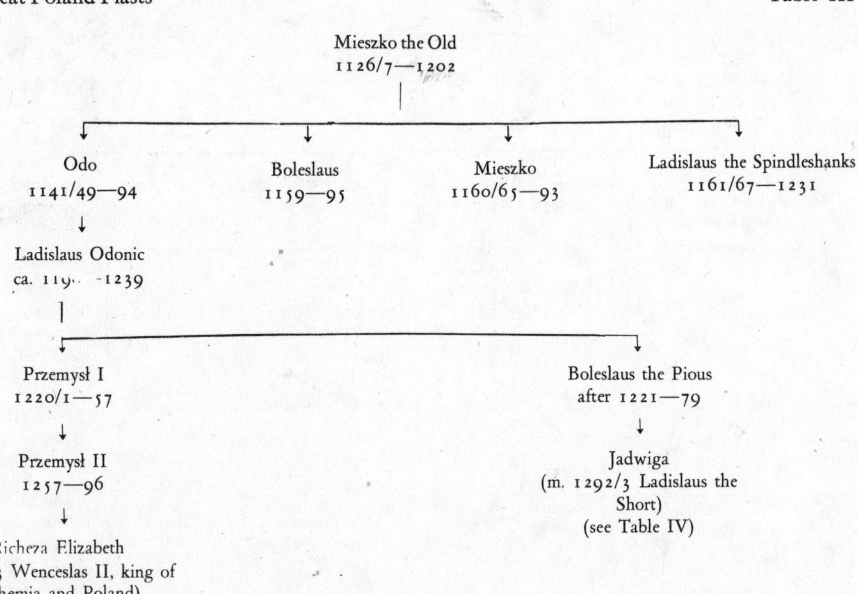
Mieszko the Old
1126/7—1202
Odo
1141/49—94
Boleslaus
1159—95
Mieszko
1160/65—93
Ladislaus the Spindleshanks
1161/67—1231
Ladislaus Odonic
ca. 119 —1239
Przemysł I
1220/1—57
Przemysł II
1257—96
Richeza Elizabeth
(m. 1303 Wenceslas II, king of
Bohemia and Poland)
Boleslaus the Pious
after 1221—79
Jadwiga
(m. 1292/3 Ladislaus the
Short)
(see Table IV)

The Little Poland, Masovian and Kujavian Piasts — Table IV

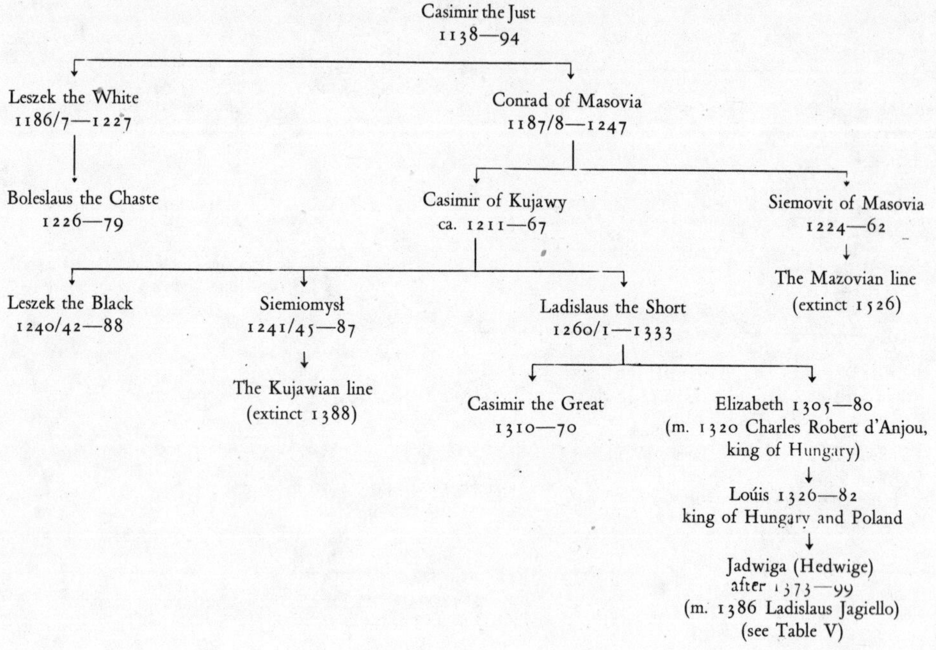

The Jagiellons and their Descendants on the Polish Throne — Table V

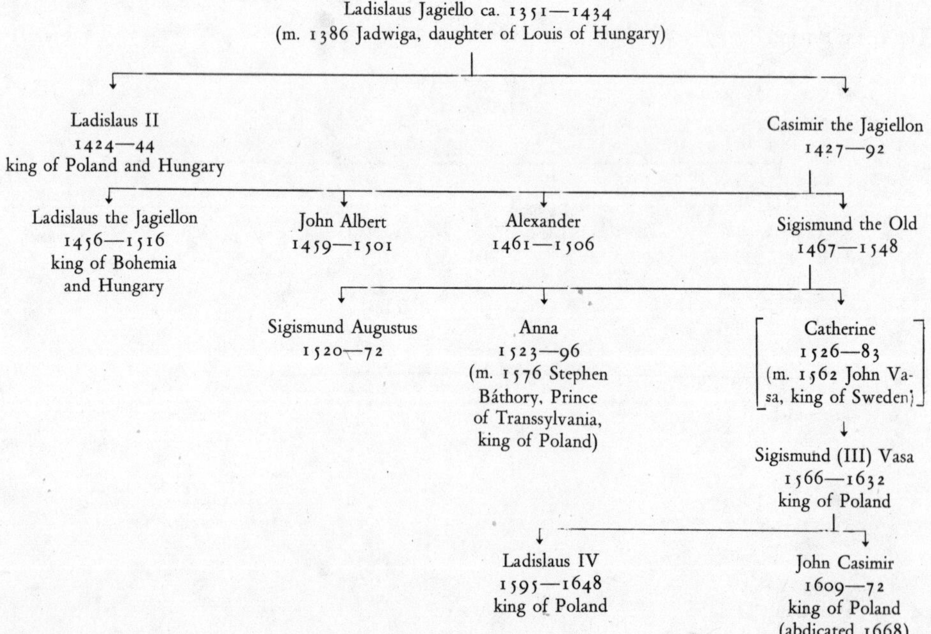

Table II

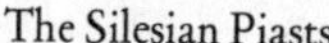

The Silesian Piasts

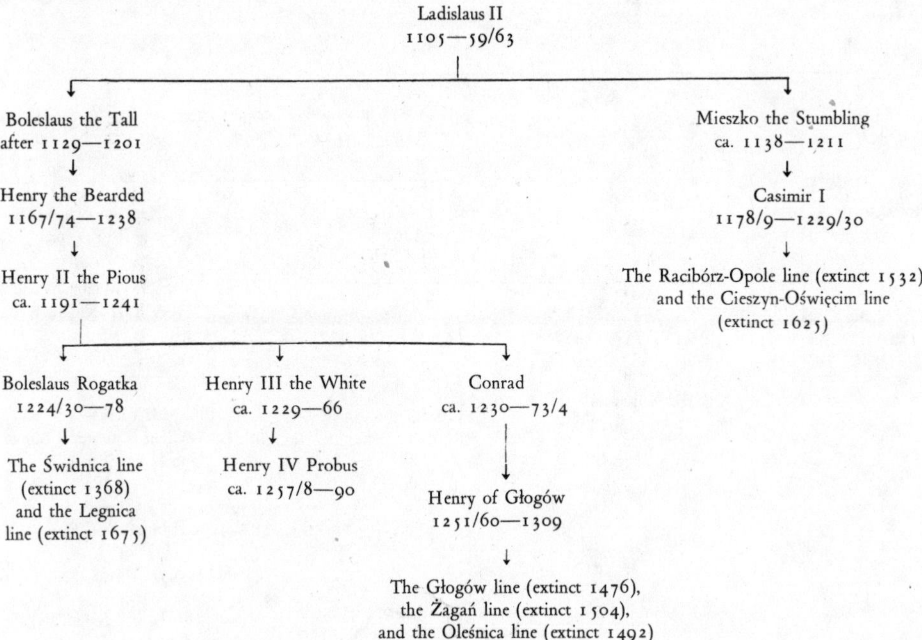

The Great Poland Piasts

Table III

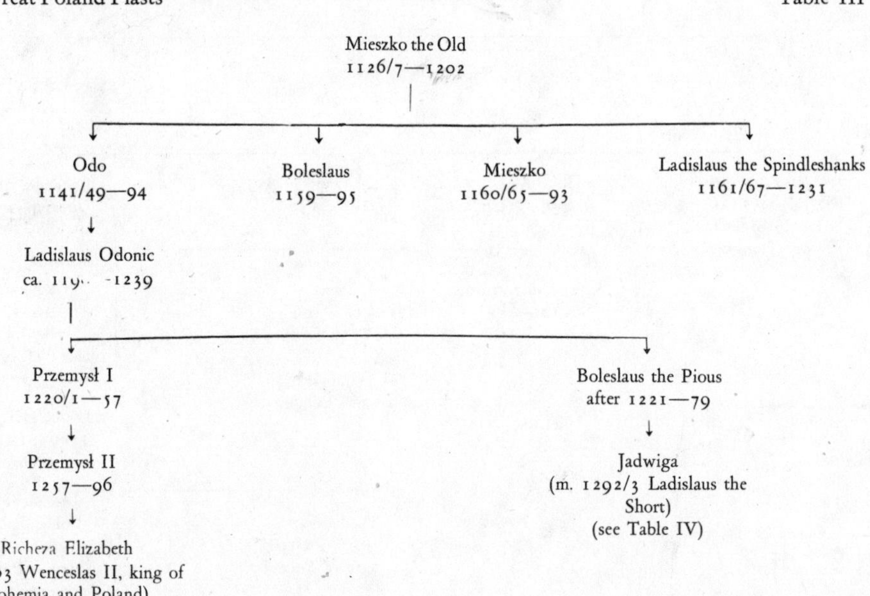

The Little Poland, Masovian and Kujavian Piasts — Table IV

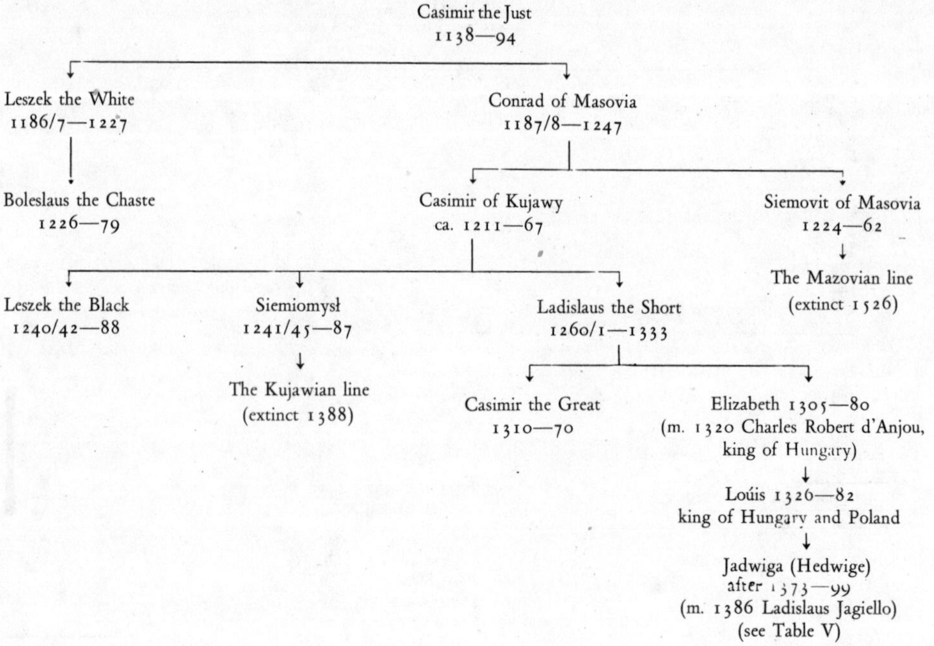

The Jagiellons and their Descendants on the Polish Throne — Table V

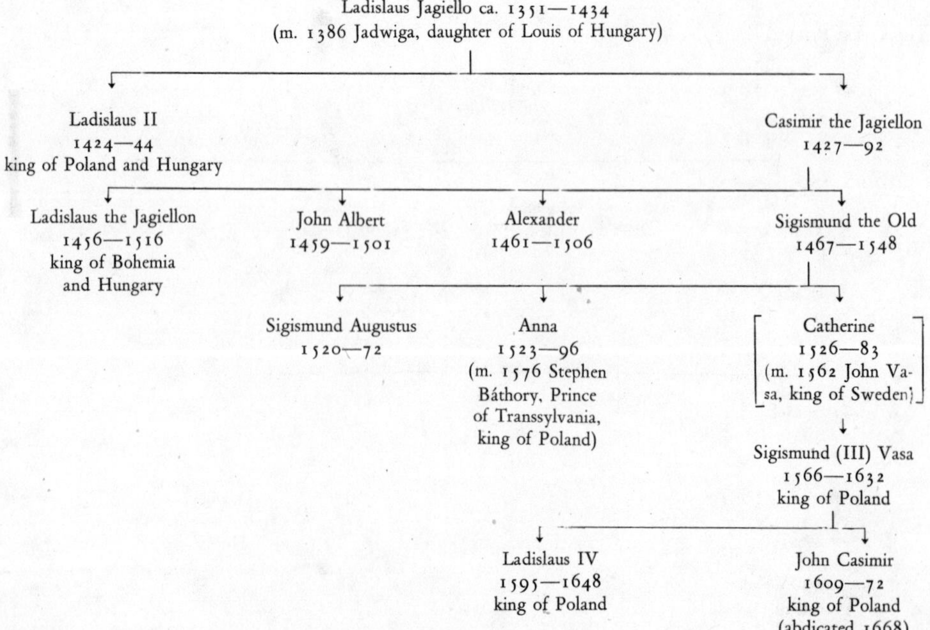

Bibliography

General Works

Dzieje Polski (History of Poland), ed. by J. Topolski, Warsaw 1976

Dzieje sztuki polskiej (History of Polish art), vol. I: *Sztuka polska przedromańska i romańska do schyłku XIII wieku* (Polish Pre-Romanesque and Romanesque art until the end of the 13th cent.), parts I and II, ed. by M. Walicki, Warsaw 1971

Europa i świat w epoce napoleońskiej (Europe and the world during the Napoleonic epoch), ed. by M. Senkowska-Gluck, Warsaw 1977

Gierowski, J. A., *Historia Polski 1505—1864* (History of Poland 1505—1864), parts I and II, Warsaw 1978

Góra, W., *Polska Rzeczpospolita Ludowa 1944—1974* (The Polish People's Republic 1944—74), Warsaw 1974

Historia kultury materialnej Polski (History of material culture in Poland), ed. by W. Hensel and J. Pazdur, vols. I—V, Warsaw 1978

Historia nauki polskiej (History of Polish science), ed. by B. Suchodolski, vols. I and II, Warsaw 1970

Historia państwa i prawa Polski (History of the Polish state and law), ed. by J. Bardach, vols. I and II, Warsaw 1964—65

Landau, Z., and Tomaszewski, J., *Zarys historii gospodarczej Polski 1918—1939* (Economic history of Poland: An outline, 1918—39), 3rd impression, Warsaw 1971

Michalski, G., Obniska, E., Swolkień, H., and Waldorff, J., *An Outline History of Polish Music,* ed. by T. Ochlewski, Warsaw 1977

Miłobędzki, A., *Zarys dziejów architektury w Polsce* (An outline history of architecture in Poland), Warsaw 1968

Polska XIX wieku. Państwo — społeczeństwo — kultura (19th century Poland: The state, society and culture), ed. by S. Kieniewicz, Warsaw 1977

Polska w epoce Oświecenia (Poland during the Age of Reason), ed. by B. Leśnodorski, Warsaw 1971

Polski ruch robotniczy. Zarys historii (The Polish workers' movement: An outline), ed. by A. Czubiński, Warsaw 1974

Rutkowski, J., *Historia gospodarcza Polski* (Economic history of Poland), vols. I and II, Poznań 1946—50

Wyrozumski, J., *Historia Polski do roku 1505* (History of Poland until 1505), Warsaw 1978

Zarys dziejów wojskowości polskiej (An outline history of Polish military system), ed by J. Sikorski, vols. I and II, Warsaw 1965—66

Monographs

Ajnenkiel, A., *Od rządów ludowych do przewrotu majowego. Zarys dziejów politycznych Polski 1918—1926* (From people's rule to May coup d'état: An outline history of Poland 1918—26), 3rd impression, Warsaw 1977

Bartkiewicz, M., *Odzież i wnętrza domów mieszczańskich w Polsce w drugiej połowie XVI i w XVII wieku* (Clothing and interiors of burghers' houses in Poland in the second half of the 16th and in the 17th cent.), Wrocław 1974

Bieńkowska, B., *Staropolski świat książek* (The old-Polish world of books), Wrocław 1976

Brożek, A., *Polish Americans 1854—1939,* Warsaw 1984

Czapliński, W., *Władysław IV i jego czasy* (Ladislaus IV and his epoch), Warsaw 1972

Czapliński, W., *Życie codzienne magnaterii polskiej w XVII wieku* (Everyday life of Polish magnates in the 17th cent.), Warsaw 1976

Czubiński, A., *Powstanie wielkopolskie* (Great Poland Uprising), Poznań 1979

Duraczyński, E., *Kontrowersje i konflikty* (Controversies and conflicts), Warsaw 1972

Garlicki, A., *Przewrót majowy* (May coup d'état), Warsaw 1978
Hensel, W., *U źródeł Polski średniowiecznej* (At the sources of mediaeval Poland), Wrocław, Warsaw, Cracow, Gdańsk 1974
Ihnatowicz, J., *Burżuazja warszawska* (The Warsaw bourgeoisie), Warsaw 1972
Jabłoński, H., *Niepodległość i tradycje narodowe* (Independence and national tradition), Warsaw 1978
Jędruszczak, H., *Zatrudnienie a przemiany społeczne w Polsce w latach 1944—1960* (Employment and social transformations in Poland in 1944—60), Warsaw 1972
Kieniewicz, S., *Powstanie styczniowe* (January Uprising), Warsaw 1972
Kowecki, J., *Pospolite ruszenie w insurekcji 1794 roku* (Levée en-masse during the Insurrection of 1794), Warsaw 1963
Kuchowicz, Z., *Obyczaje staropolskie* (Old Polish customs), Łódź 1975
Leśnodorski, B., *Polscy jakobini. Kartka z dziejów insurekcji 1794 roku* (Polish Jacobins: A page from the history of the 1794 Insurrection), Warsaw 1960
Łowmiański, H., *Początki Polski* (The origins of Poland), vols. I—V, Warsaw 1963—73
Łuczak, C., *Polityka ludnościowa i ekonomiczna hitlerowskich Niemiec w okupowanej Polsce* (Population and economic policy of Nazi Germany in occupied Poland), Poznań 1979
Maciszewski, J., *Szlachta polska i jej państwo* (Polish gentry and its state), Warsaw 1969
Madajczyk, C., *Polityka III Rzeszy w okupowanej Polsce* (Third Reich's policy in occupied Poland), vols. I and II, Warsaw 1970
Markiewicz, W., *Społeczne procesy uprzemysłowienia* (Social processes in industrialization), Poznań 1962
Modzelewski, K., *Organizacja gospodarcza państwa piastowskiego X—XIII wieku* (Economic organization of the Piast state between the 10th and 13th cent.), Wrocław, Warsaw, Cracow, Gdańsk 1975
Pajewski, J., *Odbudowa państwa polskiego 1914—1918* (Reconstruction of the Polish state 1914—18), Warsaw 1978
Piastowie w dziejach Polski (The Piasts in the history of Poland), ed. by R. Heck, Wrocław, Warsaw, Cracow, Gdańsk 1975
Słabek, H., *Dzieje polskiej reformy rolnej 1944—1948* (History of the Polish agrarian reform 1944—48), Warsaw 1972
Szczepański, J., *Zmiany społeczeństwa polskiego w procesie uprzemysłowienia* (Changes in Polish society in the process of industrialization), Warsaw 1973
Tazbir, J., *Państwo bez stosów. Szkice z dziejów tolerancji w Polsce XVI—XVII wieku* (The state without stakes: Sketches from the history of tolerance in Poland in the 16th-17th cent.), Warsaw 1967
Topolski, J., *Gospodarka polska a europejska w XVI—XVIII wieku* (Polish and European economy in the 16th-18th cent.), Poznań 1977
Topolska, M. B., *Dobra szkłowskie na Białorusi Wschodniej w XVII i XVIII wieku* (Szkłow estates in Eastern Byelorussia in the 17th and 18th cent.), Warsaw 1969
Trzeciakowski, L., *Kulturkampf w zaborze pruskim* (Kulturkampf in the Prussian partition zone), Poznań 1970
Werblan, A., *Szkice i polemiki* (Sketches and polemics), Warsaw 1970
Wisłocki, J., *Konkordat polski 1925 roku* (Polish concordat of 1925), Poznań 1977
Wyczański, A., *Uwarstwienie społeczne w Polsce w XVI wieku* (Social stratification in Poland in the 16th cent.), Wrocław, Warsaw, Cracow, Gdańsk 1977
Zielińska, T., *Magnateria polska epoki saskiej* (Polish magnates of the Saxon period), Wrocław, Warsaw, Cracow, Gdańsk 1977
Zientara, B., *Henryk Brodaty i jego czasy* (Henry the Bearded and his times), Warsaw 1975

Index

* reigned

C

E

F

G

N

S